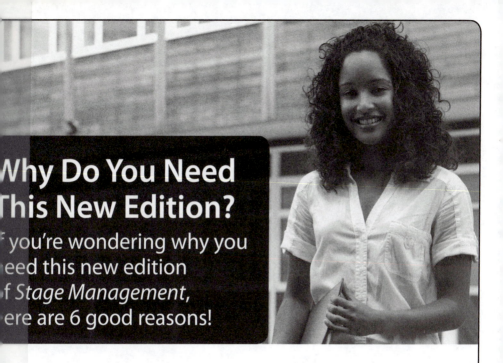

Why Do You Need This New Edition?

If you're wondering why you need this new edition of *Stage Management*, here are 6 good reasons!

1. New chapter on **working with unions** includes anecdotes from working stage managers on typical problems.
2. New **teaching strategies and classroom exercises** submitted by college instructors of stage management.
3. Updated information on the use of the **Internet and social media** in the world of stage management.
4. Added information about **associations of interest to stage managers** (AATE, PLASA) and updated information about USITT, SMNetwork, TCG, and SMA.
5. New **communication strategies** for stage managers in committee situations.
6. New **community theater production checklist** reflects how the stage manager's work interfaces with a producer's or director's agenda in community theaters.

PEARSON

Tenth Edition

STAGE MANAGEMENT

Lawrence Stern

Alice R. O'Grady

Boston Columbus Indianapolis New York San Francisco Upper Saddle River
Amsterdam Cape Town Dubai London Madrid Milan Munich Paris Montreal Toronto
Delhi Mexico City Sao Paulo Sydney Hong Kong Seoul Singapore Taipei Tokyo

In memory of Xenia Chechov

Editor-in-Chief, Communication: Karon Bowers
Editor: Ziki Dekel
Editorial Assistant: Megan Hermida
Associate Managing Editor: Bayani Mendoza de Leon
Marketing Manager: Blair Zoe Tuckman
Manufacturing Buyer: Mary Ann Gloriande
Senior Digital Editor: Paul DeLuca
Digital Editor: Lisa Dotson
Image Permission Coordinator: Lee Scher/Annette Linder
Photo Researcher: Sarah Bonner
Text Researcher: Jenn Kennett
Project Coordination, Editorial Services, and Text Design: Electronic Publishing Services, Inc., **NYC**
Art Rendering and Electronic Page Makeup: Jouve
Senior Cover Design Manager/Cover Designer: Nancy Danahy
Cover Photo: © Lance Bellers/iStockphoto

Credits and acknowledgments borrowed from other sources and reproduced, with permission, in this textbook appear on the appropriate page within the text.

Library of Congress Cataloging-in-Publication Data

Stern, Lawrence.
Stage management / Lawrence Stern, Alice R. O'Grady.—10th ed.
p. cm.
Includes bibliographical references and index.
ISBN 978-0-205-00613-7
1. Stage management. I. O'Grady, Alice R. II. Title.
PN2085.S77 2012
792.068—dc23

2011045328

1 2 3 4 5 6 7 8 9 10— —15 14 13 12
ISBN-13: 978-0-205-00613-2
ISBN-10: 0-205-00613-7

www.pearsonhighered.com

CONTENTS

FOREWORD

The best way to introduce this book is to speak well and perfectly about the author. For you can't expect a stage manager like Lawrence Stern to stand up front and blow his own horn. Someone who knows him must do it for him, and I gladly assume the task.

Now there are all sorts of virtues a stage manager must have. You will find them listed and profusely described in the pages of this book. But the supreme virtue among many is: The stage manager must arrive before everyone and leave long after everyone else is gone.

Of course that is the essence of creativity in any field you may want to mention. Those who love writing stay up until dawn to finish a story. Those who love painting work around the clock until they drop dead in their tracks. Stage managers . . . ?

Lawrence Stern is one of those superb men who quietly go about their business, keep charts, arrive two hours early and, long after the play has closed or collapsed, or both, can be found carrying out the trash, cleaning up the lobby, filling in the final forms, or holding the flashlight while the author of the play crawls around on the floor of the ladies' room helping some poor blind thing find her lost contact lens.

All this Lawrence Stern has done, and more. His passions may be quiet, but they are there. Instead of your usual slob, found all too frequently in our unhappy society these days, Lawrence Stern is one of those who gives you 150 percent of himself. I know that sounds impossible, but I have seen him do it. And this book, with its incredible amount of detail and huge compilation of firsthand knowledge, is proof of all that I say.

Frankly, I don't know how your average stage manager ever got along without this book, just as my own Pandemonium Theatre Company was never the same once Lawrence Stern moved on to other fields.

There you have it—some sort of idea of the man who wrote this book. But you needn't take my word for it. Just leaf through the book swiftly, checking chapters, pages, paragraphs. You'll soon find that a subtitle of the book could well be More than You Ever Wanted to Know about Stage Managing. Except of course, that would be foolish: you can never know enough.

Let Lawrence Stern be the best teacher you ever had. He's here. Listen to him!

Ray Bradbury
Los Angeles

PREFACE TO THE TENTH EDITION

In the many levels of live theater—educational, children's, community, showcase, and professional—there are few provisions for training in stage management. It is often assumed that anyone can do the job reasonably well who has a mind to, without previous training or experience, and the result of this is a great deal of trial and an enormous amount of error. A new stage manager typically makes his or her own kind of improvised performance, trying to carry out the functions of stage management without ever being able to find out for sure what those functions are, except by trial and error. Unfortunately, there are few places where anyone can find any written summary of useful principles or primary needs of stage management, and what they do find by gleaning from texts on directing, stagecraft, or the like is not usually appropriate to any one person's theater situation, much less to a reliable or professional standard for this kind of work. Most managers solve their problems with whatever organizational skill and inventiveness they possess—but at an unwarranted cost in time, effort, and uncertainty.

At the amateur levels of live theater, particularly in educational and community theater, the problems resulting from such a lack of guidelines for stage management are compounded by the fact that often the duties of the producer, director, stage manager, and even business manager are assumedby one person. This individual is frequently a faculty member or volunteer who has had little or no experience in stage management. It is this person who stands to profit most from this book. However, this guide is written in the hope that it will prove to be a valuable tool for all producers, directors, stage managers, and supervisors of theatrical programs, regardless of theater level or staging environment.

NEW TO THIS EDITION

In this new tenth edition, we have updated and streamlined the entire book to provide you with the most up-to-date, vibrant, and concise edition of our text possible:

- We've added a new chapter titled Working with Unions, which includes anecdotes from working stage managers that reflect the types of problems that often arise.
- We have also incorporated information about SM Network and the Stage Managers Association among other organizations of interest to stage managers.
- Additional information on using the Internet in the context of stage management has also been included.
- The charts, graphs, and illustrations used in the book have been thoroughly revised for this edition.
- Many practical forms that appear in the text may now be downloaded from **http://www.pearsonhighered.com/stern_ogrady.**
- Finally, we have included new communication strategies for stage managers to use in committee situations, and we have provided a new community theater production checklist that reflects how the stage manager's work interfaces with a producer's or director's agenda in community theaters.

ACKNOWLEDGMENTS

We are once again very grateful for the continued support of students and teachers that makes this tenth edition possible.

Thank you, working stage managers, for sharing your expertise: Bob Bones; Richard Costabile, Chairman, Stage Managers Association; Roy Harris; Lynda A. Lavin; Ira Mont; Dan Weingarten.

Thank you, theater workers: Kay Cleaves, Founder, SMNetwork; Jasper Gong, Ohlone College; Matthew Griffiths, PLASA; David Grindle, Executive Director USITT; Christopher King, Ulrich's Periodicals Directory; Brian Lawler, IATSE; Marty Nemko, Director and President of the Board, Chanticleers Theatre; Jason M. Palmer and Maria Somma, Actors' Equity Association; Kelly Prestel, AATE; Paul Puppo, Illumineering; Rom Rosenblum, Clear-Com, Inc.

Thank you, college instructors of stage management who reviewed the Ninth edition and made significant contributions to the Tenth: Kat Dunham, Edgewood College; Michael Skinner, Texas Christian University; Beth LaJoie, Nazareth College.

Thank you, Ray Bradbury, for your initial support and encouragement, remembered fondly with ever deepening appreciation.

Thank you, Pearson editors Jeanne Zalesky, Ziki Dekel, Stephanie Chaisson. Thank you Amy Pavelich at Electronic Publishing Services, Inc.; copyeditor James Dryden; and proofreader Julie Hotchkiss for your hard work in getting the Tenth together.

It's our fervent hope that the Tenth edition will make it just a little easier for beginning stage managers to get a jump start on their work and careers and will help everyone who works with stage managers to appreciate just what it is that they do.

L.S., A.R.O.

> You were my introduction to the wonderful world of stage management. In high school I was asked to stage manage a show the beginning of my junior year. I, of course, had no idea what that was. My drama teacher handed me your book, which became my bible, teaching me the fundamentals of stage management. By the time I was going to college I was certain I would be a professional stage manager. It is something I feel is still very much a part of my life and who I am.
>
> Courtesy Daryn Brown
> *Stage Manager, New York City*

ACKNOWLEDGMENTS

1

Making Things Run Smoothly

Stage managing is like riding a bicycle.
If you don't keep moving, you fall down.
—Elbin Cleveland

The cast, staff, and crew of live theater work together toward a common goal: a good performance. Theater is necessarily a group effort in professional, amateur, and educational theater. *It is a collaborative effort.* However, it is *never* a group effort of vague fellow committee members, but of associated autocrats: a playwright, a producer, a director, a stage manager, designers, and, above all, actors. Each accommodates the other and may overlap others in function when necessary, considering the variety of differing conditions for each show and every kind and level of theater. But each autocrat assumes distinct responsibilities and accepts them completely: The *producer* is the general manager who has responsibility for obtaining the personnel and resources to make theater happen. The *actors* must serve as the most essential dramatic medium, without whom no theatrical ideas or emotions can be communicated to an audience. The *director* must interpret the playwright's script through the media of actors and designers.

- **The stage manager is responsible for making the entire production run smoothly, on stage and backstage, in prerehearsal, rehearsal, performance, and postperformance phases.**

There is no definitive list of the duties of a stage manager that can apply to all theaters and staging environments. A stage manager for a comedy performed in a theater in the round might carry out specific duties that are totally different from those of a stage manager for a traveling pantomime troupe. But the function of the stage manager does not change.

- **Understanding this function is critical.** The difference between professional and nonprofessional stage managers is not whether they are paid, not whether they are members of unions, but whether they are willing and able to accept responsibility for carrying out this function. The producer, director, technical director, and other staff members are all concerned that things run smoothly, but they also have other higher-priority functions. Smooth running is the stage manager's primary responsibility. If you can and will accept this responsibility, you are an equal of the producer and director on the team that makes theater. If you do not accept responsibility for this function and simply carry out assigned duties (giving the actors their calls, supervising scene shifts), then you are a subordinate of the producer and director.

Note to the Reader

Stage Management *was never intended to be read cover to cover. It was initially a practical manual that directors and producers could hand to stage manager wannabes. It has, however, evolved into a college textbook. If you need to become an "instant stage manager," skip to Appendix A, review the list with your director and producer, check off the tasks they expect you to carry out as stage manager, and then read those pages.*

SUGGESTED CLASSROOM EXERCISE

Ask students to brainstorm what they believe are the duties of a stage manager. Write duties on a blackboard. Then ask students to state the function of a stage manager as expressed in an infinitive phrase. ("The function of a stage manager is to . . .") Write the phrase on the board above the list of duties. Discuss how each duty supports the function.

2

Characteristics of a Good Stage Manager

The ability to speak several languages is an asset, but the ability to keep your mouth shut in one is truly impressive.
—Anonymous

> What makes a good stage manager? Efficiency, organizational ability, congeniality, unflappability, knowledge of technical aspects of theater, energy and devotion, calmness under fire, and an effortless ability to announce "Ladies and Gentlemen, it's half-hour—half-hour—to curtain" on the backstage monitor, night after night after night.
>
> What makes a great stage manager? All of the above plus a love of theater and, most especially, a love of actors. Roy Harris is a great stage manager.*

Playwright Wendy Wasserstein (*The Heidi Chronicles,* 1989 Tony Award and 1989 Pulitzer Prize winner) and Andre Bishop (Artistic Director of the Lincoln Center Theater) praise Broadway stage manager Roy Harris as not only good, but great.

ATTRIBUTES OF GOOD STAGE MANAGERS

1. *Good stage managers assume responsibility.*

Effective stage managers say to themselves, "I am the one who must make things run smoothly on stage and backstage. Beyond me the buck does not pass." This is an active role, not passive. It is not merely coordination. It is not merely doing what one is told. It is not merely the sum total of the myriad little duties. It is taking charge. It is accepting responsibility.

*From the book *Conversations in the Wings*. Reprinted by permission of Heinemann. Copyright © 1994 by Roy Harris.

2. *Good stage managers keep their cool.*

Can you exercise emotional self-control during all phases of production?

You will be working with many excitable, conceited, self-centered, temperamental, volatile, sensitive, nervous, explosive people. But you will serve them best by not becoming emotionally involved in their arguments, controversies, or displays of temper.

If the leading lady stalks out screaming and crying, hand her a tissue to show her you care, but don't tell her or the director who was right or wrong in the dispute. It's none of your business. They will resolve their problems without your help.

If the producer asks for the cooperation of the cast in nonacting chores (cleaning the dressing rooms, selling tickets, publicity, etc.), don't give a noncooperative cast member a five-minute harangue or diatribe on his responsibilities. It is your job to ensure that cast members know what the director and producer expect of them—the time, the place. Post a duty roster. Hand out written memos. Phone them to remind them. You may explain. But you may not lose your temper with a cast member for any reason at all.

If a cast member is late for half-hour call, even habitually late, and fails to call the theater, you may remind, you may explain, you may plead, you may cajole—but thou shalt not lose thy cool.

In general, don't raise your voice to cast members. Reply to raised voices in calm, steady, controlled tones.

If a director or producer should reprimand you, privately or before the company, for your prompting technique (as an example) or anything else, don't sulk. Get on with the job the way they want it done.

If you blow a cue, don't get upset. Concentrate on getting the next one right.

Know your own panic response. Then control it. You have reacted to crises in the past. You know you can survive the next one. In time of panic, there must be only one question in your mind: Is there any action I can take to alleviate this situation? If so, do it. If not, keep your cool. Don't get swept up in the panic. Errors tend to compound.

Keeping one's cool means never appearing harassed, belligerent, insecure, apologetic, or imposed upon. It's not enough to be doing your job well. You've got to let the cast know by your deportment and the relaxed smile on your face that everything is under control. This gives the cast confidence. In this way, your cool may often be a positive contributing factor to the overall quality of the production.

3. *Good stage managers keep their mouths shut and their eyes and ears open.*

Do you tend to be quiet and observant? If what you say always has to do with the immediate improvement of the rehearsal or production, the cast members, crew, and staff will listen to you. If you run off at the mouth endlessly, you will have to struggle to gain attention when you have something significant to contribute. Where are you between these two extremes?

If you have a choice between shouting across the stage to a subordinate to change some gel frames and crossing the stage yourself to deliver quiet instructions, choose the latter. The cast, staff, and crew will come to appreciate the fact you are the great mover without the vocal display.

Don't waste your own time promoting yourself. Efficient work is hard to hide.

Be alert to what is going on around you. During cast breaks, stick with the director. In casual conversation with actors and staff, the director will agree to changes in lines, props, cues, or design. Can you make these changes, or cause them to be made, without further instruction?

Example

During a break, an actor approaches the director and asks to omit a troublesome line. The director agrees to the omission. You were getting a cup of coffee instead of staying at the director's side. At the next rehearsal of the scene, the actor omits the line. You prompt. The actor breaks character to advise you the line was cut. You turn to the director for confirmation. The director doesn't remember since it has been three days since this scene was last run. The actor and director discuss it. They agree to omit the line, or the director decides at this time to have the line delivered. The rehearsal resumes. Could this delay have been avoided?

Yes, there are breaks for stage managers. Of course you have to take care of your personal needs. Can you plan ahead to favor yourself? If you're in a coffee/doughnuts environment, would it be wise to bring a thermos of fruit juice and put a zip-lock bag full of trail mix, granola, or dried fruit into your kit? Don't gossip with the cast. You will often be privileged to know things that are going on at the administrative level, or between the producer and the director, or between the conductor and the harp player, or about closing date, casting history, salaries, and much more. Keep it to yourself.

If a cast member should ask you what you think of the director, staff, crew, or another cast member, try the following, delivered by rote in a loud if not sincere voice: "X is the best director (producer, scene designer, publicist, actor, actress, etc.) I've ever had the pleasure of working with." When you are no longer associated with that production, you can say what you really think, but until then, a complete, beguiling display of "I-know-how-to-play-this-game" is the most effective response.

Don't align yourself with any clique of actors within a cast. The stage manager is a friend to the whole cast. If you choose to go out after the show with one group habitually, make it clear to the others in the cast that you would also like to be with them.

4. *Good stage managers think ahead.*

Don't just sit there—anticipate!

What is the company going to be doing later today? Tomorrow? Next week? Does everyone know about it? Is everything ready? You have made a master calendar, schedules, do-lists, duty rosters, a promptbook, and checklists. All of these are instruments to help you think ahead. But there is no substitute for constant vigilance.

If something is changed suddenly, what future effects will the change have? What other changes must be made as a result of that change? Who must be notified?

One of your greatest contributions to the performance quality is making the most of every minute between first reading and final curtain. If there is any delay in rehearsal or production, it's your job to shorten that delay.

Stage managing can be compared to flying a high-performance aircraft. Once you're in the air, you can't make repairs. Once the curtain goes up, you can't stop the performance to make changes in the location of set pieces and discovered props. So pilots and stage managers both must have extensive preflight checklists.

To land a high-performance aircraft, you must take several steps prior to entering the landing pattern; the aircraft moves so fast there is no time to accomplish everything once you're into the pattern. To carry out a set change, the stage manager must also take several steps in advance to ensure that all hands are rehearsed in the execution of that change and understand their cues. Once the change starts, there is no time to do all of the things that must be done in advance if the set change is to be brought off successfully.

Serious emergencies call for both keeping cool and thinking ahead. A fire should be expected momentarily. Do you have a fire extinguisher in the control booth? Do you have another one backstage? Do you have a phone in the booth? If it's a pay phone, does dialing 911 work without coins? Do you have a cell phone? Do you know the address of the theater and the nearest cross street by heart? Is there a clear unblocked space for you to get out from behind your equipment? Can you give calm instructions to your audience in a tone of voice that will convince them to leave the theater in an orderly fashion? In a huge theater, do you have a working microphone in the booth that will allow you to reach the entire audience via the public address system? Do you know evacuation procedures? Are all the exit aisles, doors, and alleys unblocked? Will the emergency exits open? Is your scenery flameproofed in accordance with city ordinances? Is all electrical equipment wired safely?

If the answer to any of these questions is no, the stage manager and the producer are derelict in their responsibility for the safety of the audience and the cast. They have not anticipated problems.

Stage managers must force themselves out of the rut of thinking that it can't happen here. It *can* happen here, and everyone in your theater will be safer if you will just assume that it *is* going to happen here within the next 30 seconds.

Plan ahead for the worst possible type of medical emergency. Assume that a member of the cast or crew will suffer a severe injury or heart attack in the course of mounting or presenting. Do you have a company doctor? Is his office or home near the theater? Do you know the location of an all-night clinic? Have you driven there on a test run from the theater? (It is maddening to find that the clinic entrance is located on a one-way street and you will have to drive three extra blocks because you didn't make the right approach—while your passenger is losing blood!)

What's your earthquake plan?

During such emergencies, keeping your cool and thinking ahead become traits of paramount importance.

5. *Good stage managers are considerate.*

Do you have that quality of selfless caring that prompts you to give a friend your jacket when you know you'll be cold? Can you put the comfort of every cast member before your own comfort?

Is the theater warm enough? Is it possible to arrive there a little earlier to turn on the heat so that cast members don't walk into a cold theater? Can you turn on the lights so cast members won't have to enter dark dressing rooms?

Is the backstage area too drafty? Can you close some doors or make some baffles out of extra flats?

Do the actresses have to walk to their cars from the theater along a dimly lit street? Can you walk them to their cars or ask other cast members to do so? If it's raining, can you provide an umbrella?

Is there drinking water backstage and in the dressing rooms? Can you arrange for water service or provide pitchers and cups?

Have you dusted the rehearsal furniture before the cast sits down?

Do you really listen when cast members speak to you?

Can you offer your cast natural affection?

Backstage in Hollywood theaters, I found the lavish affection and terms of endearment that pass between casual acquaintances to be quite surprising. It did not seem natural to me. But insecurity seems to be a common trait among theater people, and they find warmth and affection reassuring. This display of warmth does not come naturally to all people. It is certainly not recommended if it must be forced. But if you can display a natural affection for your cast, as if they were all dear old warm friends or members of your family, why not?

Are you considerate with respect to the creativity of others? Can you effectively offer constructive criticism without stamping out creative instinct? This is often difficult to do.

Many of the creative people—scene designers, costume designers, choral directors, choreographers, and directors—carry their gifts wrapped preciously within thin skin. Yet in the theater situation no creator can work alone. The creator must communicate with and gain the cooperation of all the others on the staff to see creativity come to fruition. The stage manager, unfortunately, is frequently placed in the position of coordinating the creative efforts of the supersensitive. It requires much patience and tact.

Example

Set construction is running behind schedule. The technical director complains to you that the scene designer has no concept of economy in design and tries to present in total rather than suggesting. The technical director complains that the designer is overburdening the shop with an unconscionable amount of work.

The scene designer complains to you that the technical director has ruined more scenery than a termite on a showboat, that inefficient methods are being used in the shop, and that for two nights running, one of his ornamental set pieces has not been placed on stage because it is waiting to be repaired and that this ruins the entire aesthetic balance of the set.

Your chief concern as stage manager is to have the set for the next production ready for the take-in one night hence.

This is the type of situation that requires tactful soothing and massive doses of consideration. If you try to fix the blame at this point, you are likely to find your next production hung up. Cool off the technical director and the scene designer, separately. Commiserate with each, separately. Tell them what an incredibly good job they've been doing up to this point. Praise their strong points. Overlook their weaknesses. Sympathize with their problems. Pep them up and send them back to work. They'll get the scenery finished.

6. *Good stage managers keep their sense of humor.*

Making theater should be a happy experience for all concerned. Unfortunately, delays, deadlines, economic pressures, personality conflicts, and other factors sometimes make the process grim.

Don't contribute to the grimness. Leave your personal problems at home. Come to work with a resolve to stay happy.

"I find that most people are just as happy as they make up their minds to be," said Abraham Lincoln. Lincoln considered humor a "labor-saving device" and a "multiple-purpose tool."

Keep a smile on your face, and have a good reason for its being there. A cheerful stage manager can be a great asset to any theater group. Sometimes a cheerful word can get the whole company over a rough spot.

Knowing jokes is not a substitute for having a sense of humor. There are occasions, however, when a good theater story will put the company at ease. A successful director with whom I worked greeted each new cast with a story; it seemed to break the ice and to be effective for him. Consult Appendix C for a few of my favorite stories.

A corollary of tenet 6 is that *good stage managers do not have personality conflicts with anyone.* Holding grudges or showing hostility toward any member of the company cannot be a part of your behavior. Go home and shred your philodendron, but don't let any member of the cast, staff, or crew feel that you dislike him. It simply does not expedite production.

7. *Good stage managers are organized and efficient.*

Throughout the chapters that follow, the emphasis will be on organization and efficiency. There never seems to be enough time. Efficiency helps to buy time.

8. *Good stage managers are punctual and dependable.*

If you are not there on time or early, or cannot be depended on, you simply cannot be a stage manager.

In summary, good stage managers

- Accept responsibility
- Keep their cool
- Keep their mouths shut, their eyes and ears open
- Think ahead
- Are considerate
- Keep their sense of humor
- Are organized and efficient
- Are punctual and dependable

How do you compare?

In her mystery novel *The G-String Murders,* Gypsy Rose Lee writes, "As stage managers go, Sammy was about average, but that isn't saying much for him. I've worked for a lot of them, and I haven't found one yet that didn't think he owned the theater and everybody in it."* What an unfortunate fictional portrait. I ask all of my student stage managers to read your book. I feel it encourages them to be efficient without being offensive or despotic.

Billy C. Creamer
Theater Director
Rolling Hills High School
Rolling Hills Estates, CA

*From Gypsy Rose Lee, *The G-String Murders* (New York: Penguin Books, 1984/1941).

COMMUNICATION/MANAGEMENT SKILLS

Communication/management skills are key ingredients for success—in stage management, in business, in life. In the long run, your success in the world of theater will be more determined by your communication and management skills than by your stage management skills. Do you overrate your own personal skills? Can you improve them? Investing time in evaluating your skills can pay great dividends.

I know you believe that you understand what you think I said—but I'm not sure you realize that what you heard is not what I meant.

—Anonymous

Too often the "mouth in motion before mind in gear" syndrome catches us. Here are some conversation strategies that I have found useful:

1. Can you rephrase as a question before speaking? Instead of "Dale, you should bend your knees when you lift that set piece," could you ask, "Dale, would it be easier on your back if you bent your knees when you lift that piece?" Rephrasing as a question slows the speaker down and forces the speaker to think about what's about to be said. It engages the listener rather than telling the listener what to do.
2. Can you offer a choice? Instead of "Dale, bend your knees when you lift anything," could you ask, "Dale, would it be easier on you to bend your knees when handling that piece, or to use a dolly?" Offering a choice not only slows down the speaker, but it also gets the listener more involved because the listener has to make a decision. The listener will be more likely to follow through since his input was part of the communication.
3. Can you use open-ended questions (questions that do not call for a yes or no answer)? Instead of "Dale, can you move that piece by yourself?" try, "Dale, what's your take on the best way to move that piece?" The listener may have a better idea that would not be elicited with a yes or no answer.
4. Can you use "I" messages rather than "you" messages? Instead of "Dale, you should bend your knees when lifting anything that heavy," try "Dale, I've found

it useful to bend my knees when lifting heavy things." Sounds less like an order, doesn't it?

EFFECTIVE COMMITTEE WORK

The stage manager works in committee situations during production meetings and critiques.

Suggestions:

1. Rephrase your ideas as questions (as described above).
2. Do your homework.
3. Keep it brief.
   a. Use short sentences.
   b. Make summary brief, too.

   Example: The incoming show at your outdoor theater will require more lights than you have. From your past experience in another city, you remember that light towers were rented. You decide to present this idea at the upcoming production meeting.

4. Rather than explaining your past experience to the committee, would it be better to ask a question? "Have you considered renting light towers?" If the technical director and lighting designer have already investigated the idea, then a simple "yes" reply on their part ends the idea and saves committee time.
5. Don't offer ideas unless you have supportive information. In this example you've done your homework. You have the names of two companies that rent towers, dimensions and capacity of the two types they offer, and cost estimates.
6. To keep it brief and not take up committee time, rather than talk the committee through the information, wouldn't it be more effective to distribute copies of a graph of the information? This would allow the producer to ask the tech director to look into it, make the decision to build or rent, and move on to other business.

Management skills are closely related to communications skills. You can't have good management skills without having good communications skills.

As a stage manager:

1. Can you learn to delegate authority while retaining responsibility? This is the hardest part of management. Very often this is a survival technique. The stage manager can't do it all by himself. If you don't get people to move with you, you don't succeed.
2. Can you get people to work *with* you instead of *for* you? Can you apply the preceding conversational strategies to motivate people to get things done so they don't feel they are just following orders?
3. Can you follow up? Once you've delegated, can you find time to check out the anticipated results?
4. Can you take time to give your instructions with great clarity, making sure that you are understood, or that the director's or producer's intention, which you are passing on, is understood?

5. Can you give instructions in bite-sized portions? Instead of giving a person 20 things to do, can you give him one, check on that one when it's finished, acknowledge the person for having completed it, and then give him the next chore?
6. Can you be considerate of capabilities of coworkers by not assigning more work than you feel confident the assignees can accomplish? If you anticipate that a task will need more labor and/or time than immediately available, can you make it clear that you only expect that a start be made on the work?
7. Can you deliver instruction with calmness and self-confidence?
8. Can you check on problems and revive interest in projects by showing your interest and appreciation and by reemphasizing goals when the enthusiasm of your subordinates is flagging?
9. Can you find ways to praise coworkers? This skill is so important, yet so often neglected.

These few ideas about communication and management skills are an eyedropper's worth in an ocean of possible self-improvement.

One of my secrets of stage management is to communicate directly. Say what you mean simply and clearly. Also, I think timeliness is the best policy; get issues off your plate and move on.

Paul J. Smith
PSM Aida Broadway (1,852 performances) and national tour
Chicago Cellblock Tour and SM All Shook Up

Take time to communicate. When time is tight and you have 15 things to do and three minutes to do them, taking time to really communicate information can be the first thing to go out the window. Often I see younger SMs race through a set of instructions, then run off to get the next thing on their list done. Take the extra time to speak slowly and clearly, and then take more time to let the other person respond that he has heard and understood what you've just said. An extra 30 seconds now can save hours later.

Dale Smallwood
Production Stage Manager
Sixteen years with The Pearl Theatre Company, New York City

I think the main rules to follow are don't get defensive, don't take things personally, try to keep your cool no matter what, don't take sides, use positive reinforcement, trust your team, know when to pick your battles, and remember that not everyone is going to like you, and that's okay. Just do the job with fairness and fortitude and you'll be fine.

Francesca Russell
ASM, BARE: A Pop Opera
Dodger Stages, New York City

I have one rule in working with all people in all aspects of theater—actors, designers, stagehands, etc.—**Never, ever give an order.** There is always a way to get what you want accomplished without being bossy or officious. And if you find that you have to give an order, or make a demand, always do it with good cheer. . . . I think one of the most important things a stage manager can do is help establish a warm, friendly, relaxed atmosphere in the rehearsal room so that all the creative minds feel as free as possible.

Roy Harris, SM/PSM
Sixteen Broadway shows
Twenty productions directed by Tony Award-winning director Dan Sullivan

My Teaching Strategy

Towards the end of my class sessions, after we've been through the nuts and bolts of paperwork, blocking, prompting, and all the other essentials, I incorporate real experiences that have happened to me during my years of stage management. I write a line about the situation from the actor's point of view, and then on another slip of paper I write a line from the stage manager's perspective, giving both slips the same number. For example:

1-ACTOR: You are a hard-working ensemble member whose last exit is halfway through Act Two. You shot a rare TV appearance that airs at 11 tonight and want to skip curtain call to be able to watch it with your family and friends.

1-STAGE MANAGER: An ensemble member, who is infamous for making requests to be treated as a special case, comes to you at the 15-minute call with yet another request.

Each of my students takes a slip of paper from the "actor" pile and one from the "stage manager" pile. Then I call number 1, and those two students role-play the situation with only the information on the slip of paper. Once there has been a resolution of some sort the whole class discusses what they might have done in the same situation. It's a fun way to practice dealing with personalities, when rules can be bent, common sense, and other things that are a huge part of stage managing but can't be learned from a book. It's interesting how many students approach this in a way that may give them the desired outcome for this instance but will NOT serve them well in further relationships with the other person!

Jill Gold
Freelance Production Stage Manager & Instructor,
Occidental College

It's difficult to change. Our communication skills evolve over a long period of time and bad habits develop from childhood and linger on. Trite but true, we do not see ourselves as others see us; we reveal ourselves the moment we open our mouths, totally unaware of speech patterns that alienate others rather than "winning friends and influencing people." What can you do to identify your own problem areas? (1) Take a class in personal communications and/or management techniques. Class exercises are the best way to work toward personal improvement. (2) Study a book. Here are a few books that you might find useful:

Communications

Be Your Own Executive Coach
Peter deLisser, Chandler House Press, Worcester, MA, 1999
Messages: The Communications Skills Book
Matthew McKay/Martha Davis/Patrick Fanning, New Harbinger Publications, Oakland, CA, 2009
How to Talk So People Listen
Sonya Hamlin, HarperCollins Publishers, New York, NY, 1988
Looking Out, Looking In
Ronald B. Adler/Russell F. Proctor II, Wadsworth Cengage Learning, New York, NY, 2010

Management

Management Mess-Ups (Revised edition)
Mark Eppler, Career Press, Pompton Plains, NJ, 2006
Self-Leadership and the One Minute Manager
Kenneth Blanchard/Susan Fowler/Lawrence Hawkins, Harper Collins, New York, NY, 2005
In Search of Excellence
Thomas Peters/Robert Waterman, Jr., MJF Books, New York, NY, 2009

SUGGESTED CLASSROOM EXERCISE

Ask students to pretend that each is a producer about to hire a stage manager. Tell them to write out three qualities that they would consider essential (e.g., organized, sense of humor, dependable) and rank order those three. Then combine the lists and discuss as a group which attributes of a stage manager are most important.

3

Getting the Play and Understanding It

It takes twenty years to make an overnight success.
—Eddie Cantor

During the readings, rehearsals, and production, you must have a copy of the script and a thorough understanding of it. To expedite readings and rehearsals, make sure there are enough scripts on hand for actors and staff.

Usually, copies of the script are ordered when the rights of production are obtained from the play service (Samuel French, Tams-Witmark, etc.; see below). If, however, you are going into production with one copy of the script, or a vague memory of it, first make sure an adequate number of scripts are on hand. This may be possibly limited to determining how many are necessary, or it may mean actually picking them up.

The following information will assist you in contacting major play publishing services in the United States. Some catalogs can be ordered via e-mail or the Internet.

Anchorage Press Plays
See Dramatic Publishing Co.

Baker's Plays
7611 Sunset Blvd.
Hollywood, CA 90046
323-876-0579
fax: 323-876-5482
bakersplays.com

I. E. Clark Publications
P.O. Box 246
Schulenburg, TX 78956-0246
979-743-3232
fax: 979-743-4765
e-mail: ieclark@cytv.net
ieclark.com

Dramatic Publishing Co.
311 Washington Street, Box 129
Woodstock, IL 60098-3308
815-338-7170 800-448-7469
fax: 800-334-5302
e-mail: customerservice@dpcplays.com
dramaticpublishing.com

Dramatists Play Service, Inc.
440 Park Avenue South
New York, NY 10016-8012
212-683-8960
fax: 212-213-1539
e-mail: postmaster@dramatists.com
dramatists.com

Eldridge Publishing Co.
P.O. Box 14367
Tallahassee, FL 32317-4367
850-385-2463
fax 850-385-2463
e-mail: info@histage.com
histage.com

Heuer Publishing Co.
P.O. Box 248
Cedar Rapids, IA 52406-0248
800-950-7529
fax: 319-368-8008
e-mail: customerservice@hitplays.com
hitplays.com

Institute for Readers Theatre
P.O. Box 17193
San Diego, CA 92117-7193
619-276-1948
fax: 619-576-7369
e-mail: info@readers-theatre.com
readers-theatre.com

Music Theatre International
421 West 54th Street
New York, NY 10019
212-541-4684
fax: 212-397-4684
e-mail: Licensing@MTIShows.com
musicalworlds.com

Pioneer Drama Service
P.O. Box 4267
Englewood, CO 80155-4267
800-333-7262
fax: 303-779-4315
pioneerdrama.com

The Rodgers & Hammerstein Organization
229 W. 28th Street
New York, NY 10001
212-541-6600
e-mail: editor@rnh.com
fax: 212-586-6155
rnh.com

Samuel French, Inc.
45 West 25th Street, Fl. 2
New York, NY 10010-2751
866-598-8449
fax: 212-206-1429
e-mail: info@samuelfrench.com
samuelfrench.com

Tams-Witmark Music Library
560 Lexington Avenue,
New York, NY 10022-6828
800-221-7196
fax: 800-826-7121
tams-witmark.com

Check with your post office to determine the type of mail service you must have to ensure that scripts get to you on time. It is usually worth the cost of specifying overnight or second-day delivery, or at least first class, rather than the less-expensive book rate, to make sure that your scripts won't be delayed in the mail. UPS and FedEx are reliable.

In determining the number of scripts you will need, consider:

1. Will all speaking parts need scripts? Check your visual display of characters on stage (discussed later in this chapter) to see whether a few pages of one script can be removed for one or two other speaking parts.
2. Will the costume designer, scene designer, property master, or any other staff member need a script? The publicity person can often make good use of a script.
3. Will a follow-spot operator or any other crew member need one?
4. Will understudies or replacements need them?
5. Can the budget allow for a few extra copies?
6. Do you have copying equipment, or easy access to it? Is it legal to photocopy? (page 19)

Sides (a part of a script giving only one character's lines, each preceded by the cue for the line) may be typed or hand-copied by apprentices or the actors, if necessary.

When script shipments arrive, immediately check the content against the invoice or manifest. Make sure you have what you need. If you wait until the first day of rehearsal, you have a potential disaster!

Lock up your scripts and let them out only on a sign-out basis. Otherwise, they will disappear. It's not usually criminal intent. It may be the chorus girl who wants to read for a principal part in next week's production who loses her script on a cast picnic. This does not mean to imply that she should not be permitted to see a script in advance of a reading, but she should have to sign it out.

All scripts and sides should be signed out when issued to cast members and staff. Lock up the sign-out sheet in the same cupboard as the scripts. Scripts, sides, and scores are usually due back from cast, staff, and musicians on the day preceding or coinciding with the close of the show. (This is payday in professional companies; the cost of lost materials can then be deducted on the spot.) Post a notice to this effect and a price list on the callboard. Note your intent in the company rules.

Frequently, a cast member with just a few lines will elect to copy them rather than sign out a skimpy side, thus avoiding the possibility of losing it. You would be wise to encourage this.

Normally in musical stock and musical comedy, the scores, scripts, and sides are packaged and returned within a week after the close of the production in order to decrease rental costs. This task is usually assigned to an apprentice or the company "gopher." If a closing-night review of the past year or season is to be presented, you may want to retain one score and one script from each of the shows.

On straight playbook shows, you may allow the actors to keep the scripts, or you may ask that they return or pay for them. Determine your policy and relay it to the cast.

All too frequently, you may be held responsible for missing scripts and asked to pay for them. It is a good idea, then, to mark each script with a number so that each can be accounted for.

Scripts sometimes get tied up for unusual reasons.

Example

In casting a big-name show, an actor might be sent a script, even though there is no intent to cast that actor. You may even be called on to deliver the script to the actor's home. The script is never seen again until a few weeks after opening, when it comes back through the mail with a hard-to-read note, "Not my cup of tea," and the big-name actor's initials.

Agents for professional actors often beg directors or managers for scripts, and receive them, even though there is no intent to cast the agents' clients. The agents feel that showing the scripts to their clients is tangible proof that they are working and that their clients are being considered.

When a script is issued for any unusual reason, don't count on its being returned in time to meet your needs. It is best to replace that script immediately if you have on hand only the necessary minimum with which to begin rehearsals.

Although your responsibility for scripts may be limited, you should know how to get, replace, reproduce, lock up, control, and retrieve scripts as part of your work in expediting auditions and rehearsals.

Of even greater concern is the processing of your own script—making it into a working tool.

THE PROMPTBOOK

Turning a script into a promptbook increases the size of the margins (figure 3.1). This allows you to make all of your cues and warns (warning alerts) large and clear, and it gives you adequate room to make clear blocking notations and diagrams. It also gives you sufficient room to make production notes.

Making a Promptbook

The fastest way to convert a play script (5 × 7¼ inch) into a promptbook (8½ × 11 inch) is via a copy machine using three-hole-punched paper. See legal restrictions below.

If the promptbook cannot be made using a copy machine, cut or "unbind" the pages of a script and mount each page on an 8½ × 11 inch loose-leaf sheet (unruled) so that both sides of the script can be seen (figure 3.2, page 19).

If you are willing to use two printed scripts to produce one promptbook, paste alternate printed pages to opposite sides of each loose-leaf page.

However your promptbook is made, consider the best placement of loose-leaf page space around the printed script (see figure 3.2 for alternatives). Note that for the one-script cutout method with a loose-leaf page pasted around printed script edges, pattern 1 calls for rubber-cementing, taping, or gluing four sides of every page, whereas patterns 3 and 4 require that only two sides of each page be attached. I feel that pattern 2, which requires that three sides be attached, gives the most desirable distribution of additional space.

If you cannot spare an extra printed script and must paste loose-leaf paper around printed pages to show both sides of each printed sheet, then start by making a heavy cardboard template cut to show all the printed area of each script page (figure 3.2). With a single-edged or mounted razor, you can then cut about five loose-leaf sheets at a time to the correct size, making one loose-leaf cutout page for each two-sided leaf of printed script.

Use Scotch Magic Transparent Tape, a glue stick, or rubber cement to attach script pages to the cutout loose-leaf sheets. Rubber cement is the most forgiving. Errors can be corrected without cutting, because rubber-cemented pages can be pulled apart and restuck without damage to the pages. Glue sticks are faster and more convenient. I have found the Avery Glue Stic to be excellent. Some liquid glue sticks wrinkle the paper when dry. It is best to experiment to find the right glue stick before pasting up your entire script.

Photocopies

Copyright law and the term *fair use* are open to a wide range of legal interpretations. The play publishers listed above have various policies ranging from "No photocopying" to "It's okay under fair use if a copy is purchased for the exclusive use of the stage manager."

Blocking		Revised Blocking	Sound/Light CUES
HAMLET.			
King. With all my heart; and it duth much content me			
To hear him so inclin'd.			
Good gentlemen, give him a further edge,			
And drive his purpose on to these delights.			
Ros. We shall, my lord. ∧∧	R + G Ex UR		
[Exeunt Rosencrantz and Guildenstern]			
King. Sweet Gertrude, leave us too.			
For we have closely sent for Hamlet hither;			
That he, as 'twere by accident, may here			
Affront Ophelia			
Her father and myself (lawful espials,)			
Will so bestow ourselves, that, seeing, unseen,			
We may of their encounter frankly judge;			
And gather by him, as he is behav'd,			
If't be the affliction of his love, or no,			
That thus he suffers for.			
Queen. I shall obey you:—			
And, for your part, Ophelia, I do wish,			
That your good beauties be the happy cause			
Of Hamlet's wildness; so shall I hope, your virtues			
Will bring him to his wanted way again,			
To both your honours. ∧∧			
Oph. Madam, I wish it may. [Exit Queen]	Q Ex UR		
Pol. Ophelia, walk you here:			
Read on this book;			
That show of such an exercise may colour			
Your loneliness. (Ophelia goes up the stage)	O X U S C		Sound
I hear him coming; let's withdraw, my lord. ∧	K + P Ex UR		
[Exeunt King and Polonius]			
[Enter Hamlet]	H Ent ULX DC	H Ent URX DC	
Ham. To be, or not to be, that is the question—			Lights
Whether 'tis nobler in the mind, to suffer			
The slings and arrows of outrageous fortune			

French Scene Diagrams	Prompting	Production Notes
O H	C > "or not to be."	Spot or Sp EF?

FIGURE 3.1 If copied pages are punched on the right side, the back of the next page (which will be the front when it's bound) can be used for French scene diagrams, prompting notes, production notes, pronunciation, and prop notes.

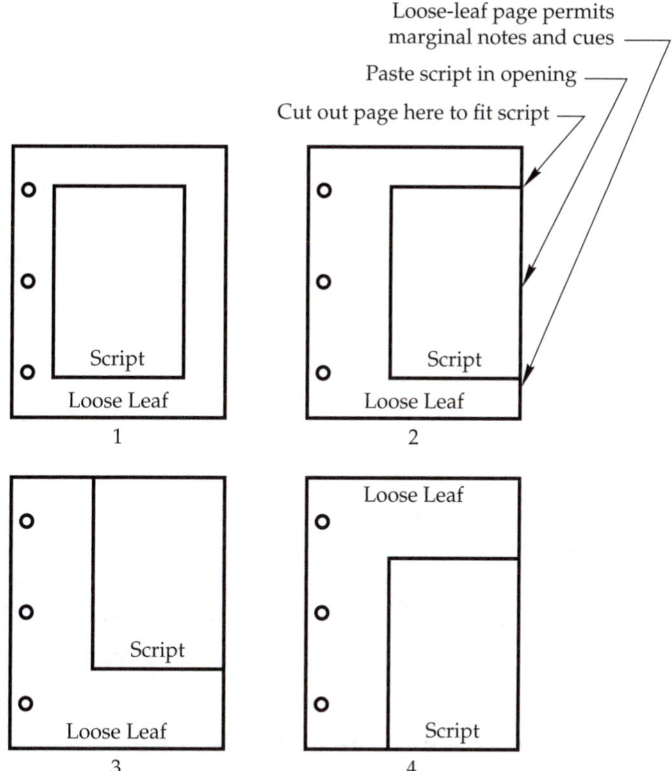

FIGURE 3.2
Four Patterns for Mounting Script Pages

If you make your promptbook by photocopying, you have the opportunity to enlarge the size of the original pages at the same time. This might help make each page more readable in the lighting backstage. What percentage of enlargement is recommended to still leave enough room for blocking notation? Experiment with one page before running off the rest. I suggest that you favor maximum space for blocking notation, cues, and production notes (figure 3.1).

Make tabs for each scene so that you can quickly turn to any scene without thumbing through the script. You can purchase tabs at a stationery store or you can make your own, using tape. Each tab should be labeled (figure 3.3). Place the scene tabs on the last page of the previous scene, not the first or second page of the scene, so that the tab will open your script properly, with the desired scene immediately displayed.

Rehearsal schedule, pronunciation guide, plots, set sketches, and cast lists should also be tabbed so that you can turn immediately to whatever information you need during a rehearsal without wasting time by shuffling through a lot of paper.

A neat, well-made promptbook is an asset, but no critic will ever review your promptbook. Great paperwork does not necessarily make great theater. It might be possible for some people to keep all of their blocking notation in their heads and make sound-and-light cue notations in the margins of uncut scripts, but most managers could not work this way, and most wouldn't feel secure or comfortable. I advise you to do whatever works best for you, but I would suggest that super organization of your promptbook is a great way to go.

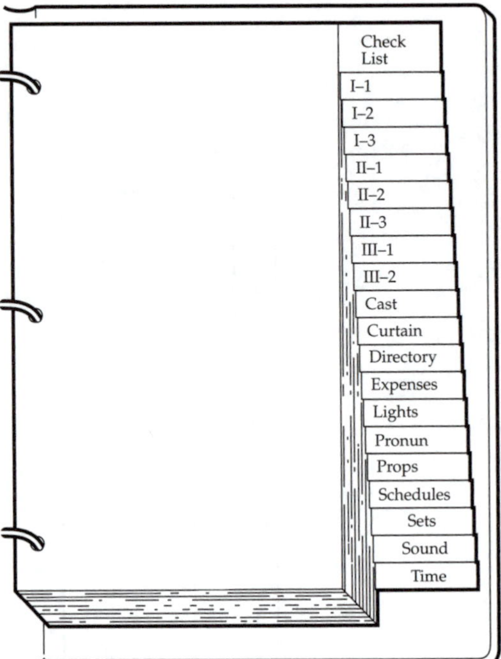

FIGURE 3.3 Page Tabs for Rapid Reference in a Promptbook. Note that the tabs are in alphabetical order so the stage manager has easy access to any information needed during rehearsal or production.

Keeping the Promptbook in a Safe Place

Once a skilled stage manager has worked on a promptbook, it becomes a valuable tool and should therefore be safeguarded.

There are two possible ways to do this. The first is that the promptbook is always with the stage manager; it even goes home with the stage manager. If anyone needs information from the promptbook in the middle of the night, that person calls the stage manager. The stage manager is so prompt and so reliable that there is never any fear in anyone's mind that the promptbook might be missing when needed.

The other possibility is that the promptbook is kept in a secure place in the theater—locked up when the stage manager is not using it during rehearsals. The idea here is that if something should happen to the stage manager, someone else could pick up the promptbook and run the rehearsal or show.

You will have to decide which of these two possibilities is best for your theater.

Allowing Access to the Promptbook

Anyone who needs information from the promptbook should ask the stage manager for that information. The promptbook is the stage manager's tool, and as a courtesy to the stage manager, no one should go into the promptbook without the stage manager's permission.

Keying or Coding the Promptbook

In educational theater, the stage manager is often advised to set up the promptbook so that anyone can read and understand all the cues and notes, as well as the blocking notation. The stage manager should make a key for abbreviations and symbols on the front page of the promptbook.

UNDERSTANDING THE SCRIPT

You must understand the script, and you must understand it well before casting and before rehearsals begin if you are to be effective. To understand it, you must analyze it and identify its problems. The word "problem" is used to mean anything that must be done to run the show.

Try to allow a quiet time of intense concentration for your first reading. It can pay off in the accomplishment of a lot of work. All of this prerehearsal work can pay great dividends in time saved during rehearsals.

As you read, use light pencil in the margins of your script to identify all possible light cues, sound cues, special effects, costume changes, or peculiarities, properties, entrances, exits, and pronunciation questions. You might want to use the following code:

L—Light cue

S—Sound cue

Ef—Special effect

P—Property

E—Entrance or exit

?—Pronunciation question

For every light, sound, and special effect, using a ruler and working in light pencil, draw a horizontal line closest to the line of dialogue preceding an oral cue, or under the description of a visual cue. This line should cross the entire promptbook page so that you can see it quite easily during rehearsals.

About a half page preceding the line, draw another horizontal line marked "warn lights" or "warn sound" (figure 3.4). In the case of two light cues and a sound cue in a tight sequence, you need put in only one warn line before the sequence, but it should be marked "warn light/sound series." It is too early to number these cues or to write them in ink, since there may well be changes during rehearsals. You will use the penciled lines to call the light and sound cues during rehearsals.

PLOTS

As you identify the problems and put in your light pencil lines, you might also wish to list the problems. A list of problems is a plot. A functional plot is one that allows your associates to obtain a complete grasp of the problems in their areas without having to refer to the script. In other words, *plots allow you to digest the script for others.*

In deciding whether making plots will be of practical value, ask yourself: If I were the sound technician on this production, would it help if I were handed a sound plot? In productions where the designers and technical people come in just a few days before opening, having plots ready is particularly valuable.

Copies of your plots should be given to all staff members concerned. Your copy should be kept in your promptbook, properly tabbed, to be changed in rehearsals as necessary.

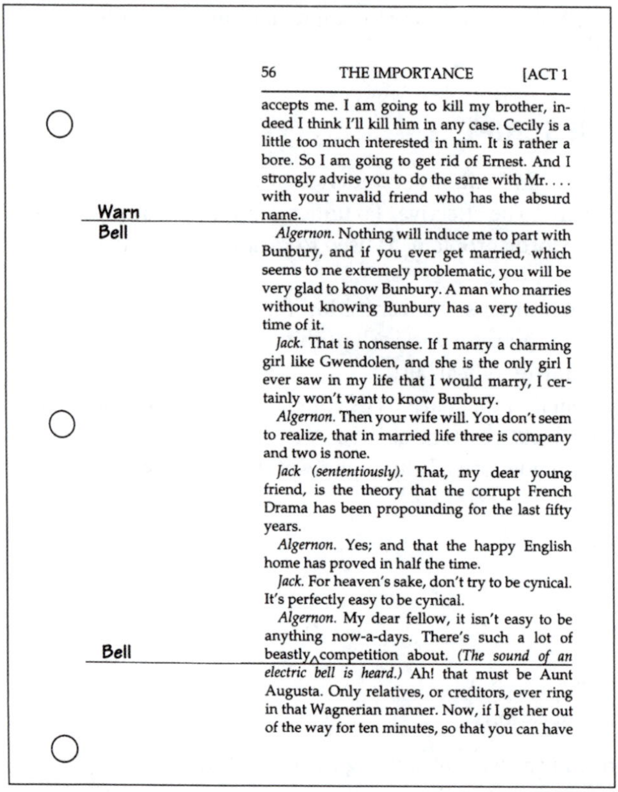

56 THE IMPORTANCE [ACT 1

accepts me. I am going to kill my brother, indeed I think I'll kill him in any case. Cecily is a little too much interested in him. It is rather a bore. So I am going to get rid of Ernest. And I strongly advise you to do the same with Mr. . . . with your invalid friend who has the absurd name.

Warn
Bell

Algernon. Nothing will induce me to part with Bunbury, and if you ever get married, which seems to me extremely problematic, you will be very glad to know Bunbury. A man who marries without knowing Bunbury has a very tedious time of it.

Jack. That is nonsense. If I marry a charming girl like Gwendolen, and she is the only girl I ever saw in my life that I would marry, I certainly won't want to know Bunbury.

Algernon. Then your wife will. You don't seem to realize, that in married life three is company and two is none.

Jack (sententiously). That, my dear young friend, is the theory that the corrupt French Drama has been propounding for the last fifty years.

Algernon. Yes; and that the happy English home has proved in half the time.

Jack. For heaven's sake, don't try to be cynical. It's perfectly easy to be cynical.

Algernon. My dear fellow, it isn't easy to be anything now-a-days. There's such a lot of beastly‸competition about. *(The sound of an electric bell is heard.)* Ah! that must be Aunt Augusta. Only relatives, or creditors, ever ring in that Wagnerian manner. Now, if I get her out of the way for ten minutes, so that you can have

Bell

FIGURE 3.4 Lightly Penciled Cues and Warns for Use During Rehearsals

If, as you read, you list problems on separate sheets of paper headed "Light plot," "Sound plot," "Special effects," "Properties," and "Pronunciation," then you will have rough plots ready.

Some acting editions of plays contain costume and property plots. They do not always contain all the information you will need, but you will be able to modify them easily (figure 3.5).

If others on the staff of the theater work on the plots you have written out, encourage them to give you a copy of the completed form for inclusion in the promptbook.

In general, you will want to cite on each plot for each entry the following: the page, the act and scene, and a full description of what happens.

Light Plot

Leave plenty of room between entries on the light plot (figure 3.6, page 24). During rehearsals, the director may add lighting effects not called for in the script and may add many dimmings and brightenings of areas.

Sound Plot

Frequently at sound recording sessions, the sound technician and staff members, each holding a copy of the sound plot (figure 3.7, page 25), select and rerecord, or create and

COSTUME PLOT	Actor Provides	Borrow	Rent	Purchase	Responsible & Date
MRS. JONES:					
Green and white silk polka dot dress					
White shoes					
Long white gloves					
White bracelets and earrings					
Pink silk fringe dress and stole					
Pink shoes and white beaded evening bag					
FRED:					
Light blue shirt					
Grey flannel pants					
Dark red tie					
Black shoes					
Red wool school jacket (Monroe High School)					
FATHER:					
Pajamas, orange and white stripe cotton					
Black shoes					
Grey suit					
Print shirt					
White shirt					
Soft grey hat					
JANE:					
Green jumper and white blouse					
White low heel shoes					
White bag					
White dress					
Light blue suit					
White gloves					
White high heel shoes					
HENRY:					
Dark blue and white stripe shirt					
Print shirt					
White shirt					
Jeans					
Grey sneakers					
Grey socks					
Tan shoes					
Light brown double-breasted suit					
Blue apron					
JEEVES:					
Black double-breasted tuxedo					

FIGURE 3.5 Costume Plot as Modified from the Script

record, sound effects. Ensure that all the needed sounds are recorded, in proper order and of appropriate length. When designers are expected to generate light and sound plots for a production, the stage manager's work on these plots serves two important purposes: (1) it familiarizes the SM with these aspects of the production and (2) it serves as a cross-check to ensure that no light or sound effects are overlooked.

Costume Plot

Besides giving some indication of the clothes to be worn (figure 3.5), also identify quick changes that will require change booths in the wings or at the tops of aisles and/or a series of changes that will require that an actor be assisted (figure 3.8, page 26).

The costume plot published in the actor's edition of a contemporary noncostume play in which each cast member wears one costume throughout might require only the director's approval. But in a musical such as *Little Me,* in which the lead plays several roles and is forever making quick changes, you will need to write a meticulous plot with cues for costume assistants and presets for costumes.

Property Plot

Note whether the prop is discovered or carried on—if discovered, where, and if carried on, by whom (figure 3.9, page 27). During rehearsals, note whether the prop enters stage left or stage right, so that if there are two or more prop tables backstage, you will know where to preset that prop.

page	lt. effect	cue	cue #	inst dmmrs	int	timg
114/64	Shop up	after Fore-man's entrance				
114/70	Shop out	David: "Whee" and Marvin's exit				
115/71	Dressing room in	following David's exit				
115/78	Dressing room out	David: "No, he's a hard-ware salesman!"				
116/78	Stage and Stage Mana-ger's area (Now the foots!) (But no worklight!)	after entrance of cast				
116/82	Stage and Stage Mana-ger's area out	David: "I am your older brother! By a former marriage!"				
117/82	Stage to general with worklight, no foots	when cast in place				
117/83	Stage down to effect of single work-light	Mother: "A very nice young man." & her exit				
117/84	Worklight out	David: "I trust I haven't kept you waiting too long."				
	Curtain calls lighting					
	Curtain lights out					
	House in					

FIGURE 3.6 Light Plot, Listing Cues. Note that cue numbers will not be established until the technical rehearsal. The columns left blank for "cue number," "instruments/dimmers," "intensity," and "timing" will normally be filled out by the light designer or the light technician working with the stage manager, depending on the staff.

Property control is discussed at greater length in Chapter 10.

While making light, sound, costume, and property plots, you might find it useful to make some notations on ground plans, property preset diagrams, and area lighting diagrams at the same time.

AREA LIGHTING DIAGRAMS

The area lighting diagram or focus chart (figure 3.10, page 28) shows the areas on the stage where the instruments are focused. It may be expanded with notes and diagrams to remind you where certain focusing is critical—for example, the lighting designer wants an instrument shuttered so that the light is exactly on a doorframe and there is no spill on adjacent flats.

In re-gelling instruments, or during other work near instruments, technicians sometimes accidentally jar the instruments out of focus. Sometimes an instrument is not tightened sufficiently when initially focused and slips over a period of time. The

	ACT SCENE PAGE	SOUND CUE SHEET	VOLUME	TONE	SPKR SLCTN	TIME	OTHER
1. Intro music		30 min prior to curtain in time	4	balance	1, 2, 3	30 min	fade out GENTLY
2. Fade out intro		to cue up 3rd cue (on "places")	—				
3. Roar of airplane	I-1	just prior to curtain	8		1	20 sec	
4. Thunder, lightning, heavy rain	I-1	"You won't be needing your raincoat."	7		2	90 sec	
5. Bells and light rain	I-2	"Hold on to my hand."	5	Treble	2	20 sec	
6. Car approach motor sick	I-6	"I don't hear anything."	6	balance	3	20 sec	
7. Motor strangles, car door slams	I-6	". . . His usual cheerful self."	8		2	10 sec	
8. Bicycles (like loud crickets)	I-10	"We'll meet you there." & ad libs (as they exit)	4 – 9 (fade up gently)		2	90 sec	

FIGURE 3.7 Sound Plot, Listing Cues. Space should be left between cues so additional cues can be entered. The last five columns are set through coordination of director, stage manager, and sound technician during rehearsals.

area lighting diagram helps you prevent such occurrences from affecting the lighting quality in a performance.

The lighting designer usually makes a complex area lighting diagram for the designer's own purposes. You can use the lighting designer's diagram or copy the important aspects of it. But for the sake of your familiarity with the lighting design, it is better if you make your own and then review it with the lighting designer.

ENTRANCES AND EXITS

Preparing for Entrance Warns

List each character, the scenes the character is in, and the pages for entrances and exits in the following way:

Irene:

I-1, 16–24; I-2, 26–30, 50–53;

II-1, 57–73, 78–83; II-2, 84–112

Constance:

II-1, 5–19; I-2, 26–45; etc.

(In Act I, Scene 1, Irene enters on page 16 and exits on page 24. In Scene 2 of Act I, she enters on page 26 and exits on page 30, then reenters on page 50 and exits again on page 53.)

You may wish to post your list of entrances and exits prior to a casting call so that actors may easily find lines to read for their parts.

You may also want to lightly pencil in warnings for entrances of actors, about a page preceding each entrance. It is not a stage manager's function to warn actors

Atlanta Opera
COSI FAN TUTTE
Principal Costume Run - Last Changed on 5-28-00

Act, scene	I,1			Shift	I,2			Shift	I,3			INTERM
est. time	35:00 - Dock & Café				67:00 - Drawing Room				85:30 - Garden			20:00 min
	EN		XT	CHANGE TIME/ PLACE	EN		XT	CHANGE TIME/ PLACE	EN		XT	CHANGE TIME/ PLACE
FIORDILIGI (Harris)	12:30 / SL	Parasol, Locket	34:00 / SL	SL	35:30 / SL	Chg to underwear	43:30 / SL	SL or SR	67:00 / SR	Chg to Day Dress	85:30 / SR	
					47:30 / SL	add dr. gown, brush hair	60:00 / SL					
DESPINA (Reuter-Foss)					35:00 / SL	maid	43:30 / SR		67:00 / SR	maid	67:00 / SR	
					44:30 / SR		57:30 / SR		72:30 / SR	maid	73:30 / SL	
									76:00 / SL	Chg to Doctor	onstage	
DORABELLA (Ziegler)	12:30 / SL	Parasol, Locket	34:00 / SL	SL	35:30 / SL	Chg to underwear	43:30 / SL	SL	67:00 / SL	Chg to Day Dress	85:30 / SR	
					47:30 / SL	add dr. gown	60:00 / SL					
DON ALFONSO (Cokorinos)	onstage		15:30 / SL		43:30 / SR		61:30 / SR		68:30 / SL	no hat	onstage	
	17:30 / SL		35:00 / SR		66:00 / SL		67:00 / SL					
GUIGLIELMO (Barret)	onstage	casual look	15:30 / SL	Mo. Rm.	45:30 / SR	Albanian	65:30 / SR		70:00 / SL	Albanian	onstage	
	20:00 / SL	Chg SL to full dress uniform	29:30 / SR									
FERRANDO (Thomsen)	onstage	casual look	15:30 / SL	Mo. Rm.	45:30 / SR	Albanian	66:00 / SR		70:00 / SL	Albanian	onstage	
	20:00 / SL	Chg SL to full dress uniform	29:30 / SR									

FIGURE 3.8 Principal Costume Run Sheet, *Cosi Fan Tutti*. This form was generated using Microsoft Excel. The costume workers use stopwatches and the production stage manager gives five-minute warnings: "Five-minute warning on Ms. Harris's quick change in the DL hallway." All warnings for costumes tell who, what, and where.

Courtesy Sean M. Griffin, ASM, The Atlanta Opera.

for their entrances during performance, but you will find that warning them during rehearsals is helpful. This aspect of rehearsal procedure is discussed in Chapter 8.

Long strips of paper rather than penciled lines may be used for entrance warns (figure 3.11, page 29). The marker warns are harder to miss than the light lines and can be completely removed from the promptbook prior to opening night. The marker can also be handed silently to an assistant to summon the actor.

From your notations of entrances and exits, you can now make up a visual display of characters on stage, a graph that shows at a glance which actors work together on what script pages (figure 3.12, page 29). This device will be invaluable to you in planning rehearsal schedules, finding appropriate pages for readings, double casting, and removing script pages to serve as sides for a minor role. The visual display should be placed in your promptbook as a reference tool.

Actors and Their Entrance Cues

During performances, actors are responsible for making all their entrances on cue. They alone have this responsibility. This arises out of understandable circumstances:

THE BEAUTY PART | Stage Right Prop Table

Act I Scene 4

PROP/SET PIECE	personal	preset	WHO/WHERE	work	SOURCE	final
coffee cup, white take-out	x		Quagmeyer	x		x
attache case	x		Hubris	x	Bill	x
script	x		Hubris/in attache	x	Lawrence	x
artist's smock	x		Hubris/in attache	x	Maria	
April Monkhood's picture	x		Hubris	x	Lawrence	x
phone, old beat up		x	on table	x		
radio, old beat up		x	on table	x		x
vase to hold brushes		x	on table	x		x
brushes		x	in vase	x	Dinah	x
small white paper bag		x	on table	x		x
push broom		x	behind easel	x		x
oil paintings		x	on chair	X		
abstract of woman		x	on easel			
bottle of whiskey in white bag	x		Quagmeyer	x		
easel, paint smeared						
table, beat up, paint smeared						
2 beat up, non matching chairs						

FIGURE 3.9 Property Plot (May Double as Control Form)

During the performance, the stage manager can only be in one place—the work area—following the book and cueing sound, lights, and curtain. Cues sometimes coincide with an actor's entrance (e.g., the doorbell rings prior to the entrance or the director calls for a subtle increase of light intensity on the door area as the actor enters). So the stage manager cannot be in two places at once, cueing and pushing the actor on stage. There might be several actors entering from more than one entrance. Therefore, out of practical considerations, it is necessary that entrances are each actor's own responsibility. In professional theater, the union insists on this. In opera, however, cues for entrances and costume changes are given routinely (figure 3.8 and page 142).

As usual, there are some exceptions to this rule. The stage manager is responsible for actors being in place when they are discovered at the rise of the curtain and when they are offstage about to enter within the first few seconds after the curtain. After calling "Places, please," the stage manager checks that all discovered cast members are in their appropriate blocked positions. The procedure for checking this, in a theater-in-the-round example, is discussed in Chapter 11 under "Shift Inspection."

There are even some exceptional exceptions: Occasionally, a producer or director overrides normal procedure and asks that the stage manager "supervise" the entrances and exits of an actor who has particular difficulties. Such an exception is discussed as an example under "The Calls" in Chapter 9.

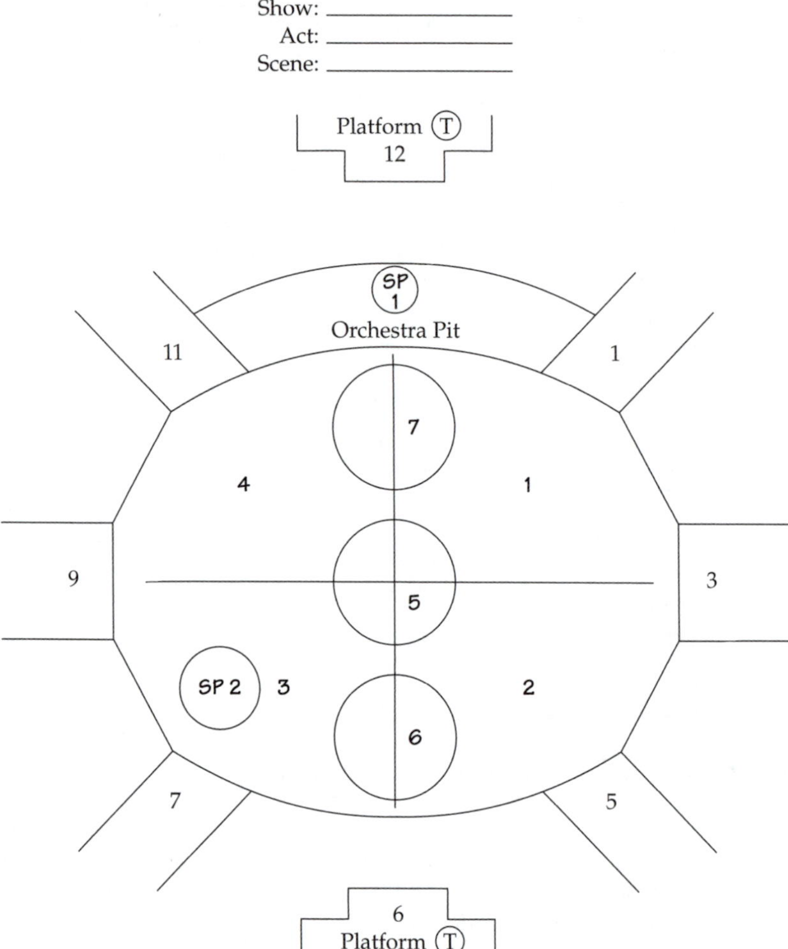

FIGURE 3.10 Area Lighting Diagram for Round Stage

During rehearsals, the situation is different. In the role of expeditor of rehearsals, the stage manager should closely supervise the entrances of cast members. In many theaters, there is no monitor system that broadcasts the rehearsals to offstage areas where the actors may wander off for fittings or to run lines. So the stage manager warns them of their entrances, following the procedures described under "Warning" in Chapter 8.

PRONUNCIATION QUESTIONS

You may wish to make a list of all words in the script about which there is a question of pronunciation. Include the pronunciation of all proper names that might be pronounced in more than one way.

FIGURE 3.11 Actor Warn in Promptbook for Quick Access During Rehearsal

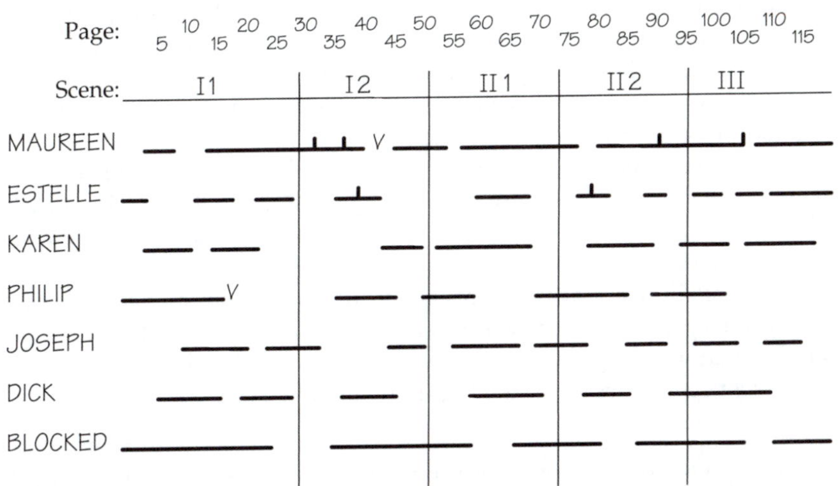

FIGURE 3.12 A Visual Display of Characters on Stage. Note that the "blocked" line allows you to see what scenes have yet to be blocked, and who's in them. The "v" denotes voice only.

Example

Middle of the Night by Paddy Chayefsky—"Mrs. Nieman." Obviously, all members of the cast should pronounce this name the same way. Should it be pronounced Nē-man or Nī-man?

List foreign words and phrases and give both the pronunciation and meaning.

> ***Example***
> *A Majority of One* by Leonard Spigelgass—“mashugina”; *ma-shoóg-i-na,* Yiddish meaning “crazy.”

List unusual and uncommon words and give pronunciation and meaning.

> ***Example***
> *The Emperor* by Hermann Gressieker—“trireme”; *trí-reem,* an ancient Roman galley with three banks of oars on each side.

> ***Example***
> *The Cherry Orchard* by Anton Chekhov—“Epihodov”; *Ep-(i)-hoé-daff,* a clerk who proposes to Dunyasha.

This list may be posted as early as the readings for the benefit of those trying out for parts. But it is especially beneficial to you, since you must pronounce the words correctly while prompting. Keep a copy in your promptbook. Also, cast members should be provided with pronunciations of character names.

SPECIAL EFFECTS

If there is only one special effect in a play, there is obviously no need for writing a plot. But if you are doing a play that calls for many, you will want to list them for consideration by the scene designer and technical director. Such a list might include a heavy fog, walls shaking, and dishes falling off shelves, a trapdoor disappearance accompanied by a flash of smoke, a sliding panel, firing of weapons, and so on. Use of fire or an open flame on stage requires a separate plot (page 232).

Making plots and lists can seem far removed from making theater happen. I am not in favor of “busy work” or unnecessary duplication of work. The fledgling SM should understand that making plots can help in the understanding of all elements of a production coming together.

Hard work in analyzing the script and identifying its problems before rehearsals begin pays off—your work becomes easier with every day that passes. Lack of preparation before rehearsals begin results in a terribly overworked and panicked feeling as opening night approaches—a feeling I've always preferred to avoid.

> I feel that two or three weeks of work on material before rehearsals start is a must, depending on how fast you can type and organize.
>
> Curtiss Marlowe
> *Stage Manager*
> *Liberty Theatre*
> *North Hollywood, CA*

SUGGESTED CLASSROOM EXERCISE

Show the class a promptbook of a recent production. Discuss the pattern of mounting pages (figure 3.2) that was used and explain why that pattern was selected.

4

Scheduling and Company Rules

If you're failing to plan, you're planning to fail.
—Anonymous

THE MASTER CALENDAR

Time, management of time, and the coordination of the cast, crew, and staff are important to every theater. In order to keep everyone on time and their efforts meshing smoothly, it is desirable to post a master calendar—and only one master calendar—at a convenient place to make it available to everyone on the staff. The master calendar can be your most effective tool for coordinating the staff.

The master calendar (figure 4.1, page 33) should be large enough so that several lines can be written legibly in the space allotted for each day. It should, of course, be developed after consultation regarding the needs of the producer or management, the department heads in various phases of production, and, above all, the director, with whom you work in a direct supporting role. The calendar should list many of the following kinds of events, but not necessarily all of them, and not necessarily in the following order:

Deadline for set drawings/line drawings (page 56)

Deadline for lighting plans

Deadline for cleaning/repairing lighting instruments

Deadline for obtaining sufficient copies of the script (page 14)

Readings/auditions (page 68)

Deadline for complete casting (page 75)

Understudy casting (page 76)

First rehearsal (page 88)

All subsequent rehearsals (page 98)

Work calls (pages 37 and 168)

Staff conferences (pages 34 and 99)
Deadline for memorization of lines (by act) (page 105)
Deadline for obtaining all rehearsal props (pages 100 and 143)
Take-in day (page 159)
Deadline for completion of sets (page 159)
Deadline for completion of sound effects (page 23)
Focus lights (page 170)
Fittings of costumes (pages 24 and 115)
Publicity picture calls (page 115)
Publicity interviews (page 115)
Deadline for reservation of opening-night tickets
Deadline for obtaining all final props (page 143)
Integration of sound effects into rehearsals (page 170)
Integration of film effects into rehearsals (page 170)
Costume parade (pages 116 and 297)
Special costume rehearsal
First rehearsal with musicians
No-actor tech/all set changes (page 189)
First technical rehearsal (page 189)
Second tech (page 189)
First dress rehearsal
Second dress
Invitational dress/previews
Flameproofing of set (pages 225 and 230)
Fire inspection (page 225)
Opening night
All performances
Understudy rehearsals (page 202)
Closing night (page 205)
Strike (page 205)
Take-out day/sets and props returned (pages 145 and 205)
All other use of the stage (page 207)

- **If you plan to have every aspect of the production in its final shape all at the same time, you are likely to have problems. But by spacing deadlines for various aspects of the production, you may check on, and overcome, small crises rather than have to face (and optimally surmount) total panic.**

SUN	MON	TUES	WED	THUR	FRI	SAT	NOTES
		1 10 STAFF CONF.	**2** 7:30 – Readings 9:30	**3** 2:00 – Readings 4:00 6:00 readings 7:30	**4** 2:00 – Readings | 5:30	**5** DEADLINE: SET DESIGN LINE DWGS.	Readings
6	**7** 1ST DAY THTR. AVAILABLE 10 AM 1ST Rehearsal (contracts) 2:00 Pub. Photos	**8** 10 AM Rehearsal 11:30 Staff conf.	**9** 10:00 Staff conf. 10:30 REHEARSAL	**10** 10 AM REHEARSAL 2:00 COSTUME FITTINGS	**11** 10:00 Rehearsal	**12** CAST DAY OFF 10:00 WORK CALL	
13 10:00 WORK CALL	**14** 10:00 rehearsal	**15** 10:00 Rehearsal	**16** 10:00 Staff conf. 10:30 REHEARSAL	**17** Deadline: Live sound effects obtained 10 AM Rehearsal	**18** DEADLINE ALL REHEARSAL PROPS 10:00 Rehearsal	**19** cast day off 10:00 WORK CALL	
20 10:00 WORK CALL	**21** CAST DAY OFF 8:00 TAPE ALL SOUND CUES MUSIC	**22** 10:00 AM Rehearsal 10:30 Staff Meet.	**23** REHRSL 10 AM ~~Staff conf.~~ deadline: Research Opening night & invitations	**24** 11:30 Rehearsal DEADLINE ALL PROPS final	**25** DEADLINE: All lines memorized 10Rehearsal Integrate Sound	**26** Take-in Day: 10 Work call 8:00 REHEARSAL RUN THROUGH	
27 9:00 Work Call SET COMPLETE 8:00 Rehearsal Run Through	**28** cast day off 10:00 Focus lights 2:00 Flame proof sets	**29** 10:00 STAFF Conf. 8:00 Tech Rehearsal	**30** DEADLINE: All costume complete 8:00 Tech Rehearsal				

FIGURE 4.1 A Master Calendar

Example

If you wait until the technical ("tech") rehearsal to check on the progress of your sound effects, you may find the tape not ready and the source CDs the sound technician expected to tape at the last minute are missing. At the second tech, the sound technician finds that backstage speaker wires are missing and there is no spare wire in the theater. So you may get your sound effects working by dress rehearsal, if then.

But if you put your sound tape completion deadline two days before your target date for sound integration at a rehearsal, and put the date of integration two days before your technical rehearsal is scheduled to run, you can afford to slip one day, even two or three, and still be ready for tech with all sound ready for plug-in. Similarly, try to plan checkpoints in other areas and get your coworkers to meet these checkpoints so that everything shapes up neatly for the first technical rehearsal.

Some deadline dates must naturally fall before others. "Take-in" day, for instance, must come before "focus lights" day, since focusing of instruments is dependent on placement and shape of set pieces. Rehearsal props deadline should precede line memorization deadline so that actors can pick up their props (or substitutes for them) as they set down their scripts.

If all staff members are required to post their requirements for use of stage and rehearsal space on the master calendar, conflicts will be avoided.

Example

The crew arrives for a work call and finds the cast on stage for an extra rehearsal. After it is determined whose needs are greater, cast or crew depart. If all of the stage requirements had been posted on the master calendar, this situation would have been avoided.

The master calendar should not be placed on the callboard or made available to the cast under normal circumstances. It must be kept away from cast members so that actors do not become confused about their rehearsal schedule or concerned about technical deadlines. All information that cast members need from the master calendar should be made available to them by other means, particularly the rehearsal schedule (see upcoming section). WordPerfect, Print Master, and Calendar Creator are three of many computer programs that can help in the fast manufacture of calendars.

STAFF MEETINGS

- **Some theaters have regularly scheduled staff conferences; most do not. If conferences have not been held in the past, you should initiate them. Having everyone on the staff gather together at a designated time to discuss problems and progress can save time and grief.**

At the preproduction or first staff meeting, get the director's concept expressed, honed, understood, and preferably summarized in writing.

During staff meetings, ask intelligent questions that will urge your coworkers to reveal specifics about what they are doing. "Everything is going just fine and on schedule" is not a satisfactory contribution to a staff meeting from any department head. It should be show-and-tell time, with every member showing diagrams and drawings and discussing the specifics.

Example

At dress rehearsal, it is found that the leading lady's costume blends perfectly into the set designer's flats to the point where all but her face and hands disappear when she stands against them. Her hoop skirt won't fit through any door on the set. Some things will have to be changed at the last minute. These problems would have been avoided if the set designer and costume designer had done "due diligence show-and-tell."

A full review of the master calendar is a good way to start the first staff meeting.

One main reason for having a production meeting with all designers, production manager, tech director, and director, as well as the stage manager, is to make sure the schedule is tailored to fit not only the tech side of things but also the cast and director's needs. Without a representative from the rehearsal point of view, many things can be overlooked, such as time built into a schedule for a spacing rehearsal on stage before tech, adding wardrobe pieces before dress rehearsal if they affect actor business, and special cue light and quick change booth needs backstage.

For a musical, especially in theaters that don't specialize in them, it's important to remind the tech crew of requirements for that type of show. Power requirements in the pit, front-of-house sound mixer location, pit setup, and other "musical" specific details need to be discussed early on in the process and built into the schedule and budget.

Aside from the mundane business aspects of production meetings, it's a nice chance for the creative team and tech crew to meet each other and feel like they're working together toward a common goal. The relationships that come out of that meeting can help avoid problems that occur when all the designers have been working single-mindedly only to collide with each other at first tech. It makes a stage manager's life a lot easier, too!

Jill (Johnson) Gold
PSM, Pasadena Playhouse

REHEARSAL SCHEDULES

- **Carefully oversee the preparation, posting, and distribution of the rehearsal schedule. If possible, the schedule should be posted at the very first reading and distributed before the first rehearsal.**

This takes a lot of coordination with everyone in a supervisory position. If you are working with amateurs who are not expected to be at the total disposition of the rehearsal schedule, you will have to coordinate the schedule with the cast as well. If you are working with professionals who are under the jurisdiction of union restrictions, you will have to work into the schedule the exact union requirements, specifying days off as well as required coffee breaks on more complicated schedules.

Once content is determined, clarity should be your chief concern in writing the schedule (figure 4.2). Make sure that for each entry you give the time, date, place, and scenes to be rehearsed. It is not enough to identify the act (Roman numeral) and scene (Arabic numeral)—for example, II-1, III-2. List the names of the cast members involved. Do not assume that cast members will know which scenes they are in. Assume the worst—that cast members will find ways to misinterpret the schedule. Take the time to make reading and understanding the schedule easy for cast members. This is not done out of contempt for actors, but out of respect: If you can free them from the mechanics of production, you may allow them greater concentration on their primary function.

Your schedule might also include a wallet-sized area with important telephone numbers that can be clipped for the cast member's wallet or purse. Numbers to be listed are (1) a coordination number or numbers that cast members can call to leave messages when supervisory personnel cannot be reached directly, (2) your home phone number,

THEATER TWENTY

5060 Fountain Avenue
phone 666 9059

Numbers You Need
(clip for wallet or purse)

Emergency	911
Coordination (Jackie)	555 2171
	555 2028
Stage Manager (Frank)	555 9887
Theater/Reservations	555 9060
Rehearsal Hall	555 9061
Yellow Cab	555 5421
Subway	555 7171
Whole Foods	555 0126
Holiday Inn	555 0253
Best Western	555 1712

REHEARSAL
SCHEDULE

Act I	Sc 1:	Rita, Arlene, Sandy
	Sc 2:	Jonas, Terry, Sylvia, JoAnne
	Sc 3:	Arlene, Jones
Act II	Sc 1:	Sandy, Dee, Norma, Rita, Arlene, Jonas
	Sc 2:	Jonas, Arlene
	Sc 3:	JoAnne, Terry, Dave, Jonas
Act III	Sc 1:	Arlene, Larry, Rita, Sandy
	Sc 2:	Terry, Jonas, Arlene

DATE	TIME	PLACE	SCENES
Sunday, Nov. 6*	1:00-5:00 p.m.	Rehearsal Hall 1	III-1
Tuesday, Nov. 8 (all lines memorized)	6:30-9:00 p.m.	Rehearsal Hall 1	I-3, II-1
Thursday, Nov. 10	6:30-9:00 p.m.	Room 203	I-2, III-2
Saturday, Nov. 12*	1:00-5:00 p.m.	Rehearsal Hall 1	II-3
Sunday, Nov. 13*	1:00-5:00 p.m.	Room 203	I-1, II-1
Monday, Nov. 14 (all costumes worn)	6:30-9:00 p.m.	Main Stage	Runthrough
Tuesday, Nov. 15	6:30-9:30 or ???? p.m.	Main Stage	Tech
Wednesday, Nov. 16	6:00-9:30 p.m.	Main Stage	Second Tech
Thursday, Nov. 17	6:30 call	Main Stage	Dress
Friday, Nov. 18	6:30 call	Main Stage	Opening

*On weekends, entrance to the building is from parking lot only.

FIGURE 4.2 A Rehearsal Schedule

(3) the home phone numbers of any other staff or supervisory personnel whose assistance may be required by members of the theater group, (4) the theater number, (5) rehearsal hall number (if different from theater number), (6) police emergency, (7) fire emergency, (8) ambulance emergency, (9) food service, (10) ticket reservations (if different from theater number), and (11) any other numbers that might be helpful as quick reference to the cast.

The rehearsal schedule need not (and probably should not) include any of the technical deadlines for staff members that are posted on the master calendar. These are not necessary for cast members. But line memorization deadlines should be included and dress rehearsals noted. Notes on parking, access to the theater and rehearsal areas, and other helpful information would also be appreciated by cast members.

If you are unable to fill the entire rehearsal schedule with specifics, it is best to post a tentative schedule, so labeled, with dates and blank spaces for the unknown variables, so that cast members can fill in the blanks when the information is available (figure 4.3).

Sometimes it is effective to staple a second copy of the rehearsal schedule into each cast member's script on the premise that the script is less likely to be lost than a single sheet of paper.

It may be desirable for you to print the following lines at the bottom of the schedule: "Open dates are not off! They haven't been set yet. Please keep your personal schedule open for additional rehearsals as called." Or you might want to write a "subject to change" disclaimer on the rehearsal schedule. Keep in mind, when first making up the rehearsal schedule, that including extra "safety" rehearsals initially and then canceling them when they are determined to be unnecessary is easier than calling extra, nonscheduled rehearsals as opening night looms closer.

In some amateur theaters, the cast may be told halfway into rehearsals that they will have to come to previously unscheduled work calls if they want to have scenery. This generally is met with much unhappiness. To avoid this, stage managers in amateur situations should plan work calls before rehearsals begin and put them on the schedule with a note that cast members will be expected to attend in work clothes.

When rehearsing a musical in one week, it becomes necessary to juggle principals, chorus, dancers, and extras between five or more different areas and still retain one's sanity. This calls for extremely careful planning of a more sophisticated schedule (figure 4.4, page 39) and the determination of all concerned to meet the schedule.

The worst problem in keeping to such a complicated schedule, where work periods are broken down to the hour and even half hour, is that the staff members—musical director, chorus director, choreographer, and costume designer—are unwilling to release the cast members they are working with at the end of the specified time period. They are always in the middle of something important and need five minutes more. It becomes difficult to cajole these creative people into keeping to the schedule.

A second problem is that a lot of cast time is lost in shepherding members between rehearsal areas. With many work areas and short work periods, a certain amount of confusion and delay cannot be avoided, but clear and careful scheduling can help to minimize it.

Is it desirable to distribute schedules? Yes, it is. It is one of the ways in which you can assist the cast beyond the minimum requirements of announcing the next call. It also saves cast members the trouble of individually copying the schedule.

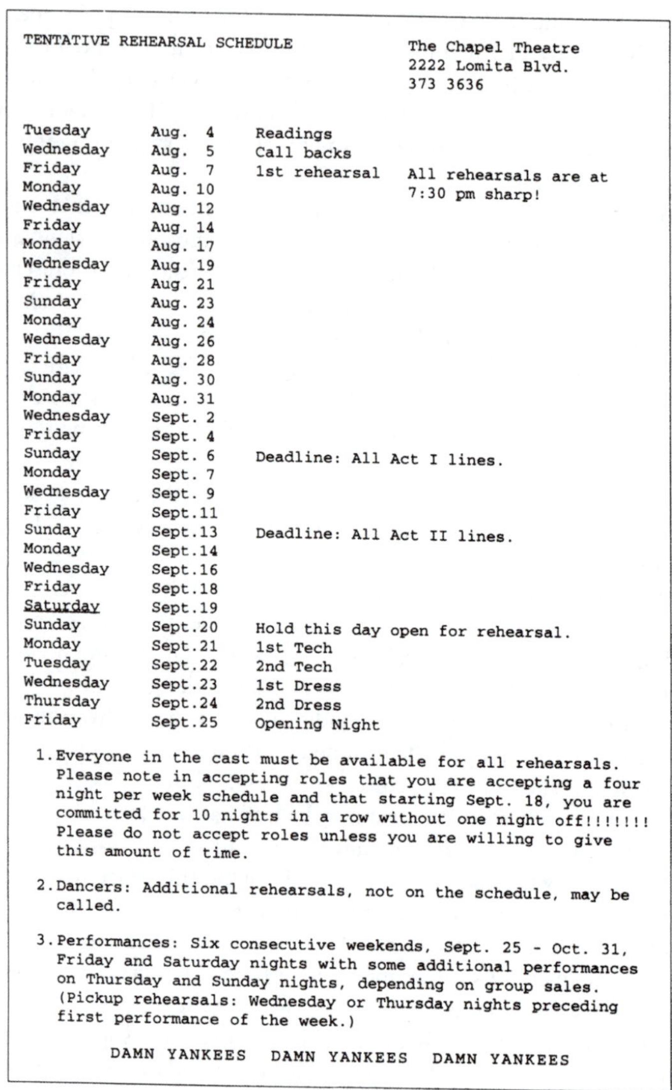

TENTATIVE REHEARSAL SCHEDULE

The Chapel Theatre
2222 Lomita Blvd.
373 3636

Tuesday	Aug. 4	Readings	
Wednesday	Aug. 5	Call backs	
Friday	Aug. 7	1st rehearsal	All rehearsals are at 7:30 pm sharp!
Monday	Aug. 10		
Wednesday	Aug. 12		
Friday	Aug. 14		
Monday	Aug. 17		
Wednesday	Aug. 19		
Friday	Aug. 21		
Sunday	Aug. 23		
Monday	Aug. 24		
Wednesday	Aug. 26		
Friday	Aug. 28		
Sunday	Aug. 30		
Monday	Aug. 31		
Wednesday	Sept. 2		
Friday	Sept. 4		
Sunday	Sept. 6	Deadline: All Act I lines.	
Monday	Sept. 7		
Wednesday	Sept. 9		
Friday	Sept.11		
Sunday	Sept.13	Deadline: All Act II lines.	
Monday	Sept.14		
Wednesday	Sept.16		
Friday	Sept.18		
<u>Saturday</u>	Sept.19		
Sunday	Sept.20	Hold this day open for rehearsal.	
Monday	Sept.21	1st Tech	
Tuesday	Sept.22	2nd Tech	
Wednesday	Sept.23	1st Dress	
Thursday	Sept.24	2nd Dress	
Friday	Sept.25	Opening Night	

1. Everyone in the cast must be available for all rehearsals. Please note in accepting roles that you are accepting a four night per week schedule and that starting Sept. 18, you are committed for 10 nights in a row without one night off!!!!!!! Please do not accept roles unless you are willing to give this amount of time.

2. Dancers: Additional rehearsals, not on the schedule, may be called.

3. Performances: Six consecutive weekends, Sept. 25 - Oct. 31, Friday and Saturday nights with some additional performances on Thursday and Sunday nights, depending on group sales. (Pickup rehearsals: Wednesday or Thursday nights preceding first performance of the week.)

DAMN YANKEES DAMN YANKEES DAMN YANKEES

FIGURE 4.3 A tentative rehearsal schedule.

Sometimes it is not enough to distribute the schedule, staple a duplicate in each script, post a copy on the callboard, and announce the next call at each rehearsal. You might "mother-hen" the schedule even beyond this. If a cast member is late, you might check to find out why, in the hope of eliminating future tardiness. If a cast member is absent, call to make sure the actor knows the next call. **If there is any change in the schedule, it is your responsibility to see that every person concerned is informed of the change.**

Keep several extra copies of the rehearsal schedule in your promptbook, always ready to hand one to a cast member who has misplaced his, one to the upholsterer who wants to know when the stage will be free so the sofa can be recovered, one to the lady who lives above the theater and wants to know when not to play her TV, and

REHEARSAL SCHEDULE

TUESDAY – JULY 14

TIME	AUDITORIUM	TENT	CHORUS ROOM	MUSIC ROOM	COSTUME SHOP
10:00		Frank			
10:30		II-5		Julie	Ravenal
11:00		II-5	Girl Sing. Dancers	Ravenal	Male Danc.
11:30	Frank, Karen	Ravenal Magnolia	Girl Sing. Dancers Male Danc.	Julie	Andy
12:00	I-1	(Lunch)	Girl Sing. (All Danc. to lunch)	(Lunch)	(Lunch)
12:30	I-2	(Lunch)	" "	(Lunch)	Parthy
1:00	(Lunch)	All Danc.	(Lunch)	Joe	Magnolia
1:30	(Lunch)	" "	(Lunch)	Andy, Parthy	Steve
2:00	I-3	" "	Girl Sing	Ravenal	Joe, Frank
2:30	I-3	Male Danc.	" "	Queenie	Girl Danc.
3:00	I-4	All Danc., Girl Sing.		Ellie, Frank	Julie
3:30	Andy	" "		Magnolia	Queenie, Ellie
4:00	Pict. Call				
4:30					
5:00		I-2			
5:30					Local Chorus
6:00	Joe, Queenie		Local Chorus		
6:30	Ellie, Frank		" "		

Notes: Today is day off for Male Singing Ensemble. Picture Call: 4 p.m. Aud. – Check sep. picture call sheet to see if you are needed. Report to costume shop, then aud.

FIGURE 4.4 A single-day rehearsal schedule.

more to all others concerned, ad infinitum. Of course, every staff member should be on your initial distribution.

COMPANY RULES

A handout of company rules is a helpful device to let cast, staff, and crew know what is expected of them (figure 4.5). Categories of rules that you will want to include are:

Backstage behavior, noise, and cleanliness

Tardiness

Guests backstage and complimentary tickets

Costume upkeep

When the rules are approved, distribute them to all concerned, preferably at the initial meeting of the company. Post a copy on the callboard.

Player's Ring Gallery
8325 Santa Monica Blvd.
December 13

The Company of
ONE FLEW OVER THE CUCKOO'S NEST

1. You must sign in each night. Never sign in for another actor.
2. Please call 555-2424 if you expect to be late for half hour call.
3. Please use the stage door, not the front door.
4. Please open and close the stage door quietly.
5. Please stay backstage after 8 pm (7:30 pm Sat.).
6. Cast members are not allowed in the box office.
7. Extremely important and emergency messages can get to you by calling 650-6920 during performances, and only that number.
8. Please leave costume laundry with SM on Sunday night after performance. You must fill out laundry slip.
9. Please stay out of the light booth.
10. Please do not speak to SM during light cues, sound cues, and set changes.
11. All cast members must take curtain call in complete costume.
12. Please smoke behind theater & not in the backstage hallways.
13. No visitors are allowed in dressing rooms during perf.
14. Please be alert to the monitors for your cues. The SM is responsible for warns only before acts, not before individual cues once the act has begun. (See your Equity rules.)
15. Please do not talk during perf. while backstage. If you must communicate, please whisper. The wall between aud. and dressing room is not sound proof.
16. Keep theater doors closed because of air conditioning.
17. Please do not congregate with aud. during intermission.
18. Please wear appropriate clothing backstage.
19. Please do not use the pay phone during the performance (because of noise).
20. Please help in Saturday night buffet cleanup.
21. Please stay out of the entrance areas during entrances & exits of other actors & during crew shifts. You can be seen by the audience.
22. Please do not use the men's room during the performance. It is noisy and near an entrance. Both men and women may use the women's room during perf., but please wait until the water has stopped running before opening the door, and hold the door to prevent slamming.
23. Use good judgment about not using the water fountain during silent moments of performance.

THANK YOU IN ADVANCE FOR YOUR HELP AND COOPERATION!

Lawrence S.
stage manager

FIGURE 4.5 An example of company rules.

Just as you want to know what is expected of you, actors want to know what is expected of them. Take time at the first company meeting to review the rules and explain the reasons for them.

Example

Tent theater rule: "Cast members must sit in the last two rows of the theater when not onstage during rehearsals." This brief rule alone seemed unjustifiable; after all, the empty seats in front were a much more convenient waiting place. The rule could have been explained in just a few lines: The asphalt surface of the center of the tent became so hot during rehearsal hours that the chair legs sank into and destroyed the surface. The back rows were not surfaced and were thus practically indestructible.

If there are good reasons for rules, make the reasons clear to cast members. This will result in greater cooperation on their part. Reasons for rules that seem obvious to you are not always so obvious to cast members—such as the fire hazard of smoking backstage. Be patient in explaining.

If there are not good reasons for rules, the rules are probably not necessary!

THE CALLBOARD

The callboard has already been mentioned as the place to post the rehearsal schedule and company rules. It is a backstage bulletin board for cast, crew, and staff (figure 4.6). It is usually located near the stage door where cast members can't miss it when they arrive and depart.

The following rules worked well during a L-O-N-G H-O-T summer in Georgia:

The fine system:

1. No bare feet at any time in the theater offices, scene shop, set or dressing rooms. First offense: $5 fine; second offense, $10 fine; third offense, dismissal.
2. Showing up at rehearsal intoxicated: immediate and irrevocable dismissal.
3. Late for rehearsals. First offense: $5 fine (waived if SM called); second offense, $10 fine; third offense, dismissal.
4. Chewing gum or smoking in rehearsal hall during rehearsal: $15 fine, doubled at recurring offenses.
5. Summer clothing not deemed appropriate (too revealing) for rehearsal (no air conditioning in rehearsal space): $15 fine, doubled at each offense.

The SM did not collect a single dime between May 23 and August 13.

Scott Ross, *Stage Manager*
Gaye Markley, *tHouse Manager*
Georgia Shakespeare Festival, 1989
Atlanta, GA

The basic items that every member of the company must be able to find are:

Emergency phone numbers (figure 4.7, page 43)

The next call (page 115)

The rehearsal schedule (described earlier)

The sign-in sheet (page 138)

Closing notice (page 205)

Company rules (described earlier)

Names of company members qualified in CPR and first aid (page 128)

First-aid information (figure 4.8, page 44) and location of first-aid kit (page 128)

FIGURE 4.6 A View of a Well-Organized Callboard. Jill Gold, Production Stage Manager, posts a notice on the callboard of the Pasadena Playhouse. Note that the callboard is spacious and well lit. It is divided into three areas: Equity, Messages, and Sign-In.

Courtesy Jill (Johnson) Gold, PSM, Pasadena Playhouse. Photo by Rato.

Blood-borne pathogens advisory and location of cleanup kit (page 119)

Location of fire extinguishers (page 225)

Some other items that you might wish to post are:

Helpful phone numbers (cab service, food service, and nearby restaurants and hotels if cast members are from out of town) (figure 4.2)

Cast list (page 83)

Favorable reviews (if favorable to all cast members—check theater's policy)

Invitations to other theaters

Advertisements of lessons and services of special interest to cast members

E-mail and Twitter messages to the cast

Duty roster (page 194)

Curtain call order (figure 13.6)

VIP list (page 198)

Firearms safety tips (figure 10.6)

When casting is complete, take down the notes regarding readings. Also, items on the callboard that are no longer timely should be removed.

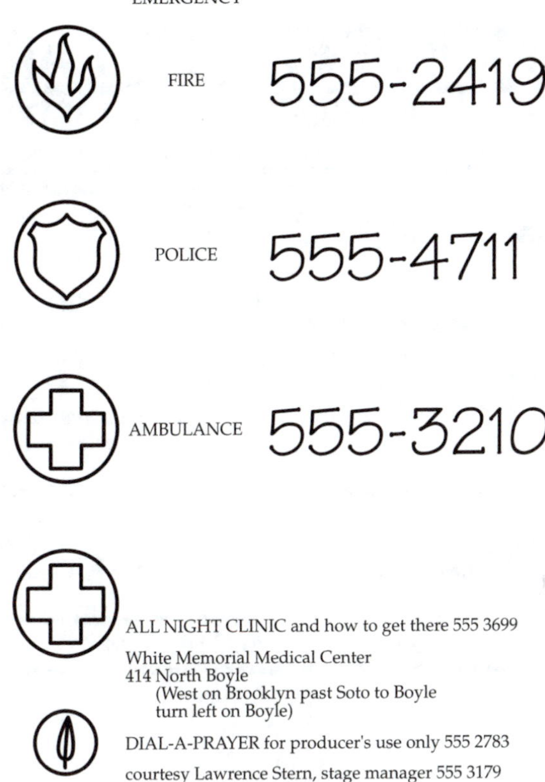

EMERGENCY
FIRE 555-2419
POLICE 555-4711
AMBULANCE 555-3210
ALL NIGHT CLINIC and how to get there 555 3699
White Memorial Medical Center
414 North Boyle
(West on Brooklyn past Soto to Boyle
turn left on Boyle)
DIAL-A-PRAYER for producer's use only 555 2783
courtesy Lawrence Stern, stage manager 555 3179

FIGURE 4.7 Emergency Phone Numbers for Callboard Display

Bring your organizational skill and artistic ability to the arrangement of items on the callboard so cast members can find what they want quickly. It might be advisable to divide the callboard into three areas: permanent, temporary, and urgent.

The callboard should be large enough to accommodate all the bulletins that must be posted without having them overlap. Make sure extra pins are available to put up additional material, and attach a pencil to your callboard so cast members can initial bulletins and the sign-in sheet, as well as make notes for themselves, without having to search for a pencil.

Electronic Callboards

Programs like Yahoo Groups and Blackboard may be set up to distribute most callboard information to the cast, crew, and staff. This should be an addition to, not a replacement for, the callboard. It cannot be assumed that everyone in your cast has regular access to the Internet or checks e-mail regularly.

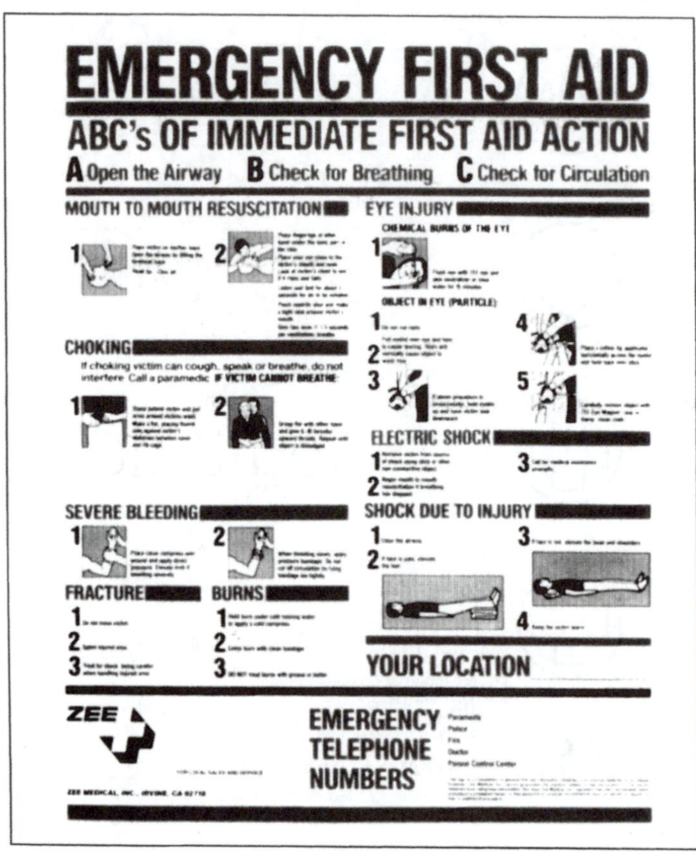

FIGURE 4.8 Example of First-Aid Information Poster That Might Be Placed on a Callboard

Courtesy Zee Medical, Inc., Irvine, California.zeemedical.com.

With your master calendar discussed and posted, staff meetings arranged, rehearsal schedules coordinated and distributed, company rules determined and explained, and the callboard made orderly, you have made a good start at making things run smoothly.

My Teaching Strategy

To understand theater communications, students work in small groups during class to (1) list staff/personnel groups that contribute to production [figure 5.1], (2) identify types of information normally exchanged (cast lists, rehearsal schedules, crew calls, etc.), (3) determine which channels of communication (callboard, Web site, phone calls, etc.) are most appropriate for each, and (4) prepare a chart displaying this information (see chart layout, page 45). When complete, class compares charts.

Type of Information	Personnel	Channels of Communication	Notes/Follow-up
Cast List	Director	Callboard	Cast Initials Call
	Stage Manager	E-mail List	E-mail Replies
	Cast	Web site	
	Public Relations		
	Designers		
Production Meeting Agenda	Director	Callboard	E-mail Replies
	Tech Director	E-mail	
	Stage Managers	Web site	

Mark E. Mallett, PhD
Assistant Professor of Theater Arts
The Richard Stockton College of New Jersey, Pomona, NJ

SUGGESTED CLASSROOM EXERCISE

Have the class brainstorm all of the events that should be included in a master calendar. Write them on the board in chronological order. Compare the list with the one on pages 31 and 32.

5

Getting Acquainted with Your Theater

A real handyman needs only three things: WD-40 to make things go, duct tape to make things stop, and a big hammer for those delicate adjustments.
—Anonymous

Every theater is unique—in the way it operates, in the organization of personnel, and in the way the staff interacts. Each unique theater has some unique expectations of how the stage manager will fit into the process of making theater.

WHO DOES WHAT?

- **The stage manager should know who reports to whom in his theater. Not only should the stage manager know to whom he is responsible, but also to whom everyone else on the staff is responsible. In the role of personnel coordinator, this information is important.**

The easiest way to find this out is to talk to people on the staff. If you are still uncertain, bring up the question at the earliest staff meeting. Even in theaters in which the distribution of tasks has been codified over the years, time may be taken at the first production meeting of a season to review and adjust for current staffing, personal preferences and capabilities of staff, and staff members' available time.

Figure 5.1 shows an organizational chart for a hypothetical theater. I know that it does not apply to your theater. There are so many variations in staff organization, names of positions, and chains of command that it would be impossible to provide in this book charts for every theater. Several factors causing variation are discussed in this chapter.

Designing an organizational chart for your theater might be desirable if you have a high turnover in personnel and you need to brief incoming personnel quickly. The more your organizational chart differs from what might normally be expected, the more your theater needs an organizational chart.

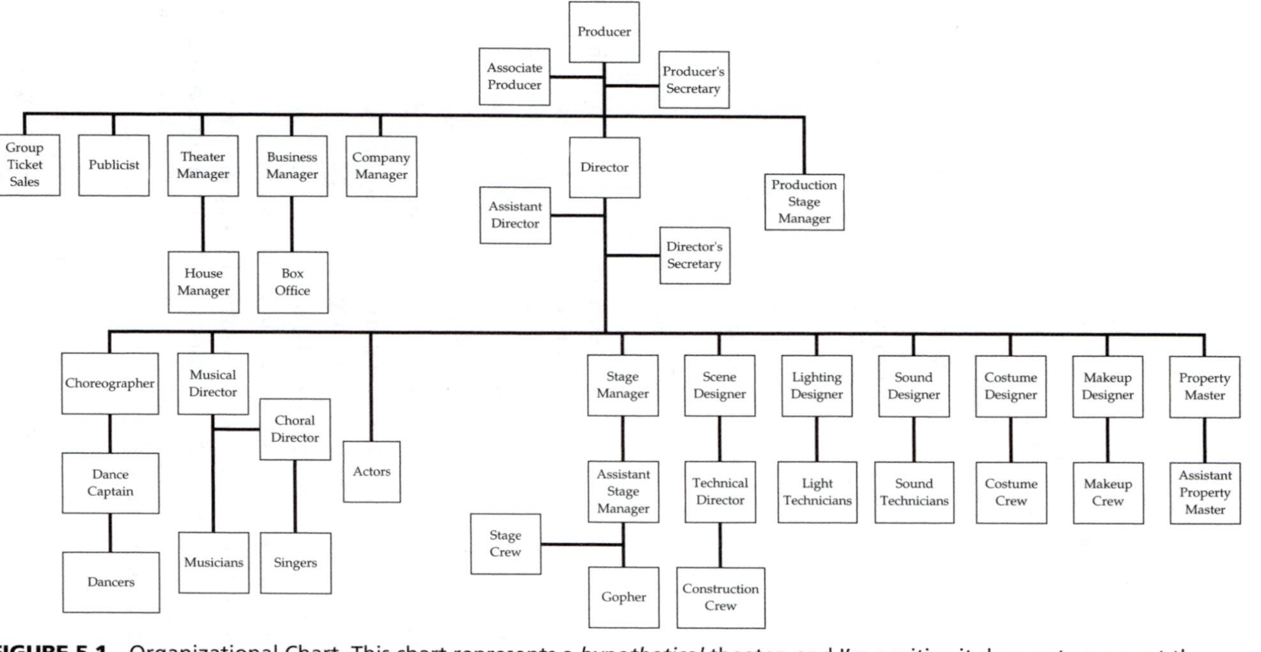

FIGURE 5.1 Organizational Chart. This chart represents a *hypothetical* theater, and I'm positive it does not represent the organization at your theater. There are an infinite number of variations in the organization of a theater's staff. Some of the causes of variation are discussed in the text. This chart shows *primary lines of responsibility only*. The stage manager, for example, reports to the production stage manager and to the producer, as well as to the director. Also, the organization shifts *when the curtain goes up*. Actors who reported to the director now report to the stage manager, and light and sound technicians who reported to designers now report to the stage manager.

Organizational structure and job descriptions vary greatly from theater to theater, and even from one production to another. Even within a given production where the structure and descriptions may be set and "understood," those involved frequently interpret this "known" organizational structure, and job descriptions, differently. Effective stage managers must be able to navigate these different structures, descriptions, and perceptions with poise and assurance. Failure to do so can result in "ruffled feathers" and a rough production process.

It is a myth that the designers and stage manager work for the director. In my view, the designers and stage manager work for the producer. The stage manager is charged with representing the producer's interests in production, not the director's. The designers work for the producer and with the director. If the director and the designers have a conflict, the producer has final say—not the director. I spend a tremendous amount of time trying to train stage managers to take a neutral role in communicating between directors and designers, to foster and encourage collaborative communication.

Ken White
Twenty-five years' experience as a professional lighting designer; eight years' experience as production manager, ECU/Loessin Summer Theatre; currently head of stage management, East Carolina University School of Theatre and Dance

[Our concepts of who the stage manager works for—see caption of figure 5.1—are not mutually exclusive. I strongly support "collaborative communication."]

The chart is not as important as is knowing who does what. Authority in the theater generally stems from function. The authority of the lighting designer over the lighting technician stems from their relative functions. The function of the lighting technician is to repair, gel, hang, wire, and focus lighting instruments. Obviously, the lighting technician takes orders from, and is responsible to, the lighting designer.

As succinctly as possible, here are the functions of the theater staff:

The *producer* obtains the personnel and materials to make theater.

The *director* interprets the script through the use of actors and designers.

The *stage manager* ensures that everything runs smoothly backstage and onstage in prerehearsal, rehearsal, performance, and post-performance phases.

The *actor* delivers the playwright's words, emotions, actions, and characterization, as interpreted by the director, to the audience.

The *technical director* executes scene designs and staging devices. (Confusion about the role of the technical director is discussed later. If you, as stage manager, have any doubts about your working relationship with the technical director, you two should talk it out. If you're unable to resolve the conflict, talk with the producer.)

The *theater manager* ensures the safe, efficient, and clean operation of the theater. (This includes care of the physical plant, box-office operations, restrooms, garbage disposal, gas, electricity, water services, and compliance with city regulations concerning the health and safety of the audience. It may include parking lot operations.)

The *house manager* greets and seats the audience and attends to the audience's comfort.

The *designer* (costumes, lighting, scene, sound, or makeup) designs plans, turning the director's and playwright's concepts into the realities that make stage illusion.

The *technicians* (master carpenter, master electrician, stagehand, etc.) turn designs into reality and operate equipment before, during, and after performances.

The *company manager* supervises the transportation and housing of the company.

There may be several other titles, real or honorary, on your staff. If you are uncertain about what they do, ask them.

The title of *production stage manager* may take on different meanings. In some theaters, it is simply an honorary title for the stage manager. Sometimes this title is assigned only when there is more than one show being rehearsed and presented in the same theater or theater complex. In this case, the function of the production stage manager is to coordinate and supervise the use of the theater's facilities, crews, and subordinate stage managers.

Sometimes the title of production stage manager is assigned to the producer's assistant. In this case, the production stage manager has no specific duties relevant to any one show but troubleshoots and supervises, reporting only to the producer.

Sometimes the production stage manager and stage manager divide duties. The stage manager works rehearsals and turns the promptbook over to the production stage manager at tech rehearsal. Then the production stage manager calls the show while the stage manager runs the stage crew. In some theaters, the production stage manager runs rehearsals and then turns the promptbook over to the stage manager who runs the show; the assistant stage manager supervises the crew; and the production stage manager sits in the audience, gives notes to the cast after each performance, and presides over upkeep and understudy rehearsals. This sharing of duties is common in musical theater and opera.

I have a major disagreement with the manner in which the relationship between the director and the designers is often portrayed. Currently, designers and directors collaborate in order to establish a point of view about a play (or dance or whatever). Working together we decide on what we believe the playwright is trying to communicate and, therefore, how we want the audience to feel or what we hope they will understand or learn through our production. After the point of view is established, the designers strive to create the world of this particular production of the play. Ongoing communication with the director and other members of the design team is vital to the success of the production. Designers strive to get to the essence of a piece, and a tremendous amount of time, energy, research, imagination, and creativity is necessary. A designer may go through hundreds of doodles, sketches, and/or models before the final design is decided upon. The director is ultimately in charge and has final say on all matters, but it is the designer who creates the design and would implement any changes to the design before and during the run. It is inappropriate for the stage manager to make changes to a design without the designer's consent, even if requested to do so by the director.

Lori Dawson
Technical Director, Lighting Designer
Skidmore College

(continued)

[I applaud producers and directors who can draw out the best from their designers through collaborative process. All of my experience, however, was with "name above the title"-type directors who wanted it done their way and attempted to focus creative input of designers within the limited parameters that the director established. In the end, we all want the best production we can get, whether we arrive there via collaborative process or under the whip of a dictatorial director. The stage manager does not establish the relationships between producer/director and designers. I'm not sure that recognizing the distinction in process is necessary to the successful functioning of a stage manager. But it's certainly worth thinking about, especially if a stage manager has a choice in selecting the atmosphere in which to work. For an excellent discussion of designer relationships in the creative process of making theater, see The Lighting Art, *second edition, by Richard H. Palmer.]*

There is no single correct distribution of duties between the production stage manager and the stage manager or between the stage manager and the assistant stage manager.

Some of the factors that determine the distribution of duties are the same factors that might influence the distribution between the technical director and the stage manager:

1. Will of the producer or director
2. Tradition of the particular theater
3. Number of people available
4. Layout of the theater
5. Personality of individuals filling the slots

In theme park operations, if two stage managers are assigned to a show or ride, they are commonly designated SM1 and SM2 [*not PSM, SM, or ASM*]. They are of equal authority—seniority is not a factor. Typically SM1 is in a booth calling the show or enabling the show from the front of house or at a stage vantage point when the show is being run by a Show Control [*computer*] System. Typically SM2 runs the show from the deck, overseeing backstage activities during the show. SM2s will frequently enable effects from backstage vantage points. SM1s typically are responsible for reporting information to management, and for interfacing with other theme park units to effect the safe and smooth operation of the venue. SM2s frequently are responsible for overseeing the running crew and ensuring that breaks and scheduling are set and executed. Both stage managers have pre-show checklists to ensure that all show elements and props are properly set. Enabling is done when people (typically performers) are interacting with show effects. Computer systems are programmed to verify the stage manager is holding down a button, which indicates it is safe for the show systems to proceed. These effects can be mechanical, like elevators, trap doors, or collapsing scenery; they can involve flame or any other element that would put performers in danger. Special Effects Technicians (SETs), who are all licensed pyro technicians, may also be assigned to a show. Their primary responsibility is to oversee the safe execution of pyrotechnic and other special effects. SETs frequently will also enable special effects.

Dan Weingarten
AEA Stage Manager and Lighting Designer

> I have stage managed four more shows now. I finally know the first prerequisite for finding an assistant stage manager: confidence. You must be able to trust this person. When you can trust your ASM, a great weight is lifted from your shoulders. Then it seems logical as to what duties you can assign.
>
> Violet E. Horvath
> *Stage Manager*
> *Arrow Rock, MO*

- **Again, the stage manager gains an understanding of who reports to whom by talking with coworkers. Problems are avoided by anticipating work that will have to be done and ensuring that all involved know their specific duties in getting that work done.**

  Some general principles to keep in mind:

1. Treat everyone on the staff with respect for his function.
2. Many hands make light work.
3. If you have subordinates, one of your responsibilities is to ensure they are not overworked. (Sometimes a stage manager feels that since she served as assistant stage manager and got the work done, she can now lean on the assistant stage manager. If you are the assistant stage manager, you have to appeal to the stage manager's ego. Explain that you are not the same terrific, outstanding, well-organized, industrious assistant stage manager that she was, and that you need help.)

Examples of Problems

1. The technical director (TD) tells you that he is in charge of the lighting designer, the sound designer, the shop foreman, and the makeup crew, as well as the stage manager. He states that he runs the crew during performances and that you (SM) call the cues. He says that you will report to him for work in the shop on scenery construction prior to rehearsals.

   Could be. In some educational and community theaters, the TD has extensive responsibility. If you feel that a different system would improve the operation of your theater, speak with the producer. If you feel that you are being overworked and/or need help (an ASM or gopher), speak with the TD and/or the producer.
2. The production stage manager (PSM) tells you that your first duty as the new ASM is to help build a fence around the theater.

   Probably. Your duties are what the PSM says they are, even if those duties don't fit your mental picture of the job. If you are a member of a union, you might complain to your union rep. Will building the fence interfere with your other duties? If so, you need to make that clear to the PSM.
3. The director's secretary tells you, the new SM, "I will be holding book [prompting] during rehearsals and will also supervise understudy rehearsals."

   How do you feel about it? Do you feel that you have lost some of the authority that goes with your title, or do you welcome the help? Or do you have mixed feelings? Perhaps you welcome the help at rehearsals yet feel that the director's secretary is not as capable of supervising understudy rehearsals as you are. Perhaps you feel that you really need to hold book during rehearsals in order to prepare yourself for running the show successfully.

This is a typical problem of the distribution of tasks among a theater's staff. The same type of problem might occur between the PSM and SM, or between the SM and ASM, or between the TD and SM. There is no correct answer for all theaters. What will work best for your theater?

Talk to the director's secretary about your feelings and discuss what is best for getting the show on most efficiently. If you fail to resolve the conflict, speak with the director and/or producer, and then abide by their judgment.

As stage managers gain experience and reputation, more responsibility is given to them. As they move on to other theaters, experience, reputation, and clout follow along, and they know enough to stipulate in advance what specific duties they will surrender to, or take from, others on the staff.

In Appendix A, you will find a production checklist from a stage manager's point of view. Please be cautioned before turning to this appendix that THE STAGE MANAGER NEED NOT DO EVERYTHING ON THIS LIST! At professional and educational levels of theater, there are many people on theater staffs to accept responsibility for doing most of the tasks on this list. Some productions, regardless of theater level, do not require that the task be done. As you review this list, check off the things that you know you personally need to do to get the show on the road. Use another symbol (?) to indicate those items you are not sure about. Then, talk to your producer and director to decide if the task needs to be done and who will do it.

PERSONAL EQUIPMENT FOR STAGE MANAGERS

In addition to your promptbook, what else do you keep handy? Actually, there is no end of little things to keep on hand to keep the show going, and it is amazing to see how the absence of a small thing at a crucial time can create havoc. For instance, it hardly seems possible that responsible people would allow a shortage of pencils to delay a rehearsal. But it happens time and again in professional as well as amateur productions.

Consider Hildegard Knef's comments on the rehearsal of the 1954 Broadway musical *Silk Stockings:*

> Today was the first reading. The whole cast sat in half-circle on the stage with their manuscripts in their hands, a paper cup of coffee beside each chair . . . nobody had a pencil. Unbelievable that actors never have pencils at first readings. Henry, the stage manager, lent his, and it went from hand to hand until finally Cy Feuer's temper snapped. "I'm well aware that you don't get paid till the opening but you could at least buy one little pencil. . . . We've wasted hours already." . . . I'd love to be able to invite a German student of Theatrical Science to attend rehearsals.*

*From *The Gift Horse* by Hildegard Knef, translated by David Anthony Palastanga (New York: McGraw-Hill Book Company, 1971). English translation copyright © 1971 by Hildegard Knef.

Let's consider some items of personal equipment you might find handy in running the rehearsal and the show.

Over a period of time, you may be able to use one or two items in the mounting of one play and one or two items in the mounting of another. It is not mandatory that you own or buy these items. It is simply handy to collect things.

As the items accumulate with each successive play, they'll overflow from your pockets and briefcase. You'll want a kit—a cardboard carton, toolbox, or tackle box—to keep everything conveniently near you in the rehearsal area.

The items listed here are, for the most part, self-explanatory. Some of their uses have been mentioned already, and you are invited to imagine a likely use for the others:

Paraffin (when a tooth filling is suddenly lost, a small piece of paraffin may allow an actor to complete a rehearsal)
Lighter flints and fluid
Matches
Paper clips
Sewing needles
Thread, black and white
Razor blade, single-edge
Masking tape, two widths
Electric tape
Two-sided tape
Scotch mending tape
Safety pins
Straight pins
Hairpins
Carpet tacks
Tacks
1-inch brads
Chalk
Pencils, many, #2
Pencil sharpener
Large eraser, art gum
Flashlight
Batteries, extra
Candle
Black ballpoint pen
Marking pens
Glow tape
Gaffers tape
Luminous paint and brush
Luminous paint solvent
Tape label maker
Graphite lock lubricant
Electric extension cord
Stopwatch
Sixty-minute timer

Ruler, 12 inch
Measuring tape, 50 foot
Architect's ruler, 1/2 inch = 1 foot scale
Tailor's measuring tape
Note cards, 3 × 5 inch
Oil, small can
Working bell and buzzer
Whistle
First-aid kit
Change, $5 in nickels, dimes, and quarters
Duplicate keys to everything
Rubber cement
Plastic cement
Plasti-tak (a putty-like adhesive)
Rubber bands
Magnifying glass
AC-DC current tester
Welding gloves (great for handling hot instruments)
Gel books
Cough drops
Throat lozenges and troches
Aspirin
Aspergum
Can opener
Salt, sugar, tea, coffee, powdered cream, bouillon, packaged soup, honey, hot chocolate
Wash'n Dri Towelettes
Paper towels
Paper cups
Nail file
Kleenex
Toothbrush and paste
Toothpicks
Dental floss
Comb
Mouthwash
Water heating element
Gummed reinforcements
Telephone extension cord
Dust cloth
Tweezers

(And don't forget that all of this is in addition to a top-of-the-line first-aid kit that must always be present.)

You will enjoy those moments when you can dip into your kit to save someone, particularly yourself, a long walk.

Good stage managers are equipped to handle anything. I suggest that you add an adjustable wrench, a collection of miscellaneous hardware (screws, nails, bolts, etc.), Post-It note pad, glo-tape, a 3-plug tap, string, soap, and garbage bags.

Neill McKay
Stage Manager
Tom Morrison Theatre and Memorial Hall
Fredrickton, N.B., Canada

I would add saline solution to the list of what a SM should have and what should be in a first-aid box; lost contacts can delay rehearsals and stop shows.

Jane Bulnes-Fowles
Stage Manager
Reed College
Portland, OR

Nail polish remover—either normal or acetone-free. It's a great solvent. I've removed magic marker graffiti, paint from my shoes, and accumulated dirt from the bottom of my makeup case.

Big J Peterson
Actor/Tech
Georgia Renaissance Festival/Six Flags over Georgia
Lilburn, GA

In my brief theater experience I have been asked for ponytail holders, barrettes, clips, or something to hold hair in place and out of the way. I do not go to rehearsals without them.

Chad Zodrow
Stage Manager
Northwestern University
Evanston, IL

The section on personal equipment for stage managers and the accompanying list of suggested items in the stage management kit is the gold standard for stage managers. I have heard of people buying kits stocked from Stern's list as gifts for their friends or family members who are beginning careers in stage management.

Stephanie Moser Goins
Instructor of Stage Management
University of Oklahoma
Former Freelance AEA Stage Manager

My Teaching Strategy

I have students bring in all the objects from their home or dorm rooms that they think need to be in a stage manager's kit. The class builds the kit. As they build, they discuss/evaluate. We then create a shopping list for the things we were not able to locate. The process can be fun, and the results surprising.

Dan Weingarten
AEA Stage Manager and Lighting Designer

STAGE DIAGRAMS

If you are starting to work in a new theater, check out the plant, record the information, analyze and apply this to your production needs, and pass on that information in a convenient, usable form. The easiest way to do this is by making a series of diagrams. Of course, if you've already done a show in this house, you should have all the information where it can be referred to quickly.

How big is your stage? Where are the sight lines? How high is the proscenium? Is there fly space and flying equipment? These are but a few of the questions your *stage diagram* should answer.

Usually the stage wings and significant surrounding space—apron, stairs leading to the stage, backstage area, and so forth—are drawn to scale. The scale of 1/2 inch = 1 foot is recommended, but any scale that is serviceable will do (figure 5.2).

When you have finished your drawing, list at the bottom the significant dimensions:

1. What is the width of the stage?
2. What is the depth (curtain line to back wall)?
3. What is the height of the proscenium arch?
4. What are the height, width, and diagonal measurements of the largest door through which scenery may pass to get from an outside street onto the stage, or in from the scene shop to the stage?

This last measurement is significant because it limits the size of scenery and set pieces. Obviously, you can't use a set piece or section of scenery if you can't carry it onto the stage.

This diagram and list of important dimensions should be filed in your promptbook.

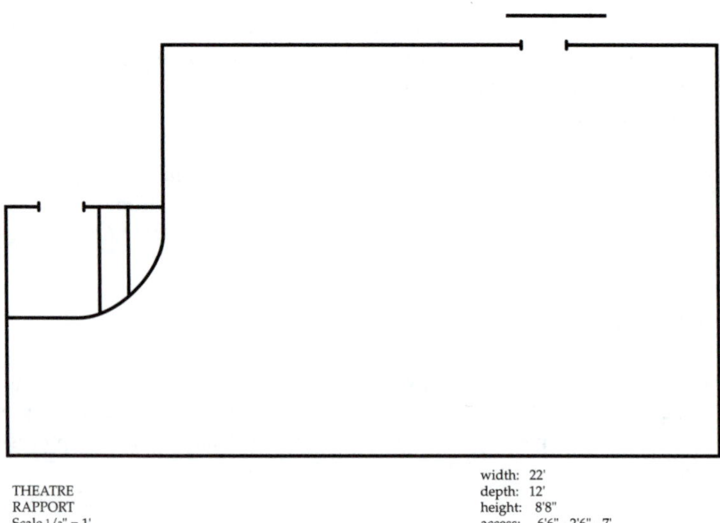

FIGURE 5.2 Stage Diagram Drawn to Scale

Some Applications

1. The set designer is on a tight schedule and won't be in town until the second week of rehearsals. The director has planned essential entranceways and windows so that she could start blocking. Now the director asks you to send the set designer information that will allow him to start his plans without actually seeing the stage.
2. You go to a warehouse to pick up set pieces. The furniture dealer offers you one of several rugs that may not be cut. What size will you need? Of course, you have that information with you and will not have to make another trip.
3. The set designer of a theater in the round presents his watercolor sketches for the next week's production at staff meeting. You ask how tall the boxy set pieces are. The set designer explains that they are 12 feet tall and that he knows they will fit through the entrances to the tent because he has measured them. You point out that they may fit through the 12½-foot entrances that you have also measured, but since the men who carry them can't very easily hold them a mere 6 inches off the ground, getting them in, on, and offstage may be clumsy and therefore slow down the scene changes. You also point out that you will have to raise the microphones that hang at the aisle positions since they are only 10 feet off the ground.

   The height of hanging microphones was, in this case, a significant dimension that you should have noted. The demands of a production sometimes determine which dimensions are most significant. If you are doing *Madwoman of Chaillot,* the stage trap dimensions become significant.

Note in example 3 that both you and the set designer were anticipating problems on the basis of sketches and diagrams rather than waiting for set pieces to be built to see if they worked.

If your theater expects to be in operation for many years, make sure that many copies of more detailed stage plans are on hand for the use of transient set designers and technical directors (figure 5.3).

If you are working at a small showcase theater or community theater in a space not initially designed as a theater, please read the following two sections on circuit breakers and diagrams of lighting instruments. If you are working in a professional theater or educational theater, skip these sections since there will be others on the staff who will be responsible. If you are not sure about where you are going to be working, take time to peruse the information.

CIRCUIT BREAKERS

Check the circuit breaker panel (electric box) at your theater. Are the circuit breakers labeled in some way to show what is on them? If not, write on masking tape or use a tape tool to identify each circuit breaker. Is there a diagram explaining what lines each circuit breaker monitors? If not, make a diagram. It is important that this information be readily available. The diagram should be posted near or on the circuit breaker panel, and you should have a copy in your promptbook.

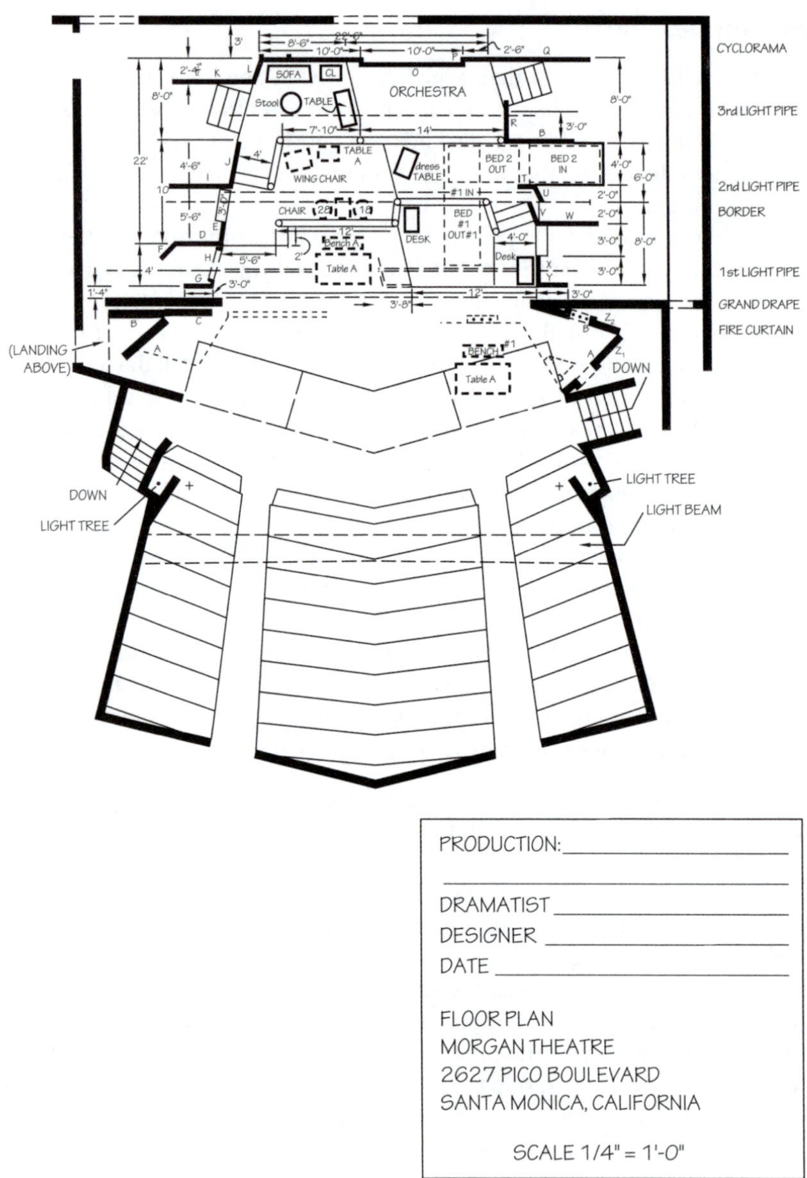

FIGURE 5.3 Stage Diagram

Courtesy Morgan Theatre, Santa Monica, California.

Take the time to check all the outlets in your theater. A current tester is an inexpensive and handy tool to keep in your kit (e.g., Circuit Master 90- 550 Volt, AC & DC; Fordham Mfg. Co. No. 101). You are not expected to repair the outlets, but you should report problems to your producer.

Although you may not be an electrician, you should be comfortable with basic principles of electricity. A source that will give you the fundamentals of electricity in theatrical application is Harvey Sweet's *Handbook of Scenery, Properties, and Lighting,* Volume 2 (Allyn & Bacon, 1995). Tuck a copy into your kit.

DIAGRAM OF LIGHTING INSTRUMENTS

Next you will want to inventory (figure 5.4) and make a diagram of the lighting instruments currently in place—type, wattage, gel frame size, and condition (figure 5.5). Indicate space available and outlets available for plugging in additional instruments (figure 5.6).

Plastic templates of various types of instruments are available. You can make your own out of cardboard (figure 5.7, page 61) to assist in making rapid diagrams of available equipment and its placement in production.

Lighting Inventory

Page _____ of ____ pages

Prepared by ________________________, on __________________, for __________________________
(name/position) (date) (theater/production)

Inst #	Type	Watts	Gel Size	Color	Plugging	Dimmer	Position	Working?

FIGURE 5.4 Lighting Inventory

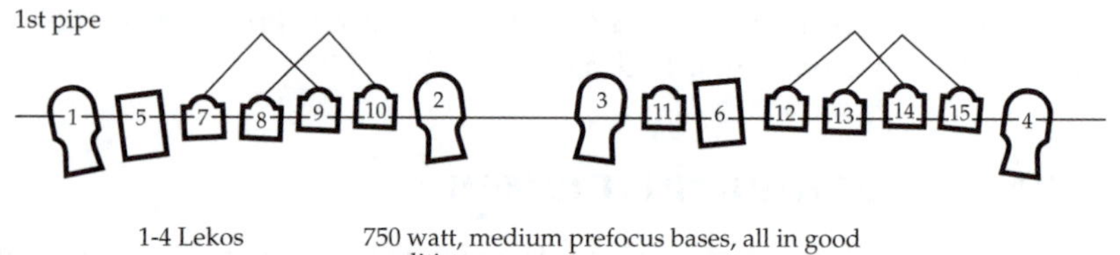

1-4 Lekos	750 watt, medium prefocus bases, all in good condition
5-6 PCs	400 watt, medium screw bases, #5 lens cracked, #6 focusing pin missing
7-15 Fresnels	500 watt, medium prefocus bases, all in good condition except #11 (#11 seems to have internal wiring problems)

Notes: No spare lamps for any instruments on hand!
Only four twofers on hand as indicated.

Ten cables run directly to board.
No ceiling plugging locations.

FIGURE 5.5 Diagram of Lighting Instruments

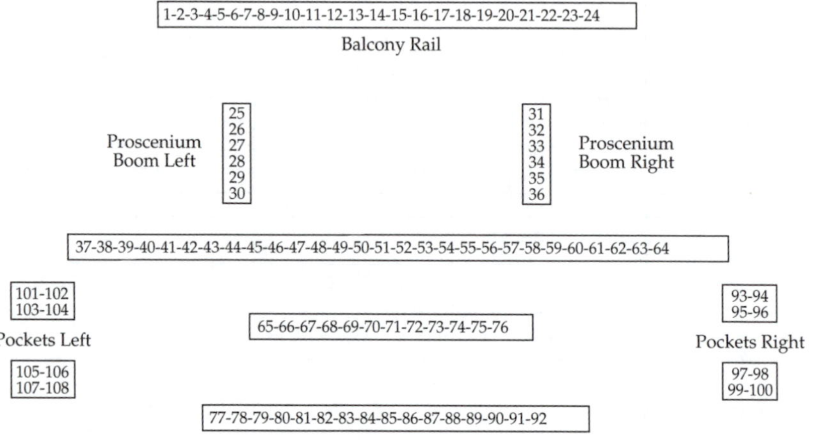

FIGURE 5.6 Diagram of Plugging Locations

While making your diagrams, check on the condition of the lighting equipment. Is it serviceable or will it need repair? Obviously, if the theater owner has rented your company 60 instruments and 10 are not working, or if a control board doesn't work, this must be brought to the producer's or management's attention. If you discover the limitations of your lighting equipment immediately, you will have time to repair, improvise, rent, or buy additional equipment. Don't wait until the tech rehearsal to find that instruments are out of order.

If the lighting designer and technicians are on hand, checking the equipment is their responsibility. But if they are not, as is frequently the case in community theater, you can save the staff and crew a lot of grief by checking out the equipment as soon as possible.

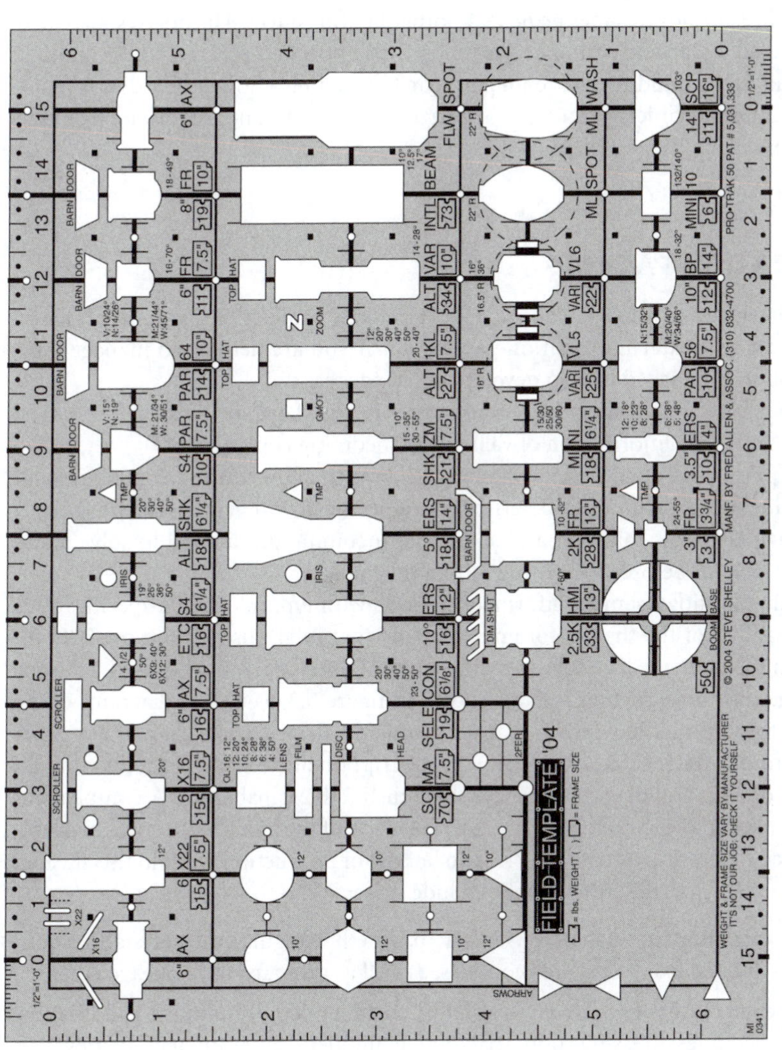

FIGURE 5.7 The Stage Fixture Field Template 2004. This template represents today's lighting instruments. Hanging weight, cut color size, and beam spread information are listed, adjacent to each symbol. Available in 1/4-inch and 1/2-inch scale.

Courtesy Steven L. Shelley, MrTemplate@earthlink.net, fieldtemplate.com.

Typical Problems

1. One of the cast members, without asking permission, brings in an electric heater to warm up the dressing room. Soon all the lights and the heater are out. You are called on to restore current. Where, if anywhere, can the electric heater be replugged?
2. The lighting designer has completed her work and left for another production. The director now decides he needs another lighting effect. The board source line is loaded to capacity; another small board will now be needed. Is there another circuit in the building with enough capacity to supply another board?
3. The sound technician can't get the buzzer to work. A lamp is working from the same outlet. Can you help?

INFORMATION PACKETS

If your theater hosts, or has the desire to host, outside productions, you may hope to find on hand a "theater information packet." Or if you are helping to manage your theater, you may be asked to help develop such a packet.

This packet should include measurements of the stage, details of the technical capability, and other information of value to an incoming company.

The purpose of such an information packet is to allow touring companies and other production companies to determine whether or how they can use the theater. It also allows the stage manager and staff of an incoming production to solve many technical problems before ever setting foot in the theater.

Figure 5.8 shows sample information sheets with typical detailed specifications on the capability of the theater for any company that might use it for a production. Along with the physical dimension specifications of the stage would be included some scaled stage diagrams, such as the one shown in figure 5.3, as well as diagrams of the rest of the theater building and diagrams showing the draw-curtain plan or any other special feature of the theater. Along with the description of electrical capabilities might be a series of electrical diagrams if these show distinctive capabilities. A complete information packet would then go on to describe many of the auxiliary services available from related professionals who are likely to be part of production work in this theater. The auxiliary services described might include these:

The availability of stage crew and help, whether regular theater staff or contracted from local area contacts, as well as standard pay scales for them

The availability of wardrobe assistants, costume people, laundry and cleaning facilities, dressing room space and equipment, and sanitary facilities

Information about customary curtain hours and customary audience preferences in attending matinees, weekday evening performances, and so on

Contacts for news and media in the area to ease the publicizing process

Transportation facilities, local and interstate, passenger and freight

Hotel and restaurant services that have proven useful to theater companies

San Jose Center for the Performing Arts (CPA)
Technical Information

412CF3F9-2FD4-1041FA.doc Page 2 of 16 Revision: January 5, 2004

FIGURE 5.8 Theater Information Packet Material. These four pages of a 16-page document reflect the range of information and the detail necessary to allow visiting companies to move into a theater. Diagrams of stage, dressing rooms, loading docks, and storage areas (not shown here) allow staff of a touring company to work out many problems in advance. Having the information available in digital form makes it fast and easy to send via e-mail to potential users of your theater.

Courtesy Bob Bones, Production Stage Manager, Michael Miller, Executive Producer, American Musical Theatre of San Jose.

San Jose Center for the Performing Arts (CPA)
Technical Information

On this same level there is a conductor's dressing room and musicians' room. Also, the pit is accessed from this area while in normal performance position.

X. RIGGING SYSTEMS

Our Grid Height is 70'-10 ½" to the top of steel. All Single Purchase Linesets can be flown out to 68'-0", Motorized Linesets to 66'-0"

A. Single Purchase Linesets:

There are 39 single purchase counterweight linesets, between 0'-10" to 32'-2" from PL. Each arbor has a 1,050 lb capacity. The locking rails (or control) of these linesets are stage right (above stage level). All of these battens are 63' in length and standard system pipe construction (Sch40 1½ pipe).

B. Motorized Linesets:

The theatre also has 16 motorized linesets - 4 variable speed motors (3.1 fps max speed) and 12 constant speed motors (1.24 fps fixed speed), between 24'-10" and 39'-9" from PL. These winch lines have an arbor capacity of 1,250 lbs. Control of the winch lines requires an operator (typically the local Head Carpenter) on the control panel, which is located on the deck DSR. Each of these winch lines are 68' in length and are a ladder truss construction.

C. Motorized Electric Bridges:

There are two Electric Bridges (ME1 & ME4 on the Hang Plot), which are hard-wired bridges with folding conduit trays to power the bridges. These two bridges are controlled from the deck (DSR) and travel very slowly. These bridges can fly out to clear 61'-0" floor.

D. Hemp Rails:

There is a hemp rail stage left and right (above stage level). It is a 2-level type with 39 pins per level. AMTSJ has over 60 spotting wheels and 30+ spotting lines at the theatre for your usage.

E. Over Stage Rigging Points:

AMTSJ has an ample amount of grid logs (3" Sch40 pipe 36" long) stored up in the grid. The grid is a standard C-channel grid.

F. FOH Rigging Points:

1. Speaker and Lighting Towers
   There are two points located 4'-0" DS of PL and 28'-3" SR & SL of CL. These points are rated for 1500# max each point. These two points can ONLY be hung motor down.
2. Lighting Truss or Center Cluster Truss
   There are four (4) points located 10'-0" DS of PL at 4'-0" and 12'-0" SR & SL of CL. These points are rated for 750# max, each point. The theatre already has four (4) ½-ton chain motors installed (motor high) in the ceiling. These can be removed to hang your motors, or you may choose to rent the theatre's.

FIGURE 5.8 *(Continued)*

San Jose Center for the Performing Arts (CPA)
Technical Information

XI. HANGING PLOT

LINE		DEPTH	Pipe to Pipe	PIECE	TRIM	WT	NOTES
PL		0'-0"	0"	PLASTER LINE			
FC		0'-3"	3"	FIRE CURTAIN			
1		**0'-10"**	**7"**	**HOUSE MAIN DRAPE**			
2		1'-4"	6"	HSE BORDER			
3		1'-10"	6"	HSE LEGS			
4		2'-5"	7"				
5	X	3'-0"	7"				
ME1	F	3'-8"	8"	1ST ELECTRIC BRIDGE			39 hard-wired circuits, loft block at 4'-2"
	F	4'-8"	12"				
6		5'-10"	1'-2"				
7		6'-5 ½"	7 ½"				
8		7'-1"	7 ½"				
9		7'-8"	7"				
10		8'-2 ½"	6 ½"	HSE BORDER			
11		8'-9 ½"	7"	HSE TRAVELER			
12		9'-5"	4 ½"				
13		10'-1"	8"				
14		10'-9 ½"	8 ½"				
15		11'-8"	10 ½"	2ND ELECTRIC			24 drop circuits
16	F	12'-4 ½"	8 ½"				
17	F	13'-2 ½"	10"				
18	F	13'-8"	5 ½"				
19		14'-3"	7"				
20		15'-3"	12"	HSE BORDER			
21		16'-0"	9"	HSE LEGS			
22		16'-8"	8"				
23		17'-3 ½"	7 ½"				
24		17'-10"	6 ½"				
25		18'-8"	10"	3RD ELECTRIC			24 drop circuits
26		19'-6"	10"				
27		20'-0 ½"	6 ½"				
28		20'-8"	7 ½"				
29		21'-2"	6"				
30		21'-8"	6"	HSE BORDER			
31		22'-2 ½"	6 ½"	HSE LEGS			
32		22'-9"	6 ½"				
33		23'-3"	6"				
34		23'-9"	6"				
35		24'-3"	6"				
W1	V	24'-10"	7"				
W2	V	25'-5"	7"				
ME2	F	27'-0"	19"	4TH ELECTRIC BRIDGE			31 hard wired circuits, loft block at 27'-6"
	F	28'-0"	12"				
36		28'-8"	8"				
W3	V	29'-9"	13"	HSE BORDER			
37		30'-5"	8"				
W4	V	30'-9"	4'	HSE LEGS			
38		31'-5"	8"				
39		32'-2"	9"				
W5	C	32'-10"	8"				
W6	C	33'-8"	10"	5TH ELECTRIC			
W7	C	34'-5 ½"	9 ½"				
W8	C	35'-0"	6 ½"				
W9	C	35'-5 ½"	5 ½"				
W10	C	36'-0"	6 ½"				
W11	C	36'-6"	6"				
W12	C	37'-0"	6"				
W13	C	37'-8"	8"	HSE BORDER			
W14	C	38'-2 ½"	4 ½"				
W15	C	39'-3"	12 ½"				
W16	C	39'-9"	6"	BACK BLACKS			

V=Variable Speed Motors, **C**=Constant Speed Motors, **F**=Fixed Position (non-kickable)

FIGURE 5.8 *(Continued)*

San Jose Center for the Performing Arts (CPA)
Technical Information

XII. CURTAINS, SOFT GOODS, MASKING AND MISCELLANEOUS

A. Main Curtain:

Guillotine, works from fly rail. Curtain is burgundy with gold trim.

B. Drapes:

6 full width black borders with chain pockets (60'W x 16'H)
6 pairs of black legs with chain pockets (16'W x 32' H)
1 full black backdrop (60'W x 30'H)
1 black traveler normally hangs on lineset 11 (2 panels 30'W x 32'H)

C. Pianos

The theatre owns a 9' Steinway grand piano and an upright rehearsal piano.

D. Odds & Ends

Theater has a 36' genie personnel lift.

There are various TV monitors around the building, which carry a closed circuit of the stage, but there is not one on the stage or at the stage manager's panel.

E. Calipers

There are two acoustic sound baffles (called Calipers) located down-stage left and right, 7' 9" down-stage of the plaster line, which when turned parallel with the house walls contribute to the acoustic accuracy of the hall. They can also be rotated to be parallel to the plaster line and act as an additional wing. They are 36' tall and 12' wide. On their off-stage side there is a standard door, which is four or five steps to another door directly to the stage.

There are light ladders and vertical bars affixed to the upstage side of the Calipers to serve as additional lighting "box boom" type positions.

XIII. LIGHTING SYSTEM

There is only one 10" conduit running from stage to the back of house. All cables (including sound, lighting, or other) MUST be run SIMULTANEOUSLY. Power available is three (3) 400 amp 3phase hookups stage left.

A. Light Control

The lighting system consists of an ETC system. There are 630 ETC Sensor A-F dimmers for the stage with another 12 dedicated to the house lights. Of the stage dimmers, 618 are 2.4kw and the remaining 12 are 6kw. The control consists of two consoles and a very sophisticated network. Primary console is an Obsession 1500. Secondary console is an Insight 2xMLM. They are networked such that either console can control any of the 1536 DMX channels at any time. If both consoles address the same dimmer simultaneously the highest level takes precedence. The 642 house dimmers are wired to the first two DMX channels. There are nine optically isolated outputs for the second two DMX universes strategically located throughout the stage for control of additional devices such as rented color changers or intelligent fixtures. The consoles are equipped with MIDI Show Control so that one can slave to the other.

B. Follow Spots

The theatre owns four (4) Lycian: 1290xlt, 2K xenon, follow spots. There are two (2) follow spot booths with 2 follow spots in each booth.

412CF3F9-2FD4-1041FA.doc Page 11 of 16 Revision: January 5, 2004

FIGURE 5.8 *(Continued)*

Information on ushers and house managerial services, ticket takers, and so forth. The packet should also include full information on the seating capacity of each section of the theater and a detailed account of parking facilities available.

Some theaters now place their technical information for visiting companies on the Internet.

My Teaching Strategy

A few times each semester, I take my stage management class into the theater, each armed with pen and paper. The class is instructed to walk the entire space and make a list of things that could be potentially dangerous and to recommend solutions (glow tape, remove, matt cable). Students map out where running lights should be placed. They also locate and check the condition of the safety equipment (the first-aid kit, fire extinguishers, disaster kit), check for clear pathways to all exits, and ensure that all electrical panels have clear access where required.

Dan Weingarten
AEA Stage Manager and Lighting Designer

SUGGESTED CLASSROOM EXERCISES

1. Have students collaborate to draw an organizational chart for your theater. Include names of faculty and staff working on current or next production. When complete, compare the students' work to the chart on page 47 and discuss the differences.
2. Teachers and students should stop laughing about the size of the trunk necessary to hold all of that junk on pages 53–54. Have students individually select ten items they think are most useful under rehearsal conditions. Combine their selections into one list.

6

Expediting Auditions and Readings

My dear boy, forget about the motivation.
Just say the lines and don't trip over the furniture.
—Noel Coward

The degree of stage manager involvement in the audition process varies with the level of theater. In some Broadway theaters, auditions are held before the stage manager is hired. In amateur and community theaters, the stage manager may be asked to perform a variety of tasks in helping the producer and director to carry out the casting process. In some cases it will just be the director and stage manager running the auditions.

In auditioning actors for roles in plays, it is desirable to make the actors comfortable and to move them quickly through an interview-audition procedure. In general, two areas are set up, one in which the actors can gather to wait and a second in which the director—and sometimes producer, musical director, choreographer, and other staff members—can interview and audition the performer.

To expedite the procedure, a stage manager might be asked to set up both areas. There should be adequate light to read by and comfortable seating. Access to restrooms should be provided for actors who wish to find a mirror to freshen up. If possible, it is a nice touch to set up a coffee/tea table to show hospitality and consideration for those who are trying out.

Since this may be a difficult time for many actors, attempt to be a cheerful receptionist. Sometimes you are the first person in the company the actor is exposed to, and the actor starts to form an opinion of the company by the way you deport yourself. Offer the same warm, friendly welcome you would want to receive if you were the auditioning actor.

You will want to write down the actors' names as they arrive so you can audition them on a first come, first served basis.

My Dance Audition Procedures

At an open dance call, I generally

1. Ask dancers to complete the audition form (figure 6.1).
2. Ask for pictures and résumés, which I attach to the audition form.
3. Give each dancer a sticker with a number that matches the number on the audition form. We usually have about 50 dancers at a call and this helps to keep track of them.
4. When the choreographer is ready, I take the dancers into the audition room.
5. I hand the stack of forms to the choreographer.
6. The choreographer will teach the combination to the entire group, reviewing it several times.
7. If there is no piano player to accompany the audition, or if the choreographer prefers a CD or tape, I will run the CD player or tape.
8. Dancers are broken into smaller groups and do the combination for the choreographer. When a cut is made, I get the names of the persons the choreographer wants to keep and read them aloud. I thank the others for coming and encourage them to audition again.
9. After the dance portion of the audition is complete, I ask all of the dancers to leave the room, to prepare their sheet music in order to return to the audition room, one at a time, to sing.
10. I escort them into the room, usually in numeric order, to have them sing, usually only 16 bars, for the choreographer, director, and music director.
11. Before they leave, I tell them the callback time, if known.

In general, I try to keep things moving along, try to keep the auditionees as informed as possible about what to expect next, and try to listen to individuals and help them with their specific needs.

Bob Bones
Production Stage Manager
American Musical Theatre of San Jose

PLEASE PRESS HARD AND PRINT Today's Date ________

Last Name First Name	Performing Union	Audition #

Address ________ Show ________

City ________ State ________ Zip ________ Role ________

Home Phone ( ) ________ Interested in Ensemble: Yes No Do You Sing: Yes No Moderate

Work Phone ( ) ________ Do You Dance: Yes No Mover Voice Part: S A T B B

Permanent Contact # ( ) ________ Singing range: low ________ to high ________

☐ Check if above information is new or changed.

Sex (M) (F) Weight ________ Height ________

Audition Song ________ Age ________ Hair ________

DO NOT WRITE BELOW THIS LINE.

Dance	Specialty	Voice	Acting
Jazz Ballet Tap			

FIGURE 6.1 Dance Audition Form

Courtesy Bob Bones.

Dance Auditions

Just a few quick notes on things to think about:

Is there room for dancers to warm up before the audition? If they can't have access to the actual audition space, where can they warm up? Is there also a space that will be available for dancers to practice the audition routine once they've learned it and they're waiting to audition?

Who provides a resin box? A first-aid kit with ice packs? Are these readily available at the studio or does your production need to bring them?

Does the producer want a videotape record of the audition, and if so, who provides the equipment, operator, etc.?

Is music live or recorded? Who is responsible for hiring/providing music?

The stage manager can either be outside the audition room (signing in dancers, answering questions about the production and the audition process, etc.) or inside (sorting résumés, running the recorded music, videotaping the dancers, etc.) but I wouldn't recommend trying to do both. I think it's important at any type of audition to be available to the performers as a source of information and encouragement, a face with a name instead of one of the anonymous people behind the table!

Jill (Johnson) Gold
Stage Manager
Sisterella, 1997 European Tour

WORKING WITH ACTORS

You can't make theater without actors. The actor is the central ingredient in making theater happen. Audiences may come to theaters to see the work of stage managers, directors, and producers, but the only people who can communicate theater magic to audiences, through ideas and emotions, are the actors. They are the only ones who can communicate this by themselves, and, if necessary, they can get along without you. But you can't make theater without the actor.

- **Regardless of your personal opinion of individual actors, you have to maintain a healthy respect for the function of the actor. And this healthy respect should be the bedrock of your relationship with cast members. As stage manager, yours is a support function. You are there to assist actors—to help them get more out of rehearsal time and to help them concentrate on their task by having everything so well organized and running so smoothly that there is nothing to distract them from their work.**

On the other hand, as the producer's foreman and the director's principal assistant, you are a supervisor of the actors' time and whereabouts. When a stage manager posts a schedule or announces a picture call, he expects the actor to be there, just as would a military commander who had given a direct order. When a stage manager has to move backstage to supervise a shift, or for any other reason, cast members are expected to yield the right of way. During performances, cast members are expected not to speak to the stage manager unless they are spoken to (with the exception of informing the stage manager of a fire or some other imminent threat to life or safety or the continuation of the performance). Cast members should know that the stage manager is responsible for the smooth running of the performance, and out of respect for that function, they should do their utmost to cooperate.

- **The actor/stage manager relationship should be one of mutual respect and mutual cooperation. As in all human relationships, this may be difficult to further codify. However, in practice, I've found it works out quite easily. Early in rehearsals, actors realize that you are concerned with their welfare and comfort, that you are eager to get the show on efficiently, and that you are quite obviously helping them. They see that what you're doing is all for the common goal of a better performance. And so they are willing and eager to cooperate with you when you exert your authority.**

Please refer to previous comments on the stage manager's relationship with cast members in Chapter 2.

Posting Notes for Readings

During casting calls, most actors will ask "the person with the clipboard" for information. You should be able to refer everyone to the notes you have posted.

If you were an actor showing up for a casting call, what would you like to know about the production?

First, is there a part in it for you? Who's putting this play on? Why? Who's directing? What's the rehearsal schedule like? Where can you get a script? On what pages does the character you're right for appear? What pages will you be asked to read?

Anticipate what the actors would like to know and post that information in the lobby or waiting area where actors can read it before filling out audition forms.

Many community theaters now post information on readings on Facebook and other social networking sites. Educational theaters may also use Blackboard, a Web site that only registered students can access.

Fact Sheet

Coordinate with the producer and publicist to get the basic facts up for the actors: who, what, when, where, and why. If possible, note on the fact sheet where the actors can obtain scripts (figure 6.2).

Character Descriptions

How old are the characters? How much do they age during the course of the play? Who played the part on Broadway? How does the author describe the character? How does the director see the character? Many actors do not have time or opportunity to read scripts and study them before they come to readings. Sometimes the scripts are simply not available to the actor until ten minutes before a reading. You can help the actors adjust to this situation by lining up this information from the script and the director and posting much of the information the actors will need (figure 6.3, page 73).

THE EMPEROR COMPANY

FACT SHEET

- **What:** *The Emperor*

  A three-act play about Nero, notoriously cruel and depraved Roman emperor (37 AD–68 AD)

- **Who:** Hermann Gressieker—author
  George White—translator and adapter
  Lou Rifkin—producer
  Charles Rome Smith—director
  Lawrence Stern—production stage manager
  Norman Houle—set designer
  Hellene Heigh—publicist

- **Where:** Cahuenga Playhouse, 3333 Cahuenga Blvd. West (Barham exit off Hollywood Freeway)

- **When:** Opens February 7, to run on weekends, four-week minimum. (See posted rehearsal schedule.)

- **Why:** To present the highly original and well-received German playwright to Los Angeles audiences and to showcase local talent.

This is an Equity production under the Hollywood Area Contract.

FIGURE 6.2 Production Fact Sheet for Auditioning Actors

Equity Paid Parts

Under some contracts, Actors' Equity Association (AEA), the union for actors and stage managers, determines which parts will be paid or not paid. Under other contracts, Equity allows producers to pay chorus members small additional fees to handle small roles. Post the paid parts list if applicable (figure 6.4, page 74).

Suggested Readings

You may wish to post a list of readings from the play with which the actors may audition. It sometimes expedites casting calls if actors can read in pairs, or even three at a time. Otherwise, you may be called on to read with the actors (see figure 6.5, page 75).

Rehearsal Schedule

If the rehearsal schedule is ready, post it. Otherwise, you might add a paragraph to the fact sheet indicating the anticipated pattern of rehearsals (e.g., "We will be rehearsing for four weeks, afternoons and evenings, Monday through Friday" or "We expect to rehearse weeknights from 7:30 to 10:30 p.m.").

THE RIGHT HONORABLE GENTLEMAN

CHARACTER DESCRIPTIONS

- ***Sir Charles Dilke*** pp. 1–14, 16–21, 29–43, 47–50, 55–67, 77, 90

  Mid-40s, air of distinction, natural commander, enigmatic.

- ***Mrs. Ashton Dilke*** pp. 1–7, 38–42, 55–57, 83–85

  Early 30s, kindhearted busybody, Dilke's sister-in-law.

- ***Mrs. Emilia Pattison (later Lady Dilke)*** pp. 7–14, 29–40, 81–90

  Mature, elegant, charming, quiet, has integrity and warmth.

- ***Mr. Joseph Chamberlain*** pp. 10–19, 42–43, 49–54, 77–90

  Statesman of Dilke's stature, at least mid-40s.

- ***Mrs. Virginia Crawford (Nia)*** pp. 14–40, 50–54, 77–85

  Vital, restless, intelligent, waspish, challenging manner, age 22.

- ***Mr. Donald Crawford*** pp. 21–27, 81–85

  Late 40s, stiff, inhibited, slight Scottish accent, formal, and pedantic.

- ***Sir James Russel*** pp. 32–44

  Distinguished, incisive, jurist, dry, mid-50s.

- ***Sarah Gray*** pp. 39–44

  Handsome woman, reserved, mid-30s, a decided cut above her station.

- ***Mrs. Rossiter (Lila)*** pp. 51–56, 81–83

  Mother of Nia, Maye, and Helen.

FIGURE 6.3 Character Descriptions for Auditioning Actors. Note that the character descriptions are either from the script and approved by the director prior to posting or generated by the director.

The lists below shall be used to determine the additional payments required when Actors on Chorus Contracts are assigned to play Roles (Parts) or to receive Specialty Payments in this Production as per the applicable Rulebook.

<u>*URINETOWN*</u>

(As viewed in April 2001 at the Actors Theatre of America—Off-Broadway)

Parts Breakdown

Principals
Officer Lockstock
Little Sally
Penelope Pennywise
Bobby Strong
Hope Cladwell
Mr. McQueen
Senator Fipp
Old Man Strong/Hot Blades Harry
Officer Barrel
Caldwell B. Cladwell

Chorus Parts and/or Specialties
Tiny Tom
Dr. Billeaux
Soupy Sue
Cladwell's Secretary
Little Becky Two Shoes
Mrs. Millennium
Old Woman
Josephine Strong
Billy Boy Bill

Note: Should a Production be sufficiently changed, either by cutting, re-writing, or re-choreographing to make questionable the category in which a particular part belongs, please consult with Equity immediately for a determination.

FIGURE 6.4 Equity Paid Parts Listing

Courtesy Actors' Equity Association.

Audition Form Format

If preprinted audition forms are not available, you should post a format and examples of the information that the company requires (see "Obtaining Information" later in this chapter).

THE EMPEROR COMPANY

SUGGESTED READINGS

Seneca	Monologue I 1-2 W/ Nero III 8-11 W/ Burrus II 9 W/ Nero, Agrippina II 6-8
Nero	W/ Actis I 11-18 W/ Poppaea II 10-15 W/ Seneca III 8-11 W/ Seneca, Agrippina II 6-8
Agrippina	W/ Nero I 2-4 & 19-21 W/ Seneca, Nero II 6-8
Burrus	W/ Seneca II 9 W/ Seneca, Agrippina I 10-11
Actis	W/ Nero I 11-18
Poppaea	W/ Nero II 10-15 W/ Nero, Seneca II 16-21
Messenger	W/ Seneca, Nero II 25
Paulus	W/ Seneca, Nero III 1-7
Thrasea	W/ Lucanus, Seneca III 12-14
Lucanus	W/ Thrasea, Seneca III 12-14

FIGURE 6.5 Suggested Readings for Auditioning Actors

Callback Schedule

If many actors are called back to read for several parts, you may want to set up a schedule so that actors can read in groups, showing how they play to one another. The callback schedule would not normally be posted for actors, as it is not necessary for them to know who else is being considered for the part they want. The schedule will help you to manage the callback period efficiently (figure 6.6, page 76).

With thorough preparation for casting calls, you show cast members from the outset that you are in total command of the situation, anticipating everything.

ACCEPTING RÉSUMÉS

In the course of casting calls, especially in professional theater, many actors and actresses will submit their résumés. These résumés generally consist of a picture or several pictures in various costumes and poses (composites); written information giving physical measurements, credits in features, TV, and on the stage; and agent's name and phone number (figure 6.7, page 77).

THE EMPEROR COMPANY

Time	Nero	Actis	Seneca	Poppaea	Paulus
4:00	Nathan H.	Betty R.	Earl O.	Liz V.	Ronald P.
4:15	John H.	Linda M.		Gina M.	Ed. M.
4:30	Barton C.			Gina Q.	
4:45	Bill C.	Liz B.	Brad M.	Dolly M.	
5:00	Glen C.	Anita M.	Ray A.	Jean S.	Mike D.
5:15	Erik D.	Dale G.	John H.	Arlene S.	Nate F.
5:30	Richard P.	Mary K.		Abigail P.	

FIGURE 6.6 Callback Schedule (not normally posted)

The purpose of a résumé is to help the director recall and contact the actor after the reading. In a production involving amateur actors, it is wise for a stage manager to secure information comparable with the résumé coverage and to keep those notes in a convenient form to help the director recall the actors in tryouts.

When you accept a résumé, look it over carefully. For amateur actors, try to secure basic résumé information. For professionals, ask the actor if she still has the same agent and if that agent can still be reached at the same numbers. Agents and phone numbers change rapidly, and it is important to make sure that the essential entries are up-to-date. Be sure to note on the résumé the part for which the actor auditions.

Sometimes the staff will want to look over the actor's résumé (or your comparable notes) before the actor is ushered in to read. This allows the staff to review the actor's background and judge his experience level before meeting him. In some other theater situations, the actor may be judged solely on appearance and reading, and résumés or preliminary notes are intentionally ignored.

After the show has been cast, don't throw away the résumés or notes. If the résumé picture is an 8 × 10-inch glossy print, it may be useful to the company publicity person as part of a publicity release or for posting in the lobby. Information on the résumé might be useful to you, the publicity person, or others. Also keep the résumés of those not cast. You might have to replace a cast member suddenly. When casting your next show, you just might remember someone right for a role by flipping through your collection of résumés.

If you save résumés for future productions, you will want to make some simple evaluation of the actor's ability and code the résumé. A suggested code is: (1) excellent, exciting actor, (2) capable actor, (3) barely competent, (4) no talent; (A) well suited to the part, (B) possible for the part, (C) not suited for the part.

The value of such a code is that in invitational readings for future productions you would not call the (4)'s to read and would start with the (1)'s. The letters, along with the names of the roles they read for, might remind you of the actors' physical types.

CONTROLLING SCRIPTS

During the casting call, you are responsible for controlling scripts. If you have not already numbered your scripts, now would be a good time to do so. Jot down the names of the readers and the script numbers as you issue them. As the actors depart the interview area, be sure to reclaim the scripts and cross off their names.

Actors will beg to take scripts home in order to prepare for callbacks. Advise these actors that scripts are needed for auditions and be prepared to point out where actors may obtain duplicate scripts.

OBTAINING INFORMATION

During auditions, at the first reading, and every time a newcomer joins your cast, crew, or staff, you will want to obtain information that you and other members of your staff can use. It is convenient to gather this information on cards (3 × 5 inch or 4 × 6 inch) or on standard-sized preprinted information sheets.

The information/audition card may be preprinted (figure 6.8, page 79), or you may post an explanation of the information you want and the format you want it in, and distribute blank cards (figure 6.9, page 80). The former method is preferable, as you are more likely to get serviceable results. Whichever approach you use, it is best to check each card as it is completed to ensure it is legible and that both sides have been completed.

Age range and union affiliation deserve special attention.

Age Range

Some actors do not feel it necessary that you know their ages. Rather than posing the sometimes awkward question of age, ask for the range they feel they can portray on stage. (You are welcome to your own opinion, but discreetly keep it to yourself.) Or, instead of asking for the age range, you might offer the following multiple choice: (1) child, (2) ingénue, (3) mature. This offends no one (except the "aging ingénue").

Union Affiliation

An actor who is a member of any of the performers' unions (AEA, SAG, AFTRA, or AGVA—discussed in chapter 18) may be prohibited by the union from performing in any nonunion production. In auditioning for showcase productions and no-budget, nonunion productions, actors have been known not to state their union affiliation on their audition cards in order to work. It is the producer's responsibility to check, or face union sanctions.

When a preprinted audition form is used, an area can be set aside ("Do not write below this line") for results of questions that the director or casting director will want to ask during interviews (figures 6.10 and 6.11, pages 81 and 82).

Joseph Behar

310 430 XXXX
SAG

Represented By:
BKI
JOEL KLEINMAN
323 . 874 . 9800

FILM

Giovanni's Room	Giovanni – Lead	Dir. Amanda Boggs
Turf	Tiery – Lead	Dir. Jerome Sable
Black & Blue	Jose – Supporting	Dir. Philip Durand
The Mediocre David Davidson	Georges – Supporting	Dir. Dan Riley
True Balance	Tim – Lead	Dir. Trevor Bennett
Vampira	Vampire	Global Media
Outer Rim	Nir – Lead	Dir. Rafael Botzer
Through The Light	Angel	Dir. Rob Dosantos

TELEVISION

Navy – N.C.I.S	Guest star	CBS
XTRM Out Doors	Host	Sports 5
Florentine	Recurring	Channel 2
Loves Around The Corner	Co – Star	Channel 2

THEATRE

Stress Test	Dupont - Lead	Dir. Sasha Litovchenkov
Foursum	Doctor - Lead	Dir. Sasha Litovchenkov
Far Away	Condemned Prisoner	Dir. Ron Sossi
Grease	Danny Zuko – Lead	Bercy, Paris
Titanic	Jack D. – Lead	Dir. Claudine Heff

TRAINING

The Ardavany Approach	Tom Ardavany	Currently
T.A School of Performing Arts	Graduate	3 Year Program
Acting Technique	Patrick Quagliano	Stella Adler – NYC
Technique and Scene Study	Lorraine Serabian	HB Studios – NYC
Acting for Camera	Valerie Kingston	TVI Actors Studio
Meisner	The Acting Corps	LA
Dance: Ballet, Tap, Jazz, Salsa	Broadway Dance Center	NYC

SKILLS

Conversational: French, Hebrew, Arabic
Flying Trapeze, Extensive Military Training, Paramedic.
Professional Horseback riding, Motor Biking, Rock climbing, Slack – Lining.
Amateur Magician, Plays an Aborigine Didgeridoo and African Djembe.

FIGURE 6.7 Sample Résumé

Courtesy Joseph Behar, actor.

The information cards or forms should be clipped to the actor's photo or composite. In school theaters, be sure to have the actors write their schedules of classes on their audition forms.

PLAYLAND THEATRE

AUDITION FORM DATE ________ # ________

Actor ________ Singer ________ Dancer ________

____

Print carefully on line above: last name, first name, middle name

____

Phone/e-mail

____

Address, city, zip

____

Union membership—Equity, SAG, AFTRA, AGVA, SEG, other

____

Agency, agent, phone, and e-mail of agent

HT: _____ WT: _____ HAIR: _____ EYES: _____ VOICE TYPE: _____ VOICE RANGE: _____

Theatrical Training and Experience: ______________________________

____

Recent Credits: ______________________________

____

Current Commitments: ______________________________

FIGURE 6.8 Printed Company Audition Form Cards

CONTROLLING FORMS

The first cast meeting after casting calls and callbacks is frequently a read-through of the script. Take advantage of a time when all the cast are present by getting the paperwork done. Take a few minutes of cast time to review the cast rules and take care of the required forms. If you fail to get it all done at once, you will have to run after individual cast members to distribute and collect forms, and this can be time consuming.

Last Name ____________ First ____________ Middle ____________

Address ________________________ City ____________ Zip ______

Phones Home ______________ Work ______________

Service ______________ Other ______________

Union Membership ☐SAG ☐AFTRA ☐AEA ☐SEG ☐AGVA ☐Other ________

Agency ____________ Agent ______________ Phone ______________

Height ______ Weight ______ Eye Color ______ Hair Color ______

Have you filled out a card? The information requested will help us remember you, cast you, and reach you. Thank you!

Front/format

Recent Credits:

Studies:

Current Commitments:

Reverse side/format

Last Name Feegle First Fred Middle Figleaf

Address 117 Marrow Bone Drive City Los Angeles Zip 90037

Phones Home (123) 555-8763 Work (123) 555-4588

Service (123) 555-3000 Other ______________

Union Membership—☒SAG—☒AFTRA—☐AEA—☐SEG—☐AGVA—☒Other Equity

Agency Talent Ltd. Agent Georgia Leech Phone (123) 555-4588

Height 6' 8" Weight 176 lbs. Eye Color Green Hair Color Brown

Have you filled out a card? The information requested will help us remember you, cast you, and reach you. Thank you!

Front/sample

Recent Credits: SHOWBOAT—Captain Andy, LILI (MGM)—Clown
DEATH OF A SALESMAN—Willy, UNTOUCHABLES—Mafia member
BREAKING POINT—Pencil Salesman

Studies: Fyodor Lerantovich Studio (NYC)
Neighborhood Playhouse (Grand Fork, ND)

Current Commitments: Tape TV Show (Sept. 2)
Tour with American Ballet Company Starting January 4

Reverse side/sample

FIGURE 6.9 Posted Model Examples for Audition Information Cards

THE ST. GENESIUS PLAYERS

The Odd Couple

CASTING

Name: ______________________________ Phone: ___________________

Address: ____

Height: _________ Weight: _________ Eyes: _________ Hair: _________

Age Range: __________________

Union: AEA SAG SEG AFTRA AGVA OTHER _____

Agency, Agent, Phone ____

Acting Experience: Use reverse side of this form to list recent credits if you are not submitting a resume.

Do not write below this line.

• Felix	smokes
• Oscar	poker
• Speed	goal
• Murray	schedule
• Roy	SM
• Vinnie	St. G?
• Gwendolyn	
• Cecily	

FIGURE 6.10 Full-Length Audition Form

Plan this paperwork session ahead of time by grouping forms for each actor into a packet. Make sure you have plenty of pens and pencils on hand. Each packet might include:

Cast keeps:

1. Rehearsal schedule
2. Company rules
3. Cast list (see the following section)
4. Guides to hotels, restaurants, points of interest (if the cast is from out of town)

You need returned:

1. Biographical data form (figure 6.12, page 83) (check with your publicity person)
2. Costume size form (figure 6.13, page 84) (check with your costume designer)

WORKSHOP APPLICATION

	TALENT
Name: ______________________	Actor: ______________
Address: ____________________	Director: ______________
	Playwright: ______________
	SM: ______________
Telephone Number: ____________	Designer: ______________
Union Affiliation:	Technician: ______________
	Singer: ______________
AEA: ______ AGVA: ______	Dancer: ______________
	Choreographer: ______________
SAG: ______ C.E.: ______	Producer: ______________
	Musician: ______________
AFTRA: ______ Other: ______	Other: ______________

Professional Background: (List any additional credits on reverse side. Attach résumé and picture, if available.)

Training: Where and with whom have you studied?

Check sessions you are interested in attending:

_____ Lecture Sessions

_____ Workshop Scenes: Assignments, observations, critiques

_____ Direction Class

_____ Production Panels: Budgeting, Stage Manager, Scenic Designer, Lighting

(Please do not write below this line)

FIGURE 6.11 Model of Workshop Application Form

3. Health insurance form (if Equity company—figure 6.14, page 85)
4. Welfare coverage form (if Equity company)
5. W-4 form (if paid company)
6. Life insurance form (if Equity company)

If you have time, print the actor's name on each of the forms before you distribute them. Then make sure to get back the forms you need. Many actors will want to take them home, insisting they have the information written down at home and they can copy it if you will just allow them to take the forms home. Don't. You may never see the forms again. Insist that they fill out as much as they can and that you must have

BIOGRAPHICAL DATA

Information requested below will be used for program notes and publicity releases. Use the reverse side to complete comments if space below is not sufficient. THANK YOU!!!!

Name: ____________________ Role: ________________

- Education:
- Theatrical training:
- First stage appearance:
- Credits:

  Most recent stage:

  Most recent film:

  Most recent TV:

  Current commitments (stage, film, TV):
- Hobbies:
- Highlight to date of your career:
- Career ambition:

If you wish to add any unusual personal facts or viewpoints that might aid in publicity, please use the reverse side.

FIGURE 6.12 Model of Biographical Data Form

http://www.pearsonhighered.com/stern_ogrady>pearsonhighered.com/stern_ogrady

all forms back before they get up from the table. Tell them you will call them at home for the information they can't remember.

"I have my biography at home." "My agent fills these in." "I'm covered by my wife's insurance." "I always forget how many of my husband's children by his first wife I'm supposed to claim." Actors, like most other people, don't like to fill out forms. Plead, cajole, and remain pleasant.

Have your tailor's tape handy for those who don't remember their costume sizes. Check each returned form on the spot to make sure that it is complete and legible.

PREPARING A CAST LIST

The ability to reach any actor immediately is of prime importance to you. The cast list is an invaluable tool in that function. The list should include the character, full name of the actor who plays the character exactly as that actor wishes the name to appear in the program, address, home phone, cell phone, work or business phone, service number, e-mail address, agent's name, and agent's phone number (figure 6.15, page 86).

COSTUMES

The costumes department needs to know your measurements. Please mark them on this sheet and return it to the stage manager. Thank you.

Name: ______________________________ Role: ______________________

Height: ______ Ft.: ______ In. Weight: _______ lbs.

Men only

- Jacket size: ____________
- Shirt: ______________

  (neck) (sleeve)
- Waist: _______
- Inseam: _______
- Shoes: _______
- Sox: _______
- Hat: _______

Women Only

- Bust: ______
- Waist: ______
- Waist to floor: ______
- Hips: ______

FIGURE 6.13 Model Costume Size Form

http://www.pearsonhighered.com/stern_ogrady>pearsonhighered.com/stern_ogrady

Check for accuracy with each cast member before duplicating.

In rare cases, actors will want to have their home phone and address withheld from all but you. Check this, too, before duplicating and distributing.

There never seem to be enough cast lists. Each cast member wants one so she can contact other cast members. The costume designer needs one. The publicist needs one. The payroll clerk needs one. The program editor needs one. The union insists on one. And as soon as you have given out your last copy, you find that there is still another person who needs one—the assistant director, the assistant stage manager, the doorman, the receptionist, the box office, or the sign painter.

You can't go too far in obtaining extra phone numbers at which you can reach an actor. Ask for any other numbers and e-mail addresses at which he can be reached when not at home or at the theater. Note these numbers on your copy against the emergency situation when you will have to reach that actor in a hurry.

You will find several uses for a well-designed, complete cast list. One should be posted near your home telephone. Another should be indexed into your promptbook for handy reference during rehearsals. You can use still another copy, with a grid overlay (figure 6.16, page 87), as a checklist. Every time you have a distribution to make,

EQUITY LEAGUE WELFARE TRUST FUND

PLEASE PRINT OR TYPE — BLUE CROSS

PROFESSIONAL NAME AS LISTED WITH ACTORS EQUITY — LAST NAME — FIRST NAME — MIDDLE INITIAL

HOME ADDRESS — NUMBER AND STREET OR AVEUE — CITY, TOWN, VILLAGE — STATE — ZIP CODE

DATE OF BIRTH — MONTH — DAY — YEAR — SEX — SOCIAL SECURITY NUMBER — FOR OFFICE USE ONLY

MARITAL STATUS — DATE OF MARRIAGE — MO. — DAY — YR.

NAME OF SHOW IN WHICH EMPLOYED

EMPLOYER'S NAME AND ADDRESS

DATE OF YOUR FIRST REHEARSAL — MONTH — DAY — YEAR — TYPE OF EQUITY CONTRACT

LIST BELOW NAME OF SPOUSE AND UNMARRIED CHILDREN UNDER 19
(Please Remember You, The Member, Must Pay For Your Dependent's Coverage)

NAME (IN ORDER OF AGE) — RELATION TO YOU — WIFE — HSBD. — DATE OF BIRTH — MONTH — DAY — YEAR

SIGNATURE

(12/90)

EQUITY LEAGUE WELFARE TRUST FUND

LIFE INSURANCE

PLEASE PRINT OR TYPE

PROFESSIONAL NAME AS LISTED WITH ACTORS EQUITY — Last Name — First Name — Middle Initial

NAME ON SOCIAL SECURITY RECORDS IF DIFFERENT FROM ABOVE — Last Name — First Name — Middle Initial

HOME ADDRESS — Number and Street — City, Town, Village — State — ZIP Code

DATE OF BIRTH — Mo. — Day — Yr. — CHECK (✓) APPROPRIATE BOXES — ☐ Married ☐ Single ☐ Male ☐ Female — SOCIAL SECURITY NUMBER

NAME OF SHOW IN WHICH EMPLOYED

EMPLOYER'S NAME AND ADDRESS

DATE OF YOUR FIRST REHEARSAL — Mo. — Day — Yr. — TYPE OF EQUITY CONTRACT

DEATH BENEFITS TO BE PAID TO: — Last Name — First Name — Middle Initial — RELATIONSHIP

beneficiary – Example: Doe, Mary A. — Number and Street — City, Town, Village — State — ZIP Code

...ed, settlement will be made in equal shares to such of the designated ... unless otherwise provided herein. ... settlement will be made to the Estate of the Insured, unless

Eff. Date of Ins. (For Funds Use Only)

PRINTED IN U.S.A.

FORM W-4 (Rev. July 1963)
U. S. Treasury Department
Internal Revenue Service

EMPLOYEE'S WITHHOLDING EXEMPTION CERTIFICATE

Print full name .... Social Security Account Number ....

Print home address .... City .... State ....

EMPLOYEE: File this form with your employer. Otherwise, he must withhold U. S. income tax from your wages without exemption.

EMPLOYER: Keep this certificate with your records. If the employee is believed to have claimed too many exemptions, the District Director should be so advised.

HOW TO CLAIM YOUR WITHHOLDING EXEMPTIONS

1. If SINGLE, and you claim your exemption, write "1", if you do, not write "0" ....
1. If MARRIED, one exemption each is allowable for husband and wife if not claimed on another certificate
   - (a) If you claim both of these exemptions, write "2"
   - (b) If you claim one of these exemptions, write "1"
   - (c) If you claim neither of these exemptions, write "0" ....
3. Exemptions for age and blindness (applicable only to you and your wife but not to dependents):
   - (a) If you or your wife will be 65 years of age or older at the end of the year, and you claim this exemption, write "1"; if both will be 65 or older, and you claim both of these exemptions, write "2" ....
   - (b) If you or your wife are blind, and you claim this exemptions, write "1"; if both are blind, and you claim both of these exemptions, write "2" ....
4. If you claim exemptions for one or more dependents, write the number of such exemptions. (Do not claim exemption for a dependent unless you are qualified under instruction 4 on other side.) ....
5. Add the number of exemptions which you have claimed above and write the total ....
6. Additional withholding per pay period under agreement with employer. *See* instruction 1 ..... $

I CERTIFY that the number of withholding exemptions claimed on this certificate does not exceed the number to which I am entitled.

(Date) ...., 19.... •48-16-77790-1 (Signed) ....

FIGURE 6.14 Forms That Professional Cast and Crew Must Complete

check off each cast member to ensure that everyone was told about a pickup rehearsal, a cast picnic, or an invitation to see a matinee of another show.

Store a copy of each cast list for your personal files. This is the only list that has both home phone and home address—information you won't readily have available if you save only a program.

In a musical stock situation with only a one-week rehearsal period, you may not know all the casting until the second day of rehearsals, which is only a few days before the printer needs that information to have programs for opening night. In such a case,

THE TORCH-BEARERS

Cast

Character	Name/Address	Home	Work	Service	E-Mail
Mr. Fred Ritter	Albert Alvarez 1058 Bramercy Dr.	753-3691 (Jerry Rosen Agency 274-5861)	870-5414	752-7975	Alall@zyx.net
Mr. Huxley Hossefosse	Ben Blahzay 3916 Melrose	232-5756 (William Barnes 273-0205)	389-7726	None	Theblahz@comm.net
Mr. Spindler	Charles Corn 12113 Redondo	268-6612 (Ted Cooper 654-3050)	231-1961	399-7171	Corney212@avl.com
Mr. Ralph Twiller	Dave Dumpling 161 S. Berendo	753-3691 (Jerry Rosen Agency)	870-5414	752-7975	73457@cropserve.com
Teddy Spearing	Earl Eastman 355 Douglas	753-3691 (GAC 273-2400)	870-5414	None	Early@early.com
Mr. Stage Manager	Frank Farley 3607 W. 3rd	732-9444 (Coralie Jr. 663-1268)	778-3557	None	Farfel@comm.net
Mrs. Paula Ritter	Gina Glass	567-6743 (Kurt Frings 274-881)	652-7934	334-0101	Gglass@avl.com
Mrs. J. Duro Pampinelli	Helen Harvey 1510 S. Vermont	665-1605 (No agent)	None	None	Offut59@sac.com
Mrs. Nelly Fell	Ida Isely 2316 McPherson	221-2074 (Kumin-Olenick 274-7281)	295-1781	752-7975	1stern@ips.net
Miss Flora McCrickett	Judy Jennings 5716 Aldana rd.	936-2325 (no agent)	627-4554	None	Jjone@comm.net
Mrs. Clara Sheppard	Karen Kristen 3130 W. 11th	870-5070 (Kendal Agency 274-8107)	None	334-0101	Karenk@avl.com
Jenny	Louise Lehrer 139 E. 27th	877-2232 (Mishkin 274-5261)	754-3024	292-1333	Landfl@sac.com

FIGURE 6.15 Cast List for Duplication and Distribution

THE TORCH BEARERS — CAST LIST / Check List

Character	Actor / Address	HOME	WORK	SERVICE	E-MAIL	Contract	8 x 10s	W2	blue x - GHI	AVAIL. TUES	Program Notes	Picnic	Pick up July 1
Mr. Fred Ritter	Albert Alvarez 1058 Bramercy Dr.	753 3691 (J. Rosen Agcy - 274 5861)	870 5414	752 7975	alall@ZYX.net	✔	✔	✔	✔	✔	✔	✔	✔
Mr. Huxley Hossefrosse	Ben Blahzay 3916 Melrose	232 5756 (Wm. Barnes - 273 0205)	389 7726	none	theblahz@comm.net	✔	✔	✔	✔	✔	✔	✔	✔
Mr. Spindler	Charles Corn 12113 Redondo	268 6612 (Ted Cooper - 654 3050)	231 1961	399 7171	corney212@avl.com	✔	✔	✔	✔	✔	✔	✔	✔
Mr. Ralph Twiller	Dave Dumpling 161 S.Berendo	758 0058 (no agent)	292 5352	752 7975	73457@crumpserv.com	✔	✔	✔	✔	✔	✔	✔	✔
Teddy Spearing	Earl Eastman 355 Douglas	665 1052 (GAC - 273 2400)	none	none	earlyman@earlyman.com	✔	✔	✔	✔	✔	✔	✔	✔
Mr. Stage Manager	Frank Farley 3607 W. 3rd	732 9444 (Coralie Jr. - 663 1268)	778 3557	none	farfel@comm.net	✔	✔	✔	✔	✔	✔	✔	✔
Mrs. Paula Ritter	Gina Glass 232 S. Serrano	567 6743 (Kurt Frings - 274 8881)	652 7934	334 0101	gglass@avl.com	✔	✔	✔	✔	✔	✔	✔	✔
Mrs. J. Duro Pampinelli	Helen Harvey 1510 S. Vermont	665 1605 (no agent)	none	none	offut59@sac.com	✔	NO	✔	✔	✔	✔	✔	✔
Mrs. Nelly Fell	Ida Isely 2136 McPherson	221 2074 (Kumin-Olenick - 274 7281)	295 1781	752 7975	lstern@jps.net	✔	✔	✔	✔	✔	✔	✔	✔
Miss Flor. McCrickett	Judy Jennings 5716 Aldama Rd.	936 2325 (no agent)	627 4554	none	jjone@comm.net	✔	✔	✔	✔	✔	✔	✔	✔
Mrs. Clara Sheppard	Karen Kirsten 3130 W. 11th	870 5079 (Kendall Agcy - 274 8107)	none	334 0101	karenk@avl.com	✔	✔	✔	✔	✔	✔	✔	✔
Jenny	Louise Lehrer 139 E. 27th	877 2232 (Mishkin - 274 5261)	754 3024	292 1333	landfl@sac.com	✔	✔	✔	✔	✔	✔	✔	✔

FIGURE 6.16 Duplicated Cast List with Overlay Grid for a Checklist

it is desirable to run off lists with just the character name so that you can fill in cast members' names on the spot as casting is finalized (figure 6.17, page 88).

You will also need a complete list of the staff and crew, with their addresses and telephone numbers. A grid overlay on such a list makes a handy coordination form to ensure that you get all schedule changes and other necessary information to every member of the staff and crew.

CONDUCTING THE DEPUTY ELECTION

At the first meeting of an Equity company, or at the first rehearsal following casting at which the entire cast is present, conduct the election of the deputy. The deputy is that cast member who will represent his fellow union cast members in all union business. You should not serve as deputy.

The union formally mails the official election form to you when your name is supplied to the union (figure 6.18, page 89). If you do not receive the form prior to your first rehearsal, call the nearest Equity office.

Take the time to read the official statement of election policy slowly and deliberately.

SHOW BOAT

OLD LADY ON LEVEE	
QUEENIE	Bertha Powell
PARTHY ANNE HAWKS	
CAPTAIN ANDY	Marvin Miller
ELLIE	
FRANK	Dian Barlow
JULIE	Beverly Alvarez
GAYLORD RAVENAL	Alan Gilbert
MAGNOLIA	Kate Miller
JOE	
WINDY	
STEVE	
PETE	
IKE VALLON	Lou Boudreau
BACKWOODSMAN	
BARKER	
FATIMA	
DAHOMEY QUEEN	
LANDLADY	
ETHEL	
MOTHER SUPERIOR	
KIM	
JAKE	
JIM	
MAN WITH GUITAR	
DOORMAN	
MISS SO-AND-SO	
MISS THINGAMABOB	
HEADWAITER	
ANNOUNCER	

FIGURE 6.17 Production Cast List with Characters in Order of Appearance

Secret ballots are desirable in large casts. This process slows the election enough to give voters time to think. In small casts, members usually reach accord in an open discussion of who might best serve. Formality is not as important as thoughtfulness. Causing cast members to reflect, rather than simply "get it over with," is a matter of tactful persuasion.

Time to conduct this deputy election—and subsequent union meetings, should the need arise—out of paid rehearsal time is guaranteed to union actors in their contracts.

FIRST CAST MEETING OR READ-THROUGH

I know one stage manager who brings from home a freshly pressed tablecloth and a bouquet of flowers in a vase to place on the first-reading table. It's a nice touch and it

To the Equity Company,
When nominating and electing our company's Deputies, please remember that the Principal Deputy represents Principal Actors and Stage Managers; the Chorus Deputy represents Chorus Dancers and Singers. Please consider that:

- the Deputy is our link to the Union;
- the Deputy has the opportunity to gain extensive knowledge about the Contract under which we are working;
- the Deputy should form an amiable working relationship with the Stage Manager to try to solve problems as they arise;
- the Deputy will have direct communication with the appropriate AEA Business Representative;
- the Deputy can be instrumental in protecting all Actors' and Stage Managers' rights and working conditions by communicating directly with Actors' Equity about any possible infractions.

Most Actors and Stage Managers who have become involved in union activity as either Councilors, committee members or Deputies, have discovered that the more we know about our rights and our contracts, the better protected we are and the greater control we have over our working conditions. The Deputy should never have any confrontations with Management. After consulting with the Stage Manager, the Deputy need only communicate with the Union to insure action. This is an important job from which the entire company can benefit.

Our Deputy, once elected, should call the appropriate Equity office and ask for the Business Representative who administers our Contract to establish communication and learn of any concessions granted for this production. Ask to be sent a Deputy kit, if you have not yet received one from the Stage Manager, and ask that the pre-paid postage envelopes be sent to you for weekly reports and for any correspondence with Equity.

The Deputy may call collect.

Your Stage Manager will read the letter on the reverse side prior to the Deputy election, and then conduct election. Please DO NOT sign this election form unless this letter has been read. No one shall be present at the election except those employed under the Equity contract for this production. A Deputy may be elected by voice vote or, if more than one member is nominated, by secret ballot.

We, the undersigned Equity members, who constitute a majority of the cast of the

(circle the applicable classification) Principals / Ensemble Singers / Ensemble Dancers

of the ______________________________ company

under a ______________________________ (type of Equity contract)

located at ______________________________ theatre

under the management of ______________________________

and opening on ______________________________ do hereby elect

______________________________ as Deputy.

______________________ ______________________

Date of this election: ______________ Deputy's local phone: ______________

Address (**not** theatre): ______________

____

FIGURE 6.18 Deputy Election Letter and Form

Courtesy Actors' Equity Association. Download from actorsequity.org starts the cast off with the warm thought that someone went out of the way to make things a little better.

What other steps might you take to improve the atmosphere of the first reading?

SUGGESTED CLASSROOM EXERCISE

Discuss the relationship of stage manager and actors in the audition process. What can stage managers do and how can they behave in order to establish an atmosphere of support and encouragement?

7

Budgeting

A theater requires two good producers: one to produce the play, and the other to produce the cash.
—Anonymous

Keeping a record of your expenses is the very least that is expected of you in the area of budgeting. If you pay any money out of your pocket to further a production, whether it is 50¢ for a phone call to an actor who is late or the C.O.D. charge for a prop delivered to the theater, make a record of it, and, if possible, get a written receipt.

You may want to use an expenditures form (figure 7.1) and attach your receipts to it. Keep the form in your promptbook so that it is with you when you need it. Periodically turn in the receipts for reimbursement.

In some instances, it is more convenient to set up a petty cash fund, from $50 to $100, depending on needs. When it has been spent, turn over the receipts to the business manager or the box office treasurer, who can advance another $50 to $100 or whatever sum has been arranged and budgeted.

In some companies, a purchase order must be obtained from the business manager before anything can be bought.

In other cases, it may be necessary for you as manager to control funds for the technical director, the costume designer, the property master (see chapter 10), and other backstage personnel. To make sure that each does not spend beyond the total budgeted for the production, you might need to use a purchase order system: Any staff member must ask for a purchase order *before* buying. You then check the budget to see if this particular expenditure is within reason, and then approve or disapprove by giving or by denying a purchase order.

The budgeted items for a one-week musical stock production could be, for example, lumber, paint, hardware, fabrics, rigging, electrics, running props, purchase props, tools, and car rental/gas. Figure 7.2 (page 93) shows the layout of an expenditures record using this example on ledger pages. Many theaters use computer spreadsheet programs to keep track of the budget, so you may very well be working from a computer printout rather than a ledger.

EXPENDITURES

____ production of "____________________" __________
(dates)

Supplier	Item(s)	Purchased by	Date	**Cost**
1.				
2.				
3.				
4.				
5.				
6.				
7.				
8.				
9.				
10.				
11.				
12.				
13.				

Page___ of___

Prepared by ________________

Lawrence Stern
Production Stage Manager
555-3719

FIGURE 7.1 Expenditures Record to Keep in the Promptbook

Download from http://www.pearsonhighered.com/stern_ogrady

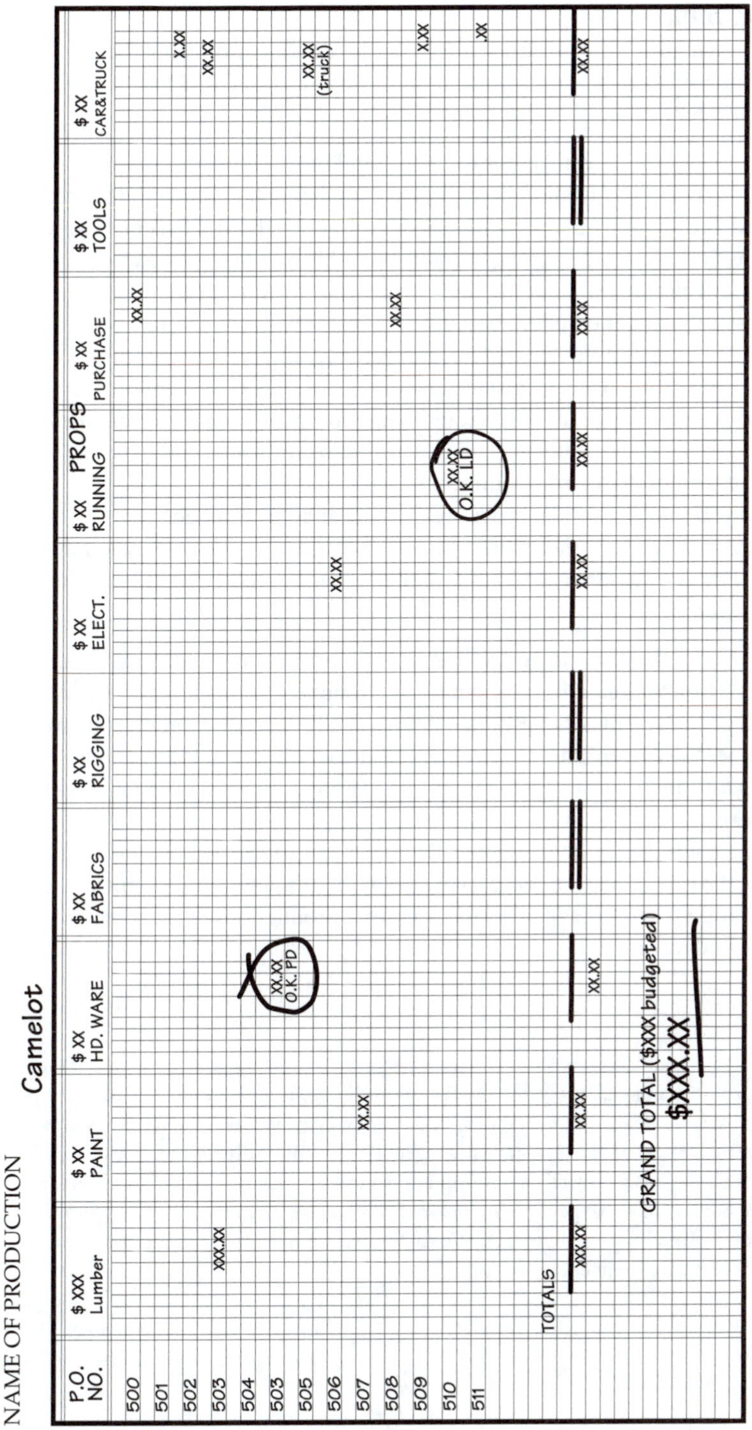

NAME OF PRODUCTION **Camelot**

P.O. NO.	$ XXX Lumber	$ XX PAINT	$ XX HD. WARE	$ XX FABRICS	$ XX RIGGING	$ XX ELECT.	PROPS $ XX RUNNING	PROPS $ XX PURCHASE	$ XX TOOLS	$ XX CAR&TRUCK
500								XX.XX		
501										
502										X.XX
503	XXX.XX									XX.XX
504										
503			XX.XX O.K. PD							
505										XX.XX (truck)
506						XX.XX				
507		XX.XX								
508								XX.XX		
509										X.XX
510							XX.XX O.K. LD			
511										.XX
TOTALS	XXX.XX	XX.XX	XX.XX			XX.XX	XX.XX	XX.XX		XX.XX

GRAND TOTAL ($XXX budgeted)
$XXX.XX

FIGURE 7.2 Ledger Page. The ledger shows columns for budgeted items with purchase order numbers listed in left column.

Example

The technical director calls you from the lumberyard to say that the materials required to carry out the scene designer's plans will cost $298. Should you issue a purchase order?

Review the budget for this show and other shows this season.

There's $240 allotted to lumber. But, being familiar with the scene design and the show, you also know there will be no flying of scenery or actors, or effects that require rigging. So you can add the rigging allocation of $40. You should also be aware of the budget situation for the season: Tools have already cost $30 over the budget because of a lost sabre saw; the last two shows were under budget by $40 and $60, respectively, in lumber, and three of the four coming shows have been staged before in past seasons; therefore, since most of the scenery is stored, they should come in under budget. Sifting these factors, and perhaps some others, while the tech director waits on the phone, you might give the purchase order number.

Or you might be under strict orders to clear all overbudget items with the business manager or other higher-budget authority. In this case, you might have to ask the scene designer to streamline the design and bring it into line with the budget.

In educational theater, the budget for a single production might have a completely different set of budgeted items (figure 7.3). Designers with a level of experience with past college productions can estimate figures at a first production meeting by evaluating whether the current show is more or less demanding than the last. Guest designers and directors and new faculty members are cautioned against overspending by others on the staff.

The contingency item is normally 10 percent of the overall budget. If not used in one of the categories that is especially needy, contingency money might get diverted into stockpiling items that can be used in future productions of the season or next season. The budget for student productions is not generally made known to the students.

> Each department head at our theater is responsible for one section of the budget. As production stage manager, I am responsible for tracking expenses for stagehands, musicians, ushers, theater expenses, and stage manager. The technical director and costume director track their expenses as well as lighting and sound expenses. Our artistic director tracks designer and director expenses. Our finance director keeps track of benefits, health insurance, and workers' comp expenses. We each input figures into separate spreadsheets that link to the master budget (figure 7.4).
>
> Bob Bones
> *Production Stage Manager*
> *American Musical Theatre of San Jose*

Date ____________

Ohlone College Drama

Individual Show Budget: Title: ________________________________

Director: ________________________ Total Budget: _____

Auditions: ________________________

Show Dates: ________________________

Rights: ________________________

Set: ________________________

Costumes: ________________________

Props: ________________________

Lights: ________________________

Special Effects: ________________________

Paint: ________________________

Rentals: ________________________

Tickets: ________________________

Contingency: ________________________ ____________

(All consultants, instructors, etc., paid out of separate budgets) Total

Separate Budget:

Publicity: ____________

Publicity Budget Covers

All Paper and Ink for: Programs
Audition Postcards
Show Postcards
Posters
Art Work
Any Photo Work

Approval:

____
Director

____
Technical Director

This budget is prepared at the first production meeting.
No changes can be made outside of a production meeting.

FIGURE 7.3 College Single Production Budget Form

Courtesy Mark E. Nelson, Professor Theatre Studies, Ohlone College.

	A	B	C	D
1	**Show 1**			
2		**Rate**	**Budget**	**Notes**
3	**Total Annual Salaries**			
4	Master Carpenter			
5	Carpenter			
6	Carpenter			
7	Carpenter			
8	Scenic Artist			
9	Scenic Artist			
10	Scenic Artist			
11	Scenic Artist			
12	Carpenter Overhire			
13	Props Overhire			
14	*Subtotal Scene Shop Salaries*			
15				
16	Draper			
17	Cutter			
18	Assistant Cutter			
19	First Hand			
20	First Hand			
21	Stitcher			
22	Stitcher			
23	Stitcher / Overhire			
24	Crafts Master			
25	Crafts Assistant			
26	Shopper			
27	Costume Shop Overhire			
28	*Subtotal Costume Shop Salaries*			
29	**Total Technical Salaries**			
30				
31	Director			
32	Assistant Director			
33	Choreographers			
34	Assistant Choreographers			
35	Musical Directors			
36	Associate Musical Directors			
37	Rehearsal Pianist			
38	Programming			
39	*Subtotal Directors/Chor/MD/Rehearsal Pianist*			
40				
41	Designer/Coordinator — Sets			
42	Designer — Costumes			
43	Designer — Sound			
44	Designer — Makeup			
45	Designer — Lights			
46	Master Elec./Asst. Designer			
47	Asst. Stage Manager (non-AEA)			
48	Prop Master			
49	*Subtotal Designers, Non-Union ASM, ME, Props*			
50				
51	Wig Crew Head			
52	Head Dresser (union)			
53	Dresser (union)			
54	Wardrobe Supervisor			
55	*Subtotal Union Dresser, Wig Crew, Wardrobe*			
56				
57	**Total Designer/Directors**			
58				
59	Ushers			
60	Police			
61	**Total Other Services**			
62				
63	AFM (musicians)			
64	IATSE (stagehands)			
65				
66	Equity Actors			
67	Stage Manager			
68	Asst. Stage Manager			
69				

FIGURE 7.4 Master Production Budget (Microsoft Excel®) for a Union House

Courtesy Bob Bones, Production Stage Manager, American Musical Theatre of San Jose. Microsoft product box shot(s) reprinted with permission from Microsoft Corporation.

SUGGESTED CLASSROOM EXERCISE

Have students brainstorm the budget items necessary to move your current production to a theater off campus for a short run. Assign a few items to each student, distribute catalogs of theatrical supply houses, and ask students to work together to determine the total cost

	A	B	C	D
70	**Total Actor's Equity Salaries**			
71				
72	Non-Union Cast			
73	Non-Union Crew			
74	**Total Non-Union Payroll**			
75				
76	**TOTAL PAYROLL**			
77				
78				
79	*Materials*			
80	Set Materials			
81	Rental Fee			
82	Cartage (rental set to & from SJ)			
83	Cartage (between shop & theatre)			
84	Dry Ice			
85	Video/Projection			
86	Video/Recording (archival)			
87	Video/Rental			
88	Sound (rental)			
89	Lights (rental)			
90	Costumes			
91	Hair/Makeup			
92	Wig Build			
93	Props			
94	Piano Tuning			
95	Stage Manager Supplies			
96	**Total Materials**			
97				
98	Guest Artist Expenses			
99	Scripts & Scores (rental duplication)			
100	Audition Expense			
101	**Total Other Costs**			
102				
103	Theatre Building Rental			
104	Theatre Equipment Rental			
105	**Total Theatre Facility Costs**			
106				
107	**Total Pizza, Tech Mtg. , & Parking**			
108				
109	**Total Contingency**			
110				
111	**Total Material, CPA, Other, Party, & Cont.**			
112				
113	**Benefits**			
114	*Workers' Compensation*			
115	Actor's Equity Association	5.48%		
116	Musical Directors/Choreographers/MD	5.48%		
117	Musicians	3.01%		
118	Total Annual Salaries	5.48%		
119	Technical Salaries	3.01%		
120	Contracted Services/Designers	3.01%		
121	IATSE	3.01%		
122	Ushers	3.01%		
123				
124	Volunteers			
125	**Total Worker's Comp.**			
126				
127	*Union Pension and Welfare*			
128	IATSE (health/welfare)			
129	Dresser (union)			
130	AEA Health			
131	AEA Pension			
132	AFM Pension			
133	**Total Pension and Welfare**			
134				
135	Kaiser (health)			
136	Payroll Tax Expense			
137	Unemployment Insurance			
138	**Total Benefits**			
139				
140	**TOTAL EXPENSES**			

FIGURE 7.4 *(Continued)*

and the price that would have to be charged for tickets to reach the break-even-point (BEP). Compare the projected cost of tickets off-campus to what is being charged on-campus for admission. (My sense is that students can endure four years of education without a clue as to how much money is required to make theater happen. The lighting board in a college theater control room, for example, is taken for granted until students know how much it would cost to rent that board for a two-weekend run.)

8

Rehearsal Procedures

The author should keep his mouth shut
when his work begins to speak.
—Nietzsche

WORKING WITH THE DIRECTOR DURING REHEARSAL

- **As the closest assistant to the director, one of your most important functions will be to assist in getting the most productive results out of the time allotted to each rehearsal. To do this well, it is important to maintain a clear understanding of the director's function and a working relationship that will help his or her aims to be carried out smoothly.**

The director is responsible for interpreting the playwright's work through the cast with the help of the staff. It is the director's artistic concept of the play that the cast, staff, and crew work to obtain.

When casting has been completed and rehearsals are under way, the director goes about his work in phases.

In the first phase, the director ensures that each cast member understands the character to be portrayed. This is accomplished at initial readings and in private discussions between the director and the actor. The director continues to influence characterization as reflected in line interpretations and business throughout the rehearsal period.

In the second phase, the director blocks—tells the actors where and how to move on stage and how to handle props.

Next, the director works on pace—the timing of lines and business, of scenes and acts. He imparts pace to the play the way an orchestra conductor imparts tempo to a symphony—one scene *presto,* another *moderato.*

In the last phase, the director works on polishing the interaction of characters with sets, with props, and, most important, with one another.

The final quality of the performance is the product of all four phases of the director's work.

(In amateur theater, work sometimes does not go beyond the first two phases by opening night. Work on characterization consists of the actors learning their lines, and blocking means they don't trip over one another. In professional theater, when a director is unable to progress beyond the first two phases, we call him a "traffic cop.")

The stage manager assists the director in two ways. First, the stage manager helps to expedite the rehearsals so the director and cast will have as much time as possible to work on pace and interaction. Setting rehearsal furniture, taking blocking notation, and warning actors for their entrances during rehearsals are examples of the duties implied by this function.

Second, the stage manager accepts the responsibility for relieving the director of all concern for the mechanics of production so that the director can concentrate on bringing about an artistic interpretation of the script. Calling all sound and light cues, scheduling crew calls, and informing the director of progress on the sets are examples of the duties implied here.

[From a small college.] We got a new director (head of theater arts department). She has one of those organic work processes; you never know anything until the last possible moment. It is quite frustrating for a tyro stage manager like myself, not to mention the design team and many of our acting students. She's not really a people person, and has a hard time communicating her ideas to the designers. She has an abrasive and demanding nature. During rehearsals, the actors are obliged to stand around until she figures out what she wants to do. Often she will preface a rehearsal with this statement: "Okay, get ready for me to lose my temper." She does. She'll single out actors and make derogatory statements about them. The show will be reblocked right up until opening night. I don't mind erasing until I have carpal tunnel syndrome, but I worry about how last-minute changes affect the quality of the show. How do I deal with a director of this nature? How do I tell her that her attitude is very negative and decreases morale?

Name withheld at request of writer
Name of college also withheld

[Working with difficult people can sometimes be the hardest part of stage management.

1. *Understand that you cannot change another person's personality or behaviors. Do not label. Do not blame. Do not accuse. Ask questions privately, not within earshot of cast or crew. Do not add to conflict. Remain calm when all about you are stamping their feet.*
2. *Focus on how the director's behaviors have an impact on your work. Analyze. Separate your perceptions of negative personality traits from the behaviors that affect your work. Remain professional. Do what you need to do to meet stage management objectives.*
3. *Use preproduction staff meetings and postproduction critique meetings to ask questions (e.g., "How many rehearsals prior to opening night should a no-more-changes-in-blocking deadline be set in order to obtain a polished performance?" "Would a no-more-changes-in blocking deadline have led to a more polished performance?" "Should that deadline be moved up in our next production schedule?").*
4. *Set limits for yourself and announce "I-messages" (e.g., "I have a low threshold for conflict. I will walk in the event of temper outbursts, regardless of source.").*
5. *Decide whether you wish to continue working with that director. Negotiate conditions under which you will continue, and come to a clear understanding with that individual.]*

The stage manager has no voice in the artistic interpretation of the script and must not intrude into this area. When prompting, for instance, he must not offer an interpretation of the lines to the actors.

What happens, then, if the stage manager notices during a rehearsal that one actor is addressing a line to a second actor that the playwright obviously intended for a third actor? The mistake is repeated at the next rehearsal. Still, the actors and director miss the obvious.

The stage manager should make a note in the promptbook and call the error to the attention of the director after the rehearsal and out of earshot of the cast. Let the director take remedial action.

Sometimes the stage manager observes basic mistakes in direction. For example, focus is drawn away from an actress's important lines by an actor moving upstage of her during her speech. The stage manager observes that the director is oblivious or condones this at rehearsal after rehearsal. What should the stage manager do?

The stage manager calls such items to the director's attention, privately and tactfully.

Now let's take it to extremes. The stage manager notices during rehearsals that the director is demanding a light comedy tone from an actress in a speech that simply won't work that way. It throws her fellow cast members off and it ruins the whole impact of the scene. What does the stage manager do?

The stage manager should judge with great care whether to discuss the matter confidentially with the director. I advise great caution until you get to know and understand the director. Certainly the stage manager should be extremely proficient in her own area before offering a director advice in another.

Although stage managers do not participate in the creative interpretation of the script, they do make a conscientious effort to identify and understand the director's interpretation so that they can retain it, if called upon to do so, in keeping the show in hand during a long run (see page 199) or blocking replacements and rehearsing understudies (see pages 202–203). Again, in these last-mentioned duties, it is the director's intent that stage managers strive to retain; stage managers do not impose their own artistic interpretation.

PRESET DIAGRAMS

- **As soon as the scene designer decides where the sets and set pieces are to be located, you should make a diagram that will allow you to place those sets (or indications of sets) and set pieces (or rehearsal substitutes) exactly where they should be (figure 8.1).**

As frequently as placement changes in the course of rehearsals, you must update your diagrams.

When it is decided which props will be *discovered* (found on the set at the rise of the curtain), add these props to your diagram with exacting specifications on just how the props are to be set (e.g., the label on a bottle should face downstage; the envelope is to be placed under the telephone with the address up and the flap open and pointing downstage).

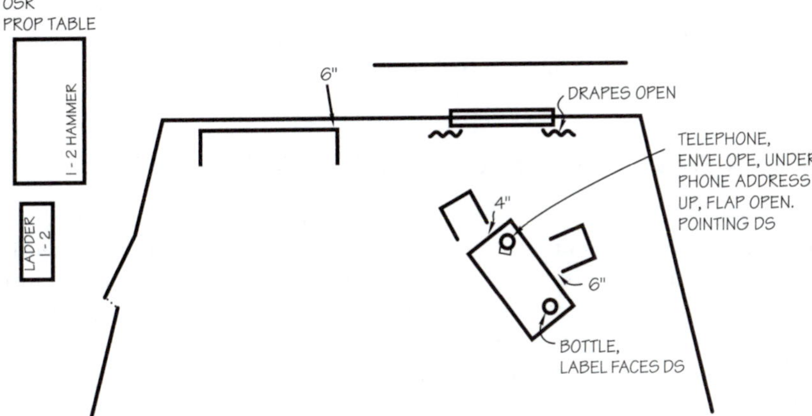

FIGURE 8.1 Preset Diagram of Set and Props

- **The purpose of the preset diagram is to allow you to make a visual inspection prior to every rehearsal and performance. You must ensure that every part of the set, all set pieces, and all props are in exactly the position that the cast expects to find them. This ritual is one of your most sacred duties.**

The preset diagram differs from a diagram of the stage (see page 58) in that it includes indications of sets and props, and it need not be drawn to scale. The preset diagram may be the same as a scene shift diagram (see pages 164, 165). Shift diagrams are placed in the crew area to help brief the crew, whereas preset diagrams are placed in your promptbook.

Examples

1. The property person is late. You know where everything goes from your diagram. You set the props in her absence and rehearsal is not delayed.
2. The crew, in setting for Act II, forgets to move a table onto the stage. During the intermission you check your diagram for Act II, realize that the table is not in place, and remind the crew.
3. An actor omits the business of closing the drapes on the set in Act II. Checking your diagram for Act III you realize that the drapes are supposed to be discovered closed. You make the adjustment.

Actors become dependent psychologically on the exact placement of set pieces and props. Their timing for business is dependent on this placement. Adjusting to misplacement puts a strain on them, and sometimes it throws them off completely.

Your preset diagram should extend to the wings and include all stacked set pieces and props that are offstage. You must check their presence just as carefully as the units on stage.

Example

A ladder and hammer, used as a set piece and prop in Scene 2, are borrowed for practical use in the shop and not returned. The items are not preset for Scene 1.

If the crew waits until its cue for the Scene 1–2 fast change to discover that the props are missing, the change will be delayed. Your inspection of the offstage set pieces and props avoids this type of incident.

REHEARSALS AWAY FROM YOUR STAGE

When stage time is not available for rehearsals, and scenes must be rehearsed in other areas, preset diagrams, drawn to scale, allow you to lay out the exact dimensions of the scene using measuring tape and masking tape and/or spare rehearsal furniture to indicate flats and doors. Physical barricades used to indicate flats are better than tape. Actors tend to move closer to the taped lines or even step over them. They later feel cramped when they get onto the actual set. Your care in setting up the makeshift rehearsal area saves the time and energy of the cast in reblocking on the actual set.

YOUR REHEARSAL CALL

Usually you should arrive in the rehearsal area 30 to 40 minutes prior to the rehearsal call, depending on how much work must be done to ready the area.

Besides arranging sets and props according to your preset diagram, check on working conditions. Sweep the stage and dust the rehearsal furniture, if necessary, and make whatever improvements you can in ventilation, temperature, and lighting.

Also prepare a work area for yourself and the director. Usually you will place a desk with two chairs in front of the apron. (Some directors prefer to use a music stand to hold their script as they remain standing during rehearsals.) Is there adequate room for your prompt script, the director's script, scratch paper, pencils, and refreshments? Ensure there is satisfactory lighting so you can follow your scripts comfortably.

Now, is everything ready to start rehearsal at the minute it is called? Or will the cast have to stand around 15 minutes waiting and/or adjusting things and not really rehearsing? Just 15 minutes of prerehearsal work by you can save two or three hours of combined cast time at every rehearsal. These hours saved and devoted to the quality of the final production are one of your valuable contributions to the production process.

REHEARSAL DUTIES

Anticipate the entire course of the rehearsal and have all working materials at hand so that you can be stationary or at the director's side throughout. As the director's closest assistant, you must be able to devote your full attention to the rehearsal because it is your busiest and most demanding work period. You have many duties and a few run concurrently:

- Calling all sound and light cues and special effects, pinpointing cues
- Spiking set pieces
- Prompting
- Warning
- Taking blocking notation
- Maintaining order
- Timing of rehearsals and performances

Calling and Pinpointing Cues

- **From the very first rehearsal, you should call every light, sound, and special-effects cue. Do this with such regularity and accuracy that no cast member ever fears for a second that you will miss a cue during the production.**

> I use those fluorescent self-stick dots in my prompt script as I work in a very dim corner during performances. They show up nicely in my blue light.
>
> Patty Kilpatric
> *Stage Manager*
> *Charles Town, WV*

No matter how many times the director reruns the same scene, you always call the cues.

At first, you go by the script. You ring the phone at the place indicated by the script and the place where you inserted your lightly penciled rough cue (see page 20). But during rehearsals, you discuss the exact pinpointing of the cue with the director. Perhaps the director wants the phone to ring two lines prior, and have the actors allow it to ring twice in order to heighten suspense as to which of them will answer the phone. Or the director decides that she doesn't want the first phone ring to come at the end of the actor's line, but three words from the end so that the actor can cross to the phone on the last words of his line. Now the cue is specific. Caret the exact point in your script. Later, just prior to the technical rehearsal, or during it, mark the exact cue with bold marking pen.

It is handy for you to have a bell/buzzer device in your kit (see page 54) to provide basic rehearsal sound effects. If you don't, simply call out "Phone," "Doorbell," "Auto horn," or whatever sound is needed. Similarly, you should call all lighting effects to which the actors must react. You call "Curtain" and/or "Lights" at the beginning and end of every act. You will also call the beginning, and sometimes the end, of all special effects: "Fog rolls in," "Vase rises from bookcase," "Rain begins," "Rain ends."

Call all cues *resolutely,* letting the cast know that you know your business and are self-assured.

Spiking Set Pieces

It is important to the actors' movements on stage that set pieces remain in exactly the same place at every rehearsal and performance. To ensure this, you not only check your preset diagrams but you also *spike* the set pieces; that is, you mark their position on the stage floor. Then, if moved accidentally or intentionally, the set pieces can be returned to exactly the same location.

Spiking is usually done with masking, labeling, spike, or gaffers tape placed on the stage at the upstage end of the set piece so that it is out of sight of the audience. An advantage of using gaffers tape is that the adhesive does not leave a residue on the stage floor when it is removed. Tape labels can be made with a portable labeling device (e.g., Brother's P-touch) and placed over masking, spike, or gaffers tape.

Spike your set pieces as early in the rehearsal process as is practical.

When many scenes are to play in the same area it becomes necessary to code the spike marks—to write on the tape which set piece plays there during which scene. Next to one tape marked "II-2 table" there might be another tape marked "III-7 chair."

Frequently shifts must be made in total blackouts or so fast that stagehands do not have time to read the tapes. In these cases glow tapes should be used, a different color for each scene.

> When using glow tape, if there is trouble with the tape sticking when just a small piece is used, or if the adhesive is not effective, it can be covered with clear packing tape so it does not wander off.
>
> Kat Dunham
> *Theatre Arts Lecturer, Edgewood College*

Prompting

- **Prompting procedure is determined by the director. You should ask the director privately, prior to rehearsals, how the cast should be prompted. How close are the actors to be held to the lines in the script? Letter-perfect? Or may they paraphrase as long as they get the sense of the line? How are the actors to call for lines? When and how are you to review lines with actors? Ask the director to brief the cast at the outset of rehearsals on just what is expected in the prompting process.**

The director's few words on the subject might go like this: "Our stage manager has been instructed to hold you very close to the script. If you deliver a line and our stage manager calls out the correct one, repeat the line as he gives it, without breaking character, and carry on. Do not argue about changing the line. See me before or after rehearsals about any possible line changes. Our stage manager will also approach you during breaks and after rehearsals to cite lines or cues that were missed. Please do not argue. Simply repeat out loud the line cited and then say, 'Thank you.' Call for lines by saying 'line,' and in no other way."

Some directors insist that the cast be held letter-perfect to the script, particularly if the playwright's reputation is great. They allow their casts greater latitude with the works of lesser-known playwrights. Some directors feel that they must update plays and encourage their cast members to experiment with and modernize the dialogue.

Certain directors insist that the stage manager throw the exact line whenever an actor hesitates or paraphrases, as well as when an actor calls for a line. Others want lines thrown only when the actor calls for them or when the cast jumps out of sequence. But they want all errors in lines brought to the attention of the cast during breaks or after rehearsals.

Some directors want cast members to say "line" when asking for a line. Others want them to snap their fingers but otherwise to remain in character. Some directors do not want their actors to call for lines at all. Some set a date in the rehearsal schedule after which actors are not to call for lines. Many directors resent any other remarks that actors throw when calling for lines, such as, "Oh, I always forget that one."

Talk it over with your director. If specific instructions are not given to the cast explaining the prompting interaction expected, start out in the way you feel is best and apply the director's criticism of your prompting technique as you go along.

- **To prompt efficiently, read the script to yourself, mouthing the words as the actors recite them.**

That way you are right there with them. Actors appreciate getting their lines immediately after they call for them. If actors and the director have to wait while you search for the line, then you are delaying the rehearsal.

When you prompt, give the actor the line in a clear, resolute, but emotionless tone of voice. Do not interpret the actor's line for her.

If line changes are made, note them in your prompt script. Prompt the new lines as if they were the old lines.

As you prompt, lightly pencil in a caret in the margin to indicate every line that was delivered improperly. Use a code to indicate the type of error, such as:

C—called for line or went up on line

P—paraphrased

BB—bobbled

L—late (cite cue to actor)

PR—pronunciation

J—jumped cue

H—handle—added extra word not in script prior to line

S—sequence, jumped out of

Use any code that works for you.

At the next break or after rehearsal, go to each actor, point out the missed line, and ask the actor to read it aloud. It is not necessary to say why you marked the line unless you are asked. Then erase the caret and code (figure 8.2).

Most professional actors are grateful for this service. If you should meet with resentment ("That's exactly what I said," "I know I missed it; you don't have to tell me"), say, "Thank you," politely, and walk away. Try it again at the next rehearsal and see how the actor accepts your help more graciously. When the actors are convinced that you are trying to help them, they are appreciative.

If there is an intentional pause prior to or during a line, mark your script with an inverted caret (^) at the pause point so that you are reminded not to prompt there (and don't panic on opening night).

Sometimes it is convenient to write out line cites during rehearsal so that you can hand each actor a list of lines that need to be reviewed. This allows you to dismiss the cast faster after rehearsal, rather than hold them while you flip through pages of the script. If the director habitually holds the cast after rehearsals to review notes with them, you might use that same time to cite lines, doing it as unobtrusively as possible, and not interfering with the director's notes.

Getting up on lines is basic to any production. You helped establish deadlines for line memorization in making up the master calendar and rehearsal schedule. Now, how can you help the actors meet those deadlines? Are you willing to run lines with them before or after rehearsals? Can you arrange extra prerehearsal sessions for cast members at which they can help each other by running lines? Can you assign a gopher to run lines with an actor who is offstage?

Start prompting with gusto just as soon as cast members are willing to put down their scripts. Let the cast know you mean to help them get up on their lines quickly

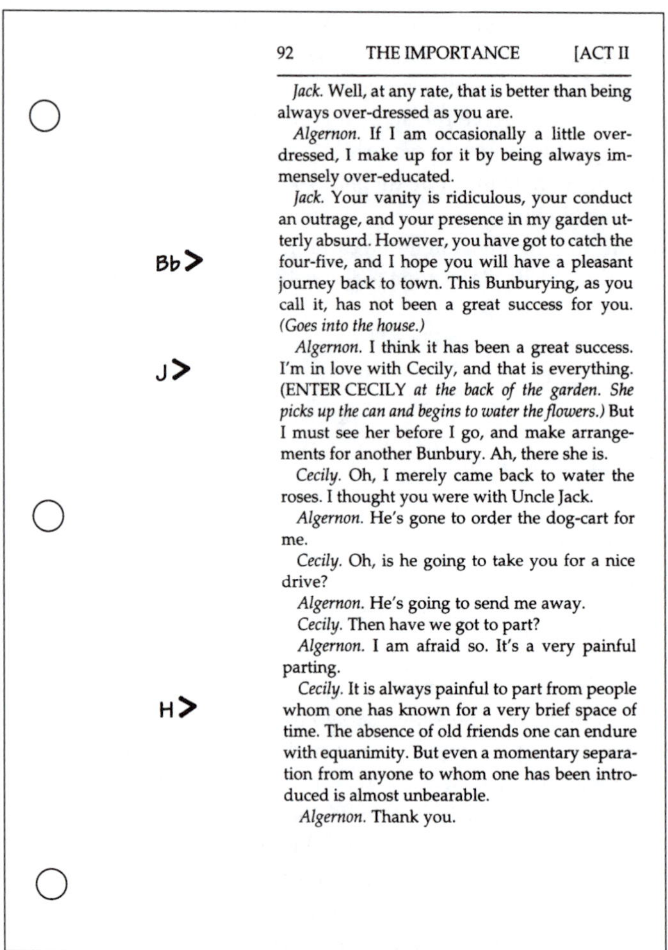

92 THE IMPORTANCE [ACT II

Jack. Well, at any rate, that is better than being always over-dressed as you are.

Algernon. If I am occasionally a little over-dressed, I make up for it by being always immensely over-educated.

Jack. Your vanity is ridiculous, your conduct an outrage, and your presence in my garden utterly absurd. However, you have got to catch the
Bb> four-five, and I hope you will have a pleasant journey back to town. This Bunburying, as you call it, has not been a great success for you. *(Goes into the house.)*

Algernon. I think it has been a great success.
J> I'm in love with Cecily, and that is everything. (ENTER CECILY *at the back of the garden. She picks up the can and begins to water the flowers.)* But I must see her before I go, and make arrangements for another Bunbury. Ah, there she is.

Cecily. Oh, I merely came back to water the roses. I thought you were with Uncle Jack.

Algernon. He's gone to order the dog-cart for me.

Cecily. Oh, is he going to take you for a nice drive?

Algernon. He's going to send me away.

Cecily. Then have we got to part?

Algernon. I am afraid so. It's a very painful parting.

Cecily. It is always painful to part from people
H> whom one has known for a very brief space of time. The absence of old friends one can endure with equanimity. But even a momentary separation from anyone to whom one has been introduced is almost unbearable.

Algernon. Thank you.

FIGURE 8.2 Prompting Cites, Lightly Penciled on Inside Script Margin

and accurately. It is easier to start out working hard than to start leniently and then apply pressure after the cast has gotten into sloppy habits.

If you can make every actor feel that you are earnestly trying to help rather than criticize, your prompting technique is good.

Prompting during a performance is a matter of the director's policy. Once a production has opened, it is generally considered unprofessional to prompt, and actors are expected to ad-lib their way out of any situation.

Warning

During rehearsals, actors may wander out of the rehearsal area. If they leave, they must always check out with the stage manager to say where they are going ("I'm going to get this sewn up in costumes," "We're running lines in the lobby"). They should also check in with the stage manager when they return (see "Entrances and Exits" on page 26).

You must think ahead. Which scene will the director work on next? You must warn wandering actors to be ready to appear. Waiting for an actor to be summoned so that a rehearsal can continue wastes a lot of time. If you observe your entrance warns (see page 26 and figure 3.11 on page 28), you can avoid such delays. If an actor is on the premises and rehearsal is delayed while waiting for that actor to appear, the fault is yours.

Sometimes an actor will be summoned only to find that the director wishes to rerun the scene prior to his entrance. It is better that a single actor be inconvenienced than that several be hung up by his absence. When you work at mounting a few plays with the same director, you will develop a sixth sense as to whether the director will press on or rerun.

If possible, don't leave your post to summon a wandering actor. Send a gopher or another actor.

During performances you are not responsible for warning actors for individual entrances, but you are responsible for warning the crew about impending shifts and the orchestra about musical cues, as necessary. (See "Actors and Their Entrance Cues" on page 28 for a discussion of exceptions.)

Taking Blocking Notation

Recording the movement of the actors helps to expedite rehearsals. With a written record of where they move on their lines, you are able to remind them when they forget. You will also use this notation to block in replacements and conduct understudy rehearsals (see page 202).

Normally you simply observe the initial blocking that the director gives the actors. Do not start to take blocking notations until the blocking starts to jell. There are several systems for making such notations.

METHOD I The stage is divided as shown in figure 8.3. Blocking notations using this method might read:

XDR—The actor crosses to the down right area of the stage.

XLC—The actor crosses to the left center area of the stage.

METHOD II (FOR THEATER IN THE ROUND) The stage is divided as shown in figure 8.4. The stage is thought of as a clock, with the orchestra pit at 12 o'clock, and then divided into four concentric circles lettered from the audience to the center of the stage.

Blocking notations might read as follows:

X3B—The actor crosses to the second ring at 3 o'clock.

X11A—The actor crosses to the first ring at 11 o'clock.

METHOD III All notations are made, regardless of the shape of the stage, with reference to the destination of the actor and the number of steps the actor takes in the direction of that destination. Blocking notations might read:

X door 2—The actor takes two steps toward the door.

X Pat 5—The actor crosses five steps toward Pat, another character.

With this type of notation, it is not possible to understand from reading a single entry where on stage the actor is located. This disadvantage should be countered by using extensive "French scene" diagrams (described on page 113).

METHOD IV (COMBINATIONS) Prior methods are combined. Blocking notations might read:

X DR door—The actor crosses to the down right door.

X2 DR door—The actor takes two steps toward the down right door.

X2 DR—The actor takes two steps toward the down right area.

X3B door—The actor crosses to the door in the 3B area.

X2 3B door—The actor takes two steps toward the 3B door.

The best method is the method that works best for you.

Most often the actors move on their lines; that is, they cross while delivering a line of dialogue. They frequently start to move at the beginning of the line and stop moving with the last word of it. So when you make a blocking notation adjacent to an actor's line, it automatically indicates that the actor is moving on the line.

If an actor is blocked to move on another actor's line—not usually the case—this must be indicated. For these instances, and for the purpose of "French-scene" diagrams, it is convenient to have a symbol for each actor:

C—Constance

I—Irene

G—George

For a large stage:

UR	URC	UC	ULC	UL
R	RC	C	LC	L
DR	DRC	DC	DLC	DL

C - Center of the stage

D - Down (toward the audience)

U - Up (away from the audience)

R - Right (actor's right facing the audience)

L - Left (actor's left facing the audience)

For a small stage:

UR	UC	UL
R	C	L
DR	DC	DL

FIGURE 8.3 Divisions of Proscenium Stage for Blocking Notation

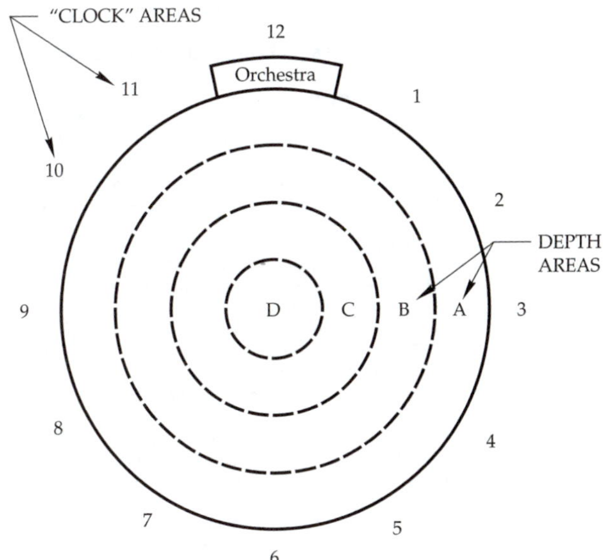

FIGURE 8.4 Divisions of Round Stage for Blocking Notation

Now, if George moves on Irene's line:

Irene: One or two? G XDR table

(On Irene's line, George crosses down right to the table.)
Or if two or more actors move at the same time:

Constance: I won't insist. XDL; I XDR; G XULC

(On Constance's line, she crosses down left, Irene crosses down right, and George crosses up left center.)

What if the actor moves before or after his line but not on another actor's line? Use carets:

Constance: ^ I won't insist. XDL

This indicates that Constance starts her cross prior to her line and finishes it with the end of her line.

Constance: ^^ I won't insist. XDL

These two carets indicate that Constance begins and ends her cross prior to her line, but not on another actor's line.

Constance: I won't ^ insist. ^ XDL

Constance starts her cross with the word indicated and completes the cross after the line.

Constance: I won't insist. ^^ XDL

Constance begins and ends her cross after her line.

Blocking notation is not an exact science. Some stage managers find that they can remember where and when an actor moves without precise notation. Others rely heavily on notation and longhand notes (figure 8.5).

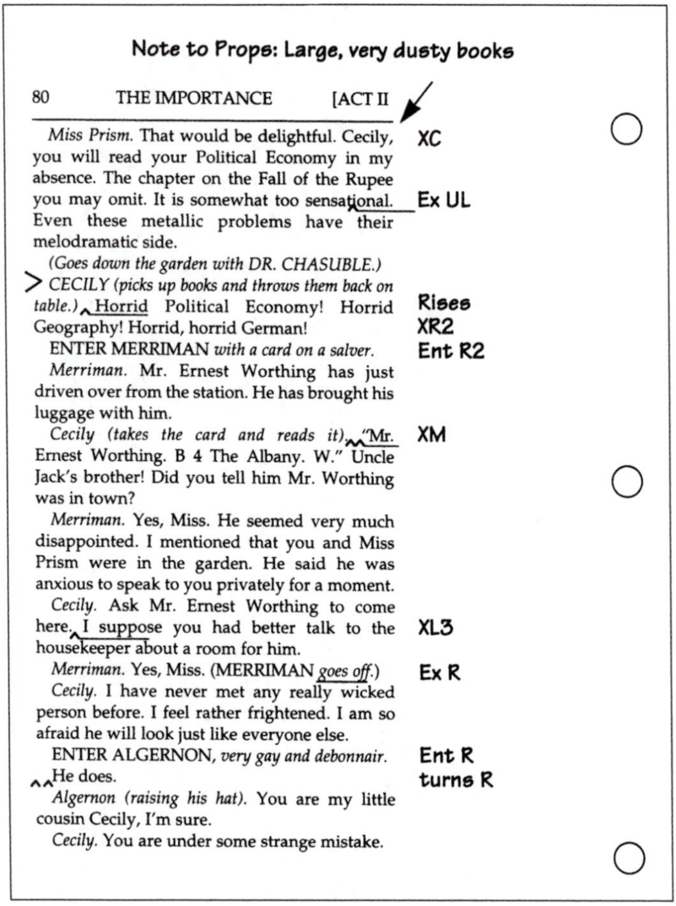

Note to Props: Large, very dusty books

80 THE IMPORTANCE [ACT II

Miss Prism. That would be delightful. Cecily, you will read your Political Economy in my absence. The chapter on the Fall of the Rupee you may omit. It is somewhat too sensational. Even these metallic problems have their melodramatic side.

XC

Ex UL

(Goes down the garden with DR. CHASUBLE.)

> CECILY *(picks up books and throws them back on table.)* Horrid Political Economy! Horrid Geography! Horrid, horrid German!

Rises

XR2

ENTER MERRIMAN *with a card on a salver.*

Ent R2

Merriman. Mr. Ernest Worthing has just driven over from the station. He has brought his luggage with him.

Cecily (takes the card and reads it). "Mr. Ernest Worthing. B 4 The Albany. W." Uncle Jack's brother! Did you tell him Mr. Worthing was in town?

XM

Merriman. Yes, Miss. He seemed very much disappointed. I mentioned that you and Miss Prism were in the garden. He said he was anxious to speak to you privately for a moment.

Cecily. Ask Mr. Ernest Worthing to come here. I suppose you had better talk to the housekeeper about a room for him.

XL3

Merriman. Yes, Miss. (MERRIMAN *goes off.*)

Ex R

Cecily. I have never met any really wicked person before. I feel rather frightened. I am so afraid he will look just like everyone else.

ENTER ALGERNON, *very gay and debonnair.* He does.

Ent R

turns R

Algernon (raising his hat). You are my little cousin Cecily, I'm sure.

Cecily. You are under some strange mistake.

FIGURE 8.5 Blocking Notation as Entered on Promptbook Page

After you have observed the first few rough blocking rehearsals, you will start to make your notations, realizing that the blocking is not yet set (permanent). It is best to take notation in light pencil. If you do not care to erase, you can make changes in columns at the side of the original blocking.

Constance: I won't insist. XDL/XULC/XRC

Using columns may be advantageous. When a director wants to go back to an earlier blocking, you will be able to tell the actors how they used to move.

After a few rehearsals when the same blocking is repeated, it is safe to assume the blocking is set. A director may still change all or part of the blocking after this point, but it is set insofar as the director expects the actors to repeat their movement unless he changes it. The time when this happens varies with the director's technique. Some directors rough block at home, using diagrams of the stage and tokens for actors. They bring in their own notation of projected blocking and start early rehearsals with firm blocking. Other directors allow cast members to drift at will as they recite their lines, and then try to arrange the drifting, sometimes called organic blocking.

Dance/Fight Blocking

Generally, stage managers are not responsible for noting exact movement of dancers/fighters. You need to note in your prompt script when the dancers/fighters enter/exit with respect to any dialogue, narration, or music score. You also need to note the duration. In dance companies, the choreographer and dance captain are responsible for remembering the moves from one rehearsal to the next in order to prompt dancers or in order to block replacements.

I punch holes on the right side of my blocking sheets so they are facing the text page (right side of my book). I write the blocking on the sheets with numbers that correspond to numbers that I write on the text page where a specific action occurs. When the action is changed to a different line, I find it easier to move the number than to rewrite the blocking notation. Props are usually noted on the blocking sheets opposite the first page of each scene *[figure 8.6]*. If there are tables with many props, I will also draw a close-up picture of just the table so that each prop can be labeled and positioned precisely.

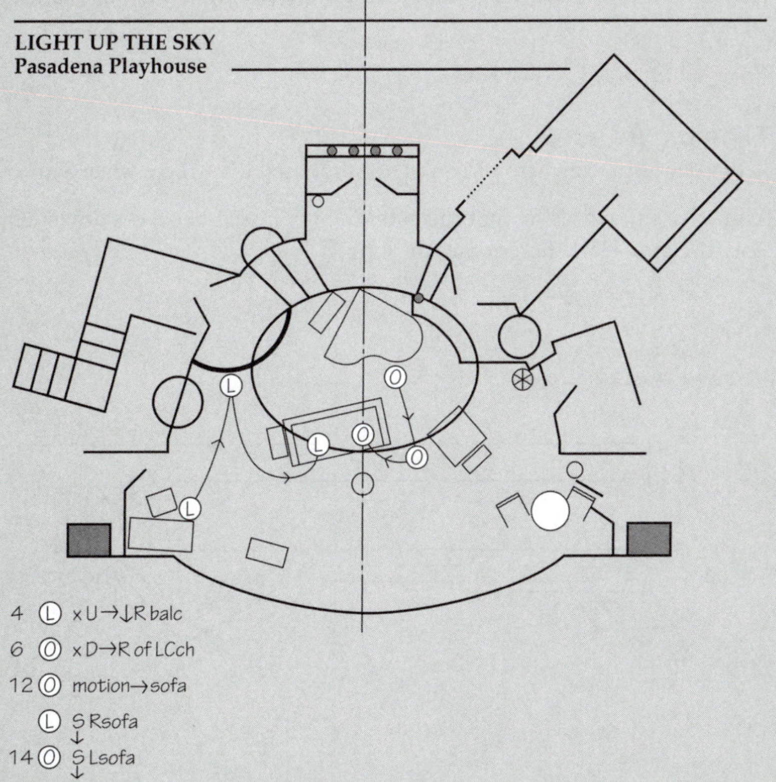

FIGURE 8.6 Computer-Generated Blocking Diagram with Blocking Notation for *Light Up the Sky,* Pasadena Playhouse. Cari Norton uses MacDraft to draw her blocking diagrams and a plastic furniture template (⅛ inch = 1 foot) to add furniture pieces.

Courtesy Cari Norton, AEA Freelance Stage Manager.

(continued)

> Most musicals that I have done use 4-inch numbers on the DS edge of the stage to help with spacing for the dancers. By placing these numbers on my blocking sheets, I can be very specific about where the choreographer has placed each dancer *[figure 8.7]*.
>
> Cari Norton
> *AEA Freelance Stage Manager*

For the stage manager who feels he must have a more precise record of dance/fight sequences, there is the camcorder. During rehearsals, a DVD played on a laptop could remind dancers/fighters of what they did the last time the choreographer/fight coach/director made adjustments. That same DVD could be used to teach a dance or fight to replacement dancers/fighters and could be attached to the archive script to resurrect the show in the future.

When you feel that the blocking is set, start to prompt on blocking.

Example A

An actor says: "I know I was supposed to move on that line but I've forgotten where."

You: "Your cross is down left."

Example B

A director says to an actor: "You're not supposed to be there when Sam enters."

You advise the director (not the actor): "She missed her cross down left three lines back on 'Hark, here comes the king.'"

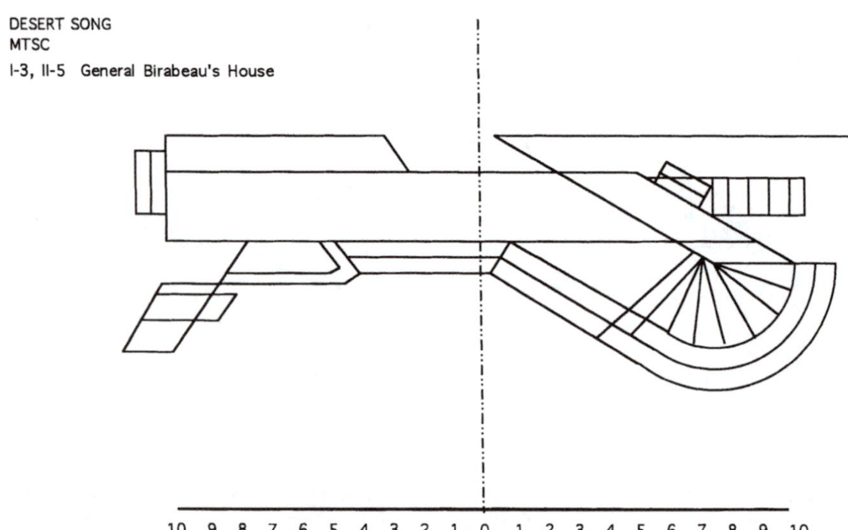

FIGURE 8.7 Computer-Generated Blocking Diagram for Musical *Desert Song*, Music Theatre of Southern California, San Gabriel

Courtesy Cari Norton, AEA Freelance Stage Manager.

In general, in the prompting of blocking, advise the director rather than the actors. If you observe actors not following their blocking, whisper to the director without interrupting the flow of the scene. Let directors decide if they want to stop and bring the error to the actor's attention, or if they want you to call the error to the actor's attention later, during a break or after the rehearsal, or if they want you to change your blocking notation in order to take advantage of what the actor has done instinctively.

Actors frequently take their crosses on the line following their cross line. The cross line triggers their memory too late. But they get where they are supposed to be in time not to upset the overall effect of the scene. This error can usually be corrected by calling the actor's attention to it after the scene is over. If you place a lightly penciled caret in the margin with an appropriate symbol, this will remind you of what the actor did wrong.

Constance: I won't insist. XDL < LX

After you have brought the late cross to the actor's attention during the break or after rehearsal, erase the caret and symbol.

Production Notes

While taking blocking notation, you should make production notes (I use the upper-right corner of my promptbook page) on (1) blocking that will require special lighting and (2) light and sound cues that will be dependent on blocking.

Example A

The director decides that an actor will sit on the apron and recite a poem with the curtain closed to cover a scene change. You realize this will call for at least one additional lighting instrument that was not in the lighting designer's original plans. You make a note. After the rehearsal, you tell the lighting designer and you change your light plot. You also place new cues in your promptbook.

Example B

The director decides that the nurse will rise and cross to a table to examine a knife before she hears a bell that summons her offstage. Formerly, the cue for the bell was the doctor's line to the nurse. You realize that the cue for the bell is now a visual one rather than an oral one, so you make this change in your promptbook immediately.

French Scene Diagrams

A *French scene* is that part of a scene or an act in which the number of characters is constant. Within a scene there may be many French scenes. Every time a character enters or exits, a new French scene is begun (named from the conventional scene designations in classical French drama).

The director usually starts or resumes rehearsing from the beginning of a French scene. It's helpful to make small diagrams of the position of the cast at the beginning of each French scene (figure 8.8).

FIGURE 8.8 French Scene Cardboard Template and Scene Diagram

If the director says, "Let's take it from the top of page 83 where Fran enters," the cast members will probably not remember where they are supposed to be for Fran's entrance. By reviewing your blocking notation just prior to Fran's entrance, you may eventually be able to determine where they are, but it will take time. But if you have made a diagram, you can say immediately (from figure 8.8), "Al is seated on the couch facing down left, Ralph is looking out the window, and Alice is standing down right center facing down left."

There are often many French scenes in every act, so you can expedite your diagramming with a cardboard template of the set and set pieces (figure 8.8). At the top of every promptbook page on which a character enters or exits, you simply copy your scene diagram. Jotting in the positions of the cast takes very little effort.

Maintaining Order

A director should never have to ask for quiet working conditions that will allow him and the cast to concentrate on their work. Be aware of any noise or other disruptions and try to remedy the situation.

Try personal contact. Approach the noisy offender and explain, eyeball to eyeball, that rehearsals require silence from those who are not on stage; that it is a matter of courtesy.

Do not hesitate to shout, "Quiet, PLEASE!" if personal contact fails.

Some people have greater tolerance of noise levels than others. If you can read Christopher Fry during a rock concert, but your director gets shell shock from seats squeaking, try to sympathize with her problem and hold the cast down to the level the director can tolerate.

Giving Rehearsal, Publicity, and Costume Calls

- **The last official voice that every actor should hear as he leaves a rehearsal is yours, giving the next call, whether that call is for a rehearsal, publicity meeting with a TV interviewer, costume call at a supply house across town, or conference with the producer.**

It should be standard procedure that every actor check out, after rehearsal or performance, with the stage manager. This might simply mean a cheerful "Good night," to which you might answer with an equally informal "See you at ten tomorrow." That informal "ten tomorrow" is an order to appear at ten o'clock sharp.

It is not enough to publish, post, and distribute rehearsal schedules. Give the calls in person, face to face. Then mentally or physically check off each cast member; if anyone left early and failed to check out with you, phone that individual to give the call.

If you are working with a large cast, divided into principals, chorus, and dancers, or other major groups, you may wish to use a special callboard.

The term *callboard* has come to mean a bulletin board where any information, including the next call, can be brought to the attention of the cast. *Special callboard* is used here to mean a board display with only the next call (figure 8.9). Rather than placing it on the general callboard, it is more effective to place the special callboard by itself near the exit through which the cast must leave.

YOUR CALL FOR

Tues. July 14
(Dates)

Principals		Time	Place
	Frank*	10:00	Tent
	Julie*	10:30	Music Room
	Ravenal	10:30	Costume Shop
	All Others	10:30	Tent
Singing Ensemble			
	BOYS	off	
	GIRLS	11:00	Chorus Room
Dancing Ensemble			
	BOYS	11:00	Costume Shop
	GIRLS	11:00	Costume Shop
Local Chorus			
	BOYS	5:30	Costume Shop
	GIRLS	5:30	Costume Shop
***Special Appointments**			
Frank	Publicity Lunch	12:00	Florentine Room
Julie	Hairdresser	6:00	Claire's 140 W. 2nd
________	________	________	________
________	________	________	________

FIGURE 8.9 Special Callboard Format, for Next Upcoming Calls

The special callboard form can be covered with plastic, glass, or even a plastic film wrap so that the blanks can be filled in with crayon and then erased with a rag.

When photo calls are scheduled in the rehearsal area—whether for publicity, cast souvenirs, or the theater scrapbook—it is often helpful to post a picture schedule (figure 8.10).

The publicity person usually decides who is to appear in the pictures. But to save time in posing the shots, you might want to preselect emotional peak scenes from the script. During the call you can then throw a line before the emotional peak and have the cast pick it up in character. If someone shouts "Freeze" when they come to the peak line, this process will usually result in an interesting tableau.

It is often necessary for the photographer to tighten the shot by moving the actors closer to one another than they normally appear in that sequence. But re-posing and rerunning is still quicker than deciding in front of the camera just what poses are appropriate.

If the picture call follows a run-through, dress rehearsal, or performance, it is desirable to start with poses selected from the last scene of the last act and work backward so that cast members are saved an unnecessary costume change.

Posting a picture call and picture schedule well in advance allows cast members to plan for the session in terms of shaving, hairstyle, makeup, costumes, and time. Careful consideration of the order of the photo shoot can save the time of actors changing costumes and crew changing scenery.

PICTURE CALL

Thursday night after performance, pictures will be taken.
Please remain in costume and change for subsequent shots.

1. Entire Cast (curtain call order)
2. III-2: "So I'll say goodnight. . ."—Arlene, Jonas, Terry
3. III-1: ". . .because I'm going to get married."—Arlene, Sandy, Rita, Larry
4. III-1: "My arms, my lips. . ."—Larry, Rita, Sandy
5. II-3: "I'm going to be frank with you, Pa."—Jonas, Dave, Joanne
6. II-3: "We going to be here that long?"—Dave, Joanne, Terry
7. II-1: "I want to go to a hotel."—Jonas, Arlene
8. II-1: "He don't look like no Cary Grant to me."—Dee, Sandy, Norma, Jonas, Rita
9. I-3: "Then start going out on dates again."—Arlene, Jonas
10. I-2: "Stop trying to fix me up with all your friends."—Shirley-May, Jonas, Terry
11. I-2: "Rosalind, do me a favor."—Terry, Vicky, Jonas, Joanne
12. I-2: "Rosalind, you know my brother Jerry."—Vicky, Jonas, Terry
13. I-1: "I'm in trouble now, Ma."—Arlene, Rita
14. I-1: "Will you get dressed and go to school?"—Arlene, Rita, Sandy

FIGURE 8.10 Picture Call Schedule

Posting the Running Order

The *running order* is a list, in production sequence, of the scenes, giving the place of the scene, the cast members in the scene, the songs or dance numbers (if any) in that scene, and special cue lines (figure 8.11). Post it on the first day of rehearsal or as soon thereafter as possible. Update it as necessary.

The function of the running order is to remind cast members of when they appear next. Why is this necessary? Shouldn't every cast member know when he appears next?

Sometimes it is confusing. In a one-week rehearsal for a musical stock show, the chorus may have rehearsed its songs in a chorus room and rehearsed its dances in a rehearsal hall. Many members of the chorus will not have gone through the show in production sequence until the "put together," possibly the day before dress rehearsal, and only two days before opening night. So, as the chorus members dash from the stage to the dressing room, they need to have an easily accessible reference to answer the questions "What do I do next?" and "Which of my eight costumes do I change into?"

TAKE ME ALONG

Running Order
Act I

- I-1 **Outside Miller Home**
  Townspeople
  "Fire Machine"
  Fire Chief, Nat, Essie, Art, Tommy, Mildred
  "Oh, Please"
  Lilly
  Reprise: "Oh, Please"

- I-2 **Macomber House**
  Richard, Muriel
  "I Would Die"
  Macomber

- I-3 **Carbarn**
  Sid, Voices
  "Sid, Ol' Kid"

- I-4 **Street (Played in Aisle)**
  Art, Sid

- I-5 **Miller Home**
  Essie, Lilly, Tommy, Mildred, Nat, Richard, Macomber
  "Staying Young"
  Art, Sid
  "I Get Embarrassed"
  "We're Home"
  "Take Me Along"

- I-6 **Picnic**
  Sid, Carter, McDonald, Nat
  "For Sweet Charity"

FIGURE 8.11 Running Order on a Large Board, Easily Legible

In the rewrite phase of a new musical, the chorus might come in for half-hour call to find that the running order has been drastically changed. The finale will be sung as the opening number, the show will be done as a flashback, and the principals will reprise the finale at the final curtain with the chorus humming the bridge from the wings. Then, the next night at half-hour call, the chorus members learn that the finale will be sung at the second act curtain and that they will reprise their Act I, Scene 2 hit song as the finale. The chorus's actual performance sequence will vary from day to day. So, in addition to briefings from the staff, the chorus members need a written running order that they can refer to in haste.

The running order should be BIG!—possibly two feet wide by three feet tall—and carefully lettered so that it is easy to read. It should be well lit and placed along the path from the stage to the dressing rooms so that cast members don't have to detour to read it. Position it in the same place from the time it is posted until closing night, so that cast members don't have to search for it.

If there is a blackout within a scene to denote time lapse (called a *false blackout*), this should be noted on the running order so that cast members will be forewarned not to enter on that blackout for the following scene. A song or line that occurs after the time-lapse blackout should be listed so that cast members will have an accurate cue for their entrance.

All reprises should be carefully designated as reprises so that there is no confusion as to whether the song or the reprise is the cue. This is a particular problem when the song and the reprise occur within the same scene.

To make the entries on your running order immediately discernible, write your song titles in one color or style of script (e.g., letters underlined), the names of the scenes in a second color or style (e.g., large capitals), the cast members involved in a third (e.g., small capitals), and special notes about cue lines and blackouts in still another (e.g., cursive script). A work of art is not your goal, but any scheme that will help cast members decipher the running order quickly is helpful.

You must call all revisions to the attention of the cast and discuss with them the problems incurred by changes.

Typed copies of the running order should be placed in the crew area and on the callboard. You are responsible for alerting all crew members (props, lights, scene changes, costumes, etc.) to changes. The crew is not expected to decipher and apply a revised running order without a briefing from you and your immediate close supervision.

When changes in the production sequence are made, the running order should not be done over, but revisions should be cited with a bold marking pen so that cast members can pick out the changes without studying the whole running order.

Summer stock running orders rarely parallel the New York productions as reflected in published scripts, so the running order must be coordinated with the staff before it is posted.

> I never had to prompt performers between acts, but I did need to post a running order. The biggest difference between circus and theater is that in theater, at no point would an actor ever walk in and say, "Gee, I don't feel like playing that one scene today; let's skip it." But in circus, if a performer is not feeling well or is injured, the stage manager has to encourage him NOT to do an act. It is an onerous task, as these professionals want to go on no

matter what. But in a show where serious injuries and even death are definite and consistent possibilities, running orders can change on a daily basis, depending on the well-being of performers.

Bradley Spinelli
Stage Manager
New Pickle Circus

Timing of Rehearsals and Performances

You should carefully time each scene, and sometimes even critical parts of scenes. The purpose of timing during rehearsals is to let the director know what the total playing time is and to let the box office and house manager know what time the show will be out and what time to expect intermissions. The purpose of timing during performances is to keep track of the pace of each scene and act.

Using a stopwatch is desirable, but an ordinary watch with a sweep second hand can be used.

Start to time scenes just as soon in rehearsal as the scenes are run without interruption. At the end of each rehearsal, advise the director of the running times, not only including how long the scenes took but also how long they took last time they were run, and the shortest time in which they were run.

As soon as every scene in the play has been timed once, give the director some projection of the total running time.

During the run, time each scene at every performance. You will find that running time of each scene varies from performance to performance. Sometimes it's audience response; sometimes it's actors who are not picking up their lines or are adding pauses; sometimes a bit of business will vary in time. There are many reasons for differences in the timing of scenes. If the director is "with the show" (attending performances regularly or even periodically), judgment as to why the times vary may be left to him. If the director has left the show, or if the show is on the road, then it is your responsibility to evaluate the running times and take appropriate action (see page 199).

If you index a weekly time chart (figure 8.12) into your promptbook, you will be easily able to make the necessary comparisons and have the information readily available to your staff.

In most theater situations you will be responsible for the timing of blackouts and intermissions. Direct the blackouts and the backstage aspects of the intermissions just as carefully as the director directs the scenes. Some of the factors involved in a blackout or intermission are changing sets, striking and/or setting props, changing position of actors, changes in costumes, patching the lighting board, and re-gelling instruments (see page 155).

During a blackout, audience attention wanders. Perhaps the first 10 seconds of a blackout are consumed in applause and/or mental reaction to what has just happened. After that, coughing, fidgeting, and conversations indicate that the audience is no longer involved with the scene that is past. The longer the audience is left in darkness, the harder it is for the actors in the following scene to regain the audience's attention, emotional focus, and/or intellectual concern.

WEEKLY TIME CHART

PRODUCTION The Bunny WEEK OF Oct. 10

	Tues Dress	Wed Dress	Thurs opening	Fri	Sat early	Sat late	Sun
Announced Curtain	8:00	8:00	8:30	8:30	8:00	10:30	8:30
Actual Curtain	8:06	8:14	8:41	8:35	8:04	10:31	8:36
I - 1	8:14 / 8	8:22 / 8	8:41 / 7	8:43 / 8	8:12 / 8	10:40 / 9	8:45 / 9
Blackout	8:14 / :30	8:38 / :16	8:48 / :25	8:43 / :20	8:12 / :20	10:40 / :20	8:45 / :20
I - 2	8:29 / 15	8:39 / 17	9:03 / 15	8:58 / 15	8:27 / 15	10:54 / 14	9:00 / 15
Blackout	8:30 / :35	8:39 / :30	9:04 / :30	8:59 / :30	8:28 / :30	10:55 / :30	9:01 / :30
I - 3	8:47 / 17	8:55 / 16	9:19 / 15	9:14 / 15	8:44 / 16	11:10 / 15	9:16 / 15
Intermission	9:09 / 22	9:07 / 12	9:30 / 11	9:25 / 11	8:53 / 9	11:20 / 10	9:26 / 10
II - 1	9:25 / 16	9:23 / 16	9:46 / 16	9:42 / 17	9:10 / 17	11:36 / 16	9:42 / 16
Blackout	9:26 / :48	9:24 / :45	9:47 / :40	9:43 / :35	9:11 / :35	11:37 / :35	9:43 / :30
II - 2	9:37 / 11	9:34 / 10	9:56 / 9	9:52 / 9	9:20 / 9	11:46 / 9	9:52 / 9
Blackout	9:37 / :25	9:34 / :25	9:56 / :25	9:53 / :30	9:20 / :25	11:46 / :25	9:52 / :25
II - 3	9:57 / 20	9:53 / 19	10:14 / 18	10:11 / 18	9:39 / 19	12:04 / 18	10:10 / 18
Total Running Time	1:27	1:26	1:20	1:22	1:24	1:21	1:22

FIGURE 8.12 Chart Record of Running Time

So it is important that you organize the proceedings during blackouts to make them as short as possible. Some directors insist that no blackouts be longer than 20 seconds. During the technical rehearsal and subsequent dress rehearsals, you must ask to run, rerun, and, if necessary, choreograph blackouts until you and the director are satisfied that they are run in minimum time.

During the rehearsals you should also time certain sound effects and special effects to figure out the length for your plots.

Example

You realize during a rehearsal that an alarm bell sound effect must last long enough to cover an actor's business of opening a safe, ransacking it, and escaping through a window, and it must also last long enough to cover the entrance of two other characters, their reaction, and the closing of the curtain. How long should a tape of that alarm bell effect be? During the rehearsals, you carefully time the business and either make a production note in your script or add this timing to your sound plot. Then at the sound session you are prepared to say, "We will need at least three minutes of the alarm bell on tape."

KEEPING TRACK OF REHEARSALS

Rehearsal Log

- **The rehearsal log is a brief diary of what happened or failed to happen at rehearsals. You should always be able to answer the question "How did we come to this state of affairs?" with specifics. It is not always possible to remember the specifics unless you keep notes. It is convenient to tab your log into your promptbook.**

Entries in the rehearsal log should include date, cast members who were late or absent, cast changes, the scene or scenes that were blocked or run, the number of times these scenes were run, delays and causes of delays in rehearsals, failure to run a scheduled scene, and any significant occurrence out of the ordinary—for example, an accident, failure to meet a deadline, or mechanical failure of equipment (figure 8.13).

If you have the opportunity to help critique a production, your rehearsal log will be an invaluable asset (see page 263).

REHEARSAL LOG

1. **Sunday, May 28** —Read through script (Mike, Will, Jackie out).
2. **Monday, May 29** —Read through again, made a few revisions (Jackie still out).
3. **Friday, June 2** —Blocked Act I to p. 17.
4. **Saturday, June 3** —Started 15 minutes late. (Dick claimed remainder of Act I.)
5. **Sunday June 4** —Jackie, Dick only—script changes.
6. **Monday June 5** —Jackie, Dick only—blocked their scenes in Act II.
7. **Tuesday, June 6** —Billy only. Worked him through all blocking as Eric's replacement.
8. **Wednesday, June 7** —Ran Act I twice. Sound session after rehearsal. (Steve was late but no delay in rehearsal.)
9. **Thursday, June 8** —Blocked Act II (except Jackie, Dick scenes).
10. **Friday, June 9** —Attempted to integrate sound but amplifier went out. Ran Act II twice.
11. **Saturday, June 10** —First run-through, integrated sound cues.
12. **Sunday, June 11** —Polished Act I, ran five times.
13. **Tuesday, June 13** —Ran Act II twice. Dick, Pandora out so rehearsal suffered; did not run Dick-Jackie scenes (Dick was shooting, Pandora's husband in auto accident).

FIGURE 8.13 Rehearsal Log with Typical Entries

Supporting Director's Notes

Immediately following rehearsals, directors often give notes to the cast. The stage manager may use this time to distribute his notes on blocking errors and line problems to individual cast members. Find a way to do this unobtrusively so that you are not distracting from the director's work with the cast. In some situations, these notes may be distributed (by both director and stage manager) via e-mail or through programs like Yahoo! Groups. In educational theater, videos of scenes can be posted on Blackboard, along with the director's notes, so that cast members can review their work at their convenience.

Rehearsal Reports

In some companies the producer or top management may require a daily written report from the stage manager. This report usually includes the same information that you keep in your log, but in a more orderly format (figures 8.14 and 8.15). If you were to keep a copy of this report, you would not have to keep a log, because the same purpose would be served.

Note that in the rehearsal report, under the heading "Engaged/Dismissed," you are expected to indicate those cast members who joined or left the company. The payroll department and Equity must be notified in these cases.

In some companies the stage manager is also required to submit a report to Equity (figure 8.16).

ACCIDENT PREVENTION AND REPORTS

In *The 776 Stupidest Things Ever Said,* Ross and Kathryn Petras cite the U.S. Occupational Safety and Health Administration for the following: "Hazards are one of the main causes of accidents." Did you laugh? If you did, you are probably not an experienced stage manager. Despite the intrinsic humor of that statement, stage managers have had too many sad experiences with hazards and accidents to find any mention of them humorous (figure 8.17).

My first experience with a theater accident occurred in an Equity production of *Enter Laughing* at the Players Ring Gallery in Los Angeles. It was staged in the round for the first time since its Broadway opening. Carl Reiner sat in at a rehearsal to give director Harvey Korman some tips on the staging.

I had helped the technical director and scene designer place a heavy wrought-iron gate used as a set piece in the actors' entrance to the stage. It was not to be moved throughout the production. In the blackout preceding the cemetery scene, sound effects of crickets and a creaking gate were heard. As the lights came up on the scene, a single spot hit the gate and the two actors. It would appear to the audience that they had just opened the gate, but the gate never moved. Because the gate was not to function at all, we reasoned that there was no need to secure it. There was plenty of room to enter and exit the stage without touching the gate (as was done in all of the other scenes of the play). Following a dress rehearsal, an actor on the way out of the theater left the dressing room and came into the theater through that entrance. The actor somehow managed to knock over the gate and injure an ankle. The wound required stitches, and the actor did the run of the show wearing a bandage.

STAGE MANAGER'S REHEARSAL REPORT

Place: Loft	**Date:** August 13
	Rehearsal started: 7:30
Call: 7:30	Lunch/Dinner Break: ---
Scenes: I-4 II-2	Rehearsal resumed: ---
	Rehearsal ended: 10:00
	Rehearsal time: 2:30
	Overtime (if any): ---
	Expenses:
Engaged/Dismissed:	Injuries: Dinah left early- See report
Absent/Excused: Al — still out sick	Late:

Remarks: Good work done on both scenes despite Al's absence. Dinah did well before she left.

Lawrence Stern
Stage Manager

FIGURE 8.14 Rehearsal Report Form

AMERICAN MUSICAL THEATRE OF SAN JOSE
Stage Manager Rehearsal Report

Show:______________________ **Date:**______________________

Scheduled Start Time:__________ Break:__________

Lunch/Dinner Break:__________ Break:__________

End Time:__________ Break:__________

Total Rehearsal Hours:__________

Set Notes:

Costume & Hair Notes:

Prop Notes:

Sound & Light Notes:

General Notes (plus injuries, illness):

FIGURE 8.15 Rehearsal Report Form

Download from http://www.pearsonhighered.com/stern_ogrady

ACTORS' EQUITY
ASSOCIATION 1913

Stage Manager Weekly Report

Do not file with Equity unless there is a violation

Name of Theater: ______________________________

Date: ____________

Violations by Actor

- List the name of the Actor
- Type of Violation (lateness for half-hour, altering directions, etc.)
- Indicate in column 1 if sufficient explanation given so that violation should be considered excused (E for excused, U for unexcused)
- Has the Actor been spoken to about this type of violation before? Indicate in column 2 (R for repeated, 1 for first time, 2 for second time, etc.)

Actor	Violation	1	2

Violations by Manager

- List only violations by Manager that have not been corrected after being informed by you, the Deputy or Equity.

Signed: ______________________
(Stage Manager)

(Use reverse side for remarks)

FIGURE 8.16 Report Form to Actors' Equity

Download from actorsequity.org

Civic's Season in Red Ink Because of Accidents

Varsity, The Stage Daily, Feb. 1994

Favorable reviews and large audiences would have resulted in a profitable season for the city-owned Civic Theatre—had it not been for accidents. *A Chorus Line, South Pacific, the Mikado, Guys and Dolls*, and *An Evening with Sondheim*, during the past season, built audiences and profits beyond expectations of previous seasons. But the season was plagued with costly accidents.

Disaster struck on opening night of *South Pacific* when an actress exiting the stage was struck by moving scenery resulting in the fracture of her arm. The performance was cancelled and tickets refunded. During a performance of *The Mikado*, a wrench fell from the grid above the stage. The union cast invoked workplace safety rules which resulted in cancelling a performance. An additional performance was scheduled to accommodate season subscribers. Ticket holders were also offered seats to remaining shows. The third and most serious accident was the collapse of a flat during *Guys and Dolls* injuring two chorus members. Litigation is pending in this incident.

The Civic Theatre hosts national touring productions of opera and ballet and is also the home of the Civic Symphony. Because of the heavy use of the facility, the theater "loads in" each show, techs, and dress rehearses it in less than one week. Management of the Civic Theatre claims that increased efforts are being made to prevent accidents.

Performing Arts

Former Israeli Foreign Minister Falls from Platform

Los Angeles Messenger, Nov. 1993

Abba Eban, former Israeli Foreign Minister, is suing the San Mateo Performing Arts Center for injuries sustained when he fell from a platform following a speech.

On January 7, Eban, 78, spoke to a full auditorium from a platform, according to a lawsuit filed Friday. When he finished his speech, he turned to exit and fell from the platform breaking his hip.

Representatives of the Performing Arts Center describe the platform as "a professional 8-inch platform that was 8 feet by 8 feet with a nonskid surface and white safety border. In the past it had been used by several other speakers, including President Jimmy Carter.

Mr. Eban's suit for unspecified damages names the Peninsula Speakers Series, the San Mateo Union High School District on whose property the center sits, and San Mateo County. The suit claims that Eban was "exposed to serious risk of injury due to uneven surfaces and a dangerous drop on the surface of said stage." It accuses the defendants of negligence.

Eban, a resident of Tel Aviv, is living in New York on a temporary teaching assignment. He was Israel's first permanent representative to the United Nations, served as Israeli ambassador to the United States from 1950 to 1959, and served as foreign minister from 1966 to 1974. He later became foreign policy spokesperson for Israel's Labor Party.

FIGURE 8.17 Accidents can happen anytime, anywhere—and result in injury, pain, lawsuits, and financial problems.

The actor felt personally to blame for the accident and did not blame the stage manager, technical director, or producer. The theater was not sued.

In retrospect, it is clear that gate should have been secured. As stage manager, I should have inspected it the first time it was placed in the entrance. I should have made the judgment that although it was a heavy piece, it still needed to be secured. I should have either advised the technical director to secure it or nailed it to the wall myself with plumber's tape. This was one of my first Equity productions, and I blame the accident on my inexperience.

So trite, but so true: An ounce of prevention is worth a pound of cure.

Whenever the stage manager is involved in an accident, there is a question about the degree of her responsibility. So here's my rule: Take the time to inspect for hazards. Adopt the attitude that anything that can possibly go wrong probably will. Pretend that an earthquake is about to happen. If you make the stage and backstage area safer than they need to be, no harm can come of it, and, hopefully, no harm will come to your cast and crew.

Here are a few backstage horror stories from stage managers who have some suggestions to pass on. Put yourself in their shoes and try to gain from their experiences.

I was in tech for a production of *Funny Girl* at Long Beach Civic Light Opera and going into a scene change for the first time. The actors and technicians had been talked through the change and it seemed that it would be a simple thing to execute. Unfortunately, as I called the rail cue that would bring in a heavy drop with a pipe weighting the bottom, one of my cast members walked downstage, right under the incoming drop. The pipe hit the actress on the top of her head.

Three people could have theoretically stopped this accident from happening: the actress, the flyman, and me. But as stage manager, it is wholly my fault that it happened. I had a view of the stage and could have stopped the incoming drop if I had seen her move into its path. Instead I was preparing for the upcoming cues and not watching as closely as I could have. The actress was okay—I was a mess!

Accidents that you aren't directly involved with are more frustrating and discouraging. For instance, on tour there are new dressers, stagehands, and new backstage traffic patterns every week. Inevitably someone will run into someone else and be injured. The stage manager is the person who will hear about it from the injured party, often in the heat of the moment of pain and fear (and usually as you're calling the hardest part of the show!). It is up to you to talk to the people involved and make sure that it won't happen again. Tact, patience, and the realization that this is not a personal attack are all important.

Anything you can do to prevent accidents will be to your advantage. Remember, if someone gets hurt, YOU have to fill out the paperwork.

Jill (Johnson) Gold
Stage Manager
Long Beach Civic Light Opera
[see her résumé, page 268]

It happened during the evening preview show of a major musical for which we had had only 15 hours of tech, including the tech earlier that day that only got through the first third. The final moment of Act I involved two actors, one carrying the other, crossing down center, and stepping onto a stage elevator that lowered from the stage into the

(continued)

orchestra pit. I called the cue for the elevator to go down. Then I heard a bang. On my TV monitor I saw the two actors fall into the trap where the elevator was supposed to be. I threw off my headset and ran out on stage. One of the actors was in the orchestra pit, and one was lying on stage. The one in the pit seemed okay, but was shaken. The actor on stage was crying and bleeding from a foot and a leg.

Someone called 911. Checked to see how serious the injuries were. Since the elevator was downstage of the curtain, 2,800 people watched. Cleared the house. Ambulance took the two actors to the hospital. The actor who had been bleeding had no bones broken but had bad cuts on the foot and leg, and some internal injuries to the leg.

At a cast meeting after the injured left, I told the cast and crew to call my office the next day so that I could tell them how the injured were doing and what the plans for the show would be. I believe the most important thing to do is to let everyone know that their well-being comes first. The show does not need to go on no matter what happens.

We had a counselor available for a couple of days after the accident to help anyone who was traumatized by the incident or just needed to talk. We delayed opening for three days until technical problems were worked out and we all felt more comfortable.

I was never blamed for this incident. I know that I am not directly responsible. It was a freak mechanical failure. But I still feel some responsibility.

This incident reinforced in my mind how important it is to put safety first. Safety awareness must start from the beginning of the production. Ask questions. Speak up if something concerns you. Trust your instincts.

When an accident occurs, make sure you call the actor's emergency contact, which you should have on file. If the actor is a member of Equity, call Equity and report the incident. Fill out an accident report and workers' comp claim form. Make sure the injured parties have the theater company's name, address, and phone number to take with them to the hospital. If possible, have someone from the theater staff go with the injured person.

Have a well-equipped first-aid box nearby during rehearsals and performance. Contents should include instant ice packs, ace bandages, Band-Aids, and ointments. You, as stage manager, or someone on your staff should be trained in CPR and first aid. It is not that expensive or time consuming to become certified, and any theater company should be happy to have someone with those skills on staff.

Bob Bones
Production Stage Manager
San Jose Civic Light Opera

Just when you think you've made a show accident-proof, something will happen completely out of the blue just to keep you on your toes. At the end of the Thenardier Inn scene in *Les Miserables,* the staging calls for Madame Thenardier to jump on top of her husband, who is leaning over a table downstage center. At the same point, the turntable begins to revolve to clear the scene to go directly into the next one. One afternoon, she jumped, the downstage table legs gave way, and both actors were pitched downstage as the turntable started to turn. The actor playing Thenardier was able to hang on to the stage and ride the revolve offstage. But Madame Thenardier went completely over and into the pit! I was calling the show from offstage right, saw the whole thing happen, and was powerless to stop it.

The worst thing about an incident like this is trying to keep the show going while trying to find out about the possibly injured. The audience had obviously seen the actress fall. Some of the cast were aware of what had happened, and some weren't. A major scene shift was in progress on stage, and the musicians had to keep playing as the actress in the pit struggled to disentangle herself from the drum set. I was in headset communication with the conductor; he might have advised me that it was not possible to continue music-wise. The production stage manager was at my side to make the decision to stop the show. An assistant stage manager ran to the pit to see how the actress was; understudies and wardrobe were alerted to the possibility of a quick cast change, and first-aid equipment was standing by. The actress was bruised and shaken but wanted to continue, and on her next entrance she got a terrific ovation from the audience!

In that case, we were really lucky that everyone was relatively unharmed. But we were prepared to deal with any scenario. The lesson to be learned here is to prepare for the worst—the best thing that can happen is that you never need to use your emergency plans.

Keeping your cool and thinking ahead are the best things to do. If you stay calm then both the company and the audience will follow your lead. Always remember that it's theater, not brain surgery. People and safety are more important than the next scene change.

Accident prevention is an ongoing, important, and often frustrating job. As stage manager, everything is ultimately your responsibility, and it is your job to ensure the safety of your company to the best of your ability. This can range from asking an assistant to edge the stage with glow tape (and then checking that it is done) to stopping a rehearsal or show in mid-scene due to some imminent disaster that only you can see.

The easiest way to ensure that your company is prepared is to talk to them briefly about safety on your first day in the theater. While on tour we meet on stage before our first sound check in any new theater to point out to the cast any changes in the setup, potential dangers offstage, and where the first-aid kits and ice packs are located. On *Les Miz,* we also set times for every new cast member to walk on the turntable and climb on the barricades before going into a run-through so there are as few surprises as possible. Even if the show is playing just one venue, make sure that everyone who is going to be on stage or in the wings has the chance to walk around in the light and learn the layout before plunging them into show conditions. Glow tape, offstage clip lights, and white tape are your friends. Use them liberally.

Jill (Johnson) Gold
Stage Manager
Les Miserables National Tour

[Please notice Jill's professional attitude. "We were prepared to deal with any scenario." When you call "Places, please," will you be able to say what Jill said?]

Always be alert to situations that might cause accidents: construction materials left on stage or backstage, materials left perched precariously on ladders and on flats, nails and boards protruding upstage of flats that might tear actors' costumes or skin, wires not secured on which to trip, sharp edges on corners in dark areas backstage, and so on. The list is endless.

Check flying cables, whether or not you have immediate plans to use them, to be sure they will hold under strain. Twist the cables open to check the condition of the inside. If they are rotten, replace them.

It takes constant vigilance to prevent carelessness and inconsideration from turning into serious accidents. Encourage all members of the staff, cast, and crew to report unsafe conditions to you; take immediate steps to correct them.

Large or long-established theaters are generally covered by accident insurance as a form of protection against suits by actors or patrons for accidents that occur on the theater premises. Most insurance companies want to have the same information about any accident that occurs (figure 8.18). If your theater does have such insurance, make sure that you have accident report forms on hand.

In the event of an accident, whether or not your theater has insurance, obtain all the information required (figure 8.18) and write a brief narrative of what happened. Ask the individual involved to write his own brief narrative, and have him sign it.

No matter how many copies of the accident form are required by the insurance company, make one additional copy for your files.

EMPLOYER

1. FIRM NAME	1A. POLICY NUMBER
2. MAILING ADDRESS (Please include city, Zip)	2A. PHONE NUMBER
3. LOCATION IF DIFFERENT FROM MAIL ADDRESS	
4. NATURE OF BUSINESS e.g., painting contractor, wholesale grocer, sawmill, hotel, etc.	5. State Unemployment Insurance Acct. No.

EMPLOYEE

6. NAME		7. DATE OF BIRTH ___/___/___ Month Day Year
8. HOME ADDRESS (number and street, city, Zip)		8A. PHONE NUMBER
9. SEX ☐ Male ☐ Female	10. OCCUPATION (Regular job title, not specific activity at time of injury)	11. SOCIAL SECURITY NUMBER
12. DEPARTMENT IN WHICH REGULARLY EMPLOYED		12A. DATE OF HIRE ___/___/___ Month Day Year
13. HOURS USUALLY WORKED EMPLOYEE WORKS _____ HOURS PER DAY FOR _____ DAYS PER WEEK	13A. WEEKLY HOURS	13B. Under what class code of your policy were wages assigned?
14. GROSS WAGES/SALARY EMPLOYEE EARNS $ _________ PER ☐ HOUR ☐ DAY ☐ WEEK ☐ EVERY TWO WEEKS ☐ MONTH ☐ OTHER _________		

INJURY OR ILLNESS

15. WHERE DID ACCIDENT OR EXPOSURE OCCUR? (number and street, city)	15A. COUNTY	15B. ON EMPLOYERS PREMISES? ☐ YES ☐ NO
16. WHAT WAS EMPLOYEE DOING WHEN INJURED? (Please be specific. Identify tools, equipment or material the employee was using.)		
17. HOW DID THE ACCIDENT OR EXPOSURE OCCUR? (Please describe fully the events that resulted in injury or occupational disease. Tell what happened and how it happened. Please use separate sheet if necessary.)		
18. OBJECT OR SUBSTANCE THAT DIRECTLY INJURED EMPLOYEE e.g., the machine employee struck against or which struck him. the vapor or poison inhaled or swallowed; the chemical that irritated his skin; in cases of strains, the thing he was lifting, pulling, etc.		
19A. DESCRIBE THE INJURY OR ILLNESS e.g., cut, strain, fracture, skin rash, etc.		19B. PART OF BODY AFFECTED e.g., back, left wrist, right eye, etc.
20. NAME AND ADDRESS OF PHYSICIAN		
21. IF HOSPITALIZED, NAME AND ADDRESS OF HOSPITAL		
22. DATE OF INJURY OR ILLNESS ___/___/___ Month Day Year	23. TIME OF DAY _____ a.m. _____ p.m.	24. Did employee lose at least one full day's work after the injury? ☐ Yes, date last worked _________ ☐ No
25. HAS EMPLOYEE RETURNED TO WORK? ☐ Yes, date returned _________	☐ No, still off work	☐ Yes, date _________ ☐ No

Completed by (type or print)	Signature	Title	Date

Form 5020 (Rev. 4)
January 1983

FILING OF THIS REPORT IS NOT AN ADMISSION OF LIABILITY

FIGURE 8.18 Accident Report Form

Latest form may be downloaded from osha.gov/recordkeeping/new-osha300formk1-1-04.pdf

About a year ago an attorney asked me to be an expert witness in a theater accident case. The crux of the matter was that during a first technical rehearsal for a community theater production on a college campus, one of the actors fell off a platform while trying to exit the stage in a blackout. As a result of the fall he injured his arm and was unable to continue with his career as a house painter. The university paid his initial medical bills, but he wanted compensation for therapy and lost income. The university said that it was not responsible for his accident and would not pay.

When I was brought into the case, I found out that the actors had never been shown the set without the stage lights on. Also, there were no running lights or glow tape to illuminate the edges of the set to help the actors see the edges.

In my testimony I said that as a professional stage manager, it is my responsibility to make sure that the cast and crew are safe at all times, and I must do whatever needs to be done to assure their safety. In this case, either the technical director or stage manager should have gone over the set prior to the first technical rehearsal to make sure the set was safe for the actors to work on, under all conditions. Or, if something was not ready, the cast should have been warned. In this case, if it was known that there were no running lights or glow tape, then the cast should never have been allowed to attempt to exit the stage in the dark. I also said that the cast looks to the stage manager as the one person who is looking out for them and if she does not perceive that there is a problem, then the cast, who have a lot on their minds, will trust that everything is okay. This is why, in this case, the actors still exited the stage even though they could not see where they were going.

A few weeks later, I learned that the injured party won his case and received additional money to pay medical bills and make up some of his lost wages.

Being involved in this case gave me a chance to evaluate my own thoughts on safety. Going into the case I looked for information in textbooks and Equity rulebooks about who is responsible for safety and what are considered safe conditions on stage or backstage. Unfortunately, I found very little on the subject.

My own experience, training, and instincts tell me that as the stage manager, I am the person responsible for the safety of all people on stage and backstage. Logically I know that I cannot keep an eye on everyone all of the time or be responsible for a decision someone may make that results in an accident. But it doesn't mean I don't try. I am fortunate in that I hire the other stage managers as well as part of the crew. So I try to hire people who share my desire to do the best show possible as safely as possible. Also, I believe that "we" set an example for everyone else and if "we" remain calm and in control, others will follow suit. I believe I need to learn everything possible about all aspects of a show so that I can anticipate any problems and deal with anything unexpected, calmly.

Bob Bones
Production Stage Manager
San Jose Civic Light Opera

KEEPING A DO-LIST

A *do-list* is a self-kept list of things you need to do. It is usually kept on your clipboard, but might just as practically be attached to the inside front cover of your promptbook (figure 8.19). Anyone who has ever made out a shopping list can write one, and anyone who has ever made out a shopping list will appreciate the necessity for one.

- **Your do-list should always be with you. Whenever staff, crew, or cast tell you anything that requires an action on your part, you should make a note of it. Any change of schedule should be noted so that you can figure out the**

Wednesday

1. Touch up staples reflecting lights
2. weight bottom of flaps swinging in draft
3. Call Norman on plans for ramp
4. Get sack of wheat paste
5. tell Nick he won't be needed Friday night
6. Call photographer for schedule

remind Chuck:

1. mortar & pestle
2. Bring in III revisions
3. Call Ray 7:00 PM

FIGURE 8.19 Manager's Daily Do-List and Reminder Checklist

consequences and deal with them. You will also want to note information that must be relayed to other staff members. Do not trust your memory. There are simply too many things to be done.

Writing something on your list implies that you will take care of it or see that it is taken care of. It is reassuring to a director to see you make a note when asked for something.

Take time at the end of each day to review your list and to assess what must be done first tomorrow and what can be delegated to others.

Keep a special area for notes for the director. In doing so, you will be functioning not only as the director's assistant but as the director's secretary. When the director promises to do something—bring in a prop, contact a scene designer with whom he has worked in the past, write a letter of introduction for a cast member who will be going to New York—jot down a note for her. After rehearsal, present your notes with tact. Obviously, if the director does not appreciate this, discontinue. You'll find most directors grateful.

Special Rehearsals for Fight/Combat and Weapons

Once the director has blocked/choreographed a fight/combat sequence, special rehearsals or calls prior to rehearsals should be scheduled to work on these sequences. When weapons are involved, the stage manager bears added responsibility for ensuring that those props are handled properly and secured when not in the hands of actors. In union houses, strict rules are enforced to ensure safety in the use of weapons. Community and educational theaters should follow those same rules. (See page 152 for AEA's *Theatrical Firearms Questionnaire* and page 153 for AEA's *Safety Tips for Use of Firearms.*) The stage manager should brief actors on those rules and to the best of his ability oversee the actors in their handling of weapons. Special rehearsals should also be scheduled for use of smoke devices, fog machines, pyrotechnics, open flame, and other potentially dangerous special effects. (See page 231 for *Notice to Fire Department* and page 232 for a fire plot.) Stage managers should familiarize themselves with the manufacturers' guidelines for safe operation and brief cast and crew members who use those devices on safety concerns.

AVOIDING REHEARSAL PROBLEMS

I'll take a few paragraphs here to throw in a little philosophy—the Gospel according to Stern—very little and not too deep.

My "Discipline of the Theater" theory is an oversimplification and can be stated briefly: The play exists only on stage when the curtain is up. Prior to performance, the play exists only in the mind of the director, and everyone works to realize her concept.* In reality, this theory never quite works. Still, it is the premise on which everyone should work, and it is a premise that serves stage managers well in deciding what their words and deeds should be.

Play production is a process of compromise. From the first casting audition, the director may find that an actor brings forth an aspect of characterization that is superior to his original concept. Or he may find that no actor really lives up to that concept, so the best available actor is cast. Either way, the original concept is changed. Compromise.

During rehearsals the director attempts to bring forth from the cast his concept. Actors experiment in early rehearsals and present the director with their concepts. Further compromise.

The scene designer talks to the director to understand the director's concept of the play and then supports the director by designing a set that will put the director's concept on the stage. It is the same with the costume designer, the lighting designer, the sound designer, and all of the other creative people concerned with the production. In reality, there are further compromises as the designers try to turn the director's inspired or approved concepts into reality.

The stage manager is concerned with this process because the inevitable compromises are sometimes preceded by confrontations that disrupt rehearsals or preproduction work and/or demoralize cast members.

Producer/Director Conflicts

Sometimes problems arise between the producer and the director. In theory, the producer is responsible for obtaining the materials and personnel to make the play happen.

*Please see box, page 49, for another viewpoint.

He generally hires or selects the director. Thereafter, the producer is supposed to work to realize the director's concept along with everyone else. But the producer hires the director and can usually fire the director. In commercial theater, the producer is concerned with possible loss of great amounts of money if the director's concept does not pay off. In theory, the producer should discuss and evaluate the director's concept before hiring him; once the producer has hired the director, she should go with the director.

In practice, however, the producer feels that her powers should allow her to influence the director, not only as to general concepts but also with respect to specifics. So there are many incidents of producers directing over the director's shoulder—pulling strings in casting, changing designs that the director and designers have agreed upon, demanding that changes in the director's realm be made up to the very last minute. Even if the producers do not subscribe to my oversimplified theory, they should honor some ethics of supervision:

1. The authority of any supervisor should not be diminished before his subordinates.
2. A person can follow the dictates of only one supervisor.

Translated into theater practice, this means that a director and producer should never discuss their differences of opinion in front of cast members, staff, or crew. Once their differences have been ironed out, all resulting changes should be announced by the director. They should not be prefaced with any disclaimers, such as, "I don't feel this way, but due to circumstances beyond my control . . ." If the director can't say firmly, "I have decided that . . . ," then he should firmly announce, "I have quit and it's up to the producer to provide another director."

As stage manager, if you should observe that producer/director conflicts during rehearsals are demoralizing cast members or disrupting rehearsals or work calls, call the director and producer aside and tactfully request that their disputes be resolved in private. It's psychologically difficult to back down in public, but significantly easier to listen to reason and to change one's mind in private.

Theater is not a democratic process in which the producer and director debate and then resolve their differences by a vote of the cast.*

It is always preferable to anticipate such problems and to discuss problem-solving procedures at early staff meetings before they erupt into rehearsal delays.

Playwright at Work

What happens when the playwright is present? The play still exists in only one place prior to the curtain's rise—in the director's mind. I know this sounds improbable, and I've never met a playwright who could accept it. But once the playwright commits his work to paper and the producer turns it over to the director, the play is a concept in the director's mind.

Of course, some changes can and should be made as the playwright and director see the play come to life. But the playwright should go to the director privately to work on changes and should not communicate directly with the cast. The director should also suggest changes to the playwright privately.

**Reminder*: Again, that's the way I see it, and I'll stick to my point of view but respect your point of view just as long as the curtain at your theater goes up on time.

I have seen playwrights angrily interrupt rehearsals because an actor paraphrased a line. I have seen casts thoroughly demoralized by director/playwright conflicts during rehearsals. If you are going into any production in which the playwright will be allowed in the rehearsal area, discuss in advance with the director, playwright, and producer what procedures will be used to resolve disputes, and particularly where disputes will be handled—in private and outside the rehearsal area, I hope.

I have the greatest respect for playwrights. None of us could work without their words and ideas. But I believe that if they cannot accept the principles discussed here, they should write novels or greeting cards, or direct their own plays.

[Here's another rule that I would like to see accepted by playwrights. I put it in brackets because I know that this is a book on stage management and not on playwriting or directing. Every director should have the right to cut 5 percent of a playwright's lines without negotiation. There isn't a play by William Shakespeare, Eugene O'Neill, Arthur Miller, Tennessee Williams, or Neil Simon that could not survive a 5 percent cut easily. It's difficult for playwrights to see this.

[I find that inexperienced playwrights become emotionally involved—in love!—with their every word, article, and comma. Directors bring a different perspective to a script. Experienced directors know instinctively when action is bogging down in verbiage, when a scene is not playing. They don't need to wait for audience reaction to know.

[When it comes to discussions or arguments between playwright and director, the playwright can always rationalize every syllable that he has committed to paper. "It reveals character." "It'll get a laugh." "It advances the plot." "It foreshadows." The playwright knows all the good writing craft reasons why every word is immortal. The director knows only that those immortal words don't play.

[If the playwright doesn't trust the director enough with his baby to allow the director to change the diapers, he ought to convince the producer to hire another director.

[But this is not a book on directing or playwriting, and stage managers do not make rules for the relationship between directors and playwrights; they only make things run smoothly by getting an understanding of what the rules are, and ensuring that everyone knows them.

[Sometimes actors approach a playwright to ask if they are giving the playwright the interpretation of the role he wants. Actually the actors are looking for reassurance or seeking praise. The playwright launches into a discussion of characterization, completely confusing the actor, not only by giving specifics that conflict with the director's but also by talking an entirely different language. Playwrights should have a stock of supportive generalizations to offer insecure actors: "I really appreciate all the hard work you are putting into this production." "I really admire the way you take direction." "I'm very well pleased with the way the director is interpreting my work and the way the cast is supporting her interpretation."

[The best time for the playwright to clarify his intent is when he is writing the play. If it isn't in the script, he shouldn't expect his presence at rehearsals to put it on the stage. If he must have contact with the cast, the playwright may give extensive notes at an early reading. But when the director and cast are in blocking, pacing, and polishing rehearsals, all further changes and clarifications should be discussed between the playwright and the director privately, and then any agreed-upon changes should issue from the director. At this point I dismount my high horse. Final advice: If you've got a system that works better for you, use it.]

Change Procedures

A "no more changes" deadline should be established at an early staff meeting. Additionally, playwrights should understand that the later any changes are made in rehearsals, the less chance there is for a polished performance.

Stage managers who are new to their work or are working with a new company should raise the issue of change procedures at the very first production meeting to arrive at an understanding among director, producer, and playwright. Tell them you or your fellow stage managers have had bad experiences in the past and that you want to prevent future problems by getting procedures spelled out in advance. If the playwright, producer, and director can't agree, or if you can't live by their agreement, find another job.

My Teaching Strategy

As an out-of-class exercise to demonstrate understanding of blocking notation *[see pages 107–110]*, I ask each student to make a specified number of pages of a prompt script. Prior to assignment, class discusses the page layouts *[figure 3.2 on page 18]* and selects the one that all will use. Students use scripts and videos of the play that have been placed on the reserve shelves of the college library. Their blocked pages are assembled into a complete prompt script, which is used for further in-class exercises on placement of light, sound, special effects and other cues.

Mark E. Mallett, *PhD*
Assistant Professor of Theater Arts
The Richard Stockton College of New Jersey, Pomona, NJ

I work with the class to tape out one of our season's sets. I speak with the TD *[technical director]* at the top of the semester to find what class date works best. During the class before the day we tape, students are given a copy of the ground plan, a basic explanation of how to read it and a demonstration of how to use a scale rule. During this class we go over the basic techniques involved in taping, the use of different colors for levels, scenes and moveable items. Next day the class works in teams of two to tape an assigned portion of the set and I assist and oversee their work as necessary.

Kat Dunham
Theatre Arts Lecturer
Edgewood College

SUGGESTED CLASSROOM EXERCISE

Arrange for one student to shadow a stage manager during three consecutive blocking rehearsals, preferably at a community or professional theater. Have the student report observations of what the stage manager did before, during, and after rehearsal.

9

Keeping the Cast on Time

Take care of the minutes and the hours
will take care of themselves.
—4th Earl of Chesterfield

The best way to predict the future is to invent it.
—Alan Kay

- **You are (of course) personally so punctual that it is difficult for you to understand those who are late. Your mental clock is 10 minutes ahead of real time. You always feel that if you are not 10 minutes early for an appointment, you're late. You know that you are being paid to think ahead. You plan ahead with master calendars and schedules. You work ahead of others, arriving at the theater before the staff and cast to open up and prepare for rehearsals and performances. You are never late.**

With that kind of orientation, and with punctuality so deeply infused into the fiber of your being, you find it difficult to comprehend how an actor can possibly show up 22 minutes late for a rehearsal. Yet it happens.

When an actor does arrive late, the rehearsal should not come to a halt while that actor is questioned. Tell the late actor what page of the script you are on, or the scene if you are off book, and ask the tardy actor to take his place. He should be advised not to apologize, but simply to get to work. If the individual is not in the scene, tell the actor which scene will be worked on next, and ask him to go over lines until needed.

Under no circumstances should you allow other cast members to wait for a late actor. Urge your director to do the scene that was scheduled. Either throw the missing actor's lines or have another cast member or understudy read the part. Make use of the time as best you can. Perhaps the director will allow you to check your visual display of characters and select a sequence that can be rehearsed without the missing actor. If there is only one actor present on time, regardless of the minimum number needed to do a scene, start working with that one actor. It is important to the play, to the on-time actors, and to the late actors that work be in progress from the minute the rehearsal was called.

At the end of the rehearsal period, discuss tardiness with the late actor, privately. First, especially in a professional situation, turn to your log in the presence of the actor and write the number of minutes he was late, ask the reason for the tardiness, and write it also. Then ask him to sign the log. In any case, confront the actor politely with the facts and ask if the rehearsal schedule was clear and if he understood what time he was expected. Ask the individual if there is anything you can do to help overcome the cause of the tardiness. Then ask if the actor needs to be called prior to the next rehearsal. If necessary, review the importance of rehearsal time, the fact that 22 minutes of tardiness represents over two hours of lost rehearsal time in terms of complete cast interaction, that not only the tardy actor but all the other actors in the scene suffer, and ultimately the quality of the play suffers. Stress the positive factors—that early arrival at rehearsals allows the actor to review lines and to run lines with other actors, that the director is going for the kind of polished performance that needs every possible minute of rehearsal time, and that since this is also the tardy actor's goal, you know you can count on future cooperation. In short, make it absolutely clear that you care and that it is important to you that actors be on time.

In professional theaters, steps may be taken against habitually tardy actors through their union, but in both union and nonunion situations, educate and stress the positive rather than threaten and punish.

Directors should not have to discuss tardiness with actors. They should be able to rely on you in this matter.

SIGN-IN SHEETS

As early as dress rehearsals, sign-in sheets should be posted (figure 9.1). Cast members should be reminded to initial in, until they get into the habit. Initialing prevents actors from placing a check mark in the wrong block. If they initial the wrong block, the error can be traced. Alternate lines of the sign-in sheet can be set up in different colors or in different indention patterns; this makes it easier to find the correct space to initial.

The sign-in sheet saves you work. It allows you to see if the cast is there by looking in only one place. If anyone has not initialed in by half-hour call, check the dressing rooms. Then phone those who are late.

Placement of the sign-in sheet on the callboard ensures that cast members will be close enough to the callboard to read any urgent new information that has been posted.

If you have a cast of two, you may elect not to post a sign-in sheet. If you have a cast of 100, you may elect to turn the sign-in sheet over to a gate man or stage door guard and have that individual check in the cast. You would still check with that individual for tardiness.

- **Calling any actor who has failed to sign in by half-hour call (see the following section, "The Calls") is an important responsibility. Nothing should get in the way of your carrying out that duty.**

Please Initial In !

ALBATROSS

SIGN IN

	TUE	WED	THUR	FRI	SAT	SUN
Frank Aletter						
Jenny Gillespie						
Pauline Meyers						
Lee Meriwether						
James R. Sweeney						
James B. Sikking						
Marge Redmond						
Paul Bryar						
Kathleen Freeman						
Dick Ramos						
Ellen Webb						

FIGURE 9.1 Sign-In Sheet for Cast Members

Examples

1. During a three-month run, the home of a habitually late actor was frequently called. His wife always answered the phone and told the stage manager that the actor had left for the theater. When the actor arrived, the stage manager explained that he had called his home. The actor complained that the stage manager was needlessly alarming his wife, who would worry about traffic accidents until he called her to reassure her that he'd arrived safely. The stage manager's complaint that he was late and the actor's complaint that the stage manager was needlessly worrying his wife were frequently voiced—until the evening that the stage manager called and woke him up.
2. On opening night of a musical, five principals and the director were late for half-hour call. None responded to the stage manager's phone calls. The stage manager assumed that they were on their way. At 15-minute call, they were still not there. The stage manager alerted the house manager and the producer. Then a chorus member remembered that one of the principals had mentioned that they were going out to dinner before the show. The restaurant was called. They had been there and left—35 minutes ago. At five-minute call, they had still not arrived. Now the producer and the house manager were pacing the lobby. An audience of 1,400 waited, completely unaware they were missing quite a drama. At curtain time, there were still no principals and no word from them. The producer's guidance was, "Stay calm,"

> but he was clearly upset. How could such a thing happen? Why hadn't they called? The stage manager was numb.
>
> At seven minutes past curtain, the principals and director arrived. Blocked road, train accident, waited to clear road, hemmed in by other cars, no way out, no phone or house visible to horizon.
>
> At 13 minutes past curtain time, the overture began.
>
> And that was the night that one of the bit players who lived next door to the theater overslept and missed his one line. The stage manager had failed to call him.
>
> In a situation of complete pandemonium, don't fail to carry out your basic duties.

During the run of any production, if an actor is late for half-hour call, she should be reminded that the half hour prior to performance is meant to be used by the actor to get into costume, makeup, and character and to relax in order to store up energy for the performance.

Actors sometimes argue the necessity of being at the theater one-half hour prior to curtain. They claim that they can get into costume, makeup, and character in seven and half minutes, they can relax at home, and they have plenty of energy. Then, too, they don't like to wait backstage because it's musty, crowded, and so on.

Regardless of such arguments, continue to expect punctuality. Call every time the actor is late and use whatever methods possible to convince the actor to be at the theater for half-hour call.

Should an actor who drives for 45 minutes to get to the theater still have the same call as other cast members? Should you call that actor's home 45 minutes prior to curtain to assure yourself that the actor is on the way? What if that same actor does not appear until 15 minutes into the first act?

Should another actor who does not appear until the third act be granted a late call? Should an actress who puts on her makeup and costume at home to avoid using the overcrowded dressing room be allowed to sign in after half-hour call?

These are but a few of the practical questions that will come up. To answer them, you must ask yourself: Can I help ensure that this actor will get to the theater on time? Can I ensure that the cast will not be rushed in putting on makeup, getting into costume, and getting into character? Can I assure myself that I will have adequate time to call actors and still carry out my other pre-curtain duties?

If an actor is ever granted a late call, the call should coincide with a period of time that you have free to check on the actor's arrival.

THE CALLS

Calls—announcements of the time to the curtain—are given in order to alert cast members to how much time they have before the play begins. The traditional calls are:

> Half hour, please.
>
> Fifteen minutes, please.
>
> Five minutes, please.
>
> Places, please.

The first three calls are given 30, 15, and 5 minutes prior to the announced curtain time. The "places" call is given after the house manager has turned the house over to you and when you are ready to run the show. Notice that "please" is a part of the call. Don't omit it.

It is traditional that all cast members acknowledge your calls with a cheery "Thank you." If cast members are unaware of this custom, you might bring it to their attention.

In some cases, the curtain will be delayed—last-minute rush at the box office, bad weather, traffic and parking problems, late arrival of theater parties, and the like. The house manager might ask you to hold the curtain for 5, 10, or 15 minutes. Relay these holds to the cast with an additional call of "Five-minute hold, please." If possible, explain to the cast the reason for the delay.

At intermissions, the calls are "Five minutes, please," and "Places, please."

Do not rely on a one-way speaker system from your work area to the dressing rooms to give the calls. You not only run the risk of mechanical failure, but you also lose that bit of contact with the cast.

A two-way communications system is only slightly better because mechanical failure is immediately noticeable and cast members have a chance to respond. A face-to-face exchange is much better.

- **Only if it is absolutely impossible for you to give the calls should you assign this duty to an assistant or call-person. But this is not a task that should be delegated. This is one of your more important duties.**

If you cannot greet and chat with each cast member as that cast member arrives at the theater, you have all too little contact. The call itself is not sufficient. There has to be dialogue between you and cast members. The subtext is, "Are you all right? Can you give a good performance tonight? Are you overtired? Did you get too sunburned? Did you have too much to drink? Do you have a stomachache?"

There is little you can do to relieve the pains and suffering of the acting condition. But hot coffee, a few aspirins, and kind words can go a long way in boosting cast morale to performance level. If you are effective, you can make just a few words and a friendly, sympathetic smile serve as a mental rubdown.

Under normal conditions you are not expected to give calls or warns for individual actor entrances once the act has begun. Actors are expected to listen for their cues in the wings or, if available, on dressing room monitors. There are exceptions, however.

Example

A big-name personality who had played the same role in hundreds of theaters in the round across the country had become so indifferent to the script and local variations in blocking that he had to be led out of his dressing room by the hand, pointed down the correct aisle, and pushed on cue. He also had to be retrieved as he exited, whenever and wherever he chose, and led back to his dressing room, as he could never remember where the dressing room was. The stage manager assigned the big name a "seeing-eye gopher."

- **If you are a new stage manager, do not worry about gaining the respect of the actors. Just assume that you already have it. You do have it by virtue of your title, and you will earn it by virtue of your work. Respect is reciprocal. The more you give, the more you can count on getting back. As soon as the actors realize that you respect them, you will gain their utmost cooperation.**

Many opera singers have done their roles three or four times, some as many as 50 or 60 times, in a variety of theaters. They may get the different productions confused. ASMs are expected to cue entrances. Standing beside the singers, ASMs give visual and verbal cues. Sometimes during rehearsals, a singer will not like the cue where the director wants it. The singer will say, "The director told me to go here." I have always told my assistants to reply, "Thank you; however, the director did not pass that on to me, so I must call it as is." The director will advise both singer and ASM if the entrance was not as intended. Opera stage managers also give five-minute entrance warns ("Ms. Smith, to stage left, please." "Children's chorus to stage right.").

David Grindle
Production Stage Manager, the Atlanta Opera

[David recommends The Da Capo Opera Manual *by Nicholas Ivor Martin, Da Capo Press (1997), for those interested in opera production.]*

SUGGESTED CLASSROOM EXERCISE

Discuss your theater's policy with respect to the tardiness of an actor or actress. Would the curtain be delayed? How long? Would an understudy be readied? At what point? Would the stage manager or someone else go on holding book? Would the performance be cancelled?

10

Department Management and Property Management

The quickest way to do many things
is to do only one thing at a time.
—Anonymous

One of my first professional assignments was as SM for the Sacramento Music Circus, a summer tent theater. The producers, who had done several shows on Broadway, tasked the production stage manager, Jack Welles, with supervising the work of the scene shop and costume shop. The shops, run by the technical director and the costume designer, worked during the days to prepare the next week's show. It got very hot during the afternoons, so the shops worked during the morning hours. We all worked split shifts, calling and running the shows at night.

Jack was my on-the-job mentor. I followed him around as he made the morning rounds, checking in with the scene shop and the costume shop. I was preparing myself for the time when I would leave later in the summer for the Fresno Music Circus to be PSM.

It all seemed like light banter, but the subtext was based in sound communications and management techniques that Jack had developed through years of experience. He wasn't telling anyone what to do, but he was seeing that everyone was on task and that there were no delays or anticipated problems.

THE STAGE MANAGER AS COORDINATOR OF DEPARTMENTS

- **If, in your unique theater, you find yourself responsible for supervising or coordinating departments, you will want to see that the department heads (1) are working, (2) are on schedule, and (3) have not run into any "insurmountable" problems.**

1. Department heads and their assistants don't usually punch clocks. But if they are not there to do the work, the production will not be able to open on time. You informally make the rounds to see if the staff is at work. It may occasionally mean rousing a late sleeper or providing transportation for someone with an unreliable auto. When you make the rounds, chat about progress on the current production.
2. Falling behind on the schedule sometimes means that a department will need more staff. Can you send over an assistant, some apprentices, or your gopher to help the shop wire on the ornamental grapes that light up? Or will you have to approach the business manager because the costumer insists on another union costume technician (at union wages) in order to accomplish the costume work on time?
3. Problem solving is frequently the same as listening well. If every department head feels able to air "insurmountable" problems to you, in doing so, the department head will usually come up with the solution. If you should observe that the department heads themselves are largely the cause of their own problems, keep this to yourself and praise their solutions.

By asking hypothetical questions ("What if . . .?" "What would happen if . . .?") rather than imposing solutions ("You should . . .") or placing blame ("You should have . . ."), you tactfully get department heads to feel that they are in command of the situation. The commander usually works harder than the person who is merely following orders.

In supervision, tact can usually get it done. (See page 9 for communications/management skills.)

Property Management and You

Assistant stage managers in England and in small U.S. theaters are often assigned to work props.

Regardless of theater level, the function of the property person remains the same—to get the props. Your usual function is to supervise. To do this, you should know all aspects of property management.

In union theaters the property person is paid for services. In community, educational, showcase, and children's theater the property person is usually an unpaid volunteer. Some people do not consider working on props particularly exciting or glamorous. It calls for someone who is methodical and persistent.

Finding and motivating a competent property person is a problem that plagues many theaters. Sometimes when a property person cannot be found, you find yourself either working as property person or retaining overall responsibility for props and dividing the prop work among the staff and cast.

Whether supervising or doing it yourself, appreciate the importance of having props available for rehearsals.

If actors can hold a prop with one hand and their script with the other, the props ought to be in place, even before the actors put down their scripts. Having props in hand helps them to memorize their lines. Using props early in the rehearsal period allows the cast and director to experiment and to develop suitable business. This is highly desirable, as it may add immeasurably to the quality of the production.

Conversely, not having props on time leads to serious problems.

Examples

1. Scenes may have to be reblocked because an actor did not allow enough room for his imagined sword.
2. The leading lady sneezes through opening night because of the bouquet. The wadded-up newspaper used as a rehearsal prop did not affect her allergies.

Property Person's Checklists

- **To help determine the extent of the property person's responsibilities, you might review the following checklists.**

BEFORE REHEARSALS Before rehearsals will the property person

1. Be responsible for hand properties?
2. Be responsible for set pieces? Which ones?
3. Be responsible for obtaining transportation to pick up and return all props?
4. Coordinate with the director, scene designer, and producer to ensure appropriate props?
5. Ensure that set pieces arrive on time for the take-in?
6. Obtain hand props as soon as possible in order to give actors maximum rehearsal time to work with them?
7. Provide temporary rehearsal props for unusual or costly props that cannot be obtained until later in the rehearsal period?
8. Give a written receipt to lenders of props and set pieces? Note on both the original and copy the condition of the prop and the intended date of return?
9. Coordinate with the producer, through the stage manager, prior to rental of expensive props?
10. Be able to give ______ hours per week for ______ weeks to this work?
11. Need assistance (an assistant property person)?
12. Report to the stage manager any difficulties encountered in sufficient time to avert a last-minute rush?

DURING REHEARSALS During rehearsals will the property person

1. Attend rehearsals to make notes of additional props, where and how props are used, which actors use them, and from which entrance they come on stage?
2. Bring in large boxes and label them by act or scene as necessary in order to store the props?
3. Set props for each scene 15 minutes before rehearsal is scheduled?
4. Lock up or otherwise secure all props after rehearsals?
5. Draw maps of prop tables and post them on or above the prop tables offstage to ensure quick, accurate checks of all props prior to rehearsals and performances?
6. Make maps of locations of props in each scene so changes of props between scenes can be made or supervised? Draw diagrams on stage surfaces (tables, bars, mantels, etc.) to indicate exact placement of props?

%$# icebag! All through rehearsal it was used empty. At dress, she (actress) filled it with ice. Why? I'll never know. It dribbled all over the stage, her, others. It was old and worn. Newspaper would have puffed it up fine. (A doctor once told me *never disrupt the body temp of an actor under hot lights,* unless in pain.) So, old ice bags, activated, are a NO NO.

Billy Carr Creamer
Associate Director, Amarillo Little Theater, Amarillo Civic Center
Amarillo, TX

[The general lesson is that all props must be used at the earliest possible rehearsal just as they are to be used on opening night.]

PRIOR TO PERFORMANCE Prior to the performance will the property person

1. Check presence and condition of all props and report to the stage manager (usually 45 minutes prior to performance)?
2. Replace expendable items (water in pitcher, tea in booze bottles, telegram that gets crumpled, etc.) prior to each performance?

DURING PERFORMANCE During the performance will the property person

1. Change properties on the stage between acts as needed?
2. Be available in the wings to assist in preparing props?

Simply put eight drops of yellow food color, three drops of red, and one drop of green into whatever bottle one is using, add water and you have perfect whiskey. (This process eliminates the bubbles that you get when using instant tea.)

William J. Buckley, III
Stage Manager, Woodstock Playhouse
Woodstock, NY

Recipe for Stage Blood

Audiences gasped every time and, visually, it held up under very close audience scrutiny. We used this recipe nightly for 10 years in the Hollywood production of *Tamara,* an unusual staging in that audiences actually followed actors from room to room and participated in the play. So they were, almost literally, right on top of the actor who was shot.

I used:

Environmentally safe "Planet" dish soap (but any dish soap will do)

3 parts red/1 part blue food coloring

Yes, the recipe is that simple. Here are the caveats:

1. Check out the balance of red to blue food coloring under lights with your lighting designer.
2. Check out various food-coloring brands until you find the right hue.
3. Check by washing the costume piece. Some brands can stain.
4. Not for internal use (bloody mouth).

Dilute the soap for a squirting effect or use it full consistency for slow drips or bloody hands.

I've tried Karo syrup (too gross, sugar based, coagulates too quickly, gets everything on stage sticky, has ruined—when tinted red—a few tablecloths and costume pieces, a pain to wash out of any delicate materials, and no matter where you hide it, the ants ALWAYS find it) and movie blood (too expensive). There are some good stage blood products I have used for "internal" use (such as bloody mouths). These are safe and minty for the actor, but still a bit stain-y for the prop guy.

To rig the appearance of stage blood, pour it into a baggie (the thin kind, NOT a zip-lock bag). Cut the baggie to your desired blood flow—a full baggie is a lot. An approximate 4-inch square shape is perfect for stage gunshots. Use freezer tape to seal the cut sides together. Pour the slightly diluted blood into the reshaped baggie. Seal the top with more freezer tape. Place in a rigged inner pocket of the actor's shirt. It becomes then a matter of the actor breaking the bag by smashing it as the "gunshot" impacts his chest. After performance just drop the shirt into the wash and the soap-blood washes out. Always do a test, though, as some companies use different formulas to make food coloring.

I have taught this recipe to many a stage manager.

Michael Angel
Property Manager
Studio City, California

AFTER PERFORMANCE After the performance will the property person

1. Check for return of all props to the property tables?
2. Store props between performances, providing secure storage for expensive props?

AFTER PRODUCTION After the production will the property person

1. Clean or repair borrowed items to ensure goodwill for future borrowing?
2. Obtain receipts for return of items borrowed, give notes of thanks, and thank contributors personally?
3. Be financially responsible for all lost props?
4. Keep a list of sources, and the types of props that can be borrowed from each, as an aid to future productions?
5. Write a critique, emphasizing problem areas, in order to help the next property master?

Although it is desirable, it is not necessary that the property person do everything reflected in the questions here. Rather than review the preceding list with the property person, present just a few items at a time or as much responsibility as you feel is acceptable at one time. A new property person might accept more responsibility gradually but might balk if presented with the whole range. It is necessary, however, that you and the property person come to a clear understanding of the exact duties.

PROPERTY FORMS

The property person can use the two forms, "Borrowed Items" and "Acknowledgment of Borrowed Items Returned," to control props (figures 10.1 and 10.2). When props are picked up, the property master fills out the "Acknowledgment" form and gives it to the lender. On the "Borrowed Items" form the program credit line that is expected

BORROWED ITEMS

_____ production of "_________________________________" _____(dates)

Item(s) Borrowed	Date Received	Borrowed From*	Date to be Returned
1.			
2.			
3.			
4.			
5.			
6.			
7.			
8.			
9.			
10.			
11.			
12.			
13.			

*Include company name, address, phone number, extension, and personal contact!

Page_____of_____ Prepared by _______________

Lawrence Stern
Production Stage Manager
555-3719

FIGURE 10.1 Property Master's Control Form and Record of Borrowed Items

Download from pearsonhighered.com/stern_ogrady

and other information are noted. When the property master returns the prop, the "Acknowledgment" form is picked up.

Receipt forms, found in most stationery stores, can be used in place of these two forms (figure 10.3, page 150). One receipt and a copy are made out for each borrowed prop. The copy is issued to the lender and retrieved when the prop is returned. The original is kept by the property master.

ACKNOWLEDGMENT OF BORROWED ITEMS RETURNED

The following items, loaned to the _________ production of "_________,"
were returned on _________ by _________ in satisfactory condition:
(date)

1.
2.
3.
4.
5.
6.
7.
8.
9.
10.

Received by:

Name: ________________
Position: ________________
Company: ________________

Lawrence Stern
Production Stage Manager
555-3719

FIGURE 10.2 Acknowledgment Form for Borrowed Items Returned

In some cases it is easier to use the prop plot (refer to figure 3.9) as a control form. If many copies of the prop plot can be duplicated, then they can be posted on prop storage boxes, placed on prop tables, and even given to cast and staff as reminders of the props they have pledged to bring in. When initial prop plots are extensive, they must be revised for prop table presets (figure 10.4, page 151).

The cost of all props that must be purchased by the theater should be carefully recorded on the property person's expense sheet (figure 7.1). For bookkeeping purposes, the property person might be asked to record expendable and permanent items on separate sheets.

Program credits and/or complimentary tickets are sometimes given for the use of props. It is important to check the producer or management's policy and coordinate with the program editor. In some cases, the lender definitely does not want a program credit. Be sure to clear this with the lender.

As soon as props are used in the rehearsals, remind the cast to cooperate with the property person by returning all props to the prop tables when they are carried offstage as part of the actor's business. Otherwise, the property person has to search the dressing rooms and even the pockets of costumes.

Great American Theater
Date Nov. 24 No. 3873
Receiver Of Shiker Bar Furnishings Inc.
Address 1038 Bluedale Road
1 finished bar, 2 bar stools $
For 3" scatch upstage end
HOW PAID | BALANCE DUE | to be returned Jan. 11, P.M. by us.
5X 820 Rediform | By Eric Spelvin, PM

Great American Theater
Date Nov. 24 No. 3873
Receiver Of Shiker Bar Furnishings Inc.
Address 1038 Bluedale Road
1 finished bar, 2 bar stools $
For 3" scatch upstage end
HOW PAID | BALANCE DUE | to be returned Jan. 11, P.M. by us.
Rediform | By Eric Spelvin, PM

FIGURE 10.3 Receipt Form Acknowledgment for a Borrowed Item. The original is kept by the property master and duplicate is issued to the lender. Both copies should specify the date of return and the condition of the prop.

As a safety factor, the stage manager is usually responsible for, and must carefully supervise, the firing of blanks, even though the weapon is a prop (figures 10.5 and 10.6, pages 152 and 153).

When the property person and others are also responsible for specific set pieces—those that will be bought, borrowed, or rented, as opposed to those that will be constructed—you must make absolutely certain that all staff members know which set pieces they are responsible for.

> About the snow: we use paper. I don't know what the exact origin of the material is. We buy it as "confetti." I suspect it may be the base material for colored confetti. It is very hard to find plain white confetti. It is also flame retardant. It sells for about $7/lb. We have about 150 pounds sitting in the wings at the top of every show (of which we recuperate probably 98 percent during cleanup). The traction on "snow" is surprisingly good, especially after being in the dancers' sweaty hands. We've had one dancer slide and fall during a performance, so far. I'm not sure whether that was caused by the "snow" or by something else like transpiration on stage. There aren't really any precautions dancers can take when they're going full out. We keep the wings downstage of the first portal and upstage of the last portal as wide as possible so that dancers can maintain a straight line until they slow down.
>
> Johan Henckens
> *Technical Director,* The Hard Nut, *Mark Morris Dance Group*
> *New York, NY*
>
> *[This unusual prop has a spectacular effect (figure 10.7, page 154), but consequences of its use must be considered by dancers and stage crew.]*

Rigoletto
Prop Table Preset—ACT I
Approximate Running time: 00:53:00

STAGE RIGHT

Scene 1
19 Gold goblets (Chorus: G. Jordan, A. Kauffman, G. Jones, K. Barnes, V. Clark, M. Cleghorn, D. Haggerty, K. Lee, G. Sterchi, E. Drew, D. Davis, J. Clark, K. Foster, M. Jaye, J. Young, D. Martin, B. Larkin, J. Jones (2))
2 Large pitchers (K. Barnes, W. Siede)
1 Silver hairbrush (N. Paul)
1 Large red fabric (M. Durham, T. Allen)
1 Large feather fan (C. Burns)
4 Combat swords with sheaths and belts (belts labeled: J. Young, D. Davis, B. Larkin, D. Martin)
1 Jester's Bauble (Potter)
1 Deck of tarot cards (K. Rosquist)
2 Bunches of practical white grapes (M. Jaye, S. Mayer)
1 Cane (P. Haynie)
2 Daggers—combat (McMillan, J. Clark)
1 Pair gloves (P. Haynie)—FROM COSTUMES
1 Hat (P. Haynie)—FROM COSTUMES
1 Necklace (L. Wood)
1 Bracelet (K. Rosquist)
1 Jester's shoulder bag (Potter)
1 Ring of keys (Potter)
1 Locket (Potter)
1 Knife inside bag (Potter)

Scene 2
1 Coin purse (Villa)
6 Torches (C. Hawkins, G. Sterchi, S. Mize, C. Hooper, G. Williamson, L. Compton)
1 Blindfold (Morrissey)
1 Wine Skin (P. Haynie)
1 Key on Ribbon (McMillan)
1 Ladder (V. Robertson)
1 Knife—must be combat knife (McMillan)
1 Mask—says THOMAS POTTER inside (G. Williamson)

RUNNING MOVES:
41:00 min.—Light torch. Give torch to McMillan.
46:00 min.—Receive and extinguish torch from McMillan.
47:00 min.—Light 6 torches and give to choristers (C. Hawkins, G. Sterchi, S. Mize, C. Hooper, G. Williamson, L. Compton)
57:00 min.—Receive and extinguish 6 torches from choristers.

CHANGEOVER from I-1 to I-2: 5 minutes
INTERMISSION SHIFT from I to II: 20 minutes

WATER SPRITZ

STAGE LEFT

Scene 1
7 Pieces of ladies undergarments (M. Durham, T. Allen)—FROM COSTUMES

Scene 2
1 Sword w/ curved guard (Bell)
1 Hairbrush (James)
1 Electric candle on small black stand (James)
1 Gag labeled GILDA (Delligatti)
1 Length of rope (Delligatti)
1 Gag labeled GIOVANNI (James)
1 Length of rope (James)

RUNNING MOVES:
48:00 min.—Give candle to James at top of SL stairs.
50:00 min.—Receive candle from Delligatti top of SL stairs. Give gag (GILDA) & rope.

NOTES: Scene 1 and 2 props should be set at top of show. Scene 1 is 14:00 min. Scene 2 is 39:00 min.

CHANGEOVER from I-1 to I-2: 5 minutes
INTERMISSION SHIFT from I to II: 20 minutes

WATER SPRITZ

FIGURE 10.4 Prop Table Preset, Act I, *Rigoletto*. At the Atlanta Opera, the property master carries out the running moves, but the ASM supervises. Both keep an eye on the clock. "Water Spritz" refers to the spraying, by a props person, of a fine mist to add moisture to the air, which opera singers appreciate.

Courtesy Sean M. Griffin, ASM, The Atlanta Opera.

Theatrical Firearms Questionnaire

If your production uses theatrical firearms, please complete this questionnaire and return it to your Equity Business Representative as soon as possible. (Note: For long-running productions, this form must be filled out every six (6) months.)

The Producer has an obligation under the Collective Bargaining Agreement with Actors' Equity Association to provide a safe place of employment. Pursuant to Equity's right to check the Producer's compliance with that provision of the Collective Bargaining Agreement, we have devised the following checklist for you to use to see if the Producer is undertaking minimally prudent safeguards when firearms are used in a production.

Name of Show:

Contract: (e.g., Production LORT, COST, etc.)

Name of Theatre: Number in Cast: Date:

Stage Manager: Deputy:

Firearms Rehearsals

It is essential that appropriate firearms rehearsals are held to insure the Actors' safety. Please confirm whether such rehearsals have taken place. If, for any reason, it is not possible to hold such rehearsals, Actors' Equity must be notified immediately.

Identify All Firearms

Please identify make or model, caliber, and load used:

Are rehearsals to check firearms angles held regularly? Yes ☐ No ☐
Weekly? ☐ Daily? ☐ Each performance? ☐

Are the blanks crimped ☐ or wadded? ☐
Have the firearms been recently certified? Yes ☐ No ☐ If so, when?
How often are firearms cleaned? Wet Cleaning? ☐ Dry Cleaning? ☐

Who is in charge of the firearms and where are they stored?

Is the ammunition stored separately? If yes, where?

Use in Production

Please identify how the firearms are used. Attach additional pages, if necessary.

Act/Scene	Number of Shots	Activity of Actors

If any Actor experiences any adverse effects from the use of firearms during the run of the production, please notify the Actors' Equity immediately. Possible adverse effects include powder burns, errant particle (e.g., a piece of casing which is propelled from the gun when fired) and eardrum problems. Also, please ensure any such injury is reported to Workers Compensation.

Please provide any other information you feel would be helpful. Attach additional pages, if necessary.

FIGURE 10.5 Equity's Theatrical Firearms Questionnaire

Courtesy Actors' Equity Association. Download the latest revision from actorsequity.org

PLEASE POST IF FIREARMS ARE USED IN PRODUCTION
SAFETY TIPS FOR USE OF FIREARMS

Use simulated or dummy weapons whenever possible.

- Treat all guns as if they are loaded and deadly.
- Unless you are actually performing or rehearsing, all firearms must be secured by the property master.
- The property master or armorer should carefully train you in the safe use of any firearm you must handle. Be honest if you have no knowledge about guns. Do not overstate your qualifications.
- Never engage in horseplay with any firearms or other weapons. Do not let others handle the gun for any reason.
- All loading of firearms must be done by the property master, armorer, or experienced persons working under their direct supervision.
- Never point a firearm at anyone, including yourself. Always cheat the shot by aiming to the right or left of the target character. If asked to point and shoot directly at a living target, consult with the property master or armorer for the prescribed safety procedures.
- If you are the intended target of a gunshot, make sure that the person firing at you has followed all these safety procedures.
- If you are required to wear exploding blood squibs, make sure there is a bullet proof vest or other solid protection between you and the blast pack.
- Use protective shields for all off-stage cast within close proximity to any shots fired.
- Check the firearm every time you take possession of it. Before each use, make sure that gun has been test-fired off stage and then ask to test-fire it yourself. Watch the prop master check the cylinders and barrel to be sure no foreign object or dummy bullet has become lodged inside.
- Blanks are extremely dangerous. Even though they do not fire bullets out of the gun barrel, they still have a powerful blast that can maim or kill.
- If the director or property master shouts, "Put the gun down," place the piece gently on the ground with the barrel pointing in a safe direction and step back quickly.
- Never attempt to adjust, modify or repair a firearm yourself. If a weapon jams or malfunctions, corrections shall be made only by a qualified person.
- When a scene is completed, the firearms shall be unloaded by the property master. All weapons must be cleaned, checked and inventoried after each performance.
- Live ammunition may not be brought into the theatre.
- If you are in a production where shots are to be fired and there is no qualified property master, go to the nearest phone and call Actors' Equity. A union representative will make sure proper precautions are followed.
- State and federal safety laws must be honored at all times.

This announcement must be posted on callboard when firearms are used in a production involving Equity members. Courtesy Actors' Equity Association.

FIGURE 10.6 Safety Tips for Use of Firearms

Download the latest revision from actorsequity.org

FIGURE 10.7 Snow Scene from *The Hard Nut* (ballet)

Photo by Catherine Ashmore, Mark Morris Dance Group, New York, NY.

SUGGESTED CLASSROOM EXERCISE

Assign a student or students to work props at your theater or at a community theater. Ask the individual(s) to evaluate the checklists on pages 145–147 to see how it relates to the reality of prop work.

11

Supervision of Shifts

All things come to him who waits, but they come sooner if he goes out to see what's wrong.
—Anonymous

When working in the round, find a way to coordinate a stage crew of 15 in making scene shifts, striking an average of five props and 11 set pieces and setting as many—in 30 seconds—in the dark—every 12 minutes—for 1 hour and 35 minutes—for a total of 14 shifts. This is the type of logistical problem that can make stage managers lose sleep and eat aspirins.

SHIFT PLOT CHARTS

A shift plot chart (figure 11.1) is a device that will help you plan and supervise scene shifts. Although this technique (and this example) is primarily applicable to productions in the round, it may also be used for complex shifts in any theater. Post the chart in the scene dock and prop area so that the crew can use it as a self-briefing aid.

Notice that the top row lists the scenes, the second row lists the cue that precedes the shift, and each row beneath describes an individual crew member's responsibility in each shift.

Make your shift plot chart BIG so that it is easily readable. Allow 2½-high-by-3-inch-wide rectangles for each separate entry. This allows you to make corrections conveniently by posting halves of 3 × 5 inch notecards over entries that must be changed.

Notice that each entry gives the following information (for an "in-the-round" production):

1. Aisle traveled to reach the stage (e.g., 1st down 11; the number *11* means the aisle at 11 o'clock if the stage is compared to the face of a clock with the orchestra pit at 12 o'clock).
2. Order number on which to travel (e.g., *1st* down 11; if a crew member is preceded by two others, that crew member is "3rd down aisle"). Controlling order helps you to choreograph the change.

TAKE ME ALONG - ACT II	II - 1 BARROOM	II - 1 BALLET	II - 2 & 3 MILLER HOME
WARN CUE	PRESET	HE READS BOOK IN BED. THUS SPAKE ZARA-THUSTRA BLACKOUT	BALLET ENDS... BLACKOUT
GEORGE RAY IATSE 1	↓7 (4:00) STRIKE PIANO SET BIRDCAGE (12) SET BLKBOX (9) ↑7	1ST ↓5 ~~SET DESK (2:00)~~ STRIKE PIANO (W. BILL) ↑5	1ST ↓1 SET DESK (2:00) STRIKE FOGPOT (3) 1↑
DENNIS IATSE 2	↓7 SET BAR (10:00) STRIKE PORCH (7) ↑7 W/HAROLD	1ST ↓11 STRIKE BAR W/ HAROLD ↑$ 11	1ST ↓5 SET PORCH (5:00) W/HAL ↑7
HAROLD IATSE 3	↓7 10:00 SET BAR (W DENNIS) STRIKE PORCH (7) ↑7 W/DENNIS	2ND ↓11 STRIKE BAR W/ DENNIS 11↑	2ND ↓5 SET PORCH (5:00) W/DENNIS ↑7
BILL C.	↓ 7 W/MIKE SET PIANO & STOOL STRIKE CHAIR (2:00) TO RCH HALL	2ND ↓ 5 STRIKE PIANO W/GEORGE 5↑	3RD ↓7 SET WINDOW ST. (6:00) STRIKE CHAIR ↑$1
MIKE	↓7 (1:00) SET 2 CHAIRS STRIKE TABLE (3) TO RCH HALL	1ST ↓1 STRIKE TABLE ↑1	3RD ↓11 SET TABLE (11:30) & CHAIR ↑7
WALLY	GATE TENT	2ND ↓1 STRIKE 2 CHAIRS ↑1	~~2ND ↓11~~ ~~SET CHAIR (11:00)~~ ~~↑11~~ FLYMAN DROP BKT.
WAYNE	GUARD INSIDE TENT	SET DRY ICE IN BUCKET (9:00)	3RD ↓11 SET STEPS (11:00) ↑11

FIGURE 11.1 Shift Plot Chart for Several Crew Members

3. Set piece or prop carried on and location it is to be placed (e.g., "Set table at 11:00"). The location designator is not an exact one, but is used to refresh the runner's memory when used in conjunction with "before and after" diagrams. (See figures 11.5 and 11.6 , pages 164 and 165.)
4. Set piece or props to be struck, and destination if other than the scene dock and prop area (e.g., "Leave at top of aisle 11 for use in Sc. 5").
5. Aisle to exit.
6. Order to exit is designated rarely—when more than one large set piece must move up the same aisle, or when fast-traveling light pieces must precede slow-moving heavy pieces to expedite the shift.

II - 4 BEDROOM	II - 5 & 6 BEACH	II - 7 & 8 MILLER HOME	AFTER PERFORMANCE
"STAYING YOUNG" reprise BLACKOUT	HELLO, OPERATOR PHONE LIGHT OUT	SCRUMPTIOUS SHORT: 9:00 REPRISE BLACKOUT	WHEN AUDIENCE OUT
2ND ↓ 1 (2:00) STRIKE DESK W/WAYNE ↑ 1	3RD ↓ 1 SET LOG CTR. ↑ 7	1ST ↓ 1 SET DESK (2:00) WITH JOHN ↑ 1	STRIKE LAMP (4:30) UNPLUG
2ND ↓ 7 SET PLATFORM W/HAROLD (ctr.) ↑ 5	1ST ↓ 11 STRIKE PLAT. W/HAL ↑ 7	1ST ↓ 5 STRIKE LOG W/HAL ↑ 7 DURING SCENE MOVE TROLLEY INTO POSIT.	STRIKE LAMP (11:30) UNPLUG
3RD ↓ 7 SET PLATFORM W/DENNIS ↑ 5	1ST ↓ 3 SET PLATFORM W/DENNIS ↑ 7	2ND ↓ 5 STRIKE LOG ↑ 5 HAVE TROLLEY TO POSITION	STRIKE PLUG (11:30)
4TH ↓ 7 SET BED OPER. W/MIKE STRIKE F.PLACE ↑ 7	2ND ↓ 7 SET FIREPLACE (9:00) ↑ 11	2ND ↓ 5 SET WINDOW SEAT (6:00) ↑ 5 PULL TROLLEY	
1ST ↓ 7 SET BED W/ BILL COOK ↑ 7	1ST ↓ 11 (11:30) SET TABLE (11:00) & CHAIR ↑ 7 AFTER WINDOW SEAT IN	↓ 11 STRIKE F.PLACE (9:00) PULL ↑ 11 TROLLEY	UNPLUG (11:30)
4TH ↓ 1 STRIKE LOG ↑ 1	3RD ↓ 11 (11:00) SET STEPS ↑ 11	↓ 11 SET LAMP (11:00) PLUG IN ← STRIKE TABLE (11) ↑ 11	
1ST ↓ 1 STRIKE CHAIR ↑ 1	3RD ↓ 7 SET 6:00 LWR. RAIL W/HAL ↑ 7	↓ 11 SET SMLL. PLG. STRIKE CHAIR ↑ 11	

FIGURE 11.1 *(Continued)*

7. If more than one crew member handles a single set piece, the names of the other crew members working on that unit are listed so that each crew member knows with whom he is to work (e.g., "with Roy").
8. If errors were made at any performance, you may put special cautions in an entry rectangle (e.g., "Watch out for hanging mike hit on opening night"). Other cautions might concern a false blackout or the rapid succession of two cues (e.g., "Hustle back to prop table for next shift").

Normally you wait until the take-in (see next section) to make up the chart because you must know definitely and exactly where the set pieces will play. Since the chart takes so much time to make, it is advisable to lay it out in advance, filling in the first column (crew members), the top row (scenes), and the second row (cues) well in advance of the take-in.

At the take-in, you see all the set pieces on stage for the first time. You should handle each piece. How much does it weigh? Should more than one person be assigned to carry it? Can it be picked up easily or should handles be added? Should wheels be built onto it or can it be moved on a dolly? Can it be carried in some other way than intended—upside down, sideways? Should it be cut in two, carried down in sections, and fastened together during the shift? Does it have sharp protruding edges that might be a safety hazard?

At the take-in, you also make changes in your scene diagrams to indicate the exact placement of each set piece as determined by the set designer. There may be still more changes during the dress rehearsal, and you must continue to update your diagrams and call changes to the attention of the crew via the chart.

- **Immediately following the take-in you should be ready to make your chart. The best way to do this is by using cutouts of paper for the set pieces. Move the paper set pieces as you calculate who should move what and when. It is a fairly complex problem, and errors are easy to make.**

When there is time and money to allow for a crew rehearsal, all of the errors may be worked out by repeating shifts until they are "greased." (Also see "Crew Briefing" later in this chapter.) But, as often happens, when crew rehearsal and dress rehearsal are simultaneous and the producer must justifiably use all available time for the cast and orchestra, which the audience will see and hear, rather than for the crew, which the audience should not see or hear, shifts must be corrected and "greased" by debriefing—that awkward process of trying to talk through what happened and visualize what changes should be made. The shift plot chart and the scene diagrams are invaluable in this process.

What sometimes happens in a union situation is that after Act I and part of Act II have consumed the entire dress rehearsal call, the producer opts to finish the rehearsal by putting the cast and orchestra on overtime; but the union crew members are sent home in order to save money. You then carry out the remaining shifts with any hands available and find yourself in the unenviable position of running some of the shifts with actual personnel involved for the first time on opening night—briefing union crew members during the scene for their moves at the end of the scene. Can you imagine the pressured chaos? The preciseness and accuracy of your shift plot chart are really significant factors in running those "no rehearsal" shifts.

The chart should be posted prior to the first crew rehearsal Crew members jot down their moves from the chart to avoid checking the chart between each scene shift. This can save a lot of walking if they have two consecutive moves up and down an aisle that is 180 degrees away from the aisle leading to the scene dock.

If you wish, you can issue each crew member a complete strike/set order (figure 11.2). This order would take the place of the individual crew member's notes and theoretically make it unnecessary to post the shift plot chart. Unfortunately, this type of strike/set order gets lost or left in other clothing. Then the crew member has to have some reference from which to copy. So you still need the chart.

TAKE ME ALONG

SET/STRIKE
ORDER for George Spelvin (IATSE 1)

ACT SCENE CUE	ENTER	SET/STRIKE/DO	EXIT
Preset		Set desk 2:00 Lay trolley track.	
I-2 "Oh, Please" reprise!!!!! blackout	First down one	Set porch rail 3:00 Strike desk 2:00 with Wayne	Up One
I-3 "I wish we still belonged to England." blackout	Second down Five	Set Lamp 4:30 PLUG IT IN!!!!!!!!!!! Strike porch rail (to rehearsal hall, not scene dock)	Up One

FIGURE 11.2 A Strike/Set Order with Typical Entries

Download from pearsonhighered.com/stern_ogrady

TAKE-IN

Coordinating with the scene designer and technical director, you share in supervision of the take-in. The *take-in* is a procedure in which all the set pieces and scenery are brought from storage, the shop, and the scene dock and set up on stage for the first time. This allows the scene designer, technical director, and you to assess your progress and problems in turning the scene designer's sketches into illusion.

- **Your responsibility is to get enough hands out to move the scenery quickly so that the take-in can be completed as soon as possible without wearing out the participants. As usual, many hands make light work.**

Your work during the take-in has been described earlier as part of your preparation for making the shift plot chart (figure 11.1). Again, you must personally handle all the set pieces and scenery so that you know what problems your crew members will encounter.

CREW BRIEFING

- **Generally, you brief the whole crew prior to their first rehearsal.**

1. Introduce crew members to one another and explain that you expect them to work as a team.
2. Cite general problems.
   a. Audience moving during blackouts.
   b. Hitting mikes with set pieces.
   c. Too much talking among crew during scenes, thus distracting audience.
   d. Necessity of crew members staying out of tent or backstage area during scenes.
   e. Necessity of having all props, set pieces, and scenery in the scene dock prior to the show, during intermissions, and after the show so that everything is out of sight of the audience and not a safety hazard.
3. Explain clock system (for round theater) or stage areas, if necessary, as well as set diagrams and shift plot chart.
4. Review safety rules.
   a. Don't run.
   b. Pointed set pieces should be moved base first so as not to spear audience members.
5. Review dress and behavior expected of crew.
   a. Don't mingle with audience.
   b. Don't call attention to oneself.

A handout to the crew is helpful in passing on important points that you've learned from experience (figure 11.3).

SCENE DOCK

The scene dock is the area in which sets and props are stored while waiting to be placed on stage (figure 11.4, page 162).

- **During the first crew rehearsal delegate the responsibility for arranging the scene dock.**

Perhaps the crew chief or a particularly alert crew member can do it. Depending on the space inside the scene dock, the arrangement of scenery and set pieces must be controlled so that everything is accessible when needed. If crew members need a set piece that is blocked by other units, they must climb over the other units and unnecessarily expend time and energy. The person placed in charge of arranging the scene dock should supervise the placement of returning sets just as carefully as you supervise their placement on stage.

- **Here are the factors to consider in designing your scene dock:**

1. The main aisle within the scene dock should not be wider than the widest aisle down to the stage, but just as wide.
2. The width of the set piece staging areas should be just slightly less than the widest aisle.

ATTENTION CREW

1. Shake hands with your new crew members. The crew is a team. Everyone must know everyone else – and be able to depend on him.

2. Think of the stage as a clock. The orchestra pit is at 12 o'clock. Aisles 1, 3, 5, 7, 9, and 11 are relative – one o'clock, three o'clock, etc.

3. The shift plot chart and diagrams of "before and after" positions of all props, set pieces and scenery are located above and on the prop table. Study them at your conv. If you don't understand, ask the SM, George Spelvin, or IATSE crew chief, Nate Spelvin, to explain it to you.

4. Follow these rules PLEASE!
   A. Don't run.
   B. Crouch at the bottom of aisles behind sight lines anticipating the blackout noiselessly.
   C. Watch out for audience moving on blackouts.
   D. Don't hit hanging mikes with tall units.
   E. Stay out of the tent when not doing your thing.
   F. Stash all props and units in scene dock prior to intermission and after show so that audience can't trip over them.
   G. Move pointed units base first so as not to stab audience members.
   H. Don't mingle with audience during intermission.
   I. Don't call attention to yourself.
   J. No talking or noise while you work or wait.
   K. Report any accident to the SM.

5. Please wear black polo shirts and black full length pants. Black tennis shoes and sox are available (free) from the costume mistress.

6. Maintain a clear aisle of 2′ in front of the prop table. Don't set any units on that area painted yellow.

7. Report any damage to any prop or unit to the property master or crew chief as soon as practical.

8. Check each night for red markings on the shift plot chart. Changes in your strike/set duties are indicated by the entire rectangle outlined in red. Study the change and discuss it with the crew chief. Red X's indicate errors made; red cautions advise you how to prevent repetitions of the error.

9. You are expected to check in with the gate man at 7:45 pm SHARP! Don't be late. In case of emergency, call the theater, 555 3558, and leave a message with the box office.

FIGURE 11.3 Handout of Instructions to Crew for Theater in the Round

3. The smaller aisles within the scene dock should be just wide enough for crew members to stand in.
4. Lines delineating the set piece storage areas should be painted on the ground.
5. Curtains masking the scene dock should open to the width of the widest aisle to the stage.
6. The scene dock should be as close as possible to the control booth so that the stage manager and the crew chief can communicate rapidly.
7. Set pieces for Act I, Scene 1 may be stored outside the tent and then brought into the main aisle of the scene dock if there are to be rehearsals on stage. Otherwise, they may be preset for the next performance after the audience departs.
8. Depending on the size and number of set pieces, they may have to be stored as far away as the shop or other storage areas and then rotated into the scene dock during scenes.
9. The scene dock should be covered in case of rain.

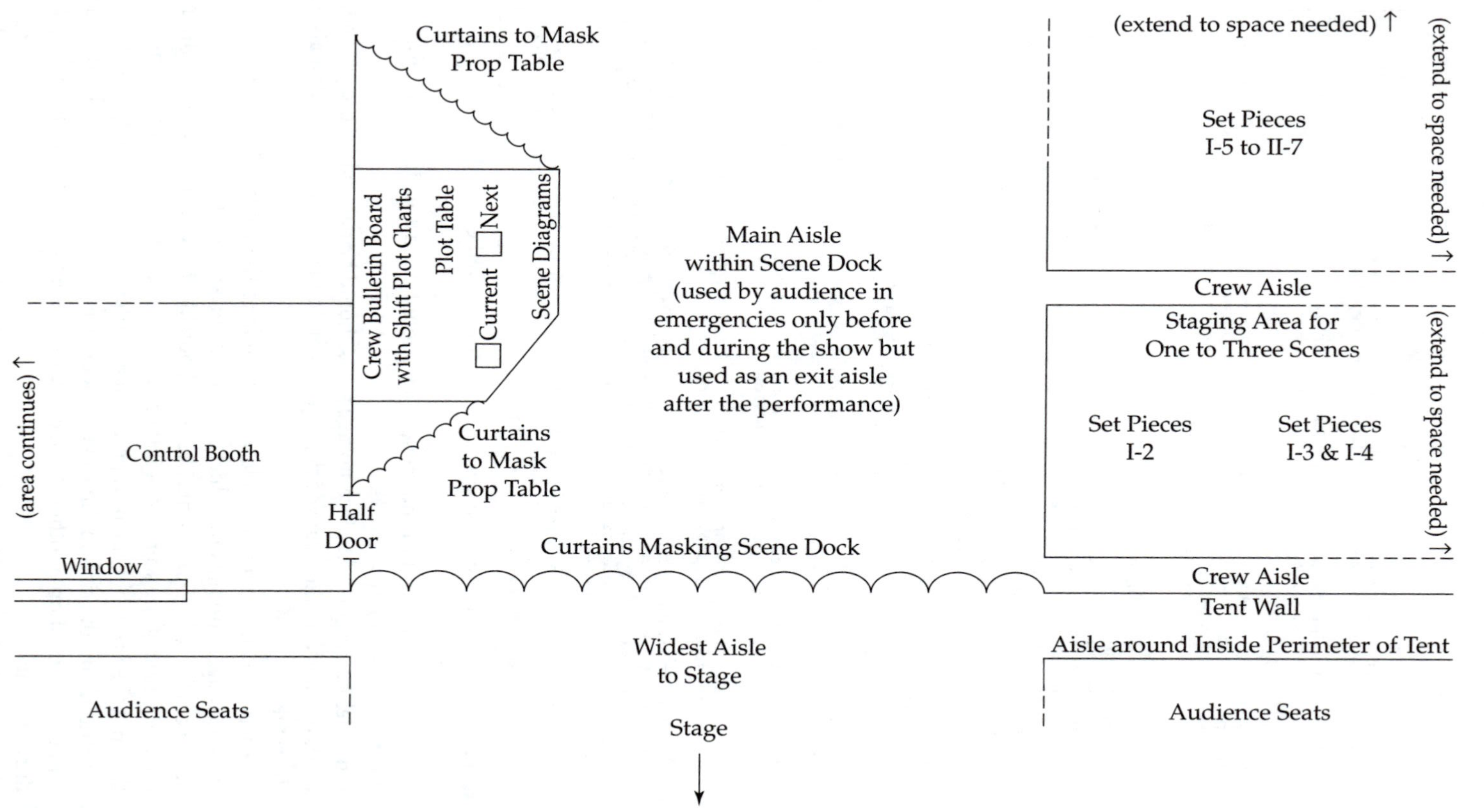

FIGURE 11.4 Scene Dock Layout

SHIFT INSPECTION

- **During the shift, you or your assistant should be on stage to supervise.**

If possible, do not assign yourself anything to carry in the shift. Keep your hands free to cope with emergencies. Attach a flashlight to your belt. Follow the crew onto the stage. Stay out from under their feet and watch carefully what they do. Check the placement of scenery, set pieces, and props. Make sure that every item from the previous scene is struck. Check that all actors who are to be discovered are in place. Check that all crew members have left the stage. For a round theater production, signal the booth, usually by blinking your flashlight from the stage, that you are ready for light and sound. Dash offstage or up the aisle as the scene commences. You should be the last person to leave the stage before the performance resumes.

Do you think you can do all of that in less than 30 seconds? Practice.

SCENE SHIFT DIAGRAMS

Diagrams of every scene can help if there are many scene shifts and many crew members. These diagrams are a visual aid that will help prepare crew members for their journeys down and up the aisles in a theater in the round (figures 11.5 and 11.6) or offstage to the scene dock. These sketches allow crew members to check their next move and refresh their memories as to the exact location and specifications for the placement of props, set pieces, and scenery.

Post these diagrams in the crew areas so that only two at a time are visible. Rotating your diagrams in "current" and "next" positions, rather than posting all of the diagrams at once, avoids confusion.

Let's look at an example. The following discussion refers to a theater-in-the-round production of *Show Boat*—Act I, Sc. 1, The Levee (figure 11.5), and Act I, Sc. 2, The Kitchen (figure 11.6).

The shift from Scene 1 to Scene 2 calls for the dropping of the hanging unit, the striking of two cotton bales, and the setting of a stool, table, and chair—not considering props. How will you assign your crew to accomplish this one shift? Study the diagrams for a moment.

Here are some considerations:

1. If there is an experienced flyman on the crew, he should drop the hanging piece.
2. Since the table is large, two crew members should be assigned to it, and the table should move down aisle 7, the widest aisle and the aisle closest to the scene dock, thus eliminating carrying the table around the outside perimeter of the theater.
3. It is generally most efficient for one crew member to both strike and set a piece. But in this situation, since there are so few set pieces to be moved, there will be hands available to do the change more efficiently by having one crew member strike only and one crew member set only.
4. Usually the fewer crew members used for a scene the better, as they have a tendency to run into one another in the dark.

In this case, a stool is to play where a cotton bale is now set. If one crew member is assigned to set the stool and strike the cotton bale, that crew member has to do the

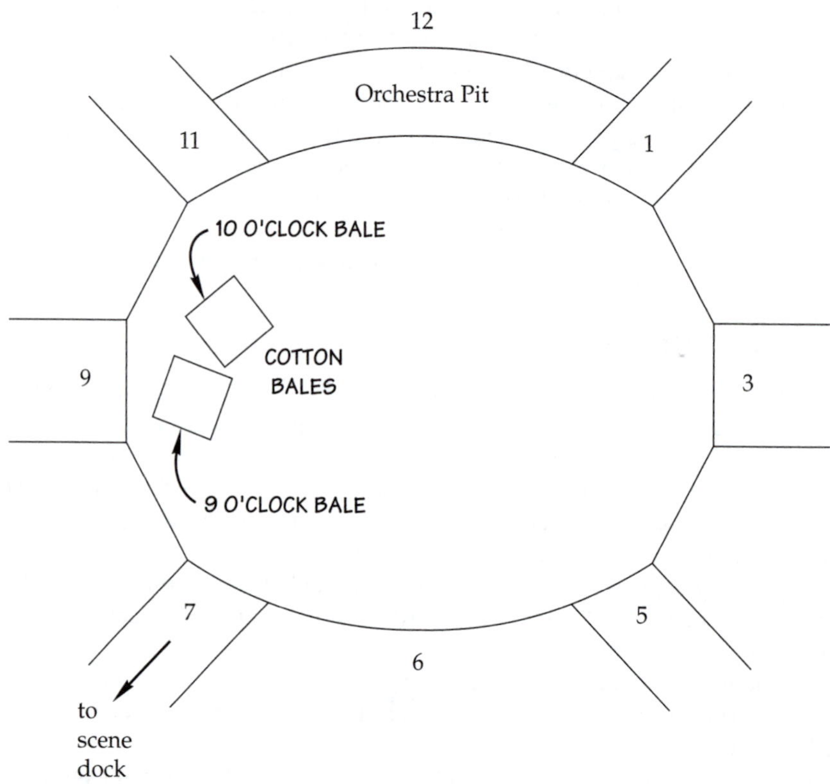

FIGURE 11.5 Scene Shift Diagram: First Scene

following: (1) run the stool down the aisle, (2) set it down, (3) pick up the cotton bale and move it aside, (4) pick up the stool and put it in place, (5) pick up the cotton bale and run it up the aisle. Yes, the move could be made this way, but evaluate the time and noise factors.

Or, you might have two crew members take care of the previously cited units, with an empty-handed striker going first to pick up the cotton bale ahead of the crew member who sets the piece that goes in its place. The striker might creep halfway down the aisle prior to the blackout and have the bale well offstage by the time the setter gets the piece down to the stage.

Or you may have the chair setter, not the crew member, carrying the stool, place the chair at 8 o'clock and strike the 9 o'clock bale, to be followed by the crew member who places the stool. (Note that it is the 9 o'clock bale, not the 10 o'clock bale, that is blocking the placement of the stool. A set piece is designated as the "X" o'clock set piece according to its most easily discernible, if not exact, clock position. Finer designations, such as the "9:35 cotton bale," just don't seem to work.)

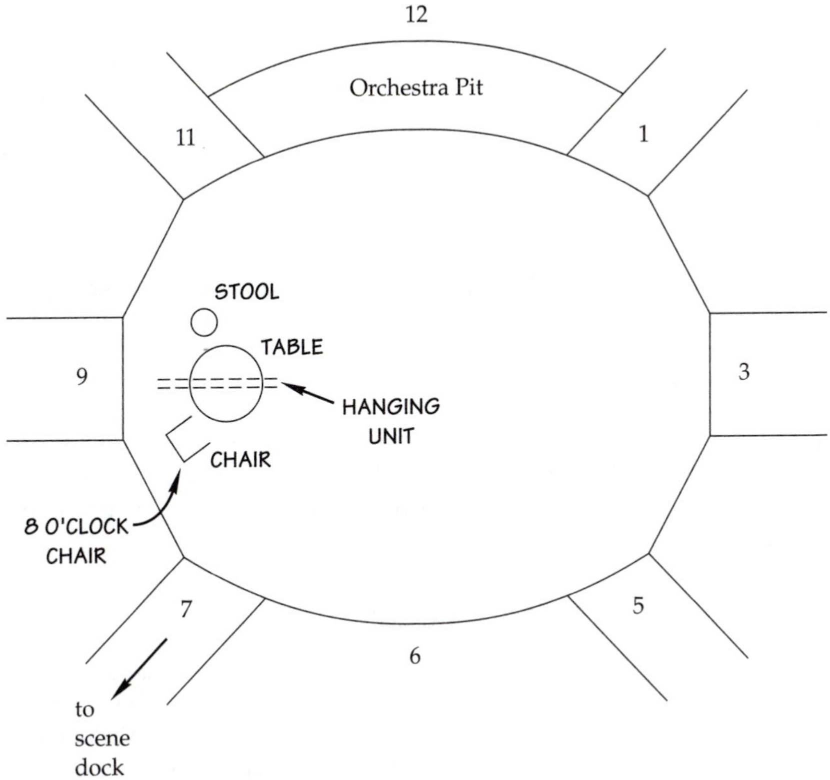

FIGURE 11.6 Scene Shift Diagram: Second Scene

> To stay neat and professional, I would never suggest shining a flashlight from the stage in the round to cue the booth. Too many customers can see the effort. Find a way to cue that is hidden from the audience.
>
> Leonard Auerbach
> *Associate Professor, Department of Theatre Arts*
> *State University of New York at Stony Brook*
>
> *[A green-gelled flashlight might be a bit less conspicuous. Or, if you can afford high tech, how about a voice-activated FM transmitter headset? Any other suggestions are welcome.]*

- **By now you can see that this simple-looking scene change needs thorough evaluation if it is to be done efficiently. These are the kinds of details that you will work out with diagrams and paper cutout set units as you make your shift plot chart.**

You must also cope with the movement of cast members. If at the end of I-1, the lights faded on two cast members standing next to the cotton bales, and, if in I-2, two different cast members are discovered seated on the stool and chair, then there is the additional consideration of four traveling cast members during the blackout.

The general practice is to specify certain aisles or wing exits for cast exits whenever possible. For entrances, cast members usually follow crew members down the other aisles. During rehearsals you may remind the director to channel cast via aisles reserved for cast exits. When this is not possible for any special reason, note it and accommodate unusual cast exits in planning your scene shifts.

It is practical to select the narrower aisles for cast exits, as these aisles are less convenient for moving large set pieces. Also consider the location of tent poles or other major fixtures in the aisles.

The importance of remembering exit blocking should be stressed to the cast. Obviously, cast members who dash up a darkened aisle in a rush to make a quick change, only to find themselves blocked, do not need to be told twice.

AUDIENCE CAUTION

Members of the audience are usually cautioned in the program to remain seated during blackouts. In many theaters in the round, the caution is repeated on the public address system prior to the performance. This responsibility usually rests with the house manager.

DISTRIBUTION OF SCENE DIAGRAMS

As soon as designs have been completed by the scene designer, scene diagrams should be made. Haste in this matter should take precedence over accuracy. In the course of building the set pieces and scenery there may be many changes. When the units are gathered all together on stage for the first time at the take-in and the scene designer sees what the set really looks like, as compared with the original perspective sketches, there are likely to be more changes, both in number and arrangement of units.

Yet if you wait until the take-in to make your diagrams, you might find yourself quite rushed. It is much more expedient to make corrections on diagrams with a bold marking pen than to wait for perfect initial copies.

Diagrams can be used at staff meetings to help everyone understand the sets for the coming production. The scene designer, technical director, master carpenter, property person, stage manager, and assistant stage manager should all be issued a complete set. The producer's secretary tucks still another set into company files for coming seasons when the show might be repeated.

The property person uses copies for preset diagrams of props.

The stage manager and the assistant stage manager use their copies to help work out their shift plot chart. They note the cast members discovered in each scene and the special-effects lighting that is initiated during rehearsals.

The technical director and the master carpenter use their diagrams to augment perspective sketches and line drawings to understand where units are to play.

The making of the diagrams is normally a responsibility of the scene designer (but they have been developed with the director's and your views in mind). You merely see to it that the diagrams are duplicated and distributed.

UPKEEP OF SETS

After opening night you are responsible for upkeep and minor emergency repair of scenery, set pieces, and lighting equipment. If, after opening night there are others on the staff (e.g., crew chief, technical director) who can carry out repair, then your responsibility is to inspect and report. You are not expected to reupholster a couch or overhaul a dimmer, but you are expected to patch, shore up, glue together, and generally keep the set fit for the eyes of the audience and the comfort and safety of the cast.

- **Have the tools on hand to carry out this function. Check to see that you have access to appropriate tools.**

FIGURE 11.7 A Well-Designed Tool Board. Orange paint was used to draw pictures of the tools on the pegboard wall. This allows student crews to return tools to the same place every time and ensures that needed tools are where they are supposed to be. It also allows Production Manager David Sword (pictured) of Santa Clara University's Department of Theatre and Dance to see if any tools have not been returned at the end of a work call.

Courtesy David Sword and Santa Clara University Department of Theatre and Dance.

FIGURE 11.8 Well-Organized Tool Cabinets. Anya Finke, Assistant Theater Manager, Cabrillo College Visual and Performing Arts Division, points to the staple guns shelf in a series of tool storage cabinets. The signs on the inside and outside of the cabinets allow student crew members to find equipment without opening all cabinets and replace equipment so that it can be found next time it's needed. Well-labeled locking cabinets are a good alternative to open tool boards when greater security is needed.

Courtesy Anya Finke and Cabrillo College Visual and Performing Arts Division.

In the absence of a staff technical director, you might find yourself responsible for the theater's tools. If so:

1. Provide a secure, locked area for storage. Disappearance and theft can thus be considerably reduced. Temporarily, the trunk of a car can serve for tool storage if there is no lockable space in the theater building.
2. No matter how small your tool collection is, it is desirable to make a tool board on which each tool is mounted and outlined or silhouetted. This allows you to determine easily which tools are not in place. It is also convenient since you can always expect to find your tools in the very same place (figures 11.7 and 11.8).
3. Painting all of your tools one color can also help to deter loss as there is no possible confusion as to whose tools they are.

In nonprofessional companies where the actors are called on to help build and paint scenery, save the company money by closely supervising the cleanup after work calls. This ensures that tools are returned, brushes properly cleaned, and paint cans tightly closed.

Close supervision in the proper use of tools can also prevent damage to the tools and to the users.

Keep on hand small quantities of the paints used on the set so that you can do touch-up work without having to buy fresh paint that matches the original. Sometimes this merely means having the wisdom to save nearly empty cans of paint until the close of the production. Date the paint cans.

SUGGESTED CLASSROOM EXERCISE

Using the scene shift charts (figures 11.5 and 11.6), have the class plan the shift and write on a chalkboard in the format shown in figure 11.1 what each member of a seven-person crew would do during the shift.

12

Running the Technical Rehearsal

If you want the present to be different from the past, study the past.
—Baruch Spinoza

The purpose of the technical rehearsal is to make a final confirmation and integration of all light and sound cues, special effects, scene changes, and curtain pulling. Every mechanical effect that should happen during the performance should happen at the technical rehearsal, and just the way it is to happen in performance.

It is during the "tech" that you will probably move from the director's side to your work area, usually in the wings, but possibly in a booth behind the audience. Advances in technology now allow stage managers to work anywhere they want to set their promptbooks.

Traditionally, the tech is the time when actors stand around, holding positions while lights are refocused, or endlessly repeating cue lines until sound cues are tightened and sound levels are set. It is usually a rehearsal at which overtime runs long and tempers run short. It need not be so.

The actors, who have rehearsed for weeks, meet the crew, who have possibly never rehearsed. The cast is impatient. They want to do their thing. They can't understand why the director, technical director, and stage manager are now giving their complete attention to the minutiae of mechanical matters that are totally insignificant compared to their performances. So think the actors. They can't understand why the crew can't get things right the first time.

You can most effectively shorten and sweeten the tech by holding a separate crew, and crew only, rehearsal of all the cues and scene changes prior to the tech—sometimes called a *paper tech*. Many tech problems can then be ironed out in advance. The crew will be able to do the work involved in smoothing out cues without the cast looking on.

- **The real purpose of the technical rehearsal should be coordination and integration of light, sound, special effects, and scene changes, not the initial attempt at each. The tech should *not* be used to finish the design or devise the effects. If this distinction can be kept in**

mind—and if time, money, and union rules will allow you to hold a separate crew-only rehearsal prior to the tech—you will be doing a great service to the director, producer, and play by supervising that separate crew rehearsal.

If this is not possible, your burden increases with respect to planning the tech, anticipating problems, and briefing crew members.

The perfect tech is one in which the actors can have the benefits of a run-through while all technical aspects are polished as the play is in progress or during breaks and intermissions.

- **This calls for good communications. If the director can talk to you, as well as the technical director, lighting designer, costume designer, and other staff members without noisily interrupting the tech, it will go more smoothly.**

Sometimes the seating arrangement of the staff can help. If staff members who do not absolutely have to be backstage will sit in the audience in the row in front of the director, the director can simply lean forward to whisper comments. All staff members should have paper and pencil. You should provide them with adequate light so that they can take notes.

Since you have moved to your work area, be it backstage or booth, the director must be able to talk to you without running or shouting. Set up whatever communication equipment is necessary.

Many theaters do not have adequate communications. Sometimes you can improvise. Two prop phones in working order, sound wire, and a battery can be hooked up to give you a link. Of course, headsets would be an improvement.

You will usually need to talk to the lighting board technician, the sound technician, follow-spot operator, curtain puller, and others during the tech and during performances. Ideally, you should be able to talk to them via headsets. You should also be able to speak to the dressing rooms and the green room without leaving your work area. (A PA system that would allow you to reach the entire audience from your work area in case of an emergency, monitor equipment enabling cast to hear the performance in the dressing rooms and green room, and a phone would round out most of your communications needs.) In recent years backstage communications have improved in educational and professional theaters, but don't take for granted that you will find optimal equipment in every theater where you work. Be prepared to improvise.

When planning for and scheduling your tech rehearsal, plan to give the staff, cast, and crew as much time as possible to work together. Any business other than the prime function of the tech should be relegated to other rehearsals. Directors should accept the fact that the tech is not the time to reblock or polish acting performances.

Cast members should be warned well in advance that they must expect to work late and that they must stay through to the end of the rehearsal.

There is a tendency for the crew to be concerned with their personal comforts and accommodations during the tech. Yes, it is important that the technician on the follow spot have a light in order to follow book. Yes, a comfortable chair is desirable, perhaps a pillow, too. And it would be worth having a phone line so the two of you can talk to one another. But the period of the tech is not the time to take care of these things. They should be seen to before or after, but not while a cast of 20 and staff of 10 are waiting to rehearse.

- **If you haven't already done so, just prior to tech is a good time for a backstage safety inspection. Walk the backstage area and check all entrance/exit areas. Place white gaffers tape, glow tape, and blinking diodes along steps and platforms that might be missed in the darkness backstage. Apply safety tape to the corners where flats butt and on any light poles and low hanging objects.**

Don't forget a blackout check. This is the time to discover unwanted spills from backstage lights left on, in the grid and elsewhere. It's good theater etiquette to warn everyone in the theater before going to blackout check.

Communications, lighting, seating, and other crew necessities and comforts should be anticipated and arranged. If these things cannot be worked out at a separate crew rehearsal, give your crew an early call for the tech and take care of these things before the cast and staff arrive.

SPIKING DEVISES

"Blink-it" and "Quarter Marker" beacons are tiny LED (light-emitting diode) lights that attach to batteries. They're easier to see than glow tape so they improve the safety factor when marking the edges of equipment such as lighting trees, booms, and monitor speakers, as well as stairs, doorways, railings, and the edges of platforms. The Blink-it is less than 1 × 3.5 × 3.5 inches and attaches to a standard 9-volt battery. The Quarter Marker is less than the size of a quarter and works with a lithium battery (figure 12.1). Both can be attached almost anywhere with gaffers tape, Velcro, or poster gum. By attaching to the stage with the LED facing upstage, dancers can find their marks in the dark and the audience can't see the lights. For further information about Illumineering products, try Nifty-Gadgets.com or sales@Nifty-Gadgets.com.

FIGURE 12.1 The Quarter Marker. LED beacons can help get set pieces, actors, and dancers on their marks in the dark and also warn of hazards backstage. Each Quarter Marker can be set to emit either red or green light.

Courtesy Paul Puppo, CEO Illumineering, IATSE stagehand, San Francisco.

A Pre-Tech Checklist

- White and/or glow tape on all level changes, lip of the stage, offstage steps/ramps, lighting instruments hanging low in the wings, floor speakers, and other protruding hazards
- Padding on low door frames, on ends of pipes on flying pieces, or on bottoms of cycs/scrims, stage weights in pathways, sharp corners on moving pieces, and other possible hazards
- Running lights in the wings and crossovers
- Working lights in stairwells, hallways, dressing rooms, outside alleys
- Stage, wings, and company areas swept and mopped (and DRY)
- Emergency exits, fire curtain switch, fire extinguishers (quick meeting with the cast to point out exits at the beginning of the first day in the theater according to OSHA rules) (osha.gov, or your state's website; in California, dir.ca.gov/dosh/)
- Rug runners over cables on the floor, down the stairs to the dressing rooms, under water stations or other slippery places, and on any hollow ramps to the stage; look for any other places that might cause cast or crew to trip (glycerin spray used in the hair room once caused a problem with slipping outside that room; there's a rug there now)
- Cables bundled and either hung high or taped to the floor
- Motors, fog machines, strip lights, and anything else on the floor in the wings either blocked off or clearly marked as dangerous
- Signs for clear crossovers/paths to wings
- Stair unit for access to the stage from the house during tech so no one tries to jump up or down
- Nonslick stage (especially for a musical or on a rake—mop with Coke or Slip-no-More) (many stages no longer use Coke because sugar contents brings ants; if you do use it, add one can to the content of a standard mop pail)
- Pretest all special effects (pyro, fog, strobes)
- Flashlights for backstage crew
- Recently stocked first-aid kit and ice packs
- Doctor and hospital numbers posted near a phone backstage

Jill (Johnson) Gold
PSM
Pasadena Playhouse, Pasadena, California

Some Tips from a Hollywood 99-Seat Equity Waiver Theater

- Above all, STAY CALM. It's not really the long hours and the repetition and the crazy pace that make tech rehearsals hellish—it's the way it grinds on people's nerves. So if you stay calm and remember that it's not the end of the world, things will be easier. The best stage managers I've worked with are the ones who make it a point to stay incredibly cool and loose during high-tension situations like tech. That calm steadiness can really work to defuse potential flare-ups between people who are at the end of their figurative ropes.

  (This isn't such a big deal in high-end professional situations where there's enough money and time to get a production done well, but in my experience, most theater [in LA at least] is underfunded and under-rehearsed due to budget and time

(continued)

constraints, and that can wear on people, so tech is usually where things gets sticky, because nobody's really ready for it to start. But tech in low-budget theater is also where the magic can happen, because it's an opportunity for people to come together to pool their creativity and inventiveness to make a great show out of next to nothing. It's all about how you look at it, I guess.)

- Remember that things are supposed to go wrong. It's nobody's fault. That's why it's tech! Tech is for finding out where the problems are, or where they will be, so that you can fix them. Don't waste your time looking for someone to blame—just work together to find out how to make it better next time.
- Have fun. I'm not saying tech is a party, but it helps to keep a good sense of humor. It just helps get you through those stressful situations, like at 11:30 p.m. when you know you've got to release the company in 30 minutes but you have 20 more cues to get through and the director is yelling at the sound technician and the actors are getting tired and bitchy—it's nice to be able to find the humor in those situations, chuckle to yourself, and then calmly but forcefully call everyone back to the business at hand.
- My favorite stage managers make sure there's food and other conveniences at tech. It's a little thing, but it's so huge to go that extra mile and take care of your company like that. I work with a fantastic producer named Elizabeth Tobias who says, "I don't believe in tech without food," so she's always got pizza or bagels or something lying around somewhere in the theatre for people to pick at. And her company members are always a little happier.
- By the way, I'm sure these are really great things for all theater people to keep in mind during tech, not just stage managers. Actors, directors, designers, and technicians could all benefit from staying calm, eating well, and having fun during tech (especially actors!). But since stage managers are sort of the "morale cheerleaders" of a production, it helps if they are the ones spearheading the effort to keep calm and loose.

Olivia Killingsworth
ASM and Actor
Met Theatre, Hollywood

Notes on Tech from a Nonprofit Equity Theater

Tech is my favorite part of the process. It's the most challenging. And the most crowded. All of the designers, the director, the cast and crew, all come together for the first time. So the pressure to make every minute of rehearsal time count is greater than ever. Thirty-eight people are in the room with you, waiting to sing a song, fly in a tree, see what the ballgown looks like under lights, or run the finale quick-change in time.

You must think even further ahead, and do that thinking for more people. You must be completely ready for the day. You plan meticulously. And you must be just as ready to shift all your priorities at a moment's notice.

For me, if it's going to go awry, it's going to blow up in the 30 minutes just before rehearsal. I once found out during half hour, halfway through a tech, that one of my interns had left—the state. She wrote us a note, and then left. But she did leave her cue sheets, and her notes were clear.

Sense of humor is the skill you need most for this job.

In planning meticulously, a lot of paperwork is generated.

1. There is a list of our goals for each day of tech, so that all of the production departments and the running crews know how far we plan to go, and which scenery we don't need today, but will need first thing tomorrow.

2. All of the crews must have their run sheets, telling them what they do and when and where.
3. The ASMs must have sheets noting entrances and exits for all the actors, and their props.
4. The calling script must have all the rough cues I've been given by the director throughout the rehearsal process, and light cues as well, depending on how your lighting designer works.

The thing I almost always forget is laying down glow tape and spiking as much furniture as I can ahead of time.

Have the god mic ready for the director and choreographer, so they can talk to and be heard by everyone easily. Have a great company manager who puts out bowls of M&Ms and fresh fruit to munch on. It all helps people stay focused and in good humor.

And then, with all these tools and people in place, you get the joy of calling that first cue, "Houselights to 50 percent." And we're off!

Kathleen J. Parsons
PSM, Rubicon Theatre Company
Ventura, California

Advice on How to Survive the Tech (from a Las Vegas Show SM)

After working the tech as stage manager for over 30 shows, here's what I've learned. First, plan each tech rehearsal very carefully. Second, keep your sense of humor. Third, do not forget about the company.

As stage managers we, of course, plan all aspects of a tech carefully. The most important thing is the schedule. You must accommodate all department needs. Make sure they are all included on the schedule. It is important to distribute the schedule to everyone and keep everyone updated with changes. The schedule becomes even more important when you work with union cast and crew. Make sure you are familiar with all union rules that may affect your schedule.

We also need to plan for things NOT to work. Plan to get things done even when things go wrong. Be creative on the fly if so needed. For example, if part of a set is not ready or does not work, move on with what does work. I once had a set that did not work for the first three days of a four-day tech. The crew would go out and manually move what would eventually be automated. That way, the cast, director, and designers had an idea of what would happen when the set did work. This also meant that I had to schedule an added rehearsal for the crew and one for set moves when it was working.

The days are long during tech. Make sure that as the stage manager you stay alert and keep rehearsal moving. You will need to get as much rest as possible before a series of tech rehearsals.

Keep the whole process moving. Always remember your end goal is opening night and the run of the show. It is easy to get bogged down in what is not happening during the tech. Focus on what IS getting done and what you can do next.

No matter how much experience you have, no matter how much training you have, a sense of humor works wonders in tense situations.

The cast, like everyone else, gets tired in a tech. It's important that they understand the purpose of the tech. Talk with the cast prior to the tech rehearsal each day and tell them what the director would like to accomplish for the day. See how they are doing during breaks if you are able. If the cast gets ignored for the "technical aspect" of the show they

(continued)

can make your day much more difficult. Keeping them informed about what's happening goes a long way.

I used to hate the tech. As I did more shows, I came to realize that the tech is the most challenging and exciting part of making theater. I love the responsibility of making all of the elements of a piece come together.

Heidi Swartz
SM, A New Day at the Colosseum
Las Vegas, Nevada

Tech from an Educational Theater's Perspective

In my experience, first tech rehearsals are often very frustrating for my students, as it's a bit like "wrangling cats." Various members of the production team are so hard at work on their individual final preparations that it becomes easy for them to lose track of time, therefore losing focus on getting the tech rehearsal started on time. The stage manager must understand that a strong, clear voice of leadership is just as crucial, if not more crucial, to a tech rehearsal than in the rehearsal room. I tell my stage managers to broadcast call times to everyone, just as they would to actors before the show, and to check in with each department just as a NASA flight director would do to get a clear for takeoff; this keeps everyone aware of how much time is left before "go" and reminds department heads that the stage manager is indeed relying on them to finish before they can begin the tech.

Stephanie Moser Goins
Instructor of Stage Management, University of Oklahoma
Norman, Oklahoma
Former Freelance AEA Stage Manager

It is a good practice for you to run the tech by yourself, giving all cues to cast and crew as if it were opening night. If the show can be run as a run-through, do so, stopping only when technical problems make it impossible to go on. In the case of a heavy technical show, you may wish to skip from technical effect to technical effect instead of running through. In either case, it is important that you have all of your cues clearly marked in your promptbook and all supporting paperwork—scene shift diagrams (pages 164–165), shift plot charts (pages 156–157), light tech's lighting sheet, and so forth—distributed and reviewed with those concerned prior to the tech.

In some cases, you may start your tech rehearsal as a run-through and then, seeing that you are falling behind, skip through the remainder of the show from tech effect to tech effect.

If time permits, it is desirable to schedule two technical rehearsals as a safety factor.

- **The technical rehearsal is one of the biggest tests of your ability, for it is the one single rehearsal where you can save the cast and staff the greatest amount of time and energy.**

There is no such thing as a cue-to-cue technical rehearsal in opera. The ASMs and volunteers, who have been told in advance not to wear white or black, "walk lights." The cue-to-cue is done with them and not the cast. The "walk lights" call precedes the technical rehearsal. During the technical rehearsals the lighting designer will smooth out the lighting cues as the show goes along.

David Grindle
Production Stage Manager
The Atlanta Opera

Few fledgling stage managers have the good sense to rig a fail-safe cue light—two bulbs at the receiving end of the cable so that if one blows the other will probably still function.

Leonard Auerbach
Associate Professor, Department of Theatre Arts
State University of New York at Stony Brook

We lead a group of student stage managers who take out professional stage managers for dinner just to talk about working as a pro. State University of New York at Purchase is a really strong technical theater school. We try to enrich our studies in various ways. We've gone up to Boston to shadow the *Movin' Out* first national tour's SM.

Jazmin Hupp
Sarah Penland
Former Stage Management BFA students
State University of New York at Purchase

SUGGESTED CLASSROOM EXERCISE

Ask one student to shadow a stage manager during a technical rehearsal and report to the class what the SM did, what problems arose, and how those problems were overcome.

13

Running the Show

There are three kinds of people in the world—those who make things happen, those who watch things happen, and those who say, "What happened?"

—Anonymous

Now comes the easy part—the production phase.

The director tells you that it's all yours. There's an audience out there. All you have to do is run the show. You have some long-range responsibilities (Chapter 15), but your basic functions should now be firmly under control.

An interesting difference between new and experienced stage managers is that the new stage manager thinks of running the show as the most difficult and most demanding part of the job, whereas the experienced stage manager thinks of it as the most relaxing part. Perhaps the reason is that the experienced stage manager has built up work habits of thorough preparation.

CHECKLISTS

- **Precurtain, intermission, and postproduction checklists will help you remember all the little things to do. These checklists should be placed into your promptbook facing the first page of dialogue and following the last page of dialogue of each act.**

A good approach is to think of someone replacing you immediately. Write out your list as if you were telling someone else what to do. List the items in the sequence in which you perform them. Don't be afraid to be too detailed (figures 13.1 and 13.2).

Leave space between entries so that you can make last-minute additions in sequence.

When you arrive at the theater, open your promptbook to your checklist and mentally check off each entry as it is accomplished. That way, when you call "places," there won't be that aggravating question in the back of your mind: "What have I forgotten?"

In stock companies where you do a new show every week or two weeks, each day may bring both a rehearsal and a performance. Instead of prerehearsal

PRECURTAIN CHECKLIST

7:00 P.M.
( ) Turn on air conditioning.
Dusk
( ) Turn on marquee.
7:30
( ) Check crew present, call late ones.
( ) Conduct light, sound check (incl. bell, buzzer).
( ) Unlock props, place on prop tables.
( ) Unlock stage door, sweep alley, empty butt cans.
( ) Unlock dressing rooms, turn on lights, check paper supplies.
7:55
( ) Final check of stage: sweep it, put all set pieces in place and all discovered props in place, set hands of clock (UR) to 3:45, and check that it's wound.
( ) Check all set pieces and props in correct positions backstage, ready for changes.
( ) Turn off work light, masking tape over switch.
( ) Bring in curtain warmers, house lights, cue start of taped music.
( ) Turn house over to manager.
8:00
( ) Give half-hour call, check sign-in sheet (post new one on Wednesdays), chat with cast, close curtain to green room.
8:05
( ) Call late actors.
8:15
( ) Turn on stage monitor, give 15-minute call, check monitor working in dressing rooms.
8:25
( ) Give 5-minute call, blink marquee lights.
8:30
( ) Await house manager's signal to call places (or give hold to cast)—call places.

FIGURE 13.1 Detailed Precurtain Checklist and Schedule

and precurtain checklists, you will want to write out daily checklists covering your procedure for each day.

Your checklists, even if geared to a specific production rather than a season of plays, would be good material to pass on to the person who succeeds you.

> You must check off on an overlay or on a tear-off sheet or some other device. That way, if interrupted, you have a record of what you have not yet done.
>
> Leonard Auerbach
> *Associate Professor, Department of Theatre Arts*
> *State University of New York at Stony Brook*

120	Walk House Check with Martha	
90	Check Sign-Ins Check with Martha	
60	CALL: **HOUR** Check Front of House	Q1 WORKS WARM
50	Main In	
45	Open House CALL: **HOUSE OPEN**	
30	CALL: **HALF HOUR** CALL: **VALUABLES** Check with Martha Check with Michael	
15	CALL: **FIFTEEN TO TOP OF ACT I** Check Front of House	
10	CALL: **TEN TO TOP OF ACT I**	
8	CALL: **PLACES** Mr. Barret Mr. Cokorinos Mr. Thomsen Chorus Supers	
5	CALL: **FINAL CALL TO PLACES** **MAESTRO TO STAGE RIGHT**	
2	**WARN HOUSE HALF AND OUT**	
0:30	CALL: **HOUSE HALF?** Mo. Cue Light ON	

House Out
Stand By LQs

Q2 WFS↑   Q3 WFS↓ Preset   WORKS OUT

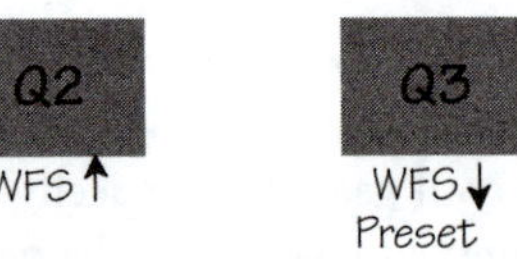

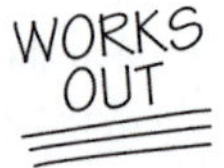

FIGURE 13.2 *Cosi Fan Tutte* Preshow Checklist/Calls. "Main in" is curtain closed. "Valuables call" allows cast members to store watches, wallets, and other valuables in large freezer bags that are kept in a secure place. Post-it notes are used for cues in the checklists, libretto, and score. Light cues are in green; places cues are in blue.

Courtesy David Grindle, PSM, the Atlanta Opera.

A few items on your checklists deserve special comment.

Sweeping the stage, including the backstage walkways between the dressing rooms and the stage, is your responsibility. You may assign this task to someone, but make sure that it's done. Following the sweeping, inspect for nails, screws, stage pegs, splinters, loose edges of rugs, or any other hazards. Only when you are willing to walk barefoot across the stage is the stage ready for the cast.

Besides checking to make sure that the worklight is off prior to curtain, check that it is on when needed and that it is on as fast as possible in order to expedite scene changes and to enable the cast to leave the stage safely (page 155). Remember that the bright stage lights will leave the cast temporarily blinded and that they will need the worklight in order not to trip over set pieces on their way out. Even if the worklight is controlled by a separate switch, and not through the dimmer board, place the cue for it in your promptbook as if it were any other lighting effect. Call for it in the same manner that you cue all other effects.

GIVING CUES

- **To run the show, you must signal or cue lights, sound, special effects, and curtain, and thus coordinate these elements with the action of the play, making them happen at precisely the right time.**

Your light pencil lines that identify cues (page 21) allow you to call the cues during rehearsals. Pinpoint them with the guidance of the director (page 103). During the technical rehearsal, or just prior to it (page 170), confirm the final cues. In your promptbook with bold marking pen lines, number the light cues and letter the sound cues (figure 13.3). Now you are ready to give the cues to the lighting technicians, master electrician, sound technicians, curtain puller, and special-effects people.

Following your script through performance, just as you did at rehearsals, give the cues clearly, firmly, and with certainty. If you do not feel clear, firm, and certain, then pretend you do. The new stage manager can be compared to a person just learning to drive a car: the new driver is afraid to step on the gas pedal. The experienced stage manager, on the other hand, gives cues with the authority of a marine drill sergeant, but in a whisper.

> I mark cues in my prompt script when they come up during rehearsals, but I don't number cues until they are given to me by designers. Occasionally we might have time for a paper tech prior to the first tech and the numbering can occur then. Otherwise it's done at the tech. I will number rail cues on my own since I am the one generating that cue sheet, but I do wait until just before tech to create that cue sheet so that it does not have to be continuously updated during the rehearsal period. Too many changes can happen during rehearsals. Although I follow any system the lighting designer uses, I let it be known that I prefer that Act I start with 1 and Act 2 start with 200. If there are added cues, they are usually point cues (37.1) because lettered cues don't go into most computer boards. I like the sound cues to be lettered (A for the cue, A1 for level change, Ax for the out cue), and I will usually request that of the sound designer. If there are projection cues or another set of cue numbers is needed for something else, I like to start with 500 or a number past any of the electrics cues.
>
> I usually sit right next to the lighting designer at the tech table, and when a new cue or effect is being built I hear it on the headset. The designer will double-check with me that I heard the number and got the correct placement. If cues have been done as work notes outside of tech time, I will meet with a designer just before the tech rehearsal and get any notes of added or deleted cues at that time.
>
> Cari Norton
> *AEA Freelance Stage Manager*

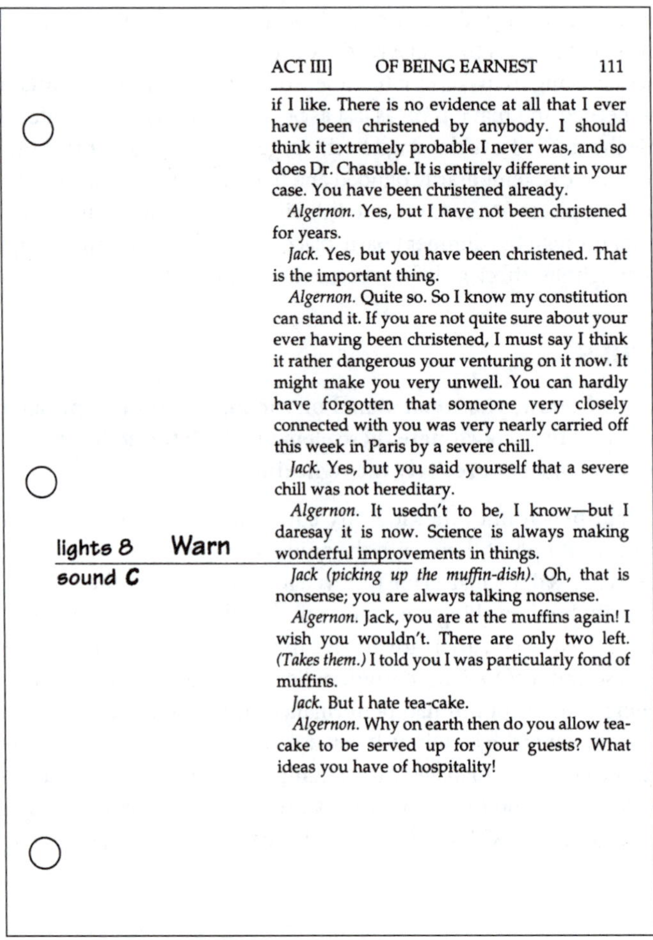

ACT III] OF BEING EARNEST 111

if I like. There is no evidence at all that I ever have been christened by anybody. I should think it extremely probable I never was, and so does Dr. Chasuble. It is entirely different in your case. You have been christened already.

Algernon. Yes, but I have not been christened for years.

Jack. Yes, but you have been christened. That is the important thing.

Algernon. Quite so. So I know my constitution can stand it. If you are not quite sure about your ever having been christened, I must say I think it rather dangerous your venturing on it now. It might make you very unwell. You can hardly have forgotten that someone very closely connected with you was very nearly carried off this week in Paris by a severe chill.

Jack. Yes, but you said yourself that a severe chill was not hereditary.

Algernon. It usedn't to be, I know—but I daresay it is now. Science is always making wonderful improvements in things.

Jack (picking up the muffin-dish). Oh, that is nonsense; you are always talking nonsense.

Algernon. Jack, you are at the muffins again! I wish you wouldn't. There are only two left. *(Takes them.)* I told you I was particularly fond of muffins.

Jack. But I hate tea-cake.

Algernon. Why on earth then do you allow tea-cake to be served up for your guests? What ideas you have of hospitality!

FIGURE 13.3 Final Cues and "Warns" Confirmed in Script with Bold Marking Pen

Generally, the cues are "warn," "standby," and "go." A cue number or letter typically accompanies the "warn" part of the cue so that the technician will know which cue to execute: "Warn sound C."

If there are sound and light cues in the same general area, you need to clarify your "warn": "Warn lights number eight, sound cue C."

The "warn" is usually given one and a half to two minutes before the cue is to be executed. This is usually a half to a full page before the cue.

The "warn" should be given in enough time for the technicians to reach their equipment for the cue, check the cue on their plot or cue sheet, and give their total attention to executing the cue. If a cue requires extensive preparation—e.g., the changing of reels or cassettes in a tape recorder—then you might wish to write a separate tech cue into your promptbook on the page prior to the "warn" (or immediately following the previous cue) to remind the technician to do this.

The "standby" portion of the cue should precede the "go" by five to ten seconds, giving the technicians enough time to place their hands in position, flex their muscles, and rivet their eyes and ears on you to await the "go." Sometimes the verbal standby is accompanied or replaced by raising the hand.

The "go" can be given verbally or by lowering the hand.

The exact nature of your cues will depend on the communications equipment backstage, your proximity to your technicians, and their ability to see you and watch their equipment at the same time.

If several cues occur in a fast sequence, and there is no time to "warn" in between them, you will "warn" and give "standby" for the series. Then give only your "go," or signal for "go," once for the whole series. If it is an intricate series of cues, it is possible that you will want to rehearse it carefully, so that the technicians can get a feeling for the timing or rhythm of the series.

Again, all cues—warn, standby, and go—are given clearly, firmly, and with certainty. **Calling cues is another of your sacred duties, *a sine qua non*.** You must be able to coordinate lights, sound, special effects, and curtain, and you do it by cueing.

Don't avoid this responsibility, and don't delegate it. Even if the light and sound technicians can see and hear the cues and follow book just as well as you can, it is still your job.

Immediately check the result of each cue that you give.

If you are fortunate enough to be working in a booth in back of the audience, you will have a good view of every effect. But if you are in the wings, arrange for a view, resorting to peepholes, mirrors, or TV monitors, if necessary.

If the cue is not immediately followed by the anticipated effect, you must be programmed as follows:

1. Don't panic.
2. Did the technician recognize and execute the cue you gave?
3. Is there a mechanical failure?
4. Is there anything you can do to alleviate this problem? If yes, do it. If not, as uncomfortable as you may be, restrain yourself.

This is true for light, sound, special-effect, and scenic cues.

One of my pet peeves—only a strong personal preference—is the necessity of using "standby" in calling cues. Once the warnings are spaced correctly in good tech rehearsals, the next order should be "Cue 48…Go." The reiteration of the cue number should serve as a sufficient standby. There is much less room for misunderstanding.

Leonard Auerbach
Associate Professor, Department of Theatre Arts
State University of New York at Stony Brook

When calling a show I use just a "standby" and "go." If there has been a really long time between cues I might also give an early "warn." (I will usually ask the operator if she would like one.) On really busy shows I find there is sometimes no need for the "standby" for electrics because there isn't even time for the operator to take his finger away from the board. On the national tour of *Show Boat,* I gave standbys to the rail and deck, but not to electrics.

Cari Norton
AEA Freelance Stage Manager

(continued)

[Rather than observing tradition, many stage managers discuss the cueing sequence with their light and sound-board operators and use the sequence that they mutually agree will work most effectively.]

There's a temptation to reach over the technician's shoulder to push a button or throw a switch. **Keep firmly in mind that the audience is much less aware of gradual changes than abrupt ones.** Bringing in the correct effect slowly is usually more desirable than immediate correction, which tends to call attention to the correction.

In the case of a mechanical lighting problem that cannot be immediately corrected, the most important principle to remember is the most basic and obvious one: The audience must see the actors.

Example

You give a cue to bring up an area. The area comes up slowly to full and a lamp blows. What should you do? Give the actors any light possible, short of shining a flashlight at them from the wings. You might bring up adjacent areas in the hopes that the actors will find some of it or gain from the spill. You might throw on a work light. As last resort you might even have to bring up the house lights. If and when the actors have enough light to continue the scene, then see how to remedy the problem.

The continuance of the play takes precedence over the quality of the lighting.

Mistakes occur in every line of work. Don't allow an error on your part to prevent you from executing all subsequent cues correctly. Don't allow errors to compound. Calm down, compose yourself, and get the next cue right.

Musical Cues

- **In musical comedy, opera, and ballet, it is often necessary that the stage manager read music and take light cues from a note in the score rather than from a word in the script.**

In such cases the stage manager has a copy of the score and marks the cues in the score, spacing "warn," "standby," and "go" as described earlier with respect to the time needed to alert the technicians. The stage manager might write a "reminder" cue in the promptbook to go to the score for the next cue, including the page number of the score. Or the stage manager might place the score pages on which there are cues into the promptbook.

If you do not read music, tell your director and don't attempt to fake it. With the director's help you can sometimes get around your deficiency by using a stopwatch. Rather than listening for a note, time how far into the music that note occurs and then take the cue from the stopwatch. If there is a fast series of cues from subsequent notes, substitute mental counts for listening to notes. Sometimes you can look for concurrent cast movement rather than notes from which to take your cues. These are all cumbersome methods, and learning to read music is preferable—and usually a prerequisite for stage management jobs in opera and ballet (figure 13.4).

FIGURE 13.4 Last Page of Score for *Samson et Dalila*. Notes given by the director prior to rehearsals are written on the score. During rehearsals and tech, the PSM adds transparent Post-it notes to indicate placement and actual cue. At the top ("SR fast to full"), the director wanted the stage-right fan, which was blowing the curtains in Dalila's apartment, to go to full speed quickly. The Post-it note ("Fans to 10") was the actual cue.

Courtesy David Grindle, PSM, the Atlanta Opera.

CUEING EQUIPMENT

Should you use verbal and hand signals, or should you use a handheld blinker light? Or should you wire in sets of red and green lights with buttons at the stage manager's desk so that you can communicate with your technicians? Some cue lights are only on/

off devices where "on" means "standby." When the light is turned off by the stage manager, that's the "go." Or should you wear TV-type headsets so that you can talk to, and listen to, your technicians?

Names in backstage communications are Clear-Com, Electronic Theatre Controls (ETC), Motorola, Nady, Sennheiser, Shure, and Telex (see Appendix D for contact information).

In voice communication, the choices are wired and wireless. Wired beltpacks (figure 13.5) require jack plates or mic cables. Wireless units are more expensive but offer greater freedom of movement. Clear-Com claims that its latest wireless systems (i.e. Tempest2400) have overcome the problems of interference formerly associated with wireless. "Clear-Com's Tempest models and HME DX Series Line use Frequency Hopping Spread Spectrum technology (FHSS) to cleverly keep our signal from either interfering, or being interfered with."

Signaling lights used in ETC's Cue Light Controller system use jumbo LEDs with more than 100 individual LEDs contained in one lamp so as to prevent burnout that might disrupt a performance. A portable panel is available so that cues may be given from the house during tech and dress rehearsals (etcconnect.com).

Theatre Projects Consultants is working with theater builders, producers, and stage managers to improve the design and utility of both the Cue Light Controller system and the Worklight Master Controller system (which regulates work lights, house lights, and blue running lights throughout a theater) (tpcword.com).

There is no best system. It's a question of what will work best for your theater. Expensive headsets won't improve the quality of your performance any more than will closed circuit TV in the dressing rooms so that offstage actors can watch the performance. More important than your cueing equipment is your consistency in using the system of cues described here.

FIGURE 13.5 Clear-Com's RS-601 Single Channel Belt Pack (with a CC-95 single muff headset). The RS-601 uses standard microphone cable. Theaters may be pre-wired with jack plates on the wall, or cables may connect the belt packs with each other and the intercom main station/system power supply. The Ohlone College Theatre and Dance Department has used several Clear-Com models over the years.

Courtesy Jasper Gong, technical coordinator, Gary Soren Smith Center—Fine and Performing Arts, Ohlone College, Fremont, CA.

TIMING CURTAIN CALLS

Learn to exercise your best judgment in timing the curtain call. Insist on ample rehearsal of the curtain call so that it will be as professional as the rest of the play.

The director usually determines the curtain call order and the effect desired in the process of having the actors acknowledge the audience's applause.

In some cases the producer or the management will have a policy on calls for every play performed in that theater. The policy may be, for instance, that the cast form a single line, in order of appearance, left to right. The policy may be that they should take only one bow, regardless of the audience response. This professional or institutional form of curtain call is hard on actor egos, since the stars are not individually acknowledged by the audience, but it usually results in the house lights coming up while the audience clamors for more. This is quite desirable compared with the call where the applause dwindles as the cast takes its last bow.

The design of the call will vary with the taste of directors and producers, ranging from the simple, as discussed, to the choreographed. I once saw a fancy curtain call add zest to an overwritten and dull last act of a musical, thus arousing some applause, but that was a highly unusual situation.

Often the planning of the curtain call is left for the very last moment and then done in haste. You can help by making a careful diagram of the call order as set by the director and by posting this diagram on the callboard (figure 13.6).

- **The timing or running of the call is another of your sacred duties. You must decide how often to bring up the lights and how long to hold them up. Judgment in this matter can come only from experience. You will quickly learn to sense how long and hard the audience will applaud. It is your good judgment that avoids the curtain closing to waning applause.**

Crank the curtain call cues into the lighting plot and rehearse these cues along with all the others. It is disturbing to endure a long blackout following the final scene

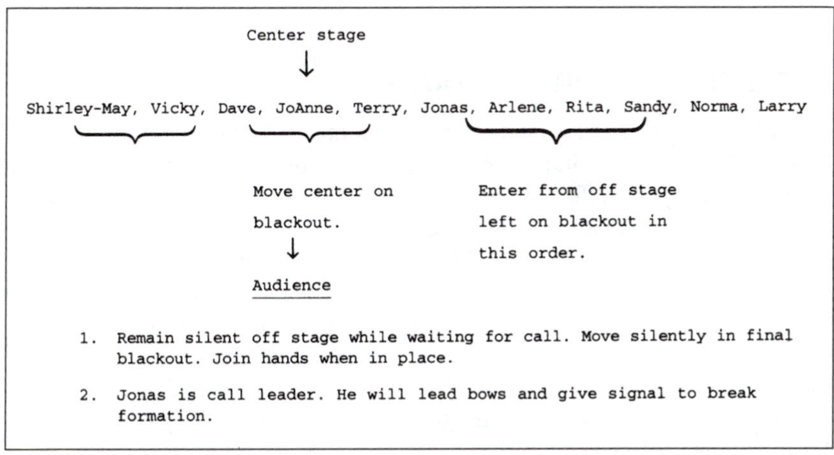

FIGURE 13.6 Curtain Call Order and Instructions

while the crew discovers that they must repatch before they can bring up the stage lights for the call. It is even more disturbing to see the house lights come up for the curtain call rather than the stage lights. We have all seen such incidents mar otherwise technically perfect productions.

When there is no curtain, and the call is conducted with lights only, a cast member should be designated the "call leader" and be given the responsibility of signaling the cast when to break their call formation and leave the stage. This will prevent a straggling exit that is discernible in the blackout. It also prevents cast members from breaking too early and being caught out of position when the lights come up.

Questions sometimes arise as to whether an actor is to appear in the curtain call and whether he must be in costume and makeup. Yes, actors are just as obligated to appear in the call as they are to appear in the play.

"I have such a small part that the audience won't miss me." "I have a date after the show tonight and I don't want to keep her waiting while I get out of makeup." "I die in the first act and I don't want to hang around for two acts." There are many excuses, but no good ones. It is best for you to include a rule on curtain-call participation in the company rules (page 39) and carefully explain to the cast what is expected.

WALKING THE CURTAIN

Have the curtain pulled occasionally during rehearsals while you watch from the audience to see how it comes together. If there are no gaps when it is closed, there may be no need to have it walked. But if the crew is available, it is always safer to have someone walk the curtain—walk out of sight behind the curtain to ensure that it closes smoothly and completely.

Walking the curtain can deter these familiar incidents:

Examples

1. The person on the rope hits a snag and thinks the curtain is closed. The actors are hung, waiting for the curtain to close completely.
2. An actor accidentally jostles a set piece, moving it past the curtain line. The curtain drags the set piece and finally overturns it.

ACCESS TO THE CONTROL BOOTH

Only authorized personnel should be allowed in the control booth. Tampering with, or unintentional playing with, sound or lighting equipment by unauthorized personnel could detrimentally affect the running of your show. It is best to post a sign, and enforce it: "No Admission" or "Authorized Personnel Only."

Is the director authorized? It's difficult for a stage manager to tell the director to stay out, especially if the stage manager has not discussed this possibility with the director prior to opening night. There is the tendency for the director to want to talk to someone during the performance, someone who will understand his or her anguish, someone who will confirm that all of the actors are not doing what they were told to do. Worst of all, the director wants to give last-minute notes or make just a little change in some cue or effect.

If you and the director have done your work properly, there is no reason for the director to be in the booth before, during, or after the performance. Make this clear in advance—that the director's presence would be a distraction. The same goes for cast members. Put this item in your company rules—you don't want anyone in the booth unless there is an immediate need to report a fire!

(Parenthetically, I don't feel that directors should give notes to cast members during intermissions. It's sometimes difficult to convince directors that the urgent things they want to say to the cast are not going to make that much difference in the second act. It's hard to limit my comments about the director's behavior. I have to remind myself that this book is about stage management and not directing. From the stage manager's point of view, there is very little you can do to keep the director out of the backstage area during intermissions. Discuss this behavior with the director in advance—such as, "I hope you're not the kind of director who comes backstage at intermissions. I've found in the past that this seems to upset cast members more than anything else.")

My Teaching Strategy

Use a feather, a marble, and a paperback book. Give one item to each of three students. Ask each to hold the prop out at shoulder height. These students will function as crew. Ask a fourth student to be the stage manager, to call cues in a way that makes all three objects hit the ground simultaneously. Ask the stage manager to experiment with styles of calling *[pages 181–184, above]* to find the one that works best. Experiment with other objects, so that falling times vary. Rotate students, so that reaction times vary. Have one student hold two objects and see how this affects the exercise. Rotate roles so that each student plays each part and has the experience of calling the cues as well as being cued. This exercise emphasizes the fact that it is not only the responsibility of the stage manager to call the cue, but also to check the result. It gives students experience in calling tight cues that must be called separately *[page 183, above]*.

Dan Weingarten
AEA Stage Manager and Lighting Designer

SUGGESTED CLASSROOM EXERCISE

Ask students to work together to write a precurtain checklist for the current or upcoming show in your theater. When complete, compare it with the one shown in figure 13.1.

14

Working with the House Manager

Never confuse the seating capacity of your theater with the sitting capacity of your audience.
—Anonymous

The function of the house manager (HM) is to ensure the audience's safety and comfort prior to a performance, during intermissions, and after the performance.

- **Understand the HM's function and coordinate with him in the total effort of assisting the audience to see the production.**

Normally, the most important item in your coordination is deciding how the HM can notify you that the audience is ready to see the production. Will the HM call you on a backstage phone or intercom and say, "It's all yours"? Or will you run the show at a prearranged time unless the HM tells you otherwise? How might the HM tell you otherwise? Should you synchronize your watches?

There must be a definite understanding between you and the HM. It seems so obvious and yet it is frequently overlooked. How often does the audience return to its seats to find a scene in progress? How often does an audience return to its seats to wait several minutes before the curtain goes up? The audience resents being rushed or having to wait, and the actors resent playing to a moving audience. But it does happen and will continue to happen if you fail to coordinate with the HM.

In large commercial theaters, HMs belong to their own union: the Association of Theatrical Press Agents and Managers (page 241). In a small company, the HM may be one of the actors and may have several other duties in addition to house managing and acting.

In some theaters the HM is in charge of the whole theater plant, box office staff, ushers, custodial staff, and so on. HM turns the house over to the stage manager for the period of the play only, and resumes total responsibility during intermissions and after the final curtain.

In a small theater the HM may double as usher, custodian, and assistant director. Halfway through the first act, the HM may turn all responsibilities over to the stage manager and depart the premises.

In a showcase theater there might be a different HM every night of the run, and it might be your responsibility to brief each new HM. The following discussion of a HM's duties was written for a showcase theater.

DUTIES OF THE HOUSE MANAGER

The HM acts as the producer's or sponsoring management's representative in greeting and seating the audience. The HM should be well dressed, well mannered, and wear a badge or ribbon to indicate his position. The house manager:

1. Obtains the reservation lists from the reservation clerk and brings them to the theater. This enables handling of future reservations at the theater as well as the reservations for the evening's performance.
2. Arrives at the theater 45 minutes prior to the curtain. Ensures the sidewalks in front of the theater, and the lobby, are clean.
3. Checks the condition of the seats and the audience area. Ensures that all fire exits can be opened easily and that alleys beyond them are not blocked.
4. Answers the phones.
5. Greets and seats arriving audience, especially VIPs, and places reserved signs on front row seats for Meryl Streep, Mike Nichols, and such.
6. Prevents the audience from bringing food and lighted cigarettes into the theater.
7. Handles reservations problems: people arriving on the wrong night, overbooked audiences, and so forth. Holds people without reservations until all those with reservations have been seated. Helps people in wheelchairs to find the most convenient aisle space from which to watch the performance. Is alert to other disabilities among audience members and tries to assist if possible.
8. Watches for causes of audience delay—rain, traffic congestion, severe parking problems, and so on—and if aware that the audience will be late, asks the stage manager to give the cast a five-minute hold.
9. When the audience is seated, the HM closes the back doors, walks to the stage door, and tells the stage manager to "take the show."
10. After the curtain rises, the HM returns to the lobby and seats people who arrive late, cautioning them that the curtain is up and asking them to be as silent as possible. (Unless seating is reserved, the HM tries to fill the house tightly from the front so that empty seats will be at the back for late arrivals.)
11. During the acts the HM again checks the sidewalks and lobby so that the audience will find these areas clean when they emerge from the theater during intermissions and after the show.
12. Find time during acts to sit for a few minutes in the audience to check the temperature in the theater and to observe any audience distractions (figure 14.1).
13. At intermission, the HM opens the back doors and outside doors to ventilate the theater. (Body heat and the lighting equipment may make the theater quite warm by the end of each act.)

[Los Angeles *Bugle*, 2001]

LETTERS

Nuisance Noises

We recently attended the visiting St. Louis Opera Company's performance of "Aida" at the Municipal Opera Pavilion on December 5. In the middle of the opera we were severely distracted by pulsating drumbeats and musical sounds which seemed to come from the ceiling of the auditorium, as if they emanated from the restaurant upstairs. It was impossible for us to get a clear hearing of the last part of the opera. In order to be sure that the vibrations from above were not somehow imaginary, we turned to a neighbor for confirmation, "Good grief!" he said, "I've been fighting it since the second act." We wrote a strong complaint after the performance, but never received any acknowlec very poor taste on the part ment to permit conflicting this to be audible to patrons formances.

Morris and Art Faye
Northeast Cucamong

Danny Bongo, public relations director for the Pavilion, admits there was no theater employee directly responsible for checking on such intrusive sounds beyond the first few minutes after the performance is under way. "Until somebody gives us the word," he said, "we have no way to be aware there's a problem." However, on December 5, a verbal complaint was made to a guard and, according to Bongo, the sound of the dance band was "totally sealed off" as a result by the end of the opera. Bongo denies that anybody involved received any written protest. But a similar complaint appeared in the Bugle's review of "La Gioconda" as performed by the St. Louis company during the same month here.

—The Editor

FIGURE 14.1 Plan Ahead to Handle Emergencies and Surprise Interruptions

14. Ensures that the rest rooms are clean and serviceable and directs the audience to the rest rooms, telephone, and water fountains.
15. Makes any necessary announcements to the audience:
    - **a.** "No smoking." The HM speaks to those individuals who haven't read the posted signs and those who don't wish to comply.)
    - **b.** Announces any unusually long delays in the curtain.
    - **c.** "Lights on in car parked outside, license number EMR 223."
    - **d.** "Is there a doctor in the house?"
    - **e.** Announces fire and other emergencies (figure 17.6, page 235). No house manager should simply yell "Fire!" Calm words should precede that word. The HM knows exactly what to do to evacuate the theater and knows the numbers to call for fire, police, and ambulance, and always carries a cell phone.
    - **f.** Announces any cast changes and omissions in the program.
16. Times the intermissions and blinks the outside lights and/or strikes chimes in the lobby and/or announces, "Curtain going up," to bring the audience back in. Closes

the back doors and the street doors at the end of the intermissions. Does not wait ten minutes to bring the audience back in, but starts them coming back after eight minutes so that they are seated and ready to go when ten minutes have elapsed.

17. If there are doctors on call in the audience, the HM takes their names and seat locations and summons them if they should get a call during the performance.
18. Answers questions of the departing audience, notes their complaints and suggestions, and passes them on to the producer.
19. Coordinates with the stage manager in securing the theater when everyone has left. Pushes up the seats and searches for lost items. Before leaving the theater, the HM must conduct a sniff test (fire inspection) of every row in the audience and every room and cranny of the theater and dressing rooms to ensure that no burning cigarettes have been left anywhere.
20. Returns the reservation lists to the reservations clerk.

Problems frequently occur when you come to your job from one theater and the house manager comes from another. You have different expectations of one another based on different past experiences.

Talk it out. Give it a dry run. Anticipate problems together. What will you each do if it rains torrents on opening night? Who will roll out the heavy-duty mats in the lobby? Who will put down the planks in the gully at the actors' entrance? How will the HM tell you from out front that the rain has delayed the audience and that she wants you to hold the curtain an additional five minutes? Since there's no cloakroom, where can the audience store raincoats and umbrellas? Does the HM lock up the theater? Do you? Or do you both share or alternate shutdown procedures? If you share or alternate, do you both know exactly what is to be done?

Anticipate emergencies together. Review what you each will do in the event of fire, civil disorder, earthquake, flood, heart attacks among the audience, animals in the audience, incredibly loud noises emanating from places unknown (figure 14.1), and hysterical patrons begging to be let out.

BLOOD-BORNE PATHOGENS

In the 1980s, the theater world became aware of the dangers of blood-borne pathogens—disease-causing microorganisms that are present in human blood, including hepatitis B virus and human immunodeficiency virus (HIV). In any accidents in a theater that involve the spill of blood, vomit, urine, or feces, safety in cleanup has become an issue for which the theater staff must plan. Who will do what and when? Will the necessary equipment be available?

In a large theater complex or university, it is usually the security staff that is given responsibility for cleanup. In smaller theater situations, the HM may be delegated the responsibility for the whole building by the producer. The stage manager may be tasked with this responsibility in the absence of others so assigned. What happens if there is a hazardous situation during rehearsals, or backstage, or in the dressing rooms during performance?

- **The stage manager should know where to find the cleanup kit or biohazard station (figure 14.2) and the instructions on how to dispose of the hazard (figure 14.3).**

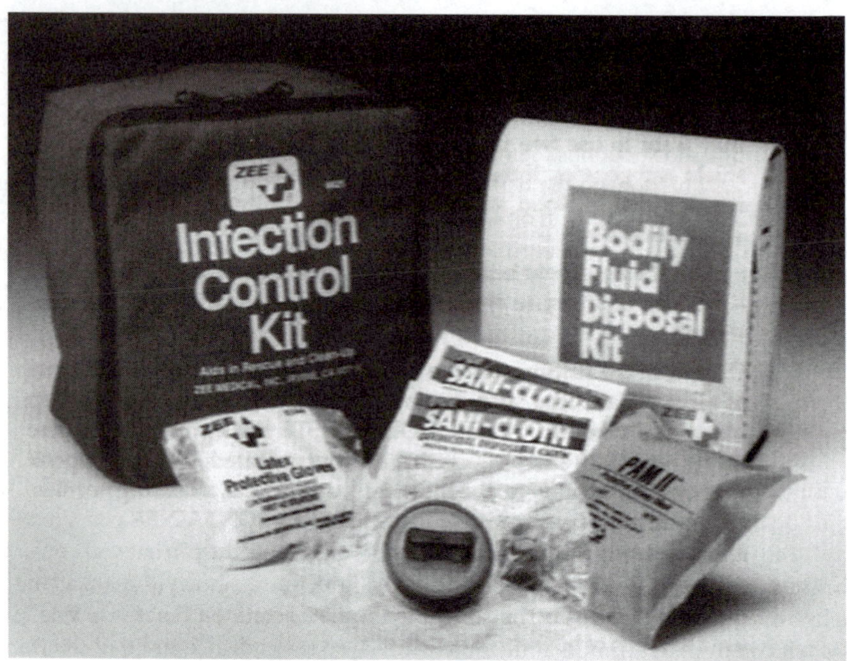

FIGURE 14.2 A Blood-Borne Pathogen Kit

Courtesy Zee Medical, Inc., Irvine, California. zeemedical.com

Keep the blood-borne pathogens cleanup kit next to the first-aid kit. Post instructions for use NEXT TO the kit as well as on the bulletin board. Cast and crew should be told in an early briefing that they are to report any potentially infectious material to the stage manager rather than attempting to dispose of it themselves, especially without proper equipment and instruction (figure 14.3).

California law, effective July 30, 1999, states that if an employer (read producer) designates an employee (read stage manager) to be responsible for implementation of first aid/blood-borne pathogen control, then the employer must provide training. Whether you have or have not been designated, it is desirable that you voluntarily seek training. Any first-aid emergency involving blood spill must be considered a blood-borne pathogen emergency. If you need further information, try the federal Occupational Safety and Health Administration (OSHA) of U.S. Department of Labor (osha.gov) or your state OSHA Web site (in California: dir.ca.gov/dosh/bloodbornefaq.html).

ROTATING DUTY ROSTERS

When there is no staff HM, and the cast must carry out the custodial duties, you may find it desirable to prepare a rotating duty roster (figure 14.4).

Example

In a showcase theater situation where there was no budget for cleanup and maintenance of the theater, the cast was called to a discussion by the artistic

1. For Liquid or Wet Blood, Use the Kit Provided

1. First, put on a pair of rubber gloves. If you have a large spill, use a pair of heavy utility rubber gloves. If using disposable rubber gloves, you may want to use two pair in case of a small hole or tear. Wear face shield and goggles. If there is a chance of getting blood on your clothing or a chance blood may penetrate your clothing, wear disposable Tyvek coveralls.
2. Spread the absorbent beads that are found in the white pouch in the Kit or use floor dry to absorb the liquid. Pick up with a dust pan or shovel.
3. Dispose of the absorbent in the WHITE BAG and tie it closed. Dispose of all materials used such as gloves, towels and any of the clean-up materials in the RED, INFECTIOUS WASTE BAG provided. If there are no needles or sharp objects that are contaminated, you may deposit the bags in the compactor. If there are sharp objects, including needles, etc., these must be disposed of in the SHARPS CONTAINER provided in the clean-up kit.
4. Clean the area with a germicidal cleaner that is provided with the kits or that are located in the designated First Aid stations. If not available, use a solution of household bleach diluted between 1:10 and 1:100 with water. Clean-up of equipment is covered in the section titled Cleaning Up of Contaminated Equipment. A WORD OF CAUTION: HANDLE INFECTIOUS MATERIALS AS LITTLE AS POSSIBLE.

2. Dry Blood Clean-Up

When cleaning up dry blood, follow the same procedures as for liquid clean-up AND wear face shield with eye protection or a dust mask and goggles to prevent ingesting dust through eyes, nose or mouth. Do not breathe any dust or get dust into any body cavity.

Equipment clean-up is covered in a following section.

3. Clean-Up of Vomit, Urine, and Feces

Put on a pair of rubber gloves.

Cover liquid with floor dry compound. Allow liquid to be soaked up into the compound. Sweep into a dustpan and dispose of in a plastic bag. Tie bag securely and place in compactor.

Clean area with disinfectant or diluted bleach solution.

4. Cleaning Contaminated Equipment

Dispose of contaminated rubber gloves, coveralls and face masks in the manner stated in Section 1.

FIGURE 14.3 One of Several Pages of a "Safety Procedures" Bulletin. Disclaimer: "The Santa Clara Convention Center is not in the business of providing advice or counsel regarding this or any other safety procedures. Accordingly, no warranty as to its adequacy or completeness is made."

Courtesy R. D. "Ray" Anderson, Director of Security, Santa Clara Convention Center.

ROSTER

Albert Alvarez	A	B	C	D	E	F	G	H
Ben Blahzay	B	C	D	E	F	G	H	I
Charles Corn	C	D	E	F	G	H	I	J
Dave Dumpling	D	E	F	G	H	I	J	K
Earl Eastman	E	F	G	H	I	J	K	L
Frank Farley	F	G	H	I	J	K	L	A
Gina Glass	G	H	I	J	K	L	A	B
Helen Harvey	H	I	J	K	L	A	B	C
Ida Isely	I	J	K	L	A	B	C	D
Judy Jennings	J	K	L	A	B	C	D	E
Karen Kirsten	K	L	A	B	C	D	E	F
Louise Lehrer	L	A	B	C	D	E	F	G
	Thursday	Friday	Saturday	Sunday	Thursday	Friday	Saturday	Sunday

A Sweep front sidewalk
B Strain sand in all four cans in lobby; move 2 outside
C Sweep/mop lobby
D Put all seats up; sweep/ mop audience area
E Clean men's room
F Clean ladies' room
G Clean dressing room tables
H Sweep dressing rooms
I Clean Green Room
J Empty all waste baskets: rest rooms, dressing rooms, Green Room (trash can behind theater)
K Resupply all paper to dressing rooms, rest rooms from supply cupboard
L Dust lobby furniture, straighten

FIGURE 14.4 A Rotating Duty Roster

director (one of the actors). They were asked how to solve the cleanup problem. All agreed that they were the only ones who could solve the problem, that they did not want to levy a tax to pay a custodian, and that their chief concern was an equitable distribution of the work. The artistic director then asked the stage manager (also an actor in the group) to set up a rotating duty roster.

The rosters were not posted in the dressing rooms or on the callboard, since cast members did not want their friends who visited after performance to see that they were expected to do chores. Instead, each cast member was given a copy of the roster. The stage manager supervised and carried out his chores.

Cast members were given the option of carrying out their assignments 15 minutes prior to or after the performance. By doing one chore before and one after the performance, they could work on chores every two nights.

By inviting the cast to participate in solving the problem, the artistic director gained their cooperation. If he had simply ordered the roster posted, it might not have worked as well as it did. A few minutes of group consultation in advance can prevent a great deal of individual dissent later.

ONE FLEW OVER THE CUCKOO'S NEST

VIP LIST

Dale Wasserman	author
Charles Faber	critic Citizen News
John Houser	critic - Herald Examiner
Phillip Scheuer	critic - L.A. Times
Jimmy Powers	critic - Hollywood Reporter
Dale Olsen	critic - Variety
Robert Lewine	agent V.P. C.M.A.
Milton Lewis	manager
Lurene Tuttle	actress
Jim Lister	cast, dir. Stalmaster-Lister Rawhide Gunsmoke
Boris Kaplan	producer
Gene Banks	casting ABC
Betty Garret	actress
King Donovan	actor-director
Meyer Mishkin	agent Mishkin Agency
Hy Sieger	agent Park-Citron Agency
Norman Pincas	producer
David Graham	agent
Bob Raison	agent Ralson-Branden Agency
Harold Swoverland	agent Swoverland Agency
Eddie Foy, Jr.	casting Columbia Screen Gems (I Dream of Jeannie)
Jack Donaldson	agent Donaldson Agency
Bob Bowser	casting Universal
Bob Shapiro	agent William Morris
Naomi Hirshhorn	producer legit
George Pal	producer MGM
Dick Lyons	producer MGM
Al Trescony	casting MGM
Meryl Abeles	Desilu 20th
Dick Berg	producer Chrysler
Bert Kennedy	director MGM writer
Dale Garrick	agent Garrick Agency

FIGURE 14.5 Portion of VIP List for the Callboard of a Showcase Theater

The stage manager also might take pains to explain where the cleanup materials are kept, how a mop wringer is used, and the importance of putting things back where they were found and reporting shortages of materials. (It was discovered, in the previous example, that a 30-year-old actor did not know how to use a mop. He had never used one. The stage manager demonstrated and the actor caught on. Unfortunately, he became much more skilled at mopping than acting.)

Not all duty rosters need be of the rotating type if the cast is willing to distribute chores in another way. Again, a group talk session in advance will help in the voluntary tapping of labor.

VIP LISTS

A showcase theater's purpose is to attract to its audience producers, directors, agents, and other very important people (VIPs) who can hire the cast members for roles in movies, television, industrial shows, live theater, and other paying jobs. Community, educational, and commercial theaters may function as showcases, even though it is not their primary purpose.

If the cast members know which VIPs have seen their performance, they can follow up the impression they've made by sending résumés and phoning for interviews. They can ask agents who have attended to represent them on the basis of their performance.

So it is desirable that the cast knows which VIPs have been in the audience. Posting a VIP list on the callboard is the easiest way to let the cast know (figure 14.5). Posting such a list is not a mandatory function of the stage manager. Anyone who takes the time to check with the box office, HM, producer, and director might make such a list. But it is one of the extra items that would demonstrate your interest in the welfare of the cast and the reputation of the theater.

SUGGESTED CLASSROOM EXERCISE

Have the class brainstorm the duties of the house manager for your theater. When arranged in chronological order, compare their list to the one on pages 213–214.

15

Keeping the Show in Hand

The dictionary is the only place where success comes before work.

—Attributed to Vince Lombardi, football coach;
Vidal Sassoon, British hair guru;
Donald Kendall, co-founder of PepsiCo;
or Mark Twain, American writer

The most difficult problem in a long-running production is keeping the quality of each performance as good as it was on opening night. If the director remains with the show, in attendance regularly and in communication with the cast, it's the director's burden. But if the director says to you on opening night, "It's all yours," and means it, then you have your work cut out for you.

- **It is your basic responsibility to retain the director's artistic intent (page 110). It is good practice for all directors in every theater environment to remind cast members that the stage manager will "give notes" after opening night.**

LONG-RUN "IMPROVEMENTS"

In a short run there isn't much of a problem. But as the actors feel more at ease in their roles, especially if the show runs for two weeks or more without the director's presence, "improvements" set in.

Here are some examples of the things that happen in extended runs:

1. *New business:* Actors sometimes feels "hung up" during the lines of fellow actors. During rehearsals and the first few performances, they were busy thinking of coming lines and business, but with their newfound ease and self-assurance, they begin to feel that they are not doing enough. So they invent new business that they feel is appropriate to their characters. They can come up with outrageous business that is highly distracting.

Or it just happens by accident. An actor trips on the set and hits the door frame, severely shaking the flat, and the audience laughs, so at the next performance . . .

2. *New lines:* A late entrance prompts two actors to ad-lib some lines while awaiting the latecomer. At the next performance the ad-lib lines are repeated on the entrance, and at the next performance the entering actor waits for the ad-lib lines.

   Or, an actor throws in an ad-lib line on impulse and gets a laugh, so at the next performance . . .
3. *Pauses:* The actor now senses that his big moment is being missed by the audience because audience focus is elsewhere. So the actor decides a dramatic pause is needed, big enough to drive a truck through. It just seems that long. Actually, new dramatic pauses and those of fellow actors only add up to one and a half minutes on your time sheet for the scene—of yawning and coughing in the audience.
4. *Handles:* Suddenly every other line in the script has as preface a new expletive ("Well"), an exclamation ("Wow"), or direct address ("You"). The actors start to make themselves "comfortable" with the playwright's lines. The crispness is gone, the pace is down, but each actor knows that the single word added is right, just the way the character would say it.

So you observe and listen carefully, and each time you hear new lines, handles, or pauses, or observe new business, you make a caret in your promptbook at the place where it occurred and note the new addition carefully. After the performance you bring the changes and improvements to the attention of the actors, privately. (Important: **In matters of acting performances, directors give notes to the whole cast, but stage managers counsel individual actors privately.**)

And that's when you hear wondrous things from the actors in justification and rationalization:

"I've grown in the part."

"It got a laugh."

"It just happened by accident but the audience bought it, so why not keep it?"

"I'm experimenting. Don't want to get into a rut."

"Got to keep that magic, spontaneous, first-time quality so I decided to do it for the first time without warning him so he'd give me a response I could play off of, but the dumdum just gave me the same tired line reading he's always been giving me."

Et cetera ad nauseum.

What do you do in the face of such static? You bring as much friendly persuasion as possible to the situation. You remind the actor of the traditional discipline of the theater—that changes in lines, pace, the interpretation of lines, and the inclusion of business are all strictly the prerogative of the director. In the absence of the director, they are now the stage manager's prerogative, and you do not approve the changes and improvements the actor wishes to make.

You may or may not go on to explain your reasons for the undesirability of the change or improvement.

Perhaps you will point out that an actor's reputation for self-discipline is more important in the long run than the change or improvement.

You might even point out that historically the worst performances of the best actors have occurred when they undertook to direct themselves.

This is a time when collaborative, supportive, therapeutic conversation skills become critical.

Finally, you simply do not argue about it. Your authority extends only as far as your persuasive influence in this matter. Never make the actor feel that an apology is necessary. If the actor gives you static after counseling, simply leave the actor with a pleasant, "Why don't you give it some thought?"

You cannot control an actor's performance. You cannot run out on the stage and twist the actor's arm. Ultimately the actor must realize what you already know—that in live theater, the stage belongs to the actors, not to the director or the stage manager. On the other hand, a production is a delicate balance of many performers' efforts, and any actor's reputation can suffer if that actor persists in upsetting it. For the really recalcitrant, the ultimate threat would be replacement with an understudy or a new actor, but this would be an administrative decision.

CAST MORALE

Sometimes the gloom in the air at half-hour call following a bad review is enough to make any stage manager feel that a comedy could not possibly be performed that evening, or that the tragedy about to be enacted on stage is nothing compared with the one backstage.

Here's how you handle the situation:

1. Don't overreact.
2. Get it out in the open.
3. Don't act elated when others are depressed.
4. Keep your own personal morale high.

It's never quite as bad as you imagine it will be before you get to the theater. Actors and actresses have a way of buoying up their own morale when they get together. Never feel that you must become a backstage court jester or psychiatrist. This is not the time for a good show biz anecdote. *Don't overreact.*

Get it out in the open. A casual, "Rough break, Sam," to an actor who has been devastated by bad reviews might get it out from the sulking level to the verbal level and allow the actor to vent his choicest invective about the reviewers. Listen. But keep it casual. Show the actor that you don't attach too great importance to it.

Don't be elated when others are depressed. You should be sympathetic enough with the plight of a demoralized cast not to want to appear to be celebrating their disaster.

Keep your own personal morale high. Your morale is dependent on the fact that you are doing a difficult job very well. Continue to do your job very well. Let the cast know, by your deportment, that it is business as usual tonight, and that you expect everyone to be on time and to acknowledge their calls cheerfully, regardless of the reviews.

Second-performance slump and "down" performances are other situations of which you should be aware.

The second performance of a run has a tendency to be a poor one. The cast, emotionally up for the opening night, experiences a letdown. The sense of urgency that attended opening night is gone. The second performance seems to be less important. Part of the challenge is missing. They know they can do it because they did it last night. And now they know how good they are. Didn't all of their friends tell them? So the cast relaxes, and the performance quality slips.

Sometimes you are simply not aware of the causes of a down performance. You observe the results. The first scene drags, the audience is unresponsive, and during the intermission it's quiet in the dressing rooms. The cast is listless.

There is no one best way to respond to second performance slump or other down performances. Judge from your past experience how best to handle the situation. Do you give a pep talk to the cast during the intermission? Do you ask them for the old pizazz? Do you individually enlist the help of the old hands in the cast and ask them to pick up the pace? Have you developed the kind of rapport with the cast during rehearsals or on the tour thus far that enables you to give them the football coach's "You guys are letting me down" routine?

If you think that you can be effective in fighting the down performances, then you should try to do so. But don't feel it is an obligation. Simply make sure you do not contribute to poor cast morale.

BLOCKING REPLACEMENTS AND REHEARSING UNDERSTUDIES

Traditionally, as the closest assistant to the director, you are presumed to have the duty of blocking in replacements and rehearsing understudies. In reality, you rarely get to perform these duties. Sometimes the director wants to do it. Sometimes other staff members step in. Sometimes there is simply no need to block replacements or rehearse understudies.

- **Of course, you should be ready and able to do it since you have the blocking notations in your promptbook.**

Rehearsing understudies or replacements is unlike original direction in that you should attempt to prepare the understudy or replacement to fit into the already mounted play. In most cases, replacements and understudies have the opportunity to observe the cast and take their own blocking notation during a rehearsal or performance.

If working with an Equity company, review the rules concerning understudies with the producer. Some contracts require that understudies be present at the theater, while other contracts require that the understudies simply be on call. Union stage managers are not allowed to work as understudies. Assistant stage managers may act or understudy, depending on the contract. If unsure, check with your Equity office.

Append the names and phone numbers of potential replacements and understudies to your cast list so you are able to reach them when the need arises. Since you never can tell when you will need a replacement, it is a good idea to keep the résumés submitted during auditions along with your notes of evaluation.

> Before the final performance of a production of Wagner's *The Flying Dutchman* in Richmond, VA, for which I was an Assistant Stage Manager, we received a call at the theatre 75 minutes before curtain that the tenor singing the role of Erik was undergoing emergency surgery at a local hospital. The cover *[understudy]* for the role was also cast as

the Steersman and needed to sing that part in the show as well. When called to the production office, the cover admitted that he knew the music, but had never had a staging and didn't know the blocking. Any hopes of teaching him the blocking, in less than an hour, for a major role like Erik were out of the question.

We realized that it was possible for him to sing his on-stage role as well as sing the part of Erik from the pit since, fortunately, both characters were never on stage at the same time. The head of the company then turned to me and said, "You fit the costume. You walk the part." So, I went to costumes and wigs, spent Act I reviewing the blocking and then went on stage, without script, to essentially mime the role of Erik for his appearances in the last two acts. At the end of the evening, the singer and I received a standing ovation in our tandem bow. So my paying attention in rehearsal paid off.

David Grindle
Production Stage Manager
The Atlanta Opera

UPKEEP OF SETS AND COSTUMES

On the very mundane level, the stage manager of a long-run production becomes responsible for the upkeep of the sets and costumes.

Every member of the cast should be encouraged to report to the stage manager any part of a set piece or set that is becoming worn or unserviceable. This might range from a door that is sticking, to a hole in a flat, to a loose cable backstage.

The stage manager should try to stay ahead of the cast by inspecting sets, set pieces, and costumes periodically and carrying out minor repairs before the cast members notice the need.

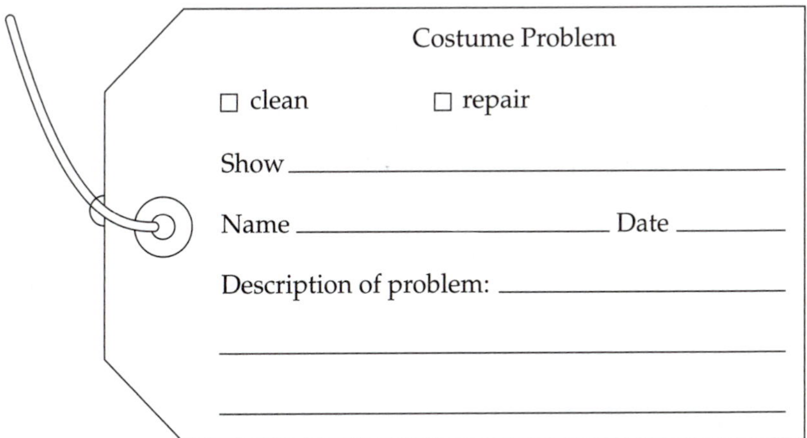
Costume Problem

☐ clean ☐ repair

Show ____________________

Name ____________________ Date __________

Description of problem: ____________________

____

____

FIGURE 15.1 Costume Tag. Tags with eyelets, and preferably wire ties, are available in stationery stores. When you have a large cast, it is important that you get the right costumes back to the right actor. Tags should be left in the dressing rooms, and actors should be informed via company rules when and where they are to turn in costumes for cleaning or repair.

The stage manager is also responsible for seeing to it that costumes are laundered and repaired when and if necessary (figure 15.1).

SUGGESTED CLASSROOM EXERCISE

Plan inspection of the set of your current production to cite those things that would need upkeep if the play were to run for an extended period.

16

Closing and Moving/Touring

Someone is always doing what someone else said could not be done.
—Anonymous

When the show has completed its run, it is time to strike—tear down the sets and return or store the props and costumes. It is usually desirable to clear the stage area as soon as possible after the last performance.

In union companies the close of the show is announced two weeks in advance by a closing notice signed by the producer and posted on the callboard.

STRIKE PLAN

- **To accomplish the strike efficiently, write out and distribute a strike plan. This plan lets each person involved know what is expected (figure 16.1). Coordinate the plan with all concerned department heads.**

Will the actors or only the crew be involved in the strike? In a union theater situation, cast members do not participate in the strike. In educational, community, and showcase theater, they usually do.

If you are working in a union situation, your strike plan will be brief. It will advise the union crew of their call. Along with the producer, business manager, or production manager, evaluate the amount of time required and review the applicable union rules and pay scales to determine whether the strike can most economically be carried out during a night call following the final curtain, or delayed for a future date, even possibly the day that the next set is to be brought in. Evaluate availability of storage space, storage cost, and trucking costs.

It is wise to review the strike plan with the union crew before finalizing it.

If the staff technical director is responsible for strike supervision, the stage manager will follow the TD's directions. Can you help the TD to plan the strike?

In a nonunion situation, it is usually best to accomplish the strike as soon after the final curtain as possible. Tools and transportation should be well planned so that your cast, staff, and crew will have everything on hand they need to accomplish the strike. Have enough bags and boxes to get all of

THE TORCH-BEARERS

STRIKE NIGHT PARTY
Sunday, June 14
11 PM – 1 AM

General

1. Strike can be completed in less than 2 hrs. with the cooperation of all.
2. Please bring hammer and/or crowbar plus at least one large corrugated paper box suitable for packing.
3. Please change out of costume and make-up and into work clothes as soon as possible.
4. Urging final night guests to leave as soon as possible will expedite.
5. Remove your own personal costumes, make-up, and props to your cars as soon as possible to facilitate cleaning of dressing rooms.
6. Stay off the stage because of falling flats and flying hardware, tools, & crew members, unless specifically assigned there. (Use side doors to go between dressing rooms and aud.)
7. Upon completion of assigned tasks, see stage manager.

Assignments

Crew: Dick, John, Fred, Barry (others):

- A. Strike front rows of chairs in aud.
- B. Bring in stairs, garbage cans, place in aud. near DSL.
- C. Remove sconces, place in one box; all furn. in aud. near DSR.
- D. Remove all portable lighting equip. to storage room, rear aud.
- E. Remove all flats, braces, rigging to aud. near DSL.
- F. When stage strike complete, replace curtains, move furniture to patio.
- G. Dick will be in charge of further refining crew assignments.

Doug:

- A. Oversee removal of all items from stage.
- B. Supervise replacement of curtains front and rear.

Len & Hoke, Brett & Ben:

- A. Form 2 teams to work in aud. near DSL area to accept flats, rigging, stage pieces from crew.
- B. Remove hardware & break down to smallest desirable parts.
- C. Store all hardware in box.
- D. Remove all parts to patio & store as directed.
- E. Bring screw driver and/or pliers; work gloves desirable to avoid splinters.

Karl:

- A. Turn on patio lights.
- B. Organize patio area for quick future removal of all materials.
- C. Show Len, Hoke, Brett, Ben where & how to store flats & materials.
- D. When all materials stored, instruct crew to bring out furniture and supervise placement.

Jeanne, Barbara, Margaret, Evelyn, Marlene, Beatriz:

- A. Clean Dressing rooms.
- B. Store costumes to be ret.

Harvey and Bandy: See me for prop forms

- A. Pack all props in boxes.
- B. List contents of box on outside.
- C. Insure with completed forms that we will know what goes where & to whom on Tuesday, June 16th when furniture & props will be returned.

If you anticipate any strike night problems please see me.
Thank you all in advance for the swift, pleasant strike.

FIGURE 16.1 Strike Plan Handout

the props and costumes properly packed and out of the theater and enough back seats, trucks, and trunk space to accommodate all of the set pieces, scenery, props, and costumes. Cleaning implements should be in plentiful supply, too, so that the theater can be left clean for the next production.

Most cast members actually enjoy the strike if they know what is expected of them. There is usually a letdown that follows the closing performance, which is buffered when the cast members continue working together for the brief period of the strike. There is a sense of urgency, team play, and accomplishment present at the strike that makes it quite enjoyable.

During the strike don't tie yourself down with repetitive manual tasks. Observe and supervise. Delegate authority to others, particularly when there is more than one area. Can an actor be put in charge of the shop area while you are on stage? Can one supervise an even smaller area, like a loading dock? Actors who suddenly remember long-lost hernias and war wounds at the mention of the strike have been known to do vast amounts of work when named supervisor.

Be especially aware of safety problems during the strike, and take time to caution everyone about the most basic of potential dangers: watch where you step; don't step on nails and tools; don't fall into the pit; don't use power tools that you have not operated before until you have been instructed in their use; look above for falling scenery and tools.

Start the strike with a safety lecture and caution workers when you see dangerous practices.

The strike may well be the last chore that cast members see you do. Make a good final impression by carrying out the strike with the same calm and meticulous organization with which you managed the rest of the production.

CHANGEOVER SCHEDULE

In cases where the theater will not have a dark night between two consecutive productions, it is necessary to prepare a changeover schedule. This schedule is actually a combination of strike plan, setup plan, and rehearsal schedule that aids in smoothing out the transition from one production to another. It tells who has use of the stage space during the critical hours of transition. It coordinates the personnel of the outgoing production, the incoming production, and the house staff (figure 16.2).

Before posting it, coordinate the schedule with the producer, business manager, production manager, and staffs of the incoming and outgoing productions.

During the changeover, be on hand to supervise the on-the-spot adjustments that become necessary.

Examples

1. When construction takes longer than anticipated, and it frequently does, keep the master carpenter from coming to blows with the choreographer of the incoming show who expected those all-important ramps to be in place at the beginning of the rehearsal period and not left for last.
2. Be forearmed with the authority to make decisions as to whether 10 members of a union will be paid for an additional four-hour call because their services are required for 15 additional minutes (when the union requires a four-hour minimum pay period). Discuss contingencies with the producer. Find out what authority you have to commit his money.

Send all personnel concerned a copy of the changeover schedule and post copies on the callboard, in the shop, and in the crew lounge area.

JOHNNY MATHIS/U2 ELEVATION			
Friday	July 15	8 A.M. to noon	Electrics
		1–5 P.M.	Carpentry
			Props
			Electrics
Saturday	July 16	open	
Sunday	July 17	1–6 P.M.	Sound
		8 P.M.	Half Hour
		8:30	Curtain MATHIS Show
		end performance	Begin strike
Monday	July 18	12:00–3 A.M.	Strike/Set
		3–6 A.M.	Full Orchestra
			Dress Rehearsal
		6 A.M. to 12 noon	As needed
		1–6 P.M.	Technical Cleanup
			(no performers)
		8 P.M.	Half Hour
		8:30	Curtain U2 ELEVATION

FIGURE 16.2 Changeover Schedule Between Two Productions

MOVING THE SHOW

All moves are alike and all moves are different. They require coordination of staff, crew, and cast in moving the cast, crew, and equipment.

- You are moving your production from one theater to another. Your lease ran out but your advance sales are great so you have to find another house.
- You tried out in Azusa and now you're opening in West Covina.
- You are on a national tour, either via train and/or plane to major cities or by truck and bus to the hinterlands.
- Your children's play is traveling to all the elementary school auditoriums in town.
- Your industrial show will tour 38 cities in two and a half months.

In any of these situations, here are some of the steps you will want to take:

- Prepare and distribute an itinerary.
- Caution the cast/crew on travel deportment.
- "Mother-hen" the cast on the road.
- Supervise the load-in, setup, strike, and load-out.
- Pave the way with letters to business agents, host theater owners, and so on. Request the host theater's info packet (page 62)

Serving as assistant lighting director on national tours of *Tommy* and *Company*, I loaded in the lighting rig with union crews, focused the show, called the cues for up to six follow spots, then struck it all and moved on to the next venue. I work closely with stage managers throughout the production process. From the SM I expect a preliminary production calendar, contact sheet, and rehearsal reports (if there's any information pertinent to lighting). Once the show has been teched and the tour begins, I give the stage manager (1) follow-spot cue/track sheets, (2) light cue list, (3) focus charts, and (4) magic/cheat sheet. I keep a production notebook in the lighting road box, which has all the plots, paperwork, and advance information that is sent to the theater prior to our arrival.

A good SM knows whether a special is off-focus, or if the actor forgot the blocking, and has the initiative to remedy the situation. The best SMs know their shows inside and out and really watch what's happening on stage every night, becoming both director and lighting designer once the show has opened.

Ben Kato
Assistant Lighting Designer
Jeffrey Finn Productions

Here's my best advice for moving a show:

Do your homework in advance. Call ahead about six weeks in advance to your local contact (tech director, production manager, or house carpenter, whoever is in charge of handling the needs of the tour) and go through your list of requirements. You can develop that list by starting with the tech rider for your show and making up your own form or checklist of things you'll need upon arrival.

The list of requirements is determined by the tech rider. Each show has a different rider depending on the needs of the show. For example, one show like *Lion King* might need 40,000 pounds of weight for the fly rail, whereas a show like *Chicago* might only need 12,000 pounds. No two shows will ever have the same tech rider. The tech rider is also part of the contract between the producer and the presenter. (The presenter is the local person who put up the money for the show to come there and is usually the person who signed the contract with the producer or general manager.)

Work directly with your own head road carpenter for the tour to see what items *will be advanced* and what *you need to advance*. Your head carpenter (HC) on the tour should be your working partner and you need to develop a good working relationship with the HC. The HC runs the stage on load-ins and load-outs.

Help keep the communication up to date between the local presenter (or the presenter's representatives), your carpenter, your company manager, and any on-site management with whom you've been dealing.

The more information everyone has in advance, the better the load-in goes. Be sure the local theater staff and crew have an up-to-date tech rider. If not, fax or e-mail one to them as far in advance as possible, but at least a few months before you arrive. Tech riders should be mailed out three months before your arrival. Phone advances or visits should take place about six weeks before you arrive. Tech riders are also attached to the contract with the theater, but I always play it safe and send out copies directly to the tech staff at the theater. Producers are not always good about getting them to the local house crew. You can never send out too many tech riders. The more people who have them, the better, and the less chance of something not getting covered.

After you've moved a show a few times you'll probably discover some new things you need to take care of in your advance phone calls, so update your work form every few

(continued)

weeks until you've got a good working tool for yourself. Part of stage managing is finding your own system and finding what works for you. No two SMs do it the same way.

Know when to work with the local house crew and presenter and when you need to fight for what the show needs. Sometimes it can be a fine line. Never try to be everyone's best friend. If they all like you, you're not doing your job, because we all know you can't please everyone. Better they learn to respect you first for the job you do; they can learn to like you (or not) later on. Try not to alienate the local crew and staff, because chances are you'll be back there again one day, and their memories of the past visit will be as good as yours. And, as a wise old stage manager told me many, many years ago as I started out in this business, "You're only as good a stage manager as your head carpenter will let you be."

Lynda A. Lavin
Production Stage Manager
Eleven national tours and currently touring with
Thoroughly Modern Millie!

[See figures 16.5, pages 212–220 and 16.6, page 221.]

Itineraries

The first thing you need is an itinerary, whether you are moving across the street or across the nation (figures 16.3 and 16.4). What day are you making the move? What time? What is your destination? What's the new address (with zip code)? What's the new phone number (with area code)? What is the rehearsal and performance schedule during the period?

Planning the itinerary is not necessarily your responsibility, but you should contribute. Think through the moves in advance. Has enough time been allotted for setups? Anticipate problems. Have all of the union rules been considered (e.g., union casts may not travel on their day off)?

It is your responsibility to make sure that every member of the cast and crew has a copy of the itinerary.

Touring Agreement

Caution the cast and crew about deportment expected on the road (figure 16.7, page 222). You are expected to be a model for the rest of the company. Advise the company members if things get out of hand. In the absence of a regular company manager on the road, you may be expected to do some "mother-henning." Tactfully remind cast members that their health, as it affects their performances, is the first concern of the management, and it is for that reason you are cautioning them to take care of their health.

The most common occurrence for touring companies is simply making too much whoopee once out of town, resulting in reduced energy levels that bring down the quality of performances. You can't always prevent such things, but you can caution. If tactful influence fails and an actor's performance suffers as a result of offstage activities, inform the producer or the management.

Lost Sheep Productions, Inc. 12308 Brackland Ave.
Los Angeles CA 90033-3905
ITINERARY—SPRING TOUR—Air Transportation

	Hotels
March 16 Leave Los Angeles Southwest 72/4 P.M.; arrive Miami 9 P.M.	Ramada Inn Airport Everglades 2275 W. State Road 84 Ft. Lauderdale FL 33312 954-584-4000
March 19 Leave Miami United 395/2:55 P.M.; arrive Jacksonville 3:57 P.M.	Ramada Inn 1153 Airport Road Jacksonville FL 32218 904-741-4600
March 21 Leave Jacksonville Continental 151/1 P.M.; arrive Tampa 2:17 P.M.	Manger Motor Inn 200 Ashley Drive Tampa FL 33164 813-223-2456
March 24 Leave Tampa Continental 462/12 P.M.; arrive Pensacola 1:15 P.M.	Town House 16 West Cervantes Street Pensacola FL 33225 904-438-4511
March 26 Leave Pensacola Southwest 865/3:15 P.M.; arrive Birmingham 4:33 P.M.	Parliament House 420 18th Street Birmingham AL 35445 205-323-7211
March 28 Leave Birmingham American 285/8 A.M.; arrive Memphis 9:30 A.M.	Holiday Inn 200 W. Georgia Avenue Memphis TN 38103 901-523-0102
March 30 Leave Memphis United 589/10:45 A.M.; arrive Chattanooga 12:28 P.M.	Towne House 831 George Avenue Chattanooga TN 37401 615-266-1255
April 1 Leave Chattanooga United 736/8:30 A.M.; arrive Charlotte 10:45 A.M.	Manger Motor Inn 1187 Tenth Street Charlotte NC 28202 704-332-3121
April 3 Leave Charlotte United 710/2:40 P.M.; arrive Atlanta 3:33 P.M.	Marriott Hotel 47 Cain Street Atlanta GA 30303 404-688-6500
April 6 Leave Atlanta United 431/2:55 P.M.; arrive Cleveland 4:30 P.M.	Pick Carter Hotel 407 E. 9th Street Cleveland OH 44107 216-771-7200
April 9 Leave Cleveland American 257/11:25 A.M.; arrive Los Angeles 3:20 P.M.	

FIGURE 16.3 Itinerary for a Touring Company

BURT BACHARACH				NOVEMBER		ITINERARY		
DATE	LEAVE	ARRIVE	HOTEL	PLACE OF ENGAGEMENT OR REHEARSAL	TIME CONCERT	TIME RHSL	CALL NEXT DAY	NOTES
THUR. NOV. 19	NO GROUP	TRAVEL	NONE	ATM RECORDS 1416 N. LABREA LOS ANGELES STAGE #1-555-2711	NONE	7 PM	NONE	PARK IN BACK LOT
FRI. NOV. 20	NO GROUP	TRAVEL	NONE SOUND PSL HOLIDAY INN HYLAND ST. 555-3714	LONG BEACH ARENA 270 E. LAKESIDE LONG BEACH CALIF.	8:30 PM	4 PM	NONE	BE AT AIRPORT 1 HR. BEFORE DEPARTURE
SAT. NOV. 21	PERSONNEL AUTO TO TERMINAL #116 (LA)	ARRIVE 1:30 PM SALT LAKE BUS & LIMO	HILTON 200 W. SIXTH SALT LAKE	SPECIAL EVENTS CTR. UNIV OF UTAH 619-555-3719 SALT LAKE CITY	8:00 PM	5 PM	11/22 9 AM	NOON CKOUT. TRVL. W/SAL MONTE TO HOUSTON 11/22
SUN. NOV. 22	SLT. LAKE WAL 5 11:00 LAS VEGAS NAT 2 2:30	L. VEGAS 11:00 HOUSTON 6:50	CHECK RIVIERA HOTEL THEN TO HOUSTON & SAME HOTEL		NONE	NONE	NONE	MERCER McCUNE
SUN. NOV. 22	SLT. LAKE WEST. A.L. 4:10 @ 1:31	DENVER 2:58 555-7010	SHERATON 777 PARK McCUNE & CAR	NOTE: WAIT IN COFFEE SHOP FOR MERCER	NONE	NONE	PUNCH NONE	BURNS

FIGURE 16.4 Itinerary for a Touring Musical Show

MILLIE NATIONAL TOUR

Technical Requirements

In the following pages, we will outline for you the technical requirements for the touring production of "THOROUGHLY MODERN MILLIE!" Your cooperation and advance preparation will facilitate an efficient load-in and load-out. We hope to cover all areas of concern, but if you have additional questions after going through this document please feel free to contact us with further questions.

MINIMUM STAGE REQUIREMENTS

Minimum proscenium width opening: 40′ 0″ (20′ 0″ left and right of center)
Minimum stage depth (from first working set): 37′ 0″
Minimum stage width: 74′ 0″ (37′ 0″ left and right of center)
Minimum grid height: 65′ 0″
Minimum width between fly floors: 50′ 0″ (25′ 0″ left and right of center)
Minimum height clear under fly floors: 26′ 0″
Minimum size loading door: 8′ 0″ wide × 9′ 0″ high

SEATING HOLDS

Sound console: See Sound Department
Follow spots: See Electrics Department
Sightlines: TBD

GENERAL REQUIREMENTS

1. Please mail a copy of current local union contracts to the New York office mailing listing the prevailing local union rates at least six (6) months prior to the engagement.

FIGURE 16.5 Tech Rider—Millie National Tour Technical Requirements

Courtesy Mike Isaacson and Fox Associates, producers of *Thoroughly Modern Millie!* National Tour.

2. Please fax or mail a copy of the current hanging plot (line set positions) to the New York office as soon as possible.
3. Please mail a complete and detailed ground plan and section on the stage and house (in scale) to the New York office as soon as possible. Also, please include a copy of the dressing room layouts.
4. We require the following for both the in and out:
   1 2-ton 6′ forklift and qualified operator (2 if required by local conditions, e.g. no level truck dock)
   1 pair fork extensions
   1 36′ genie lift
5. It is imperative that all areas of the stage, fly system, backstage, loading docks, dressing rooms, storage areas, and productions offices be completely clear and broom clean prior to the start of the advance loads-in.
6. All personnel called for all load-in, load-out, and performances of the production must be qualified in their department and prompt for the starting times of all calls. ALL STAGEHANDS EMPLOYED ARE EXPECTED TO BRING BASIC TOOLS (E.G., A HAMMER, PHILLIPS SCREWDRIVER, SLOTTED SCREWDRIVER, CRESCENT WRENCH, PLIERS, AND A TAPE MEASURE).
7. **ANY STAGEHAND SHOWING UP FOR WORK OR SHOW CALLS SHOWING ANY SIGNS OF DRINKING OR SUBSTANCE ABUSE WILL BE DISMISSED ON THE SPOT, AND REPLACED AT LOCAL PRESENTER'S EXPENSE (IF ANY).**
8. It is expected that when a stagehand begins working in one department that the stagehand will continue in that department for the duration of load-in. Further, it is expected that when a stagehand accepts a job on the running crew, that said stagehand will remain on the job for the duration of all performances. In the event that a stagehand must vacate a position, then his replacement must have a training period of a minimum two performances under the direction of the current employee prior to assuming the position alone.
9. Some stagehands will be required to wear black clothing in order to avoid being seen while in the wings.
10. This production travels in seven (7) 53′ tractor-trailers. One of these will arrive for the spotting call/advance load-in. Four of the remaining six trucks will arrive for the start of the load-in on the first day. The remaining two trucks will arrive the morning of the first performance. For the load-in and load-out please arrange to have all available parking spaces in the immediate area of the loading dock clear and available for trailer parking and unloading. It is extremely important that the movement of the trucks not be obstructed by cars parked on the streets and lots surrounding the theatre. The Local Presenter is responsible for obtaining all proper permits for trucks/trailers during load-in and load-out.
11. A portion of the running crew will be called to work up to one and one-half (1½) hours prior to each show to preset the stage while others will be called at half-hours.

<u>**CARPENTRY DEPARTMENT**</u>

1. Fly system and the stage area must be cleared of all scenery, electrics, drapes, **band shells,** scenery and projection screens prior to the load-in. *This is absolutely essential.*
2. The musicians are in the pit for the production. Before our arrival, the pit must be in its lowered position and seats removed.
3. There must be 20,000 lbs. of weight, over pipe weight, available on the loading gallery before the arrival of the production. This weight should be doubled (40,000 lbs. over pipe weight) in a double purchase house.

FIGURE 16.5 (*Continued*)

4. Carpenter must be able to lag into deck, which must be level and structurally sound.
5. Line sets must be kickable and should be set according to current house hanging plot (line set positions)
6. We require no less than 40 spotted lines with 2 wheels per line and a commensurate amount of ⅝" hemp, available at the time of the advance spotting call.
7. **A phone line should be made available backstage for the Automation Carpenter for the run of the show. This line should have access to long distance via a 1-800 number.**

IF YOU ARE UNABLE TO COMPLY WITH ANY OF THESE REQUIREMENTS, PLEASE NOTIFY US IMMEDIATELY.

ELECTRIC DEPARTMENT

1. POWER REQUIREMENTS
   A. **AUTOMATION REQUIRED POWER:** 1 200-amp 208VAC 3-phase Y-power with ground and neutral. Power should be fused and have a disconnect switch with lugs.
   B. **LIGHTING REQUIRED POWER:** 3 400-amp 3-phase 5-wire with ground switches. Power needed within 50′ of dimmer rack location. Rack location to be determined by Road Electrician.
   C. **SOUND REQUIRED POWER:** Unique (AUDIO ONLY) 3-phase 200-amp service with isolated ground—may not be shared with any other powered systems (e.g., dimmers, automation motors, air conditioning etc.). Power needed within 50′ of amplifier racks. Rack location to be determined by Road Sound Operator.

   House power feed must maintain a minimum of 208 volts and be configured in a "Y" phase. If the voltage drops below 208 volts, the computer controlled motor effects may not work properly. The production requires a water pipe or earth ground. If a water pipe is provided, it must be a filled pipe. A standpipe is not acceptable. If the power feeds do not terminate in a location as specified above it is the responsibility of the local presenter to provide the necessary feeder cable, etc. to ensure that the power feed terminates as specified.
2. Before the start of the load-in, all on-stage electrical pipes <u>must</u> be cleared of instruments and their raceways and feed cables.
3. Please supply the New York office with any local electric restrictions or codes. If specific permits are required, it is the responsibility of the local presenter to secure these permits prior to the start of the load-in.
4. The local presenter must provide sufficient cable and plug-in strip boxes for 20 music stand lights located in the orchestra pit.
5. The production requires the presenter to provide three (3) matched 2kw Lycian Follow spots. Follow spots should be central at the rear of "High Balcony" level. Audience heads/hands should not interfere with follow-spot beams when audience stands in the back row. If the spots are blocked or three spots cannot fit into the booth, soundproofed scaffolding will need to be erected in the balcony section of the auditorium and within sightlines determined by the production staff. Since the placement of these scaffolding towers may eliminate some seats from possible public sale, the presenter should hold and not sell the rear balcony seating sections until released by the production staff during the load-in. Please discuss this situation with the production staff in advance. These follow spots have to be in position and checked that they are in good working order prior to the load-in and can in no way be part of the load-in work calls. **The touring electrician will check the**

FIGURE 16.5 (*Continued*)

follow spots to make sure of their condition. Any work he deems necessary will be at the cost of the local promoter. A spare lamp must be included in case of lamp failure.

6. We require an area approximately 6′ deep and 8′ wide for our lighting consoles with a clear view of the stage. This may be set up in a tech booth or in the back of the orchestra seating. If no such space is available for this position, seats may need to be removed to accommodate it. Please discuss this with the production staff in advance.
7. This production utilizes the following positions:
   - Balcony Rail, or hardware to supply. If no balcony rail, it will be necessary to block the four (4) center seats in the first two rows of the balcony.
   - Front of House Truss and Focusing Track Near Box Boom
   - Far Box Boom

   If adequate positions do not exist, they will need to be installed. Please discuss with the production staff in advance.

SOUND DEPARTMENT

1. We require an area 10′ deep and 12′ wide for our sound mixing position which must be near the center line at the rear of the orchestra section of the house (no more than 100′ from the stage) within the seating section and within sight of the center cluster. Any seats must be removed prior to the beginning of the load-in. The console area provided must be level, with a flat surface. Easy access and egress to sound position by sound operator is necessary throughout the performance. The show cannot be mixed from a closed room or room with a window. Under all circumstances, our production will run and use its own multi-cable to and from the sound position and the stage area.
2. We will tie into the house cluster, where appropriate, with two feeds. Upper and Lower Control of the cluster is necessary along with the ability to bypass house EQ and Delays on the cluster. If no center cluster exists or is deemed by the Production Sound Engineer as inappropriate for our use, we will provide a center cluster and truss. If house chain motors installed for this purpose are not available, please inform the New York office immediately. We will in some cases be able to utilize the house sound truss for our cluster—we require a truss capable of supporting 750 lbs. Should the house truss not meet our needs, we will provide a truss which will be 16′ in length (maximum of 2′ × 8′ sections). The house chain motor points must be appropriately spaced in order to rig the production truss if it is required. Any existing, proscenium speakers or towers must be removed prior to the beginning of our load-in. If they are not removed by the time the load-in begins, the promoter will have to hire additional manpower, at his expense, to complete the removal. The show will need full access to hang necessary surround speakers, delay speakers and video equipment in the theater.
3. We carry a complete sound system and insist that our own console, microphones, playback devices and speaker system be used. We reserve the right to use our own speaker system exclusively. If it is determined by our soundman to be advantageous, we will tie into your house sound and/or paging system with a 600-ohm LINE LEVEL output and use it in addition to our system. We will require full access to all house sound, paging, video and hearing-impaired systems.
4. During the load-in period, the theater lobby will be used as a work area for the sound department. If possible some or all of the sound equipment will be moved into the theater through the lobby. In an effort to protect the lobby

FIGURE 16.5 *(Continued)*

floors, the presenter may wish to provide protective covering: either heavy canvas drop cloths or 4′ × 8′ one-quarter inch (1/4″) Masonite with all seams taped. Such floor covering (if required) should be in place prior to the start of the load-in.

5. This production will utilize 40 channels of UHF Wireless Radios, 10 channels of UHF HME Comm. and at least 8 channels of UHF Motorola walkie-talkies. The use of walkie-talkies or other wireless used by local television crews while filming in the theater is not allowed.
6. The MILLIE Sound Department personnel will require a small sized dressing room or other office space preferably located close to the stage for the preparation of wireless microphones and other work related to the running of the show. This room may be shared with the hair and or wardrobe as a quick-change location. (see Dressing Room Requirements)
7. **A phone line should be made available at the sound console position for the run of the show. This line should be compatible with a modem if possible and should have the ability of accessing long distance via a 1-800 number.**
8. A functional dressing room paging system is required. This system should allow patching from our systems via a 600-ohm LINE LEVEL input. If the theater does not have functional paging speakers in all backstage areas (including dressing rooms) please inform the New York office immediately.

PROPERTY DEPARTMENT

1. We require a professional upright piano (not a console), on a piano dolly, which must be tuned (A=440) before the first rehearsal in each city and thereafter every week. The piano is for rehearsal purposes only.
2. We require 20 music stands with clip lights and chairs in the orchestra pit for the musicians.
3. Please be certain that there are at least 70 chairs total for use in the dressing rooms, backstage, and in the orchestra pit.
4. We required black carpeting or black velour for the front and back walls of the pit as well as the pit floor.
5. Push brooms, mops, buckets and a vacuum must be available.
6. One large refrigerator located within easy access of the cast and crew.

WARDROBE DEPARTMENT

1. At least 6 15-amp 115-V circuits are required in the wardrobe area.
2. In the wardrobe area, there must be 6 6′ or 8′ worktables and 10 chairs, 10 rolling racks, and 2 large garbage cans.
3. Local presenter must provide 2 full size washers and dryers on the premises for show use only. Washers must have individual cycle capabilities and water levels. Dryer must be 220 volts. Coin-operated machines will be at the expense of the theatre. Appliances must be in full running condition on the first day of the load-in.
4. Crew Information: It is imperative that the same nine (9) people work the load-in, load-out, and performances. Of the nine (9) personnel, two must be experienced stitchers. Ideally, the composition of the wardrobe crew should be five females and four males. All dressers need to be proficient in reading and speaking English.

FIGURE 16.5 *(Continued)*

5. Crew Calls: There will be two four-hour work calls each week, on days to be determined by the wardrobe supervisor based on the performance schedule (usually Tuesday and Friday). The wardrobe crew will also be called for a one-hour continuity call before the half-hour call before each performance.
6. A fully functioning utility sink with hot and cold running water will be needed for the cleaning and rinsing of costumes and wigs. This sink must be nearby the wardrobe and wig rooms yet separate from any sink used by theatre custodial and cleaning staff.

HAIR/WIG DEPARTMENT

1. At least 3 20-amp circuits are required in the wig area.
2. The wig area must be well-lit.
3. In wig area, there must be 3 6′ or 8′ worktables with 1 lighted mirror space, 1 height-adjustable chair, and 1 trashcan.
4. A deep sink with hot and cold running water (see Wardrobe Department #7) is required.
5. Crew Information: It is imperative that the same two (2) people work all of the performances. The hair crew will be called from one hour prior to half-hour through the end of the performance.

ORCHESTRA REQUIREMENTS

1. The production travels with a conductor and two musicians. In addition, we require 13 local musicians for total of 16 playing musicians. Our orchestra contractor will be in contact with the local musicians union to coordinate the hiring of these musicians.
2. Prior to the first performance, the musicians will be called for the following rehearsals:
   - 1 3-hour note rehearsals
   - 1 1-hour sound check
3. Advance music will be sent to the local musicians at least 2 weeks in advance of the first scheduled rehearsal.

DRESSING ROOM REQUIREMENTS

1. Our company consists of 25 performers, 1 conductor, 2 traveling musicians, 3 stage managers, 2 company managers, 11 stagehands 2 wardrobe, 2 hair.
2. The dressing room requirements are as follows:
   5 – Principal (1-person) Dressing Rooms
   2 – 2-person Rooms
   2 – Large Chorus (12 people) Rooms
   1 – Conductor Dressing Room
   1 – Crew Room
3. All performers' dressing rooms must be cleaned—floors, make-up tables, mirrors, sinks and bathrooms—prior to the START of the load-in and maintained daily. Their rooms must be well-lit with burned-out bulbs replaced daily. They must have hot and cold running water, wardrobe racks, etc. in accordance with Actors' Equity Association requirements. Drinking water (fountains and/or water coolers) must be accessible in the dressing room area and backstage. Clothing hooks shall not serve as a substitute for wardrobe racks. Chairs, not stools or benches, are required

FIGURE 16.5 *(Continued)*

at each space to be used by a performer. Bathroom facilities must be well stocked with soap, toilet tissue, and paper towels.

4. Additionally, we will need the following rooms for staff personnel, which must be able to be locked:
   i. Room for Company Management with 2 private telephone lines with call-waiting and/or call roll-over plus a third private telephone line for a fax without call waiting, with no rollover features, accessible to AT&T Long Distance. If the third line does not have modem capabilities, a separate modem line will be required. Phone lines must be checked and fully operational by the commencement of the load-in. All phone lines should be direct lines. If the phone lines for Company Management and Stage Management are controlled by a switchboard, the phone lines must be operational from 9:00 a.m. to 12 midnight for everyday during the engagement including days when the theater is dark.
   ii. Room for Stage Management with 1 private telephone line with call-waiting. If this line cannot also serve as a modem line, an additional line with modem capabilities will be required. Phone lines must be operational by the commencement of the load-in.
   iii. Room for Wardrobe Department (see Wardrobe Requirements)
   iv. Room for Hair/Wigs Department (see Hair/Wigs Requirements)

SECURITY INFORMATION

1. We require security personnel for each performance to arrive at the theater one hour before each performance and remain at the theater until the last company member has departed. Throughout the engagement, all areas used by the company must be secured to the satisfaction of the company's representative.
2. The Company Managers and Stage Managers must have access to their office space during business hours. Arrangements must be made with the Company Manager for office access and keys.
3. Any property of the THOROUGHLY MODERN MILLIE! tour—including scenery, costumes, sound and lighting equipment (whether owned or rented), props, and equipment, are for the sole use of the Company. The Local Presenter may not utilize any property for any use (including but not limited to performances, presentations, and speeches on the set) without the prior written consent of the Producer.
4. The house cannot be opened to the public before the half-hour prior to the advertised curtain time.

MANAGEMENT REQUIREMENTS

1. Please mail the following to Nina Lannan Associates, 1450 Broadway, Suite 2011, New York, New York, 10018, as soon as possible:
   - List of the theater personnel and presenting organization's personnel with their private office numbers and home phone numbers if possible.
   - List of local doctors to include general practitioner, ear, nose, and throat, chiropractor, podiatrist, dentist and OB/GYN, and appropriate hospital or medical center for emergency treatment; as well as a listing of local transportation, laundry facilities, drug store, grocery stores, health clubs, post offices, and nearby restaurants and hotels.
   - A copy of the house-seating plan, which includes all seating areas.
   - Company house seat locations, with prices inclusive of any and all facility/restoration fees.

FIGURE 16.5 *(Continued)*

2. In the event of a change in cast, it will be necessary for the ushers to place printed announcements in each house program at no additional expense to producer. The production stage managers will supply these pre-printed announcements to the house.

ESTIMATED LOCAL CREW REQUIREMENTS

The following is an estimate of the number of local stagehands needed and approximate call times. Actual numbers of personnel may vary depending on local circumstances. These call times may increase or decrease and a final determination of personnel and call times will be made by the Head Carpenter.

PRE-ENGAGEMENT SPOTTING ADVANCE CALL @ 1 p.m. of First Day

4 hour call

1	Head Carpenter
11	Carpenters
1	Head Electrician
7	Electricians

LOAD-IN*

The estimated Load-in call is 12 hours spread over 2 days as follows:
Day 1 4 hours 7 p.m. to 11 p.m.
Day 2 8 hours 8 a.m. to 5 p.m.

The estimated Load-out call is 7 hours. Load-out will begin immediately following the final performance. **THIS IS A PRELIMINARY CALL. WE WILL ADVISE YOU OF THE FINAL CALL AT A LATER DATE.** This is also the minimum call and is subject to local conditions.

	IN	RUN	OUT
Carpentry	16	7	16
Electrics	14	4*	14
Sound	6	1	6
Props	4	2	4
Wardrobe	9	9	9
Hair	2	2	2

Loaders AS NEEDED

*If local conditions allow the house electrician to perform deck cues, the number of local electricians can be reduced to 3.

If union requirements demand the Local Presenter supply lunch and/or dinner for the locals crews during load-in, between performances, or load-out, meals will also be provided for the traveling crew, stage managers, and cast (if applicable) and the cost will be a local documented expense. The Head Carpenter will coordinate any required meals with the Local Presenter prior to the load-in.

WORK CALLS

In addition to the wardrobe work calls listed in Wardrobe Requirements #6, there will be one 4 hour work call each week that will require the following local crew:

1	Head Carpenter
4	Carpenters
1	Head Electrician

FIGURE 16.5 *(Continued)*

PRESENTER AVAILABILITY

1. The Presenter or a representative must be available at all times to the Road Carpenter and the Production Stage Manager from one hour prior to the load-in to the end of the final performance. This person must be able to make decisions on behalf of the Presenter.

SUMMARY OF MATERIALS TO BE MAILED TO THE NEW YORK OFFICE

- Union contracts with prevailing rates
- Hanging plot (line set positions)
- Ground plan and section in scale of stage dimensions and dressing room layout
- The location, size, and access of the loading door
- Local electric restrictions and codes
- Names and phone numbers of Carpenter/Tech Director, Electrician, Theater Manager, Concessions/ Souvenir Manager, Presenter Contact
    - House seating plan and Company House Seat locations and prices
    - Doctor and local orientation list

Be advised that failure of the Local Presenter to meet the requirements of this rider may dictate additional time or labor and result in additional expenses. The expenses shall be deemed a fixed expense and borne solely by the Local Presenter.
If there is any further information you require, or if you anticipate any difficulty in meeting the needs as stated above, please contact:

Jim Brandeberry, General Manager
C/o Nina Lannan Associates
1450 Broadway, Suite 2011
New York, NY 10018
(phone)
(fax)

Tour Personnel

Title	Name
General Manager	Jim Brandeberry/Nina Lannan
Production Manager	Christopher C Smith
Production Stage Manager	Lynda A. Lavin
Company Manager	Roeya Banuazizi
Production Electrician	Jimmy Maloney
Head Electrician	Ger Switzer
Follow-spot Operator	Noah Switzer
Moving Lights Technician	
Sound Designer	Jon Weston
Sound Board Operator	Bill Ruger
Wireless Microphone Coordinator	
Production Carpenter	Bryan Oard
Flyman	Bill Gregory
Automation	Richard Force
Asst Carpenter	Scott Beck
Properties Supervisor	Nick
Asst Properties	Linda Whittwer
Wardrobe Supervisor	Gerbie Connelly
Hair Supervisor	Ruth Carsh
Music Contractor	John Mille

FIGURE 16.5 (*Continued*)

Thoroughly Modern Millie-Advance /Phone Information Form

City: Costa Mesa California
Theatre:Performing_Arts Center
Presenter: Clear Channel/Judy Morgan Phone: *714-xxx-xxxx* E-Mail: Jmorgan@xxxxx.org
Tech Contact: John Smith!Prod.Mgr. Phone: 714-xxx-xxxx E-Mail: Jsmith@xxxxx.org
Other Back Stage Contact: Jim Brown 714-xxx-xxxx (I.A. Rep.)
House Mgr: Marge O'Harrah Phone/Fax: 714-xxx-xxxx E-Mail: Mohanah@xxxxx.org

Late Seating Policy: At request of the show Stuffers: Must be delivered out front to Head Usher 2 hrs. before half hour

Rehearsal Piano: Delivery Date: Already on sight. Storage Location: Off Stage Right Tuning: Tues. 11:00

Dressing Room Information:
Stage Mgr: Basement, Rm A Phone: 714-xxx-xxxx Fax: 2322 Internet Access: Wireless
Co. Mgr: Basement, Rm. B Phone: 2323 Fax: same as SM Internet Access: Wireless
On Stage Phone Line/Internet Access: Wireless
Water: (2 Coolers/25-5 gallon bottles & Cups): Delivered on Monday

Cast Rooms: (Floor and Room Number)
Millie:Star I S.R Jimmy/Trevor: Star 2. S.R.Bun Foo/Ching Ho: Star 3 S.R.
Muzzy:Basement Rm D Miss Dorothy: Basement Rm. EMeers/Flannery: Basement Rm. F
Conductor: Basement Rm. C
Mens Chorus (8: Basement. Chorus A Women's Chorus (8) :Basement. Chorus C
Hair Dept: Basement. Chorus B Sink? 3
Wardrobe:Basement, Ward Room Phone:2325 # of Washers/Dryers:3/3 Sink(s)2__

Front of House Locations:
Lights (6 ft D.x 8 ft. W): Back of Orch Section. Hs. L.
Sound:(l0 ft D x 12 Ft W): with lights. Total space is 24 wide by 8 deep
Do seats need to be removed: Space is already cleamed Is floor level: Yes
Location for Orchestra Read: Rehearsal Room A on 3r~1 Floor
Signed Perf: Sat. Matinee Location of Signers: Off Stage Left, on platform #of Signers: 2
Type of House Curtain: Track___X___Guillotine
Access to FOH from Backstage: Pass door off_stage right in the hallway. Steps SL & SR

Misc. Information:
Pay Phones: By the stage door Vending Machines: Soda machine by stage door
Stage Door Location: Back side of_the building on Sunflower Street
Door Man's Hours: 8:OOam-12:00 midnight
Rehearsal Room(s): Rm. C on 3rd floor Mirrors:Yes Barres:Yes
Is the room available to the cast: Before shows for warm up only__________Is there a charge for the use of the room: No (No food or drink allowed in the rehearsal rooms, per the house request.)

Notes:
-Advance Call for Crew. Mon. 1:00-5:00 pm, Dinner 5:00-6:00 Load in begins 6:00-11:00 pm.
. Evening door person is Connie.
-Possibility of T.V. stations at the load in on Tuesday AM
-Another show loading into the Black Box Theater the same day as us. Using a different loading dock.
-Audience meet and greet after the Sunday matinee. Ask cast for volunteers.
-Remind the cast of new cast members joining us this week.
-Happy Birthday to Darcie.
-Fax cast list and late seating hold information to Judy Morgan.

FIGURE 16.6 Advance Form. Note that most of the information above is taken directly from the preceding tech rider. The stage manager needs to have only certain information from the tech rider and doesn't want to pore through an eight-page document to find it each time it is needed.

Lynda Lavin, Production Stage Manager, *Thoroughly Modern Millie!* National Tour.

TO: LOST SHEEP PRODUCTIONS, INC.
12308 BRACKLAND AVE., LOS ANGELES, CALIFORNIA 90033

Gentlemen:

It is my understanding that all personnel employed by, and who will travel with, the Lost Sheep road company must agree to the following:

That while we are in the employ of Lost Sheep Productions, Inc., we will conduct ourselves in a manner that will not bring any adverse criticism to Lost Sheep Productions or its clients.

That our manner of dress will be businesslike, neat, and in good taste, particularly when traveling.

That we will travel with the group as assigned and ask for no changes or deviations from travel schedules and itineraries. All travel departures are final and no changes can be made except by Lost Sheep Productions or representatives who have been instructed that the only change that can be made is a change for the entire group. The reason for this is that changes affect price and budget.

It is our understanding that we are on a job and a business trip and not on a paid vacation. The show and any rehearsals are to take first consideration in any planning of extracurricular activities.

That when technical rehearsals are called, all personnel involved are expected to put the same effort into them as into the performances.

That all personnel will be prompt at any and all calls for fittings, rehearsals, or performances as called by the stage manager.

Agreed To: ____________ / ____________
(name printed) (signature)

Date: ______________

FIGURE 16.7 Touring Agreement for Cast and Staff

On the tour I was responsible for making sure that all luggage was on and off buses/carousels/luggage carts. I tipped all porters, bellhops, and bus drivers each time we moved into a city, and I coordinated color coding and tagging all bags so that they were delivered to the correct hotels. Hopefully there's a company manager as well, which we had. But he wasn't always with us on travel days and the bulk of travel duties fell on the SMs. I was also in charge of Equity breaks and food stops.

Jill (Johnson) Gold
ASM, City of Angels
Shubert Theatre, Los Angeles

On the McCartney concert tour they were forcing the crews not to eat meat while the show was in the venue. Everything was soy and tofu, and we were not allowed to bring our own food. It was very disturbing to a lot of people.

Sean P. Crandall
Local Crew Member
Paul McCartney Concert Tour

[Does the tour management have the right to impose dietary rules on the crew? Are the rules made clear to the crew prior to their being hired?]

LOST SHEEP PRODUCTIONS, INC.
12309 Brackland Ave.
Los Angeles, California 90033
(213) 555 6246/sid@sidrswld.com
www.sidrswld.com

Mr. Victor N. Otorino
General Manager
The Civic Light Opera
2020 Lake Shore Drive
Cleveland OH 44176

Dear Mr. Otorino,

On November 18, 2005, we will be setting up the Lost Sheep production of *The Magnificent Eight.* Our truck should arrive on Thursday at 11 A.M.

We would appreciate your taking the necessary measures to clear any alley or passageway to allow our truck access to your loading dock at that time. It is essential that our truck be allowed to unload immediately upon arrival. Can an operator be placed on duty on your freight elevator until we have finished carrying in our equipment?

Our stage manager is Lawrence Stern. Chris Papadapoulos is our head road carpenter.

When we unload, we would like your house electrician to be on hand to answer questions of our technical crew. We will be carrying all of our own stage draperies, specialty lights, PA system, and projection equipment.

We will be coming in on a yellow card and we will be employing union stagehands. Chris will be in touch with your local business agent concerning calls for local workers to assist us.

We will need a grand piano, tuned to 440 pitch, a piano bench, and a 12 × 12 rug for the musicians at stage right.

We look forward to working with you in your facility.

Sincerely,

SID REDWOOD
Executive Producer

FIGURE 16.8 Advance Letter to Host Theater Manager

Overseeing the Arrival

- **The packing, padding, and care of sets, props, costumes, and technical equipment concern every department head. You coordinate with them in planning every move. You are the overseer of the move.**

It is particularly important that set diagrams be accurate and that all flats be marked with accurate butting guides so that crews who have never seen the assembled set can put it together with ease.

On arrival at a new location you first go to the theater. Inspect the premises to ensure that your setup plans are workable (pages 56–66). Assign dressing rooms and make sure they are in serviceable condition. Supervise the setup and check your personal equipment. Greet the new crew members who will run the show and review the running order, lighting sheet, sound plot, and shift plot chart with them (pages 155–160).

Before leaving the theater, post your local address and phone number on the callboard so that it is available in an emergency for the management of the theater and the local crew members.

Then check with the cast to ensure that their hotel accommodations are satisfactory.

Advance Letters

In very large companies there are sometimes advance people who go to a new location ahead of the company to prepare for their arrival. Sometimes an assistant stage manager may be dispatched in advance. But in many cases the problems of a traveling company can be anticipated and smoothed out via letter (figure 16.8). Letters requesting specific support (to hotels for accommodations, to business agents of unions for local personnel, to host theater owners, etc.) are usually sent out over the signature of the producer or company management. You can contribute to these letters by letting management know what problems you anticipate or encounter; for example, difficulty of hotels cashing checks for cast members on paydays, unavailability of an elevator during a load-in, and so on.

Calling a special staff meeting to brainstorm a move or series of moves can save time and money on the road.

> For the stage manager who travels and needs to focus a show quickly and efficiently, I have found that it is most helpful to grid the stage by dividing it into squares with numbers across the foots and up the center line. That way positions and hot spots can be identified and recreated with great precision. The only additional information needed is shutter information and gel color.
>
> Leonard Auerbach
> *Associate Professor, Department of Theatre Arts*
> *State University of New York at Stony Brook*

SUGGESTED CLASSROOM EXERCISE

Brainstorm a strike plan for a current production and put it in chronological order. Compare it with the strike plan shown in figure 16.1, page 206.

17

Fire/Evacuation

The most stringent protection of free speech would not protect a man falsely shouting fire in a theater and causing a panic.
—Oliver Wendell Holmes, Jr.
*In U.S. Supreme Court opinion (*Schenck v. U.S.*)*
(often misquoted)

Do not allow your dreams to go up in smoke. Practice fire safety.
—Anonymous

- **The first day you step into a theater as stage manager, check out the fire prevention/control equipment—extinguisher, sprinkler system, phone—because every day after that, you are the first line of defense against fire—on stage and backstage.**

It happened within the last 10 minutes of a production of *You Can't Take It with You*, in the round. From the booth I could not see the grid. I noticed that the audience was looking up at something in the ceiling. I went into the house to check it out. One of the wooden three-fer connectors had shorted and melted the connector of the instrument. The flame was getting bigger and closer to the ceiling. I rushed back to the booth, turned on the house lights, and announced an evacuation. The house manager pulled the fire alarm. One of the cast members, a volunteer fire fighter, grabbed an extinguisher and shot it into the air to put out the flame. With the audience (about 215) outside, I asked the cast to finish the show, altering the blocking from in the round to in the parking lot. I didn't actually see it because I was dealing with the fire department. I asked the cast to do a quick curtain call. The audience was very appreciative, even though they could not hear a lot of it, due to the noise of the fire engines and firemen. At the time, it was the worst incident I'd ever had to deal with. I was nervous and scared. We were very lucky. If the flames had gotten to the sprinkler system, there would have been extensive water damage to the theater.

Jorge Delgadillo
Stage Manager,
Hale Centre Theatre, Gilbert, AZ

(continued)

The fire was small and not obvious, so there was no panic. A smoke machine that was built into a set piece caught fire. While overseeing the running crew, I smelled the smoke and realized that it was not normal. I called the stage manager in the booth, grabbed a fire extinguisher from a few feet away, and put the fire out as he called the fire department. We stopped the show and made the standard announcements to the audience telling them that technical difficulties were causing us to stop the show. Following procedure, I then evacuated the cast and crew as we waited for the theme park fire department to come and inspect the building to make sure it was safe to go back in. About 20 minutes later we went back into the building and prepared for our next show. The smoke machine was replaced the following morning.

Dan Weingarten
AEA Stage Manager and Lighting Designer

On tour I was always prepared for inspection by the fire marshal. All Production Stage Managers, and their Head Carpenters, had to have their paperwork in order, regarding open flames, i.e., candles, cigarettes, etc., that would be used in the production, along with the presentation of a book of swatches of all the drops used. A match would be held directly to the swatch, by a fire marshal, to ensure that the scenery had been chemically treated with fire retardant. No Permit—No Performance!

We were even better prepared for inspection in Boston, Hartford, and Las Vegas.

In Boston, The Coconut Grove Night Club fire on November 28, 1942, claimed 492 lives. In Hartford on July 6, 1944, 167 people died in the Ringling Bros. Barnum & Bailey Great Circus Fire. (Prior to 1944, the way to waterproof canvas was to coat it with paraffin. It was bits of these hundreds of pieces of canvas that floated down and stuck to the victims' skins that contributed to so many excruciatingly painful deaths, along with those that had the misfortune of being trampled, as the sold-out performance of over 2,000 souls tried to make their way out of the tent.)

Finding your way out, in case of fire, was the first thing my crew and I would look for in any Las Vegas showroom. On November 21, 1980, the MGM Grand Hotel fire resulted in 84 deaths and 679 injuries. The way showrooms were then designed, with room-length tables and customers seated shoulder to shoulder, back to back, there was little hope for any audience member in the event of a fire. I knew a lot of those rooms well, in my years with Shirley MacLaine's nightclub act.

Now Nevada has the toughest fire sprinkler law in the world. I was given a tour of the MGM Grand (now Bally's Hotel & Casino), prior to its reopening. My host asked me to look at the ceiling and observe the extraordinary number of sprinklers. He said they were thinking of attaching seat belts to the gaming chairs—if the sprinkler system was ever activated, the clientele would have to float to safety due to the amount of water coming down on them.

Bryan Young
Production Stage Manager
Broadway, National & International Tours

[Note: In his 45 years of backstage experience, Bryan Young never had to run for a fire extinguisher once. But that's 45 years of awareness and vigilance.]

LIMITATIONS

It is not the stage manager's responsibility to know all of the fire/evacuation regulations, laws, and codes of all of the governing entities (state, county, and city). Nor is the SM responsible for knowing whether the theater was built in compliance with the fire/evacuation-related building codes. If you are working in a venue that was not designed as a theater (e.g., storefront to community theater), it is not your responsibility to know if the conversion to a performance space included upgrading to meet codes. This is the theater owner's and/or producer's responsibility. The stage manager's responsibility is for the safety of cast and crew, for knowing how to apply all of the equipment and procedures that will ensure their safety, and for knowing how to react if there is a fire or if the cast/crew needs to be evacuated.

For those stage managers who want to know more about state, county, and city fire law/code, visits to your local fire department and law library are recommended. Most cities no longer publish their fire code in hard copy, but it is typically available via computer, and many cities use the standard codes of the International Code Council (ICC), (see Resources below).

Occasionally, requested or not, fire marshals inspect theaters just prior to the opening of new productions to check fireproofing, exits, no smoking signs, and so on. Theaters have been closed and performances postponed as a result of such inspections (figure 17.1).

(*Los Angeles Bugle,* July, 2000)

STAGE NEWS TODAY

*

The Awareness Theater, recently closed by the fire marshal, has relocated temporarily at the Psychiatry Center Auditorium at the UCLA Medical Center where Bella Harpman is directing two one-acts by Harry Rose on Friday and Sunday nights. The plays are "Big Sol" about an aging convict who fantasizes about the blonde he murdered so effectively that he has his cellmate seeing things, and also "One Time Charlie" which deals w[illegible] an opium addict who drops [illegible] peddling dope on horseba[illegible]

Mrs. Harpman says [illegible] versity will reinstate [illegible] ness Theater, starti[illegible] other members of [illegible] Students' Guild [illegible] while the thea[illegible] duction on [illegible] cal Center [illegible] ovation [illegible] theater [illegible]

(*Varsity, The Stage Daily,* February, 2001)

FIRE DEPT HALTS SHOW OF LIVING THEATER

Performances of Living Theater at USC were canceled this weekend after fire safety code violations were alleged by fire marshals.

A tactical alert was called by police Friday after notification that fire safety codes were apparently being ignored and that too many people were being allowed on stage. Refunds were made available.

(*Los Angeles Messenger,* February, 2001)

USC LIVING THEATER CALLED OFF

Performances of the Living Theater Saturday night and tonight were canceled at USC following apparent violations of fire safety regulations.

Police called a tactical alert on the campus Friday evening after learning that fire safety laws had been violated and that too many persons were occupying the [illegible]r-sized stage at once in [illegible]on of regulations.

[illegible]rsity executive di[illegible] university rela[illegible] said that the per[illegible]nce had been can[illegible] because the theater [illegible]nd staff were "inade[illegible] to assure that the [illegible]ssary compliance with [illegible] safety codes and audience safety would be carried out in accordance with municipal regulations."

Refund information is available by telephone at the following numbers: 555-7834, 555-6093, 555-8427.

FIGURE 17.1 A Theater in Violation of Safety Laws Can Be Closed Down

Frequently in small theaters, scene designers and technical directors build into the audience, covering exit lights and no-smoking signs, and blocking exit aisles with scenery. You should act to prevent or correct this.

- **Review fire safety with the producer and the entire theater staff.**

If you are working in an Equity company and feel that the producer is failing to comply with regulations, thus endangering safety, and you have already discussed the problem with the producer, then take the issue to your union and let the union take up the issue with the producer.

If you are in a nonunion theater situation and can't convince your management or producer to make the theater fire-safe, quit. Then call for fire, police, and building code inspections as a concerned citizen. People die in theaters as the result of negligence. As a stage manager, the lives of your cast, crew, and audience may depend on your understanding of the importance of fire safety (figure 17.2).

(*Varsity, the Stage Daily*, August, 2000)

PROP BURSTS INTO FLAMES AS PLAY REACHES HIGHLIGHT

Murfreesboro, Tenn., Aug. 15—Just as Mark Antony was about to deliver his "Friends, Romans, countrymen" speech in praise of Julius Caesar he was left speechless when a fire out on the stage of the Anders Theater during a Rebel Theat pany performance of the Sh ean play last night.

The blaze ignited a 151 foam and fiberglass but u which dominated the Jap stage throughout the pla veloped the stage props the rest of the seventee ater before the eyes of tators.

Stage Manager re nounced what spectators knew, that there was a fire, and asked patrons to leave as quietly as possible. More than a thousand spectators occupying three-fourths of the theater building managed to file out without panic. Shortly afterward four fire rigs arrived to quench the blaze, although stagehands and actors had already acted to douse the flames.

(*Varsity, the Stage Daily*, February, 2001)

FIRE DEPT HALTS SHOW

After a thirty minute delay, during which debris was removed and further precautions were taken against the outbreak of any other fire, patrons were permitted to re-enter the theater, still smoke-filled, and the play continued with Chuck Kitting as Antony resuming his eulogy of Caesar. Most of the audience waited out the firefighting efforts and returned to watch the end of the play. The biggest ovation of the evening went to five members of the Murfreesboro Fire Department as they marched out with full equipment shortly before the play was ready to resume.

FLAMES CALL OFF LIVING THEATER

(*Los Angeles Messenger*, February, 2001)

Performances of Living Theater at USC cancelled this after fire ...

FIGURE 17.2 On-Stage Fire Can Threaten Your Production Anytime, Anywhere

STAGE MANAGER'S FIRE/EVACUATION CHECKLIST

Before rehearsals begin

1. Discuss fire safety with producer.
   - A. In absence of house manager, who is responsible for front of house?
   - B. If venue was not designed as a theater, what equipment (exit signs, fire extinguisher, sprinkler system) was added to meet fire codes for performance space?
   - C. Will producer place fire/evacuation info in the program or make precurtain announcements on fire/evacuation procedure?
   - D. Review fire/evacuation announcements (see figures 17.5, 17.6, 17.7, pages 234, 235, and 236 respectively).
2. Check out fire/evacuation equipment/procedures.
   - A. Where are fire extinguishers? Read tags. Do you know how to operate? If you have never used one, practice. When was maintenance last done? Most extinguishers have to be replenished every two years.
   - B. Is there an alarm system? Where? What do you have to do to activate?
   - C. Do you have a phone with which to call the fire department? Do you know the number of the station in case 911 is not working or overworked?
   - D. Where is the closest fire station? What is the estimated response time?
   - E. Where are the exit signs? Are their lights all working? Is any scenery or lighting/sound equipment making the exit signs less visible?
   - F. Do you have a microphone backstage with which to speak to the audience? Do you know how to use it, unassisted?
   - G. Are the emergency announcements posted near the microphone?
   - H. Where is the circuit breaker panel?
   - I. Where are first-aid supplies?
3. Include fire safety and evacuation in company rules.
   - A. No smoking in dressing rooms or backstage. (Designated smoking area?)
   - B. No electric appliances (heaters, coffee makers, etc.) in dressing rooms without prior approval of stage manager.
   - C. Evacuation routes for cast, crew.
   - D. Designation of location to regroup after evacuation. (Is there an all-night coffee shop near the theater?)

During readings and rehearsals

1. Review fire safety/evacuation with cast/crew. Discuss applicable company rules.
2. Lead cast/crew on backstage tour, pointing out fire extinguishers, exit routes, and potential hazards. Are all exit hallways uncluttered?
3. Discuss dressing room fire safety.
4. Explain post-fire/evacuation regroup location, pointing out that you must be able to account for every member of cast/crew.
5. Conduct sniff test (no smoldering cigarettes in waste baskets).

During production

1. Place inspection of exit lights on precurtain checklist.
2. Are you ready for an unexpected visit by a fire marshal five minutes before curtain?
3. Conduct sniff test as part of locking-up routine.

Postproduction

1. Leave a note for next stage manager (or even to yourself) on your use of fire equipment and anything that should be known about your experience with fire/ evacuation.
2. Conduct sniff test after the strike or the last time you leave venue.

I have a very close relationship with the Atlanta Fire Department. We discuss any new regulations. New fire marshals who visit the theater are always impressed at how well prepared we are, mostly because we started by going to the AFD many years ago to ask them what they require. We also try to keep them abreast through casual conversation of new theater technologies. Before opening night, I fax * a list of the use of fire to the fire chief. The most important thing is that I hide nothing from him. If a fire marshal shows up five minutes before curtain and wants a demonstration of everything we are using—its ignition, its extinguishing—I do it and hold the show.

Dave Grindle
Production Stage Manager
The Atlanta Opera

*[*See figures 17.3, page 231 and 17.4, page 233.]*

EVACUATION

Like many other aspects of stage management, an hour of preparation is worth many, many hours of remorse afterwards. In the event that you should need to evacuate cast, crew, and audience, you will be under pressure and will need to remain calm. This is not a good time to be thinking about the exact wording to fit the circumstances or weighing the ethics of what you are about to say. If you have considered various scenarios for emergency evacuation—fire backstage, fire on stage, fire in the lobby, fire in the building, fire in adjacent building, or bomb threat, and talked through them with producer and house manager, then you can prepare an evacuation announcement appropriate for each situation and have these announcements posted near your backstage microphone.

The place: Major West Coast Touring Company Host Theatre. The show: The First National Tour of *Bubbling Brown Sugar,* Cast: 23, Band: 11.

Though it was a Saturday matinee, the house was sold out. Everyone was excited because our San Francisco run had been wonderful. The house was packed for every performance. We were in "places." I had cued the house to half, the top of the show electrics, and the conductor to start the overture. Just as the overture ended, the house lights were going out, the stage lighting was changing, and the dancers and principals were making their first entrances singing the theme song from the show, I noticed the house manager walking hastily toward me. "We have to evacuate the theater. There's a bomb threat." She hurried away to the front of house.

Inexplicably, I became extremely calm. There was a microphone off stage right used for announcing to the audience any understudies that might be going on, other announcements, or emergencies. I didn't know what I'd say. I flashed the sound man who apparently already knew about the problem. He picked up immediately. I asked him to make the off-right mic hot. "Done," he said.

(continued)

728 West Peachtree St
Atlanta GA 30308

Phone 404.881.8801
Fax: 404.881.1711

The Atlanta Opera

Fax

To:	Captain Nathaniel Grissom	**From:**	David Grindle, Production Stage Manager
Fax:	404-853-7093	**Pages:**	1
Phone:	404-853-7062	**Date:**	07/17/00
Re:	Live Flame in Cosi fan tutte	**CC:**	Sarah Wikle

☐ **Urgent** ☐ **For Review** ☐ **Please Comment** ☐ **Please Reply** ☐ **Please Recycle**

Captain Grissom-

I wanted to advise you as to our plans for use of live flame for the upcoming Atlanta Opera production of *Cosi fan tutte* at the Fox Theatre.

In the final scene of the opera (approximate 3 hours after the show starts) we are planning to use six (6) tiki torches (the backyard Kmart type) and 2 candelabra. The tiki torches will be brought on and placed in fixed spots on the set and then lit. The candelabra will be carried lit by two chorus men. One man per candelabra.

The burn time for these items will be approximately 20 minutes for tikis and 10 minutes for the candles.

As we have not yet staged the final scene, I do not have a precise plot to fax you. Once have that, I will get it to you.

The following is a list of rehearsal dates and times when the live flame is scheduled to be used on stage. The times are for the complete rehearsal, the actual use of flame will occur sometime during the time frame indicated.

Friday, June 2 7p-10p

Sunday, June 4 7:30p-10:30p

Monday, June 5 7p-10:30p

Tuesday, June 6 7p-10:30p (there will be an invited audience at this rehearsal)

Thursday, June 8 8p performance

Saturday, June 10 7:30p performance

Sunday, June 11 3p performance

FIGURE 17.3 Notice to Fire Department of Intended Use of Fire. Dates and times of both rehearsals and performances are given. All persons who handle fire receive careful instruction and precautions.

Courtesy David Grindle, PSM, The Atlanta Opera.

I could see the conductor from where I stood. I remember taking a deep breath and telling myself to remain calm. From the number-one wing down right, I held up my left hand to get the attention of the conductor as I held the microphone in my right hand. I very calmly said into the microphone, "Ladies and gentlemen. Ladies and gentlemen, may I have your attention please." By this time, the conductor noticed me and had stopped the band. I remember the sound of confusion as each musician realized that something was wrong. The bewildered look on their faces begged the conductor for an explanation as the sound of their instruments dropped out one by one. Now the only sound that could be heard was my voice.

I began waving my left hand to the principals and dancers indicating that they should come off stage. Again, there was that look of bewilderment on their faces. I repeated into the microphone, "Ladies and gentlemen, your attention please." By this time, everyone on stage could hear me, and they began to exit the stage and come toward me. The musicians grabbed their instruments and exited off left where a stagehand told them to exit the building through the stage door. "Ladies and gentlemen, due to a small problem with some electrical equipment, we ask that you please leave the theater at this time. Please remain calm. There is what appears to be a small chance of fire in the basement. It is with your interest in mind that we ask you leave the theater at this time. We are confident that the show will go on, but at this time please leave your seats and exit the theater. The ushers will help you. Thank you for your cooperation."

All the actors and stagehands were heading toward the backstage door as I grabbed the script and followed them. Out of the corner of my eye, I could see the show curtain coming in. We exited into the street where we stood two blocks away from the theater in the cool spring breeze for over an hour. We joked about the things that the musicians, stagehands, and cast members had chosen to take with them. We all laughed when the drummer said, "I'm so glad that the drum set is rented."

Though the search of the building by the bomb squad and their dogs did not yield a bomb, we were happy but a bit apprehensive about going back into the building. The threat was confirmed as a prank. The matinee went on an hour and a half late. Food was brought in between shows. I found it amazing that cast members, stagehands, and all company members cooperated and did not complain. It wasn't until after the evening performance, as I was walking to my hotel that I began to feel fear. My hands began to shake. It was then that I was grateful that no one had panicked. I acknowledged and marveled at how everyone cooperated during an emergency that could have had a very different ending.

Femi Sarah Heggie
Production Stage Manager
Recipient 2003 Audelco Award

During my prep week, I always find the evacuation routes, fire extinguishers, first-aid, and emergency supplies, but fortunately I've never had to use them. I also always make sure that I have a public address microphone, communications with the house manager, and prepared announcements (see figure 17.6) in case an audience needs to be evacuated. I guess I have been very fortunate. In my nine years as an Equity stage manager, I have never had a fire.

Cari Norton
Stage Manager

[See figures 17.5, 17.6, and 17.7]

The Atlanta Opera
MACBETH
Fire and Pyro Plot

Act I Scene II

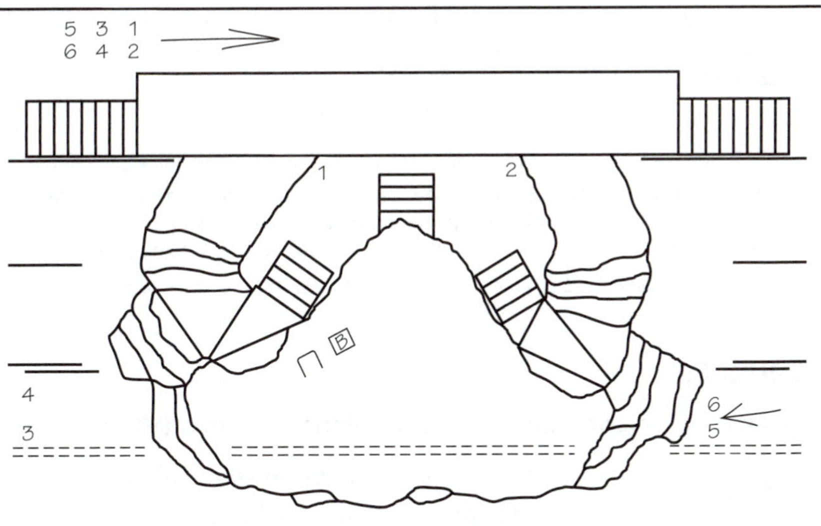

Live Flame		*F/x*
Top of Scene	Brazier lit (see map for placement) (B)	No Pyro, Fog, or Dry Ice in this scene
6:00	Flash paper thrown on Brazier by Lady Macbeth	
9:30	Brazier extinguished and struck DL by chorus men (T. Tunnell and G. Jones)	
23:00	6 torches carried on by Supers from SR to SL (Brown, Seide, Chrestensen, Coyle, Haynie, Smith)	
27:30	Torches extinguished by supers using dead man switch built into torch	

FIGURE 17.4 Fire Plot, *Macbeth*, Act I, Scene II. Fire and special effects are listed on this plot, which is submitted along with notification.

Courtesy David Grindle, PSM, The Atlanta Opera.

EVACUATION ANNOUNCEMENT

"May I have your attention please? Please, may I have your attention? A situation that is not immediately threatening requires us to evacuate the building at this time. We ask that you please walk to the nearest exit. The ushers will be available to assist you and will direct you to a safe gathering point. Thank you for your cooperation."

(Repeat as necessary.)

FIGURE 17.5 Emergency Evacuation Announcement Used at the American Musical Theatre of San Jose (California). The stage manager has a bullhorn stage right in case the power goes out and he cannot communicate via his public address microphone.

Courtesy Bob Bones, Production Stage Manager, American Musical Theatre of San Jose.

RESOURCES

International Association of Venue Managers, Inc. (IAVM)

"To educate, advocate for, and inspire public assembly professionals, worldwide."

The International Association of Venue Managers (formerly International Association of Assembly Managers) was founded in December 1924, as a result of the meeting in Cleveland, Ohio, of six enthusiastic building managers with a vision of the future of public assembly facility management. IAAM membership has risen sharply in the past 20 years, as have its supportive services, including conferences and trade shows. In 2008, the conference and trade show was combined into one event, July 25–29 at the Anaheim Convention Center. A topic of interest to stage managers was "Soft Target Awareness," which reflected the changes in evacuation procedures in the light of possible terrorist attacks in the post-9/11 era.

In November 2010, IAAM changed its name to International Association of Venue Managers.

Kris Williams
International Association of Venue Managers
972-538-1006
IAVM.org

International Code Council (ICC)

The International Code Council, a membership association dedicated to building safety and fire prevention, develops the codes used to construct residential and commercial buildings. Most U.S. cities, counties, and states that adopt codes choose the International Codes developed by the International Code Council.

500 New Jersey Ave. NW, Sixth Floor
Washington, D.C. 20001
888-422-7233
iccsafe.org

HOUSE ANNOUNCEMENT

Casting Change

Ladies and Gentlemen. May I have your attention please. Welcome to __________. In this evening's performance, the role of __________, usually played by __________, will be played by __________. Thank you and enjoy the show.

Technical Problem

(Brief stop)
Ladies and Gentlemen. May I have your attention please. We are currently experiencing some technical difficulties on stage. Please bear with us and the performance will continue in just a moment. Thank you for your patience.

(Intermission)
Ladies and Gentlemen. May I have your attention please. We are currently experiencing some technical difficulties on stage. At this time we will take an early intermission. Please feel free to leave your seats, and we will ring the lobby chimes as soon as we are ready to continue the performance. Thank you for your patience.

Possible Fire:

Ladies and Gentlemen. May I have your attention please. We have been notified of a possible fire somewhere in our building. For your safety, and the safety of those around you, we are going to evacuate the theater until the fire department tells us it is safe to resume the performance. Please stand and calmly exit to the exit door nearest you. Please notify an usher if assistance is needed. Move away from the building to a safe distance, and we will notify you when it is safe to return to your seats. Thank you.

Noticeable Fire:

Ladies and Gentlemen. At this time we need to ask you to exit the theater building. For your safety, and the safety of those around you, please stand and calmly exit to the exit door nearest you. Once again, please stand and calmly exit to the exit door nearest you. Move away from the building to a safe distance, and we will notify you when it is safe to return to your seats. Thank you.

Earthquake:

Ladies and Gentlemen. Please crouch down as low as you can in your seat and cover your head with your hands. We are experiencing a small earthquake and it will be over shortly. DO NOT ATTEMPT TO LEAVE YOUR SEATS AT THIS TIME. Actors, please exit the stage into the wings. Once again, crouch down low in your seats and cover your head with your hands. Please remain calm and remain in your seats.

FIGURE 17.6 Emergency Announcements. Cari Norton finds that many theaters now have evacuation announcements posted in the control booth. In case they don't, however, Norton has her own.

Courtesy Cari Norton, Stage Manager.

EVACUATION PROCEDURES
FOR THE CENTER FOR THE PERFORMING ARTS

In the case of an emergency requiring the evacuation of the building, a decision made by the police, events coordinator, CLO manager on duty and the stage manager, the following steps are to be taken backstage to evacuate.

1. The Stage Manager will stop the performance, if it has not already stopped, and through the microphone backstage that goes into the house system, go on stage and direct the audience as to what to do. If power is out, the stage manager will use the bullhorn that is located stage right.
2. The Stage right ASM and the IA steward on the call will make sure that everyone on stage, on the rail, in the immediate backstage rooms stage right, and the loading dock area are evacuated.
3. The Stage left ASM will go upstairs and make sure the dressing rooms are evacuated.
4. The orchestra conductor will make sure the pit and lower-level rooms are evacuated.
5. The security guard will stay at the stage door to make sure people exiting that way do so safely and quickly.
6. The Stage managers, steward, and orchestra conductor should then meet the security guard at the backstage door and let the others know that backstage is evacuated. Then go to the meeting place outside the building on the Park Ave. side.

FIGURE 17.7 Evacuation Procedures Used by the American Musical Theatre of San Jose (California)

Courtesy American Musical Theatre of San Jose.

SUGGESTED CLASSROOM EXERCISES

Have students draw a slip of paper containing an emergency situation and give, within 30 seconds of the draw, an emergency evacuation announcement. Have class discuss the appropriateness of the announcement to the situation and evaluate announcer's delivery.

Take a tour of your theater building to demonstrate use of fire prevention equipment and point out potential fire hazards.

18

Working with Unions

A verbal agreement isn't worth the paper it's printed on.
—Sam Goldwyn

"You can't join Equity until you have a job in an Equity company, and you can't get a job in an Equity company until you are a member of Equity." This seeming paradox is often quoted but quite misleading. As soon as you can convince an Equity producer or director that you should be the stage manager, the doors of the union will open to you. Equity is not one of the closed unions where nepotism reigns or where "blood is thicker than talent."

If it is your intent to become an Equity stage manager, don't wait for an Equity job to get acquainted with the union. Understand the benefits and disadvantages of union membership. Go out of your way to meet a union stage manager. Discuss working within union restrictions, advantages and disadvantages. If you live in a city with an Equity office, get to know the people in the office. The union office is not a placement service, but the union staff is in a good position to know what producers are anticipating productions or casting. Bulletin boards in the union offices frequently display information useful to stage managers. Sometimes the union has available handouts, such as lists of union-approved theaters where you might apply for work.

An Equity card is what one should strive towards, not start with. We recommend that stage managers (and actors) get as much experience as they can before accepting an Equity contract. An Actors' Equity Association card does not guarantee you work. This is attested to by the high unemployment of both actors and stage managers in our union. There are from one to three stage managers in any given production, as compared to whatever the number in the cast. So finding jobs is even harder for a stage manager than for an actor. Stage managers limit their experience possibilities by getting their Equity card because they cannot work non-Equity once they join the union. Experience is the only way for a stage manager to perfect his/her craft. I recommend that a stage manager get as much experience

(continued)

as possible before accepting a job as an Equity stage manager. I cannot stress enough that experience is a most important aspect of a stage manager's future potential.

Martha R. Jacobs
Stage Manager, New York City

[Martha is currently working in an administrative position in live theater in New York City. Her work as a stage manager led to her current position.]

I am often asked why stage managers are members of Actors' Equity Association (i.e., in the same union with the actors). I believe it is the right place for us to be. The main reason is this: of all of the many people and disciplines that come together to make a show happen, only two are there together every day and/or night, from the first rehearsal to the final performance—the actor and the stage manager.

Ira Mont
National 3rd Vice President (office held by a stage manager)
Chair, Eastern Region Stage Manager Committee
Actors' Equity Association

If you accept a job as a stage manager or actor with an Equity company, you must join the union. Thereafter you may never legally work in a non-Equity company without first getting a waiver from Equity (figures 18.1 and 18.2).

Actors' Equity Association (AEA)
165 West 46th Street, 15th Floor
New York, NY 10036-2501
212-869-8530
fax 212-719-9815
actorsequity.org

Los Angeles Office
6755 Hollywood Blvd., 5th Floor
Hollywood, CA 90028
323-978-8080
fax 323-978-8081

Chicago Office
557 West Randolph St.
Chicago, IL 60661
Chicago, IL 60603
312-641-0393
fax 312-641-6365
877-232-1913 ext. 815 audition hotline

Orlando Office
10369 Orangewood Blvd.
Orlando, FL 32821-8239
407-345-8600
fax 407-345-1522

Once in a union position, you may quickly find it necessary to deal with members of other unions, depending on the size of your theater staff:

American Federation of Musicians
afm.org (national)
Local 47, Hollywood
817 N. Vine
Hollywood, CA 90038-3715
323-462-2161
fax 323-461-3090
local47@afm.org
promusic47.org (local)

American Guild of Musical Artists (AGMA)
1430 Broadway, 14th Floor
New York, NY 10018
212-265-3687
fax 212-262-90088
AGMA@musicalartists.org
musicalartists.org

Definition of the Duties of a Stage Manager

- A stage manager under Actors' Equity Contract is, or shall be obligated to perform at least the following duties for the Production to which s/he is engaged, and by performing them is hereby defined as the Stage Manager:
- Shall be responsible for the calling of all rehearsals, whether before or after opening.
- Shall assemble and maintain the Prompt Book which is defined as the accurate playing text and stage business, together with such cue sheets, plots, daily records, etc., as are necessary for the actual technical and artistic operation of the production.
- Shall work with the Director and the heads of all other departments, during rehearsal and after opening, schedule rehearsal and outside calls in accordance with Equity regulations.
- Assume active responsibility for the form and discipline of rehearsal and performance, and be the executive instrument on the technical running of **each** performance.
- Maintain the artistic intentions of the Director and the Producer after opening, to the best of his/her ability, including calling correctional rehearsals of the company when necessary and preparation of the Understudies, Replacements, Extras and Supers, when and if the Director and/or the Producer declines this prerogative. Therefore, if an Actor finds himself/herself unable to satisfactorily work out an artistic difference of opinion with the Stage Manager regarding the intentions of the Director and Producer, the Actor has the option of seeking clarification from the Director or Producer.
- Keep such records as are necessary to advise the Producer on matters of attendance, time, health benefits or other matters relating to the rights of Equity members. **The Stage Manager and Assistant Stage Managers are prohibited from the making of payrolls or any distribution of salaries.**
- Maintain discipline as provided in the Equity Constitution, By-Laws and Rules where required, appealable in every case to Equity.
- Stage Manager duties do not include shifting scenery, running lights or operating the Box Office, etc.
- The Council shall have the power from time to time to define the meaning of the words "Stage Manager" and may alter, change or modify the meaning of Stage Manager as herein above defined.
- The Stage Manager and Assistant Stage Managers are prohibited from handling contracts, having riders signed or initialed, or any other function which normally comes under the duties of the General Manager or Company Manager.
- The Stage Manager and Assistant Stage Managers are prohibited from participating in the ordering of food for the company.
- The Stage Manager and Assistant Stage Managers are prohibited from signing the closing notice of the company or the individual notice of any Actor's termination.

FIGURE 18.1 Equity's Definitions of the Duties of a Stage Manager

Courtesy Actors' Equity Association. Latest revision may be downloaded from actorsequity.org.

Responsibilities of the Actor

Please Post Please Post

Equity requires management to meet all of its responsibilities under its contract with Equity. In turn, members have certain professional responsibilities to the producer, to the production and to fellow Equity members. All Equity members **must:**

- Be on time for all rehearsals and half-hour calls.
- Notify the Stage Manager as soon as possible, and certainly before half-hour, if ill or unable to reach the theatre on time.
- Remember that, even though places for each act will be called, you alone are responsible for all of your entrance cues.
- Observe all reasonable rules of management not in conflict with Equity rules.
- Cooperate with the Stage Manager and Assistant Stage Managers, Dance Captain and Fight Captain.
- Take proper care of, and make no unauthorized changes in, your costumes, props, or makeup.
- Maintain your performance as directed.
- Appear at curtain calls in complete costume and make-up.
- Go to your Deputy in cases of disagreement. If a disagreement cannot be resolved by the authorities backstage, refer it to the appropriate Equity Business Representative.

Your Stage Manager is obligated to report violations to Equity and Equity will, when necessary, call before a Membership Relations Committee any member who violates these rules.

Discipline is a sign of professionalism. Maintain a professional attitude at all times.

FIGURE 18.2 Equity's Responsibilities of the Actor. Note the references to the stage manager.

Courtesy Actors' Equity Association. Latest revision may be downloaded from actorsequity.org.

American Federation of Television and Radio Artists (AFTRA)
5757 Wilshire Blvd., 9th Floor
Los Angeles, CA 90036-3689
323-634-8100
fax 323-634-8246
losangeles@aftra.com
aftra.org

260 Madison Ave.
New York, NY 10016-2401
212-532-0800
212-545-1238

International Alliance of Theatrical Stage Employees (IATSE)
1430 Broadway, 20th Floor
New York, NY
212-730-1770
fax 212-730-7809
iatse-intl.org

American Guild of Variety Artists (AGVA)
363 Seventh Avenue
New York, NY 10001-3904
212-675-1003
fax 212-633-0097
agvany@aol.com
americanguildofvariety artistsagva.visualnet.com

American Guild of Variety Artists (AGVA)
4741 Laurel Canyon Blvd., Suite 208
North Hollywood, CA 91607-5915
818-508-9984
fax 818-508-3029
agvala@earthlink.net
http://home.earthlink.net/~agvala/agval.html

Association of Theatrical Press Agents and Managers (ATPAM)
62 W 45th Street, Suite 901 | New York, NY 10036
212-719-3666
fax 212-302-1585
tsanchez@atpam.com; atpam.com

Teamsters Local 399
Studio Transportation Drivers
P.O. Box 6017
North Hollywood, CA 91603-6107
818-985-7374
Fax: 818-985-0097
office@ht399.org
ht399.org

International Alliance of Theatrical Stage Employees (IATSE)
Local One (formerly Local 922) IATSE
Sound Designers, Lighting Control Board Operators, Carpenters, Lighting Directors, Spotlight Operators
320 West 46th Street
New York, NY 10036-8399
212-333-2500
fax 212-586-2437
wngai@iatse-local1.org
iatse-localone.org

Screen Actors Guild (SAG)
360 Madison Avenue
New York, NY 10017
212-944-1030
fax 212-944-6774
TTY 212-944-6715
nypr@sag.org
sag.org

Screen Actors Guild (SAG)
5757 Wilshire Blvd., 7th Floor
Los Angeles, CA 90036-3600
323-954-1600 or 800-SAG-0767
fax 323-594-6603
TTY/TTD 323-549-6648
sag.org

Stage Directors and Choreographers Society
1501 Broadway, Suite 1701
New York, NY 10036-5653
212-391-1070
fax 212-302-6195
sdcweb.org

The Western Region Stage Manager Committee tries to educate stage managers, members, and producers on the roles, duties, and abuses of stage managers. It represents the voice of stage managers within the western region of Actors' Equity Association. The committee would like to remind stage managers that we maintain an interest in and stand in support of their work. In turn, AEA is responsible for serving and assisting stage managers in any grievances, overtime claims, or other problems that might occur with the company that has employed them.

(continued)

The committee encourages you to contact us if any need arises. Please keep us informed about the progress and problems you encounter. We are interested in what stage managers have to say.

Call and get involved.

James T. McDermott
Chairman
Western Region Stage Manager Committee
Actors' Equity Association
323-634-1750

[The Eastern Region Stage Manager Committee is currently chaired by Ira Mont. Call the NYC Equity office—212-869-8530—for information. The Central Region Stage Manager Committee is currently chaired by Malcolm D. Ewen. Call the Chicago office—312-641-0393—for information.]

As closely related unions for performers, SAG, AFTRA, and AGVA have reciprocal agreements as to when and how their members may perform in jurisdictions of the other unions. The producer normally handles arrangements with the unions and ensures that all members of the cast are members of Equity or have been cleared by Equity to work in the production.

Union composition of a staff varies from theater to theater, depending on size and on the arrangements that producers have made with union locals. In a small union house, all of the cast may be Equity, and there may be only one non-Equity union member, an IATSE master electrician.

In another larger house, there may be three IATSE members (carpenter, lights, props); two theatrical wardrobe attendants members; five treasurers and ticket seller members in the box office; two members of ATPAM (publicist and house manager); and five musicians from the AFM (who are paid to play bridge in the wings during a play in which there is no music).

In a huge outdoor theater, Teamster truckers may refuse to leave their trucks and enter the stage area to pick up scenery, insisting that the scenery be loaded out by IATSE stagehands and handed to them on their truck, while IATSE stagehands will refuse to get on a truck, insisting that Teamsters must be present to stack the scenery.

In still another tent theater, four well-paid IATSE crew members may work right alongside six nonunion "apprentices" who are not paid at all; both union and nonunion crew members do the same work, but at the end of the union work call period, the union workers go home while the nonpaid "apprentices" continue to work to the end of the rehearsal period.

The stage manager need never contest the inequities of union regulations. This is a responsibility of management or the producer. Understand the rules that apply to other union members with whom you work: hours, minimum calls, overtime rules, and working restrictions and jurisdictions.

Examples

1. A union property master PM may be prohibited from moving lighting equipment, so the PM looks on while the master electrician, who might be a friend and a member of the same union, toils.

2. A union carpenter may be paid to be on hand for a show in which he has no duties other than pulling the curtain, but his union rules will not allow him to use that paid time to work on the sets of the next show that follows in the same house for the same company.

Start by asking the producer or administrative manager for the information you will need to know about union calls to enable you to plan work calls most efficiently.

If the producer cannot give you sufficient information, request permission to call the business agents of the unions to get this information. Usually the producer or business manager will want to handle this for you.

Discuss work rules with the individual union members concerned. In informal chats find out what union members feel are their obligations to their employer, as well as what they consider the benefits of their union membership.

In the long run, the more you know about the work rules of the other unions, the more money you will be able to save the producer in scheduling calls.

Union rules cannot be summarized here, since they vary from local to local, and since they are also dependent on agreements that each producer makes with each local business agent. It is a mistake to assume that wage scales, hours, and work restrictions are not locally negotiable, regardless of nationally distributed union literature. Stage managers do not negotiate, but producers and business managers do.

Inexperienced stage managers are frequently apprehensive about working with IATSE personnel for the first time. Perhaps this is because the veteran IATSE members are often much older than the new stage managers. There is nothing to fear. Treat members of all other unions with professional courtesy. Give them the same respect for the job they are doing as you expect for yours. Assume they are trained specialists who know exactly how to carry out their work once you have scheduled it.

It is wrong for a stage manager to harbor contempt or resentment for a member of another union because of perceived inequities. Think of those three AFM musicians who were paid to play bridge in the wings. They were there because a contract specified that a minimum number of musicians would be hired during the season. Remember that union rights and benefits are negotiated by unions to protect their members from exploitation. There are good reasons for what may seem to be obvious inequities.

In San Jose, with the Andrea Bocelli concert tour, the production manager asked me to send the orchestra on stage at 7:45, even though we knew the concert would not start till 8:15. Sending them to the stage 30 minutes before they were to start playing was overly cautious, and yet that is what the production manager insisted on doing. I tried to talk him out of it, but he wanted to ensure that all of the musicians were going to be on stage and ready to play at the prescribed "go" time. In my experience, union musicians I worked with had never been late. I did everything I could to warn the production manager that it was likely to cause overtime, about which the musicians had warned me, but he was so insistent, that I sent the musicians to the stage. I also let the orchestra's managers know. As anticipated, the concert ran long, incurring 15 minutes of overtime, which for 80 musicians was no small amount of money. The producers of the concert wanted to know why they had been hit with this overtime charge. Fortunately the orchestra managers came to my defense and informed the producers that I did indeed

(continued)

warn everyone about the impending overtime. The musicians were paid. The producers were not at all happy.

Dan Weingarten
Stage Manager, New West Symphony
Andrea Bocelli Concert Tour

My business partner and I, working as set construction subcontractors, built sets for a small, nonprofit opera company that was performing in an IATSE venue. The set we built had to be installed and struck by union stagehands. Although I asked, I could not get the union steward to give me the rules on breaks and overtime. After closing, the producer told me that he had been billed for overtime. Since that incident, I have worked as both an AEA stage manager and as an IATSE stagehand. After becoming a member of IATSE, I served as event manager for the same venue (years after the opera company folded). As a building representative, I strongly suggested that clients be extremely organized and use their time wisely. Our building steward was very conscientious in giving clients accurate estimates that were usually in line with the final billing.

Name withheld at writer's request

I've been working with IATSE crews as an ASM since 2003, and since 2008 as a PSM. Our theater company has a contract with our local IA.

After getting the local to lower its hourly rates in a rather heated debate, our company acquired brand-new moving lights. The lights were met with mixed feelings. Some of the crew were pleased to work with the new equipment, and others were hurt that money had been spent on the lights while they took a cut in pay. Within days after the new lights were set up, a five-member camera crew was brought into the theater to tape the dress rehearsal of a show. I had sent an e-mail notice to staff members a few weeks prior (costume and technical [TD] directors) and had included a video notice on our theater schedule, which was handed out to all crew on the first day of load-in. When the IA steward noticed the camera crew setting up, the steward yelled at our TD. When the TD would not respond, the steward yelled at the ATD. Both claimed to know nothing about the camera crew, so I said that it was all my fault. I had sent the e-mail notice to the TD and had assumed the TD would notify the IA. I apologized over and over, but nothing would calm the steward down. The steward then yelled at the camera crew asking if they were professionals and getting paid, to which they responded "Yes." A solution was reached between the TD and the steward: two A/V IATSE would be hired for all calls at which camera crews were present.

I have since spoken with our company's ED about changing company policy to allow me to send video notices to our IA steward (as my TD had preferred that any communication with IA go through the TD) so that this situation can be avoided in the future. I also intend to spend more time reading our contract with IA so that I can be aware of those special situations that require additional crew.

Name withheld at writer's request
PSM in California

I tour all over the country with Hal Holbrook's *Mark Twain Tonight!* and other ongoing productions, like the *Ella* tour that I'm doing now. Many of the houses we play are IATSE houses, and EVERY local has its own rules, which affect whether or not a stagehand can cross departments (work on lights AND sound AND props, etc.), whether a stage manager can handle (or even touch!) props or scenery, and, of course, what the minimum call is. I can complete the load-in for *Mark Twain* in four to five hours. Most locals have a four-hour minimum, and the added hour would cost extra, sometimes even at a premium rate. I was shocked when I came upon a local where I found, after the fact, that the minimum for load-ins was eight hours. After conferring with the producer, the promoter and a fellow stage manager, I determined that there was nothing I could have done to help in this situation.

Rich Costabile
Stage Manager Mark Twain Tonight!/Ella

I've been a member of AEA for 33 years, and a member of AGMA for 15 years. I've worked with over 300 IATSE Locals, including Local 1 in New York, the Musicians Union and ATPAM, the Company Managers union. Each have their own set of rules and regulations and all I can say is, "Respect the rules and their contracts as much as you want them to respect yours." Many times it gets very complicated when trying to schedule all the different departments, but it's all doable. The rules are there for a reason so learn them, work with them, and respect them. Remember that the rules are there for two reasons: (1) Someone was abused or taken advantage of, so a rule was voted on to prevent it from happening again or happening to others, and (2) because some producer agreed to it. That's what collective bargaining is all about.

Lynda A. Lavin
Production Stage Manager, Twelve National Tours

I'm a firm believer that we—actors and crew—are one family. So on the first day of tech, we do a brief meet and greet with full cast and crew saying their names and what they do. On my first Broadway show 21 years ago (*The Heidi Chronicles*), I'm afraid I didn't see the crew as real people and didn't do any kind of introduction, and there were some problems that I know now wouldn't have happened; for example, there was some animosity between two actors and a stagehand that I'm sure wouldn't have happened if there had been proper introductions. Stagehands have a tendency to act very self-sufficient and like they don't need any special attention, but they are people the same as actors. At the end of a show, I always thank everyone over the headset for a good show. In previews, I make sure when, let's say, a new transition from one scene to another has gone into the show, to say a personal thank you to the carpenter and other stagehands who were responsible for the new move. I also host a brunch every Sunday before the matinee, to which everyone on the show—cast, crew, and front-of-house—can bring in something and take part in eating what other people have brought. (These brunches were the germ for three books I wrote, the final one called *Brunch over Broadway*, which includes 88 recipes culled from 12 years of Sunday brunch.)

Roy Harris, SM/PSM
Twenty-one Broadway shows
More than 20 productions directed by Tony Award-winning director Dan Sullivan

There are currently 386 IATSE locals. Each local may be working under slightly different rules regarding mandated breaks, time for meals between matinee and evening performances, minimum crew, situations that require additional crew, whether a given craft may assist another craft, minimum overtime, etc. It is important to remember that costs and conditions vary from facility to facility for a myriad of reasons such as how long the building has been open, the size of the facility, the area standards for comparable work, and the

(continued)

particular strength of the local union. More importantly, any wage or working condition that exists in the facility is a byproduct of the collective bargaining process and was agreed to by both sides, management of the facility and the local union.

My best advice to new stage managers is to adopt the Boy Scout motto: "Be prepared." Think ahead and get the information you need from your producer. Talk to the event coordinator for your venue or the union steward. Reach out to the union and discuss specifics in advance and build rapport. If you're with a touring company, study the technical rider, which usually gives the specific rules and costs for the venue. Better to be prepared than surprised.

Brian Lawlor
International Vice President I.A.T.S.E.

My Teaching Strategy

After teaching union rules, I create and distribute daily schedules with AEA (LORT contract) rule violations for work hours and calls. Students are asked to find the problems, explain why the scheduled items violate the rules, and explain what they would do to adjust the schedule to fit the rules, or state what the financial repercussions would be if the schedule remained as written.

David Grindle
Production Manager
Indiana University Dept. of Theatre

SUGGESTED CLASSROOM EXERCISES

Invite a union member or union representative to speak to your class.

Arrange for students to interview union members and report their findings to the class.

19

Organizing Information

All plays are problem plays, the problem being to get the play produced.
—Anonymous

The world is in the midst of an information explosion. The availability of books, magazines, newspapers, radio and TV broadcasts, microfilm, photocopies, and Internet information is often overwhelming. As the amount of information available increases, the stage manager must decide how to organize it so that she can make use of it.

LOCAL THEATER

Check out your local theaters. Contact educational, showcase, community, and children's theaters to get on their mailing lists. You will soon receive information about who's doing what, and you will receive more complete and accurate information than you can find in your newspaper.

Go to the theater as often as possible. Make notes in your programs as to outstanding acting and technical credits. Save your programs.

NEWSPAPERS, MAGAZINES, AND INTERNET INFO

Read local newspapers and national magazines regularly. Scan the Internet for play reviews, advances in theater technology, and other theater-related news. Making a scrapbook of theater information is the easiest way of keeping abreast of live theater (figure 19.1).

Clip local reviews of plays. Note the technical credits. You may soon discover, for instance, that just a handful of people are getting all the good lighting reviews. Even if you have never worked with these people, you will start to know who they are.

You will also be able to determine trends. What types of plays are being done by the many community theaters in your area? What types of plays are the educational theaters doing? The showcase theaters? The commercial theaters?

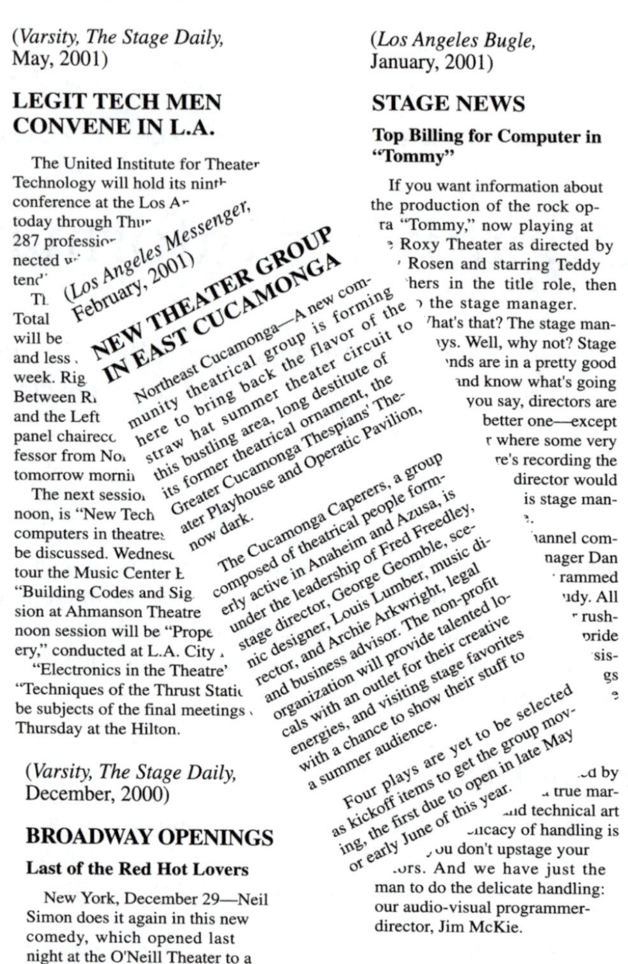

(*Varsity, The Stage Daily,*
May, 2001)

LEGIT TECH MEN CONVENE IN L.A.

The United Institute for Theater
Technology will hold its ninth
conference at the Los A…
today through Thu…
287 professio…
nected …
ten…
Th…
Total
will be
and less …
week. Rig…
Between R…
and the Left
panel chaire…
fessor from No…
tomorrow morni…
The next sessio…
noon, is "New Tech
computers in theatre…
be discussed. Wedne…
tour the Music Center …
"Building Codes and Sig…
sion at Ahmanson Theatre
noon session will be "Prope…
ery," conducted at L.A. City …
"Electronics in the Theatre"
"Techniques of the Thrust Stati…
be subjects of the final meetings …
Thursday at the Hilton.

(*Los Angeles Messenger,*
February, 2001)

NEW THEATER GROUP IN EAST CUCAMONGA

Northeast Cucamonga—A new community theatrical group is forming here to bring back the flavor of the straw hat summer theater circuit to this bustling area, long destitute of its former theatrical ornament, the Greater Cucamonga Thespians' Theater Playhouse and Operatic Pavilion, now dark.

The Cucamonga Caperers, a group composed of theatrical people formerly active in Anaheim and Azusa, is under the leadership of Fred Freedley, stage director, George Geomble, scenic designer, Louis Lumber, music director, and Archie Arkwright, legal and business advisor. The non-profit organization will provide talented locals with an outlet for their creative energies, and visiting stage favorites with a chance to show their stuff to a summer audience.

Four plays are yet to be selected as kickoff items to get the group moving, the first due to open in late May or early June of this year.

(*Los Angeles Bugle,*
January, 2001)

STAGE NEWS

Top Billing for Computer in "Tommy"

If you want information about
the production of the rock op-
ra "Tommy," now playing at
… Roxy Theater as directed by
… Rosen and starring Teddy
…hers in the title role, then
… the stage manager.
…hat's that? The stage man-
…ys. Well, why not? Stage
…nds are in a pretty good
…nd know what's going
you say, directors are
better one—except
… where some very
…e's recording the
director would
is stage man-
…
…annel com-
…nager Dan
…rammed
…udy. All
… rush-
…pride
…sis-
…gs
…
…d by
… true mar-
…nd technical art
…icacy of handling is
… you don't upstage your
…ors. And we have just the
man to do the delicate handling:
our audio-visual programmer-
director, Jim McKie.

(*Varsity, The Stage Daily,*
December, 2000)

BROADWAY OPENINGS

Last of the Red Hot Lovers

New York, December 29—Neil
Simon does it again in this new
comedy, which opened last
night at the O'Neill Theater to a

FIGURE 19.1 Likely Items for a Manager's Scrapbook

The experimental theaters? By reading nationally published reviews of Broadway and off-Broadway openings, you can learn to anticipate which of these plays will later be done by certain local theaters.

Which local producers do consistently good work? By judging the type of plays they do and the quality of their work, which producers would you prefer to work for? Which could you learn the most from? The largest, most plush plant in town may not be doing the kind of work with which you would want to associate yourself. By going to the theater and reading reviews, you can discover the theaters in which you would most like to work.

Also, clip articles on all aspects of production and reviews of new books about theater.

A subscription to one or more of the trade papers might provide you with good current information.

Trade Papers

Back Stage East
770 Broadway
New York, NY 10003-9595
646-654-5700; 800-562-2706
backstage.com

Back Stage West
5055 Wilshire Blvd., 6th Floor
Los Angeles, CA 90036-6103
323-525-2356; 800-562-2706
fax 323-525-2226
backstage.com

Hollywood Reporter
5055 Wilshire Blvd., #600
Los Angeles, CA 90036-4396
323-525-2150 or 866-525-2150
fax 323 525-2377
mailbox@hollywoodreporter.com
hollywoodreporter.com

Variety
Los Angeles Office
5700 Wilshire Blvd., Suite 120
Los Angeles, CA 90036-5804
323-857-6600
fax 323-857-0494
variety.com

Variety
New York Office
360 Park Ave. South
New York, NY 10010
212-337-7002
fax 212-337-6975
variety.com

Magazines

TDR (The Drama Review)
MIT Press
5 Cambridge Center
Cambridge, MA 02142-1493
617-253-2889
fax 617-577-1545
journals-orders@mit.edu
mitpressjournals.org

Dramatics
Educational Theatre Assoc.
2343 Auburn Avenue
Cincinnati, OH 45219-2819
513-421-3900
fax 513-421-7077
lckelley@etassoc.org
schooltheatre.org

Live Design
249 W. 17th Street
New York, NY 10011
866-505-7173
livedesignonline.com

Plays and Players
Mineco Designs Ltd.
Northway House
1379 High Road
London N20 9LP England
44-181-343-8515
fax 44-181-446-1410

Technical Brief
Yale University, School of Drama
222 York Street, Yale Station
New Haven, CT 06520
203-432-8188
fax 203-432-8129
technicalbrief.org

Ulrich's Periodicals Directory (2011) contains 783 active titles related to theater. It is available at many libraries, both in hard copy and on the Internet—but access is only via licensed entities, such as libraries. The directory is published by ProQuest, 789 E. Eisenhower Pkwy., Ann Arbor, MI 48106, proquest.com. The editorial address is Serials Editorial Dept., 630 Central Ave., New Providence, NJ 07974-1506. Ulrich's hotline: 800-346-6049.

GUIDES TO GOODS AND SERVICES

Where can you get lighting supplies in a hurry? Where can you send someone to repair a damaged wig? Who has Max Factor pancake makeup in 7A on hand? Anticipate needs. Do an Internet search for the nearest theatrical supply houses, costume shops, and hardware stores in your area. Print out the results and add them to your promptbook.

How many times have you driven to a supply house only to find on arrival it doesn't have what you need in stock? Call ahead.

You are only a mouse click away from names, addresses, and Web sites of suppliers at the following Web addresses:

PLASA	plasa.org
TechnicalTheater.com	technicaltheater.com
World's Greatest Lighting Manufacturers	ewholesalelightingblog.com/2/lighting-manufacturers.html

Here's a sampling of manufacturers:

Altman Stage Lighting Company, Inc.
57 Alexander Street
Yonkers, NY 10701-2714
800-425-8626
212-569-7777
fax 914-963-7304
rleonard@altmanltg.com
altmanltg.com

Apogee Sound, Inc.
50 Spring Street
Ramsey, NY 07446
800-443-3979
fax 800-999-9016
apogeesound.com

BASH Theatrical Lighting, Inc.
3401 Dell Avenue
North Bergen, NJ 07047-2348
212-279-9265
manta.com/c/mm38lym/bsh-theatrical-lighting-corp

Clear-Com Intercom Systems
850 Marina Village Parkway
Alameda, CA 94501
800-462-4357
fax 510-337-6699
sales@clearcom.com
clearcom.com

Colortran-Leviton Controls Division
20497 SW Teton Avenue
Tualatin, OR 97062-8812
503-404-5500; 800-576-6080
fax 503-404-5600
800-576-6060
info@nsicorp.com
colortran.com

Dudley Theatrical
3401 Indiana Avenue
Winston-Salem, NC 27105-3403
336-722-3255
fax 336-722-4641
sales@dudleytheatrical.com
dudleytheatrical.com

Eastern Acoustic Works
One Main Street
Whitinsville, MA 01588-2238
800-992-5013
800-322-8251
eaw.com

Eastern Costume Company
7243 Coldwater Canyon Avenue
North Hollywood, CA 91605-4204
818-982-3611
fax 818-982-1905
cust.serv.@easterncostume.com
easterncostume.com

Electrol Engineering, Inc.
500-A Bynum Road
Forest Hill, MD 21050-3051
410-638-9300
fax 410-638-2878
dimmers@electrol.net
electrol.net

Electronic Theatre Controls, Inc.
3031 Pleasant View Road
Middleton, WI 53562-0979
800-688-4116
fax 608-831-4116
mail@etcconnect.com
etcconnect.com

High End Systems, Inc.
2105 Gracy Farms Lane
Austin, TX 78758
800-890-8989
fax 512-837-5290
info@highend.com
highend.com

Kliegl Bros.
5 Aerial Way
Syosset, NY 11791-5502
516-937-3900; fax 516-937-6042
klieglbros.com

Meyer Sound Laboratories, Inc.
2832 San Pablo Avenue
Berkeley, CA 94702
510-486-1166
fax 510-486-8356
techsupport@meyersound.com
meyersound.com

Mackie Designs, Inc.
16220 Wood-Red Road, NE
Woodinville, WA 98072-9061
425-487-4333; 800-258-6883
fax 425-487-4337
sales@mackie.com
mackie.com

Martin Professional, Inc.
700 Sawgrass Corporate Parkway
Sunrise, FL 33325
954-858-1800
fax 954-858-1811 or 888-298-4776
martin@martinpro.com
martin.dk

Musson Theatrical TV Film
890 Walsh Avenue
Santa Clara, CA 95050-2640
800-THEATER; 408-986-0210
fax 408-986-9552
info@musson.com
musson.com

The Phoebus Co., Inc.
2800 Third Street
San Francisco, CA 94107-3502
415-550-0770; fax 415-550-2655
lighting@phoebus.com
phoebus.com

Rosco Laboratories, Inc.
52 Harbor View Avenue
Stamford, CT 06902-5914
800-767-2669
fax 203-708-8919
info@rosco.com
rosco.com

Strand Lighting
267 5th Avenue, 4th Floor
New York, NY 10016
212-213-8219
fax 212-532-2843
sales@strandlight.com
strandlighting.com

Strong Entertainment Lighting
4350 McKinley Street
Omaha, NE 68112-1643
800-424-1215
fax 402-453-7238
paul@strong-lighting.com
strong-world.com

Tomcat USA, Inc.
2160 Commerce Drive
Midland, TX 79703-7504
432-694-7070
fax 432-689-3805
sales@tomcatusa.com
tomcatglobal.com

Studying a few catalogs will help make you aware of the industry that is ready to back up the theater. It will help you keep abreast of new products. What do you know about quartz lights? Black light? Foam scenery? Solid-state communications equipment?

Request samples, swatches, and gel books. Services and demonstrations are sometimes available from manufacturers who wish to promote their products. Can you get a lighting-equipment sales representative to come to your theater to help you analyze the problem of augmenting your lighting equipment for a particularly heavy show? Can he help you with the know-how to create special effects?

Before you buy, compare products carefully. Not all the factors about a product are stated in brochures. Evaluate cost, durability, repair costs, availability of spare parts, capability of the product, ease of cleaning, ease of repairing or replacing worn parts, proximity to a repair facility, ease in use, unique advantages, and peculiar disadvantages.

CONTACT FILE

In your electronic organizer or personal digital assistant (PDA), assemble information: names, street addresses, e-mail addresses, Web sites, and phone numbers for people, theaters, and businesses that might be helpful to you in the future. Make entries for actors, producers, directors, designers, technicians, costume designers, suppliers of equipment, sources of props, and unions.

You may be able to help in casting by keeping tabs on the various fine actors that you discover in plays that you see. Make an entry for each actor whose work impresses you. Get addresses and phone numbers as well as agents' names and numbers. Go out of your way to see the actors in the next play that they do.

BOOKS

Have available a few books on theater that can recharge your intellectual batteries—the type of book that you can read more than once and still find interesting and helpful. These might be considered your "clothesline" books, giving you the basic information that will allow you to assimilate other information, pinning it up on the "clothesline" in your mind.

What seven books would you take with you to another planet if you expected to establish a live theater there? Perhaps the seven books listed in figure 19.2 are a good start for your own personal library. It is better to know seven books well than to own a huge collection of books with uncut pages.

Extensive bibliographies for every theater arts subject can be found in your local library.

"What Seven Books Would I Take to Another Planet if I Expected to Establish a Live Theater There?"
(a small, prejudiced, but useful selection)

ACTING

Actors on Acting
Cole, Toby, and Helen Krich Chinoy
Crown, distributed by Random House, 1995

DIRECTING

Directors on Directing
Cole, Toby, and Helen Krich Chinoy
Macmillan, distributed by Prentice-Hall, 1990

MAKEUP/COSTUMING

Stage Makeup
Corson, Richard, and James Glavan
Allyn and Bacon, 9th ed., 2001

The Costume Technician's Handbook
Ingham, Rosemary, and Liz Covey
Heinemann, 1992

SCENE DESIGN/SET CONSTRUCTION/LIGHTING

Scene Design and Stage Lighting
Parker, W. Oren, and Harvey K. Smith
Holt, Rinehart & Winston, 7th ed., 1996

HISTORY

History of the Theatre
Brockett, Oscar G., and Franklin J. Hildy
Allyn and Bacon, 10th ed., 2008

PLAYWRITING

Playwriting: How to Write for the Theater
Bernard Grebanier
Barnes & Noble, a division of Harper & Row, 1979

FIGURE 19.2 Seven Titles to Start a Theater Library. This list of seven books has changed little over the last 10 years despite the fact that hundreds of titles have been published in the last decade. *Mea culpa*. I have not kept up with the literature. Still, I am reluctant to make changes as I know the books recommended are good. So I ask my readers: If you know of a book in any of these areas that has a clearly superior ability to illuminate an aspect of theater for a potential stage manager, please let me know.

In addition, if you are interested in a program of directed reading, many graduate schools of theater arts publish graduate reading lists. Contact the university nearest you. Or you may wish to add your name to the mailing lists of the several publishers who specialize in books on theater arts.

Allyn & Bacon, Inc.
75 Arlington Street, Suite 300
Boston, MA 02116
617-848-6000
pearsonhighered.com

Cornell University Press
Sage House
512 East State Street
Ithaca, NY 14850-4499
607-277-2338
cornellpress.cornell.edu

The Drama Bookshop
250 West 40th Street
New York, NY 10018
212-944-0595
800-322-0595
dramabookshop.com

Drama Publishers
260 Fifth Avenue
New York, NY 10001
212-725-5377
fax 212-725-8506
info@quitespecificmedia.com
quitespecificmedia.com

The Fireside Theater
Member Service Center
6550 E. 30th Street
P.O. Box 6375
Indianapolis, IN 46206-6375
800-688-4442

Indiana University Press
601 North Morton Street
Bloomington, IN 47404-3797
800-842-6796 or 812-855-8817
fax 812-855-7931
credit card orders 800-842-6796
iupress.indiana.edu

The Internet Theatre Bookshop
info@stageplays.com
stageplays.com

Miami University Press
356 Bachelor Hall
Miami University
Oxford, OH 45056
513-529-2602
muohio.edu/mupress

KEEPING CURRENT WITH THE TECHNOLOGY OF THEATER

Here are five suggestions for keeping abreast of the incredible technology that is now available.

1. *Join USITT*

   The United States Institute for Theatre Technology
   315 S Crouse Ave Suite 200
   Syracuse, NY 13210
   800-938-7488
   usitt.org
   info@office.usitt org

USITT is the member service organization for design and technology professionals in all areas of live entertainment. Membership is encouraged from theater planners, owners, clients, architects, engineers, and designers; city officials, builders, administrators, and managers; educators, writers, critics, playwrights, performers, and directors; designers and makers of stage scenery, lighting, machinery, furnishings and equipment; stage managers, arts managers, and front of house personnel; and designers and technicians in all theater disciplines.

USITT arranges meetings, programs, discussions, tours, and demonstrations. It also publishes a magazine, *Theatre Design and Technology*, in addition to a newsletter, *Sightlines*, newsletter supplements, a membership directory, and an annual report, as well as regional newsletters and reports.

The Annual Conference & Stage Expo is usually held to further promote an exchange of information between outstanding professionals and theater people who share concerns and who can help you solve professional problems. It's at the conference that the Stage Management Mentoring project has helped novice stage managers for over 20 years by providing mentors. The conference is attended by thousands.

USITT partners with industry leaders to create training opportunities for the professionals of tomorrow. Through these partnerships, USITT seeks to augment the education of the next generation with the expertise of those in the industry.

Membership benefits include discounts on publications, hotels, and car rentals. Beyond this, the USITT annually honors individuals, services, innovations, and publications that have made outstanding contributions to the performing arts.

It was the USITT that brought about the use of a standard protocol for communication between control boards and dimmers (DMX 512). Most U.S. manufacturers of theater lighting equipment now provide for the protocol even if they feel that their own is more effective. This allows a theater to use a control board manufactured by one company with dimmers made by another. USITT is also actively involved in the establishment of standards for teaching theater technology and design as well as promoting research and development such as funding the initial research in the use of LEDs for theatrical purposes.

2. *Subscribe to* Live Design

Live Design
249 W. 17th Street
New York NY 10011
subscriptions 866-505 7173
idcs@pbsub.com
http://livedesignonline.com

This magazine features articles on new theater technology and novel theater applications of technology developed for architectural and other purposes. Much of the new technology is reflected in advertisements. Every year the January issue features a "Technical Literature Guide" that lists product brochures, catalogs, specification sheets, newsletters, and other descriptive materials available from companies that manufacture, distribute, and provide services for theater. Products and services include lighting equipment, scenic materials, costumes, special effects, flameproofing, and rigging. The annual June issue features a directory of many companies that manufacture, distribute, and provide services for the theater.

3. *Attend the annual LDI trade show*

Lighting Dimensions International
Penton Business Media, Inc.
800-927-5007
http://ldishow.com

Lighting Dimensions International (LDI) is an international trade show of lighting, sound, and special effects for clubs, concerts, theater, television, and films. It has become the *de facto* tech products trade show of the entertainment industry. There are booths where you can try out new equipment, as well as workshops, exhibits, and other events. Many manufacturers, both domestic and foreign, introduce their new products at this show. The show is held in the fall. Visit its Web site for schedule and registration information.

4. *Browse the World Wide Web (WWW)*

Here are just a very few of the companies that have pages out in cyberspace. Appendix D has an expanded list.

Barbizon	barbizon.com
Chimera	chimeralighting.com
Dove Systems	dovesystems.com
Eastern Accoustic Works	eaw.com
Electronic Theatre Controls, Inc.	etcconnect.com
High End Systems	highend.com
Iridion	vari-lite.com
Premier	premier-lighting.com
Strong	strong-world.com
Tomcat	tomcatglobal.com

5. *Research software that can be applied to stage management*

From word processing to spreadsheet programs to databases, many software programs are now available that can be applied to theater-making and stage management.

COMPUTER-AIDED DESIGN AND DRAFTING (CADD)

Computer programs used by draftspeople and engineers, called computer-aided design and drafting (CADD), can also help scene and lighting designers. In addition to increasing accuracy in the drafting of sets, CADD programs allow you to make changes very quickly, store drawings, and create a library of drawings that can be recalled and reused. In selecting a printing device, consider dot matrix, laser, and plotters. The better the quality of your output, generally the higher the cost of the printer. As in the selection of light boards, it's important to talk to people who have used the programs and equipment, and then shop around. An increasing pool of people is qualified to apply CADD and other computer programs to the challenges of theater production.

An intriguing application of CADD programs is in the area of costume design. Patternmaker is a full-featured garment design program for the PC with both DOS and Windows versions. Software runs on any PC with Windows 95 or better, to support most commonly available digitizers, printers, and plotters up to 72 inches in width. As with CADD scene design, the acquisition of a satisfactory printer is a major concern since the best application of the software is to produce a clear pattern. A free demo of Patternmaker may be downloaded from the Internet at patternmakerusa.com. You may also join an online discussion group at the same Web site.

POLICE, FIRE, AND MUNICIPAL REGULATIONS

Be aware that police regulations, fire laws, and municipal codes may control the operations of all theaters, if and when applied (figure 19.3).

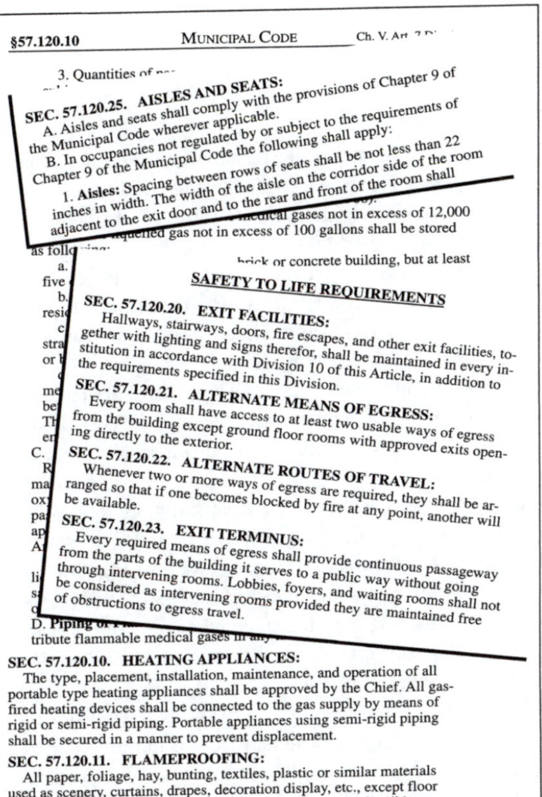

§57.120.10 MUNICIPAL CODE Ch. V. Art. 7

SEC. 57.120.25. AISLES AND SEATS:

A. Aisles and seats shall comply with the provisions of Chapter 9 of the Municipal Code wherever applicable.

B. In occupancies not regulated by or subject to the requirements of Chapter 9 of the Municipal Code the following shall apply:

1. **Aisles:** Spacing between rows of seats shall be not less than 22 inches in width. The width of the aisle on the corridor side of the room adjacent to the exit door and to the rear and front of the room shall

SAFETY TO LIFE REQUIREMENTS

SEC. 57.120.20. EXIT FACILITIES:

Hallways, stairways, doors, fire escapes, and other exit facilities, together with lighting and signs therefor, shall be maintained in every institution in accordance with Division 10 of this Article, in addition to the requirements specified in this Division.

SEC. 57.120.21. ALTERNATE MEANS OF EGRESS:

Every room shall have access to at least two usable ways of egress from the building except ground floor rooms with approved exits opening directly to the exterior.

SEC. 57.120.22. ALTERNATE ROUTES OF TRAVEL:

Whenever two or more ways of egress are required, they shall be arranged so that if one becomes blocked by fire at any point, another will be available.

SEC. 57.120.23. EXIT TERMINUS:

Every required means of egress shall provide continuous passageway from the parts of the building it serves to a public way without going through intervening rooms. Lobbies, foyers, and waiting rooms shall not be considered as intervening rooms provided they are maintained free of obstructions to egress travel.

D. Piping ... tribute flammable medical gases ...

SEC. 57.120.10. HEATING APPLIANCES:

The type, placement, installation, maintenance, and operation of all portable type heating appliances shall be approved by the Chief. All gas-fired heating devices shall be connected to the gas supply by means of rigid or semi-rigid piping. Portable appliances using semi-rigid piping shall be secured in a manner to prevent displacement.

SEC. 57.120.11. FLAMEPROOFING:

All paper, foliage, hay, bunting, textiles, plastic or similar materials used as scenery, curtains, drapes, decoration display, etc., except floor covering and furniture upholstery, shall either be non-combustible or flameproofed in an approved manner. This Section does not prohibit the use of ordinary window curtains in guest or patient rooms.

FIGURE 19.3 Typical Theater Safety Regulations

These regulations vary with each city and within cities, depending on the size of the theater. They are generally written in the form of ordinances and sections of the city code. The ordinances and codes are available in the offices of city administrators concerned and in public libraries. Unfortunately, not all regulations pertaining to live theater are neatly grouped together. They may be found under such diverse headings as "Rules Governing Cafe Entertainment and Shows," "Assemblage Occupancies," "Safety to Life Requirements," and others. See Chapter 17 on fire and evacuation procedures.

Experts are usually available to assist theater owners and producers who may call to request inspections of their facilities or submit plans for approval. The stage manager does not normally do this.

If you are involved in opening a show in a building that has been newly converted into a theater, ask the producer or management if local regulations have been checked. The number of people allowed in the building, the number of off-street parking spaces necessary, and even the amount of lavatory space are all the subjects of city regulations.

ORGANIZATIONS

Stage Managers' Association

The Stage Managers' Association, founded in 1982, is a professional organization of stage managers who work in theater, dance, opera, industrials, special events, and other venues. Through meetings and events in the New York area and nationwide, its Web site stagemanagers.org, and regional activities coordinated by its members, the SMA seeks to create a network through which stage managers can share ideas, educate themselves, and build strong relationships. Although the SMA is not a labor union, its membership includes members of AEA, AGMA, AGVA, AFTRA, DGA, and other unions, as well as non-union, career-minded stage managers. The SMA welcomes all stage managers who feel they can benefit from the opportunity for discourse with their colleagues. All are encouraged to contribute their energies to the Association's growth. Stage Managers' Association. P.O. Box 275, Times Square Station, New York, NY 10108-0275; stagemanagers.org; on the Web site, click on Contact the SMA.

September, 2007 saw the 25th anniversary of the SMA's founding, as well as the anniversary of Actor's Equity Association's adoption of its proposal to add five seats to AEA Council specifically for stage managers. At the SMA's urging, AEA changed its officer structure so the third vice president would be a stage manager. In 1995 the SMA was instrumental in the creation of three office staff liaisons for stage managers, one in each AEA regional office (pages 241–242). The liaisons serve as ombudsmen to AEA business staff members for the resolution of stage management issues.

In 2010, the SMA organized a day-long event in NYC, "Theater: A View from the Wings," at which three panels of distinguished theater professionals—general managers, directors, and new media technologists—shared their insights with the audience of stage managers and others in the theater industry. The day was capped off by the presentation of the Del Hughes Award for Lifetime Achievement in the Art of Stage Management to Susie Cordon, Alan Hall, and Porter Van Zandt.

The SMA now has regional representatives in 22 states. Social/professional events have been held in Philadelphia, Minneapolis, Pittsburgh, Denver, Tulsa, San Diego, Washington DC, Seattle, Los Angeles, Chicago, Greensboro, Rochester, Cleveland, Dayton, Indianapolis, and many other locations. Operation Observation has enabled many stage managers to observe their peers at work in rehearsal and during performances in New York City and nationwide. Notices of well over 1,000 job openings have been e-mailed directly to members since 2003. The SMA's Web site, stagemanagers.org, is a great resource for information about the organization and about stage managing, including an online directory of members (with uploadable résumés), which is searchable by a number of criteria, an extensive list of links to extremely helpful Web sites, listings of regional representatives, and the various committees that help make the SMA an effective and influential organization.

Courtesy Richard Costabile
Chairman

SMNetwork

SMNetwork (smnetwork.org) is one of the oldest online gathering places for stage managers. Founded by Kay Cleaves in January of 2000, the site is an information hub for the international backstage community. The format has evolved to a bulletin board setup with features, including the "Been There, Done That" database of members' production history, community-wide trivia contests, and regional sub-boards for recommendations about working in various areas of the world. Membership stands at over 3500 registered accounts. Members arrange regional meetings (as in Washington DC, New York, and the Boston area). Discussion topics include mentoring younger stage managers, how-to's, tips, and job-search strategies. The site also provides coverage of less-commonplace performance types such as dance, opera, circus, cruise ships, and industrials. Membership, although not required, is still free and grants access to hidden areas of the site, including a collection of sample résumés. This site is worth your time. Cleaves and her staff of moderators have done an excellent job of maintaining a Web site that allows all stage managers to communicate easily.

Theatre Communications Group

Theatre Communications Group (TCG), a national organization for the American theater, was founded in 1961 with a grant from the Ford Foundation to foster communication among professional, community, and university theaters. Today, TCG's constituency has grown from a handful of theaters to nearly 700 member theaters and affiliate organizations and more than 12,000 individuals nationwide. TCG offers its members networking and knowledge-building opportunities through conferences, events, research, and communications; grants approximately $2 million per year to theater companies and individual artists; advocates on the federal level and serves as the U.S. Center of the International Theatre Institute, connecting its constituents to the global theater community. TCG is the nation's largest independent publisher of dramatic literature; TCG also publishes the award-winning *American Theatre* magazine and ARTSEARCH®, the essential source for a career in the arts. In all of its endeavours, TCG seeks to increase the organizational efficiency of its member theaters, cultivate and celebrate the artistic talent and achievements of the field, and promote a larger public understanding of, and appreciation for, the theater. 520 Eighth Ave., 24th Fl, NY, NY 10018-4156; 212-609-5900, Fax: 1-212-609-5901; tcg@tcg.org; tcg.org

PLASA

PLASA is the lead international membership body for those who supply technologies and services to the event, entertainment, and installation industries. As a proactive trade association, it looks after the interests of its members and seeks to influence business practices and skills development across the industry. PLASA owns and manages the PLASA Show and PLASA Focus events and publishes leading industry magazines *Lighting&Sound America*, *Lighting&Sound International*, and *Protocol*.

At the beginning of 2011, PLASA and ESTA—the leading trade association representing the North American entertainment technology industry—merged under the PLASA name, to create a strengthened organization with a worldwide membership of over 1,100 companies and individuals.

(continued)

PLASA is actively involved in the development of standards and directives worldwide. In North America, PLASA leads the ANSI-accredited Technical Standards Program (created by ESTA), which is responsible for developing standards and recommended practices that facilitate the use of new and existing equipment and promote safe working conditions in the industry. Under the TSP, PLASA facilitates a number of industry-led working groups focusing on camera cranes, control protocols, electrical power, fog and smoke, follow-spot position, performance floors, photometrics, rigging, and stage lifts.

In North America, PLASA offers the Entertainment Technician Certification Program (developed originally by ESTA), which delivers rigorous assessments for professional technicians, awarding certifications to entertainment electricians, arena riggers, and theater riggers.

630 Ninth Avenue, Suite 609
New York, NY 10036
212-244-1505
info.na@plasa.org
plasa.org

American Alliance for Theatre and Education

AATE was created in 1987 to serve the needs of theater artists and educators who work with young people. AATE has grown to become a large, worldwide network of teachers, directors, producers, playwrights, and others—all of whom share a commitment to theater and young people.

Members of AATE receive a subscription to *Incite/Insight* (published bimonthly); *Youth Theatre Journal* (published biannually); *AATE Member Update* (published biweekly); access to the online AATE Membership Directory and Forums; discounts on regional events, including National Theatre In Our Schools Month mini-conferences, the AATE National Conference (held in Lexington, Kentucky, in August 2012) and workshops, including the Theatre Leadership Institute (held in Washington, DC in November 2011); free membership to Fractured Atlas to gain access to health and liability insurance; the opportunity to become involved in programs and projects of the Alliance and its networks; and networking opportunities with professionals dedicated to quality theater and drama/theater education for young people.

The AATE Web site, aate.com, promotes networking among theater artists and educators. Contact AATE at 7979 Old Georgetown Rd, 10th Floor; Bethesda, MD 20814; 301-951-7977; info@aate.com; Skype us: aateoffice; follow us on twitter: aateoffice; facebook: facebook.com/aateoffice

Courtesy Kelly Prestel
AATE

The Theatre Sound Mailing List

Using the Internet effectively to help sound people communicate is the Theatre Sound Mailing List (brooklyn.com/theatre-sound). You can read about bugs in specific equipment and how to overcome them, recommendations of certain equipment for specific applications, needs for sound effects with immediate response as to where to get them or how to make that effect, plus job openings. Kudos to Jim Bay for maintaining this site, which brings together sound designers, sound board operators, sound instructors, students of sound, and sound equipment manufacturers and distributors—more than 600 people in 17 countries.

SUGGESTED CLASSROOM EXERCISES

Ask students to write to a few manufacturers (pages 250–252) to obtain current catalogs.

Have students visit a library to examine *Ulrich's International Periodicals Directory* at ulrichsweb.com and select the magazine that they feel would be most useful.

20

Correspondence

If experience is such a great teacher,
why do the lessons always seem late?
—Anonymous

As stage manager, you will have little need to write extensive correspondence, but you will want to consider writing a letter to the next stage manager, critiques, letters of recommendation, and thank you notes.

A LETTER TO THE NEXT STAGE MANAGER

Turnover of stage managers is frequent. Sometimes they are there for a season only, and next season a new person is holding the clipboard, starting anew, running into the same problems that you ran into last season. Sometimes stage managers are replaced in the middle of a season, and sometimes a theater has a different stage manager for every single production.

No matter what your length of service, you have learned things that your replacement can only learn by time-consuming research or trial and error.

Where did you take the tape recorder to be serviced last time it broke down? When was the last time it was serviced? How frequently should preventive maintenance be done?

Where is the key to the metal bulb protectors for the dressing room lights?

Who services the air-conditioning units?

What ceiling outlets are on what lines into the booth?

What mistakes did you make that the next stage manager should avoid?

What working diagrams and templates, applicable to this theater only, can you turn over to your replacement?

There are many little things that only you know. When you leave, the staff cannot be expected to pass this information on to the new stage manager. Some of it may be trivial. Some is important. But all of it would help the new stage manager to adjust to the job more easily.

- **If you are not going to be around to break in the new stage manager, why not leave a letter to make the adjustment easier? Simply write**

the same kind of letter you would like to find if you were coming to the job instead of leaving.

CRITIQUES

The purpose of a written critique is to help you to improve your work on future productions. It is intended to remind you of mistakes you made, problems you solved, and methods you devised. It need not be formal and it need not go anywhere. Don't feel that you have to turn it over to a producer or director because you wrote it. It is for you.

Experience is a great teacher. If the critique reminds you of your experience, it will be a great self-improvement aid. As history students know, mistakes of the past are too soon forgotten and too often repeated.

- **In your theater career what seems unforgettable to you today will be just a hazy, useless memory tomorrow unless you write it out, review it, and apply it.**

As you start into your next production, review your old critiques to see how you can contribute more effectively to better theater.

It is the exceptional theater that holds critiquing sessions following productions or seasons. If you should be asked to contribute to such a critique, select one significant item from your written critique to present. Using your most tactful manner, present that one item from the point of view of how best to improve the next production or season. Make sure your suggestions are concrete. Don't offer vague censure or praise. Remember the effective critique should be concerned with locating the "curse" rather than the "culprit." Be hesitant to give adverse criticism on techniques or devices that have produced desired effects.

LETTERS OF RECOMMENDATION

- **You can help capable people with whom you work by writing letters of recommendation for them (figure 20.1). It will help their morale to know that their work was appreciated, and it may help them to secure better jobs in the future.**

Use the theater's letterhead stationery when available.

In your letters of recommendation: (1) cite the exact work the individual performed; (2) give your evaluation of that work; (3) state whether you would or would not wish to work with the person again in the same capacity; (4) evaluate the individual's potential for doing other related work, and for advancement; and (5) give your title and relationship to the individual.

If the individual was property master this season, do you think the person might make a good assistant stage manager next season? If the person was assistant stage manager, do you think the individual is ready for stage manager, business manager, or technical director?

If you feel that you have performed well in your position, don't be reluctant to ask for a letter of recommendation from your immediate supervisor.

Copies of letters of recommendation may sometimes be enclosed with résumés when applying for a job.

The Limelight Theatre

September 19, 201X

To Whom It May Concern
C/O Mr. George Spelvin
234 Limelight Avenue
Aptos CA 95001

This summer I had the pleasure of working with George Spelvin. He was the company "gopher," a title given in summer stock to the first person called upon when there is work to be done.

As a member of the stage crew George set and struck scenery down and up the aisles of our theatre in the round, seven nights every week. During the day his duties varied. He assisted me as shipping clerk, errand runner, and truck driver. He helped the property master in collecting and returning props. On loan to the technical director he helped build sets. He painted scenery, props, and the stage.

It was always a pleasure to assign George to a job, because you knew it would be done right–the first time. He always accepted assignments cheerfully and was alert in seeing if there was a better way to do a job. Despite his long hours George was always willing to do a little more, and often recognized and did work before I could assign it.

George earned the respect of the production staff and cast members for his dependability and quiet, courteous, unassuming ways.

I would be very pleased to work with George again. I feel that he is ready for an assignment of greater responsibility. He would make an excellent assistant stage manager.

Sincerely,

Lawrence Stern

LAWRENCE STERN
Production Stage Manager

FIGURE 20.1 Letter of Recommendation from a Manager

THANK YOU NOTES

Don't forget to write thank you notes, letters of thanks, or letters of appreciation. Let the capable people with whom you worked know that you cared.

ALWAYS give notes! I had a few jobs early on in my career where I apparently didn't make a good impression, but no one bothered to tell me. I thought I was doing a great job. So I continued in some bad, but very fixable, habits until someone finally gave me a note, and I realized what I'd been doing all along. So now whenever I have anyone working under me—assistants, crew, etc.—especially if they're young, I always make sure to let them know when something's wrong. Even if I've already made up my mind not to hire them again, it will make life easier for everyone while they're here—and for the next person who does hire them. And if you are a production assistant (PA) or intern, never be afraid to ask how you're doing.

Adam Grosswirth
PSM Here Lies Jenny *(off-Broadway)*
Seven Years of Experience as a Professional SM

SUGGESTED CLASSROOM EXERCISE

Ask any students who worked in any capacity backstage on the last production to write a critique of their own work, identifying any problems they encountered, and explaining what they would do in the future to overcome similar problems.

21

Getting a Job

I honestly think it is better to be a failure at something you love than to be a success at something you hate.
—George Burns

Go confidently in the direction of your dreams. Live the life you have imagined.
—Henry David Thoreau

YOUR FIRST JOB AS STAGE MANAGER

There is no minimum number of college credits that qualifies an individual to become a professional stage manager. Outside of educational theater situations, no producer (or anyone else who hires stage managers) will ask to see your college diploma, your high school diploma, or any other kind of certificate. Producers might ask to see your résumé and will probably ask you about your past experience.

The two factors that count most heavily are your feeling of competence and your ability to sell yourself. If you have read this book this far, understand it, and feel that you can apply everything in it, you are ready to stage manage. Now, can you convince someone else that you are ready?

- **In seeking your first job, apply immediately as stage manager at the theater closest to your home. If you are not accepted, ask if you may work as assistant stage manager, property person, assistant property person, or on the crew. Once working in any subordinate position, demonstrate your competence and tell the producer you want to work your way up.**

The frequent pattern is that if you're hired as props, no matter how competent you prove yourself, you will always be seen by that producer as props. So, with the experience you have, start applying to other theaters for positions of greater responsibility. Later, when you have worked at another theater as stage manager, the producer for whom you propped will welcome you back as stage manager.

The best time to get a paid stage management position is when you already have a job in community, educational, or showcase theater. This might mean taking a bread-and-butter daytime job while you work in community theater* at night until you can get the necessary experience and credits.

If you are considering going to college with a career in theater in mind, visit possible campuses and talk to the students who are in the theater program. It is too easy to be misled by advertisements and catalogs. Ask students the following questions:

1. How many main stage and little theater productions are put on every year? Some colleges provide the opportunity to make theater happen. Others have limited production opportunities, even though they may have fine academic programs. Your concern is whether you will have a chance to work. In some schools where there are many productions every year, there may also be large numbers of students. Will you be a small fish in a large pond? Perhaps it would be better to go to a smaller school where everyone works without waiting to be in the junior class. Ask the students about this; they know.
2. Does any one faculty member teach with passion? Well, if not passion, a point of view? Well, lacking a point of view, how about a sense of joy? You can't write to a prospective teacher and ask, "Will you light my fire?" But you can ask the students if they can endorse an enthusiastic faculty member. Again, the students generally know.

By the time you have discussed these two questions with prospective fellow students, you will have a good idea if you will fit into their theater community just from the vibes you get.

Many different atmospheres are available in which to study theater. Check around at junior colleges, private and state-supported colleges and universities, and independent theater programs before making up your mind. Don't feel trapped if you don't find what you want the first semester; you can usually transfer credits to other institutions.

RÉSUMÉS

A résumé is a letter of introduction that you write on behalf of yourself to a prospective employer.

Put yourself in the recipient's shoes. What does the prospective employer want to know about you? Your past experience is most important. What have you done? Put your most recent credit at the top of the page. With whom did you work? At what theaters? The faster the prospective employer can find this information, the better (figure 21.1).

It's a good idea to list the names of a few prominent cast members along with your credits. It is name-dropping in its most obvious and honest application.

Your address and phone number(s) are essential on your résumé. Note that race, religion, national origin, and age are not included.

Send your résumé out regularly to every theater in town, and if you're willing to travel, to selected theaters out of town. Every three months is not too often. It is impossible for you to know exactly when a theater will be in need of new personnel.

*If all of your previous experience has been in educational theater, be prepared to adjust. See Appendix F for an example of a community theater's practices.

JILL GOLD
AEA Stage Manager
626-296-XXXX

NATIONAL TOURS

ASM	Wicked	Dir. Joe Mantello
	Les Miserables	R.J. Alexander
	City of Angels	Michael Blakemore
	The Unsinkable Molly Brown	John Bowab
		Chet Walker
	La Cage Aux Folles	Gene Saks
	Bye Bye Birdie (reh/1 stop)	
	Sisterella (PSM - European tour)	

PASADENA PLAYHOUSE

PSM 29 shows including:	Can-Can	David Lee
	Moon over Buffalo	Glenn Casale
	The Old Settler	Sheldon Epps
	Only a Kingdom	Scott Schwartz
	Do I Hear A Waltz	David Lee
	A Class Act	Lonny Price

REPRISE THEATRE COMPANY

PSM 22 shows including:	How to Succeed...	Marcia Milgrom Dodge
	Sunday in the Park...	Jason Alexander
	Mack and Mabel	Arthur Seidelman
	Kiss Me Kate	Michael Michetti
	Gigi	David Lee

McCOY/RIGBY ENTERTAINMENT

PSM 18 shows including:	A Chorus Line	Kay Cole
	I Love You, You're Perfect...	Joel Bishoff
	Annie	Glenn Casale
	Smokey Joe's Café	Jeffrey Polk

GEFFEN PLAYHOUSE

PSM	Quills	Adrian Hall
	Atlanta	Adrian Pasdar/Randy Arney
	Equivocation	David Esbjornson
	Step in Time	Josh Ravetch

HOLLYWOOD BOWL

PSM	Music Man	Gordon Hunt
	Mame	Gordon Hunt
	Not the Messiah	Eric Idle/John Du Prez

REFERENCES

Gilles Chaisson	**Tom McCoy**	**David Lee**	**Gordon Hunt**
Prod. Director, Reprise	Producer, McCoy Rigby	Director	Director
(213-555-1234)	(213-555-2345)	(213-555-3456)	(213-555-4567)

FIGURE 21.1 Jill (Johnson) Gold's Résumé. What a pleasure it is to present Jill's résumé. Jill first wrote to *Stage Management* when she was a student at Occidental College. Now look at her credits! After four years of national tours, she is now a freelance PSM and instructor in stage management at her alma mater.

A résumé is usually worthless unless it is followed up with personal contact. Start with a phone call. Ask if your résumé arrived. Then ask if there are any openings now or if any are expected. Ask if you might drop by for a chat to get acquainted and to be kept in mind for some future opening. At the very least, get the name of the person who actually hires the stage manager at that theater.

In your contact file keep a record of the theaters to which you've sent your résumé and the names of the people to whom you've spoken in your follow-up phone conversations. Note their comments carefully. Who is the stage manager now? Could you work without salary on the crew until a paying slot opens up? During pre-opening rush, could you work with the crew just to get acquainted with their staff?

Hiring is usually done face to face, and personality may be a much more significant factor than experience. For the novice it is important to realize that although you may be the best stage manager in the world, there are directors, production managers, and producers who will not care to work with you because they feel that your personality will not mesh with theirs in what they consider to be the best interest of production. Over the years they have become able to make this evaluation instantaneously. It is something that does not lend itself to open expression in the interview process. If you are rejected and feel there is no reason other than the interviewer's feelings against you, trust that judgment and try someplace else.

For those whose upward career path takes them into theater management, check out the International Association of Venue Managers, Inc. (see Resources, page 234).

The trade papers rarely contain advertisements for stage managers. It is definitely a producer's market, with supply exceeding demand in situations where the stage manager is paid. If the job is dreadfully underpaid, it is almost impossible to get competent people to serve as stage manager. This means the novice can easily gain the valuable experience needed if she wants to work up to the level of the professional stage manager.

Do not underestimate yourself. Send your résumés to theaters you feel require greater experience than you possess. You may make a valuable contact that will pay off later. Or you may be hired for a slot far above what you're seeking by a producer who recognizes your potential.

When you are "at liberty," you will have plenty of time to send out résumés and to update your contact file so that you can get off your next round with far less effort. From your file you will be able to pull the addresses of the theaters, and you can send them out marked to the attention of the specific individual who does the hiring.

It is a Hollywood aphorism that "the best time to get a job is when you have one." Even if you are happily employed in what seems like a long-range situation, get out your résumé regularly and keep up your contacts.

Some people with experience in stage management are able to find work in the related fields of television, movies, and advertising. Jobs in these fields are just as scarce or scarcer than in live theater. If you search for a job in television, movies, or advertising, you may be competing with people who have studied those specific fields at the college level. Sometimes executives in those fields recognize the organizational and people skills that are honed in stage management.

Figure 21.2 is the résumé of a person whose career path has shifted from live theater into television production. Leslie Ann Kent studied theater at the college level and then worked as a stage manager. She had several live theater productions under

Leslie Ann Kent

Production Management

"Maybe This Time" (a Stabilizers video)	Avocado Films	Patrick Welborn
Chip's Hardware	Artist in Torment Productions	Michael Jung
Everything I'm Not	Artist in Torment Productions	Jonathan J. Casson
1989 Solo Showcase	University of the Arts	Walter Dallas

Stage Management

New World Order	California Institute of the Arts	Kelly M. Johnston
Caught in the Act (an Improvisational Comedy Troupe)	California Institute of the Arts	Anne West
An Evening of Cabaret	Colorado Shakespeare Festival	Richard Devin
The Rivals (ASM)	Colorado Shakespeare Festival	Joel Fink
L.A. Showcase '92	Odyssey Theater	Roxanne Captor
Mardi Gras with Queen Ida's Zydeco Band	California Institute of the Arts	Christopher Gratton
Tempest (ASM)	Modular Theater	Craig Belknap
Drums in the Night	California Institute of the Arts	William Kasper
The Importance of Being Earnest (ASM)	Colorado Shakespeare Festival	Joel Fink
L.A. Showcase '91	Odyssey Theater	Peter Frisch
Bonjour la Bonjour	The Off Ramp Theater	Judy Goff

Additional Experience

Dr. Quinn, Medicine Woman (production assistant)	CBS Entertainment Productions	John Liberti

Bachelor of Fine Arts - Theater Management — California Institute of the Arts - May 1993

References available on request

FIGURE 21.2 Résumé Showing Transition from Live Theater to Television Production. Leslie Ann Kent read *Stage Management* while in college. She worked as a stage manager in several live theater productions before looking for work in television production.

Courtesy Leslie Ann Kent, Production Assistant, CBS Entertainment Productions.

her belt before working in film and television. (The production assistant title in television seems equivalent to gopher in live theater.)

PERSONAL MAILING LIST

In addition to mailing out résumés to prospective employers, you may wish to keep up your contacts with people in the business by regularly sending them notes on your progress, invitations to shows you're doing, and programs of shows you've done. Think also about holiday greetings.

E-mail and social networks make it easy to let your theater acquaintances know what you're doing—and it can pay off in many pleasant ways.

Three months after your present show closes, 10 members of your cast, staff, and crew may be working in 10 different theater situations. Each represents a possible introduction for you to another set of directors and producers. But three months after you close you may run into an actor with whom you worked nightly, and the actor may not even remember your name.

The theater scene is fluid and forgetful. To exploit the former quality, you have to overcome the latter.

Your personal mailing list might consist of all of your cast lists with crew and staff members added.

The best thing about being a production assistant is that you have nowhere to go but up. You get to watch all of the departments function simultaneously. There are about 110 people on a set at any given time working in many different departments. Over the last year, there is not a single one that I have not helped out in some capacity—some many times. Being a production assistant gives you the opportunity to get closer to the people who can teach you what you want to learn.

Production assistant is a common first job for industry insiders. Most of them have been a production assistant at one time and understand that a person in that position aspires to move up. If you show enough intelligence, diplomacy, and skill, people will notice and, hopefully, remember you.

Leslie Ann Kent
Production Assistant
Dr. Quinn, Medicine Woman
CBS Entertainment Productions

I worked for many years outside of New York as a nonunion stage manager. When I came to New York, I stage managed showcases for about two years, getting paid next to nothing—working with Equity and non-Equity actors. One of the actors I worked with recommended me to a producer, and I got an interview. I know that the actor's recommendation helped, but I had to put myself on the line—let the producer know that I had the experience and the background that would make me an asset to his company. I got the job and the Equity contract. Once that job was over, I was back looking for paying work and stage managing Equity showcases—to keep growing as a stage manager until I landed my next Equity job—and so it continued for the seven years I actively stage managed as an Equity stage manager.

Martha R. Jacobs
Stage Manager
New York City
[Martha's work as a stage manager led to her current administrative work in live theater.]

LONG-RANGE GOALS

Where are you going, stage manager? Do you want to stage manage for the rest of your life? Do you want to find a big, cushy theater with stable management and move in to stay—to age 65 or senility, whichever comes first?

There seem to be too few career stage managers in the business. There are many aspiring actors, aspiring directors, aspiring producers, and aspiring writers who call themselves stage managers. There are many stage managers who are on their way out of the theater—on their way to law school, teaching English, programming a computer, or selling shoes. Stage management seems frequently to be a phase rather than a career.

If you make a career of it, you can hope for a salary of $683 to $1254 per week in regional theaters, depending on contract. Smaller-sized theater salaries begin at $226 per week. If you get to Broadway, your salary might go as high as $2480 per week as production stage manager for a musical. For latest contract information, contact your Equity office.

But that's the optimistic viewpoint. Expect feast and famine, periods of high pay and periods of unemployment.

> Now that AEA has a 401K plan, put the maximum in. Also, invest as much as humanly possible.
>
> Paul J. Smith
> *PSM Aida Broadway (1852 performances) and national tour*
> *Chicago Cellblock Tour and SM* All Shook Up

If you want to know what it's like to be a highly paid Broadway SM, please read "The Stage Manager: Off-Broadway or On, the Buck Stops Here." This February 1987 article in *Smithsonian* details SM Alan Hall's work on the Broadway musical *Smile.* For more insights reflecting the life of a Broadway SM, read any of Roy Harris's books: *Conversations in the Wings* (1994), *Eight Women of the American Stage* (1997), or *More Recipes & Reminiscence*: a *Celebration of My Friends in the Theatre* (2006).*

Unlike many careers, stage management does not offer regular promotions, hours, vacations, and retirement. A few benefits are provided by union membership, but it is up to the individual to plan career progress. Promotions are yours for the getting, the hustling, and the self-promoting. If you plan to be a career stage manager, evaluate your own aggressiveness as a significant factor in your potential career. If you are not aggressive, you will drift from one union minimum situation to the next.
I believe it is important to stress to students the reality of life in the theater. Staying employed often requires that you must go to where the work is, meaning it's difficult to put down roots.

> Students need to understand that although this may not seem important to them at the current moment in their lives, there will come a time in which they wish to settle down and find themselves craving a lifestyle that is more stable and conducive to establishing and supporting a family. Early in their careers, students may be faced with difficult choices—taking a job may mean long hours away from home and many days throughout the year touring away from friends and loved ones.
>
> Stephanie Moser Goins
> *Instructor of Stage Management, University of Oklahoma*
> *Former Freelance AEA Stage Manager*

*Career SM Roy Harris's Broadway and off-Broadway credits include 11 plays directed by Tony Award-winner Daniel Sullivan. Wendy Wasserstein's 1989 Pulitzer Prize-winning *The Heidi Chronicles* is one of these plays.

A big-name visiting director at our school said that no one important he had ever met started out as a stage manager. I'm pushing to be the first.

Jill (Johnson) Gold
Theater arts student Occidental College, CA

*[Former stage managers don't wear miniature gold clipboards around their necks. So sometimes it's hard to tell. Your visiting director had obviously not met Humphrey (*Casablanca*) Bogart, Dale (*Man of La Mancha*) Wasserman, or Gordon (Mark Taper Forum) Davidson. Hal (*Pajama Game, Fiddler on the Roof*) Prince started his Broadway career as third assistant stage manager. I'm sure that these four (actor, writer, director, producer) do not exhaust the list. (William Shakespeare was a stage manager before he wrote his first play. Is that why his plays contain no stage directions?) Stage management is not a mandatory prerequisite for any other job in theater. But it is a potentially valuable way to enter the competitive world of the theater and meet others who can help you along the way.]*

If stage management is just a phase for you, take this advice: Get out just as soon as you can and do your thing. Stage management demands too much of your organizational ability, energy, time, and emotional juices for you to think of it as a bread-and-butter job to support your real interest in life. When you have stage managed three or four shows in two or more theaters, you will have a fair understanding of the job and certainly adequate background for any related theater work. It won't take you more than six months of steady work to know if you want to make it a career. Then if you want to be an actor, director, producer, writer, or shoe salesperson, get out and act, direct, produce, write, or sell shoes.

But if you want to be a stage manager, give it all you've got. Be a *great* stage manager!

I've come a long way since my last letter. I am an Equity stage manager, and have worked the past three years at the Mark Taper Forum (for, ironically, Gordon [Davidson], who was indeed a stage manager and who consequently demands a great deal of his stage manager teams). My best advice is to start wherever you can, experience any and all aspects of theater, and make it known to those around you what your ultimate goals are. I began as an intern in the Taper casting office and told *everyone* that I wanted to stage manage. That information reached someone who needed a production intern, a position which let me prove myself as well as learn the ways of professional theater. I was offered a year-long position as resident production assistant, which enabled me to work with various directors, designers, and stage managers. Then they needed a stage manager for *Moby Dick: Rehearsed*, and here I am, one year later, resident production stage manager in a brand new four-theater complex.

Jill (Johnson) Gold
Production Stage Manager
Los Angeles Theatre Center
Los Angeles, CA

My Teaching Strategy

Students are required to keep a daily journal. It can be very simple. They can relate anything they want: their feelings about a current project, about their personal life, about their classes, or anything else. They can praise and complain to their heart's content. The purpose is to know themselves better and express themselves more fully. Kind of an odd technique for the teaching of stage management, but I feel that self-knowledge and self-expression are so important. I usually read their journals midway through the term to see how they're coming along.

—Roy Harris
Production Stage Manager
Instructor, Columbia University

SUGGESTED CLASSROOM EXERCISES

Ask the students to write their résumés. Have students exchange and critique résumés.

Ask two students to role-play job interviews at a community theater. After role play, ask the two students to read Appendix F and repeat role play.

APPENDIX A

Production Checklist from a Stage Manager's Point of View

A CHRONOLOGICAL APPROACH AND PRIORITIES

Don't be deterred by the size of the job!
Begin with the possible. Begin with one step.
—G. I. Gurdjieff and
P. D. Ouspenski
(Russian philosophers)

Those two priceless abilities: first, the ability to think. Second, the ability to do things in the order of their importance.
—Henry L. Doherty

YOU DO NOT HAVE TO DO ALL OF THE ITEMS IN THIS CHECKLIST! You need to know if the task needs to be done and who in your theater will do it. If you determine that the stage manager needs to do it, you may still be able to assign the task to a coworker or subordinate.

In the first hardcover edition of *Stage Management*, the following chart appeared as endpapers. In the subsequent five softcover editions, it appeared prior to the first chapter. In both cases, this chart's placement reflected my hope that it would help the novice stage manager get a basic understanding of the job and allow the reader to access critical information directly, without reading the book from cover to cover.

Generally, reader reaction to this chart has been favorable. Some producers told me that they amended it for their own production checklist. The negative reaction was that it intimidated students and amateurs ("I can't possibly accept a job where I have to do all that!").

My hope is that now that you have found it, you will use it to help you determine what you have to do to get the show on the road.

Hopefully, you understand that YOU DO NOT HAVE TO DO ALL OF THE FOLLOWING, and you're ready to turn the page.

SUGGESTED CLASSROOM EXERCISE

Collectively review this list to select items that are appropriate to the work of stage managers at your theater. Have the class write an abbreviated list that could be used as a stage manager's guide at your theater.

A Chronological Approach and Priorities

Task	Page	Priority*	Coordinate with
Before Rehearsals Begin			
Check out fire prevention equipment	225	A	Producer, Tech Dir
Get things to run smoothly on stage and backstage	1	A	
Gather equipment	52	B, E, F	
Be aware of police, fire, and municipal regulations	256	A	Producer, Tech Dir
Get to know the theater	56	B	
Inspect safety conditions	122	A	
Make a diagram of the stage	56	C	Tech Dir
Make a diagram of lighting instruments	59	C	Tech Dir, Light Design
Keep a do-list	191	B	
Make a promptbook	17	A, B, D	Director
Identify the problems of the script	20	A	Director
Hold preproduction staff meetings	34	C	Producer, Director
Write out plots	22	B, C, G	Dir, Technicians
Make master calendar	31	B, C	Everyone
Distribute rehearsal schedules	35	B, C	Producer, Director
Arrange the callboard	41	C	Producer
Post emergency numbers	43	A	
Distribute/explain company rules	40	C, G	Producer, Director
Keep a budget and record your expenses	91	A	Producer
Obtain audition forms	77	B, C	Producer, Director
Prepare staff, crew, cast lists	83	C	Prod, Dir, Staff, Crew
Make supply directory	250	E	
During Readings and Rehearsals			
Post notes for readings	71	B, C, D, F, G	Prod, Dir, Publicist
Accept résumés	77	E	Director

*Priorities depend on the staging environment and the staff of the theater. What might be a priority A task in a showcase theater in Los Angeles might be a D task in a professional touring company playing in Los Angeles.

Task	Page	Priority*	Coordinate with
Control scripts	77	B	Director
Make preset diagrams	100	A	Dir, Tech Dir, Sc Des
Prepare for rehearsals	102	B, D	Director
Brief cast, crew on safety, fire evacuation	122, 160, 229	A	Producer, Director
Post running order	117	B, D	Director
Supervise department heads	143	C	Prod, Dept Heads
Control required forms	79	C	Producer, Director
Conduct deputy election	87	B	Union, Cast
Keep cast on time	137	A, B	Director, Cast
Distribute itineraries	210	C	Producer, Cast
Distribute touring agreement	210	C	Cast
Post duty roster	194	C	Everyone
Make checklists	178	B	
Supervise props	144	A	Prop Mast, Prod, Dir
Distribute scene-shift diagrams	163	B, C, D	Scene Designer
Contribute to advance letters	223	C	Producer
Maintain order	114	B, E	Director
Call rehearsal cues	103	A	Director
Take blocking notation	107	B, C, D	Director
Make French scene diagrams	113	E	
Spike set pieces	103	A, C	Tech Dir
Prompt	104	C	Director, Cast
Give rehearsal, publicity, costume calls	115	A	Everyone
Warn cast	106	E	Director, Cast
Keep rehearsal log	121	E	
Submit rehearsal reports	122	B, G	Producer
Time rehearsals	119	B, D	Dir, House Manager
Post photo calls	116	E	Publicist, Dir, Costumes, Cast
Work on take-in, brief crew	159, 160	C, B, D	Scene Designer, Dir, Tech Dir, Crew
Make shift plot chart	163	C, D	Tech Dir
Supervise arrangement of scene dock	160	C, D	Tech Dir

(continued)

Task	Page	Priority*	Coordinate with
Supervise technical rehearsal	170	A	Director, Tech Dir
Choreograph scene changes	155	B, D	Tech Dir
Prepare area lighting diagram	23	C	Light Designer
Post sign-in sheets	138	B, C	
Place curtain call light cues on lighting sheet	187	B	Director, Light Techs
Secure rehearsal area/theater, conduct sniff test	229	A	Producer
During Production			
Post scene-shift diagrams	163	B, C, D	Tech Dir
Give calls (prior to curtain)	140	A	Cast
Caution audience	166	C	Producer
Call late actors	138	A	Cast
Coordinate with house manager	190	A	House Manager
Give cues	181	A	Technicians
Check immediate effect of each cue	183	A	
Supervise shifts	163	C, D	Tech Dir
Inspect shifts	163	B, C, D	Tech Dir
Time performances	119	B	Director
Walk the curtain	188	D	Tech Dir
Time curtain calls	187	A	Director
Maintain sets	203	B, C, D	Tech Dir
Be aware of cast morale	201	A	Cast
Keep the show in hand	199	A, C	Director, Cast
Post V.I.P. list	197	F	Producer
Rehearse understudies, block replacements	202	C	Producer, Director
Secure theater, conduct sniff test	229	A	Producer
Postproduction			
Distribute strike plan	206	B, C, G	Tech Dir
Post changeover schedule	207	C, G	Producer, Tech Dir
Supervise moves	208	A, B, C	Producer
Write letter to next stage manager	262	F	
Write critique	263	D	
Write letters of recommendation, thank you notes	263, 264	F	

Task	Page	Priority*	Coordinate with
Secure theater, conduct sniff test	229	A	Producer
In General			
Make contact file	252	E	
Make a theater information packet	62	C, F, G	Producer, Tech Dir
Get acquainted with unions	237	C, E	
Send out résumés	267	A	
Read theater news	247	E	
Keep in contact with theater acquaintances	270	F	
Start a theater library	252	F	

KEY

A. I've got to do this first. The quality of the production will be adversely affected if I don't.
B. I've got to do this because if I don't, time and energy of staff and cast will be wasted.
C. Someone else may do this well, but I've got to make sure it gets done.
D. I can assign this task to a subordinate if I make sure it gets done.
E. I'll do it if I have time, and it would help, but we'll survive without it.
F. A luxury; leave it for last.
G. This might be helpful for another show in a different theater, but will be useless here.

APPENDIX B

Forms

Try to be a problem solver, not just a problem.
—Elbin Cleveland

Many forms and checklists are used by a stage manager in the course of his work. Not all of the forms are necessary for every production. All of the following have been explained in this book. For quick reference, they are listed here in alphabetical order with page number.

*These forms may be downloaded from pearsonhighered.com/stern_ogrady. Other stage management forms may be downloaded from pearsonhighered.com/stern_ogrady.

MY TEACHING STRATEGY

Students are asked to design form templates using readily available software, which include spaces for date, time, theatre, and initials of person reading the form. Students are asked to use font, point size, and typographical variety— boldface, italic, underline, etc.—to make forms readable and effective whether printed or read from a monitor.

Mark E. Mallett, PhD
Assistant Professor of Theater Arts,
The Richard Stockton College of New Jersey, Pomona, NJ

SUGGESTED CLASSROOM EXERCISE

Select and list those forms that are used at your theater. Have students make a book of master forms that will be used in your future productions.

APPENDIX C

A Few Theater Stories

A sense of humor is part of the art of leadership, of getting along with people, of getting things done.
—Dwight D. Eisenhower

Knowing jokes is not a substitute for having a sense of humor. There are occasions, however, when a good theater anecdote can be helpful.

1. The wedding of the daughter of a famous Hollywood character actor brought out many producers, directors, and agents. As the proud father escorted the bride down the aisle, this whisper was overheard: "Will you look who they got to play the father!"

2. The old circus worker came home drenched from a storm. For years his job had been to follow the elephants in the parades and clean up after them.

   His wife pleaded with him. "Why do you do it? You're past retirement age. It's bad for your health—out in all kinds of weather. Please, I beg you, retire."

   "What," he replied, "and give up show biz?"

3. The novice actor was elated by a call from his agent. It was just a one-line walk-on in a historical play, but it was work. The actor who was to do the part had been taken ill. The play opened that night. The agent explained that he would get his costume and full particulars at the theater.

   "By the way," said the agent, "your line is, 'Hark, I hear a cannon.'"

   On the way to the theater the novice rehearsed his line: "*Hark*, I hear a cannon." "Hark, *I* hear a cannon." "Hark, I hear a *cannon*." He was absolutely determined to deliver his one line well.

   He got into his costume and the stage manager briefed him. His cue would be the firing of the cannon.

   He went on stage. He waited. His moment was coming. He became more and more excited. Finally the cannon exploded.

   And the novice delivered his line as follows: "What the hell was that?!!"

4. Cecil B. De Mille was about to shoot his greatest, most costly epic scene. He had stationed his three best cameramen strategically. In the scene, a herd of elephants stampeded through a primitive village, an earthquake swallowed up half the village, a tidal wave covered everything else, and, as the waters receded, a volcano erupted spewing hot lava and burning the remaining huts. Then the Yugoslavian army on horseback, dressed as the hordes of Genghis Khan, swept through the remains, raping and pillaging, only to be in turn swept off by a tornado.

   Eighty-seven assistant directors and the headquarters staff of the Yugoslavian army held the thousands of extras in place. Three hundred and seventeen special effects men readied the wind machines, dynamite, and chicken feathers.

Then C.B. gave the command, "Lights, cameras, action."

And it all happened beautifully—the elephants, earthquake, tidal wave, lava, burning, the Yugoslavian army, raping, pillaging, and the tornado. And when the last chicken feather had settled to the ground, Cecil B. De Mille knew that he had produced the most incredible sequence ever captured on film.

"Did you get that, Dick?" he asked his ace cameraman. "Gosh, C.B., I forgot to take the lens cover off the camera."

"Never mind," said C.B. "Did you get that, Roger?" he asked his second cameraman.

"Oh, boy, C.B. I forgot to load the film."

"Never mind," De Mille said and shouted up to the third cameraman on the dolly, "Did you get that, Arthur?"

Arthur shouted back, "I'm ready when you are, C.B."

5. The Boy Scout saw a nun trying to cross a busy intersection near Broadway. He offered to help her.

"Oh, thank you, young man, but I can make it."

"Please, sister, let me help," said the scout. "We're supposed to do good deeds."

When they had crossed, he said, "May I ask what order you're with so I can tell my scoutmaster?"

"Oh, for Pete's sake," she said. "I'm with *The Sound of Music.*"

6. The last act of a college's production of *Hedda Gabler* was building to its melodramatic conclusion in which Hedda takes the pistols, which the playwright had so conspicuously planted, and exits into the library to shoot herself. After a shot is heard, Tesman crosses to the library door, peers offstage, and announces to the audience, "Shot herself. Shot herself in the temple. Fancy that."

The student actor playing Tesman waited for the shot. Finally he heard—click, click. He crossed to the library door, peered offstage, and said, "Oh my God, she stabbed herself to death."

7. We were rehearsing a play called *Golden Boy*. Charlie Lynch was playing the part of Tom, a prize-fighter, and Dorothy Kilheffer was playing the part of Lorna. These two are in love. In the process of finding out they are in love they have a violent quarrel. During this quarrel he says to her, "I wouldn't look at you twice if they hung you naked from a Christmas tree."

At this moment I heard a quite audible gasp from John Schaeffer (president of the college). I thought to myself, "Uh-uh, we may be going to get the blue pencil." But we went on without interruption.

At the end of the scene Dr. Schaeffer called Dotty to him and said something to her in a rather agitated whisper.

After rehearsal I asked Dotty what happened. He had said to her, "Dotty, that's a terrible thing for a man to say to a woman. That's the worst thing he can possibly say. Don't worry, Dotty, if they hung you naked from a Christmas tree, I'd look at you twice." (Darrell D. Larsen, retiring after 35 years as director of theater for Franklin and Marshall College, *Alumnus Magazine*, July 1962).

8. Sammy Ginsburg had been in show biz for 80 years as a stunt man in a circus. His specialty was diving 100 feet into a barrel of water. As he began his act, he addressed the crowd.

"Ladies and gentlemen, good evening. Tonight for the 47,453rd consecutive time you will see me climb up on this 100-foot ladder and dive into this barrel of water."

A hush fell over the audience. The drums started to roll.

"Of course," Sammy continued. "it's not like in the old days. I've been doing this same stunt for 65 years, and I'm a little slower now—my arthritis." He reached for the ladder and moaned. "Also a little bursitis. I have it in my right arm. But I have to go on with the show because I'm the sole support of a family of fourteen."

He slowly pulled himself up on the second rung and groaned low again.

The crowd became apprehensive at the sight of this old man groaning up the ladder. "Don't jump," shouted a member of the audience. Soon several others joined in and it became a chant, "Don't jump, Sammy, don't jump." Finally the whole audience was standing up, chanting, shouting, imploring Sammy not to go through with it.

"Okay, okay already," said Sammy, stopping his climb and addressing the audience. "The next performance is at 10:30."

9. Edward G. Robinson once said that you could always tell if he was a good guy or a bad guy in a movie by the angle of the brim of his hat. If it was up, he was usually a detective, and if it was down, he was the heavy. While filming a flick in which he was a terrible villain, his hat brim suddenly popped up.

"What did you do?" asked a friend.

"What could I do?" replied Robinson. "Why, I arrested myself, of course."

10. When Cecil B. De Mille arrived at the Pearly Gates, St. Peter asked him to produce a film.

C.B. said no.

"But you can use all the greatest talent we have here," St. Peter persisted. "Directors: Stanislavsky, Eisenstein, Griffith . . . "

"No," said C.B.

"Actors: Barrymore, Gable, Cooper, Bogart . . . "

"No," said C.B.

"Composers: You can have Beethoven, Tchaikovsky, Mozart, Gershwin, Hammerstein . . . "

"Well," said C.B.

"Writers: Shakespeare, Shaw, O'Neil, anyone you want."

"Okay," said C.B., "with talent like that, how can I refuse. I can start this afternoon."

"Great," said St. Peter, "but first I'd like you to read this girl I know. She sings."

11. Dustin Hoffman was scheduled to shoot a scene from the movie *Marathon Man.* He arrived on set looking totally bedraggled. Sir Laurence Olivier asked what had happened. Hoffman explained that in order to prepare for his scene as a runner, he had stayed up all night running. "My dear young man," said Olivier, "have you thought of acting?"

12. A lovely Hollywood lady was complaining to her friend that she couldn't sing. The friend sympathized. "And I can't dance." The friend sympathized. "And worst of all, I can't act."

"Why don't you give up show business?" her friend asked.

"I can't quit. I'm a star."

13. The rabbi was running late when he arrived at the funeral. Flustered, he tried in vain to find the notes that would help him to personalize his eulogy. "He was so loved by his brothers. Although they all live far from here, they have gathered with us to pay their last respects. His brother . . . "

"Arthur," someone whispered.

" . . . his brother Arthur," continued the rabbi, "is from . . . "

" . . . a doctor in Cleveland," the same person whispered.

"Cleveland," continued the rabbi, "where he's a doctor. And his brother . . . "

"Leonard," came the whisper.

"His brother Leonard is . . . "

"an accountant in Kansas City," whispered.

" . . . here from Kansas City where he's an accountant. And his brother . . . "

"Sam," whispered.

"and his brother Sam, who . . . "

"An agent in Hollywood," whispered.

"Sam enchanted evening, you will meet a stranger . . . "

14. Phillip runs into his old friend Elliot, an actor on Broadway.

"How are you, Elliot?"

"Terrific. Couldn't be better. I've been running over at the Helen Hayes Theatre for the last three months, and it looks like we'll run forever. Before that I shot a spaghetti Western in Yugoslavia. My TV series is in reruns nationally. I've been selected as spokesperson for Campbell Soup, and my last three commercials are all still running. And Neil Simon wants me to do the lead in his next play. But enough about me. How about you? How did you like my last movie?"

15. The late Ruth Gordon was performing in a play. The phone on the set rang, and she knew it was her cue, but she went up on her lines. She picked up the phone, turned to the actress standing next to her, and said, "It's for you."

16. A director dies and goes to heaven. On his very first day there he is delighted by St. Peter's tour of the Heavenly Civic Theatre. The actors in rehearsal are first rate. The facilities are without equal—state of the art lighting, sound, and stage equipment. "This is terrific!" exclaims the director, "I can't imagine what hell must be like."

With a snap of his finger, St. Peter transfers the director to the Satanic Civic Theatre. The director is equally impressed—from the chandeliers in the lobby to the ornate barber chairs in the makeup room, the facilities are equal. "I can't see any difference," protests the director.

"No," says St. Peter knowingly. "but in heaven the critics aren't allowed at opening night."

17. A producer and a writer are on their way to Palm Springs for a weekend to work on a script when their car breaks down in the desert. They walk and then crawl across the burning sands. Finally, almost totally dehydrated, they come upon a tiny stream of cool water. The writer scoops up some water in his hands and is about to bring it to his lips when the producer throws some desert sand into the water in the writer's hands. "Why did you do that?" shouts the writer.

The producer answers, "Just trying to help you fix it up a little."

18. An actor returns home to find his home burned to the ground. He asks his neighbor what happened. The neighbor says, "Sorry to tell you, but your agent came to your home, beat up your wife and kids, locked them in the basement, stole your TV and VCR, and torched your house."

"What," stammers the actor incredulously, "my agent came to my home?!"

19. Two guys are sitting in a bar. One asks, "What's your IQ?"

"One eighty-five," replies the second.

"How do you feel current subparticle quantum research will impact on Einstein's theory?" They chat for a while.

In another part of the bar two others are talking. "What's your IQ?" asks the first.

"It's 120," answers the second.

"Did you catch the Dodgers game last night?"

They chat. In a dimly lit corner two others are talking. "What's your IQ?" asks the first.

"About 39," replies the second.

"Have you read any good scripts lately?"

20. Experiencing stage fright while waiting in the wings, Renee Taylor noticed that Helen Hayes was crossing herself.

"Will that help me? I'm Jewish."

Ms. Hayes answered, "Only if you can act."

21. Julie Andrews tells a Moss Hart story. They were rehearsing for *My Fair Lady* in London. The rehearsals were going badly. Hart complained to his wife Kitty Carlisle that if these were the old days, he would have taken Julie to the honeymoon suite of the Savoy for private rehearsal time. He was sure that would have improved the production. Kitty said fine, go right ahead.

Julie concluded the story by saying that "the honeymoon suite of the Savoy is just marvelous," (after a pause) "I've been told."

22. Long ago on Broadway, it was the stage manager's responsibility to deliver dismissal notices to actors who had rehearsed, but would not be used in the run of the show. If the actor was not personally notified by the end of dress rehearsal, the producer would have to pay him for the run of the show.

One worried actor took to sneaking out of the theater during the last week of rehearsals in the hopes of avoiding the stage manager. But alas, after dress rehearsal, and after hiding in a closet for hours, and just as he was exiting the theater from a fire escape, he heard the stage manager calling him. He accepted the small envelope, read the contents, and smiled. "What a relief. My mother died."

23. He stepped from the stage to scant applause. As he removed his buskins, his mother approached.

"What was that, son?"

"Acting."

"That's acting?"

"Yeah, Mom. I'm an actor."

"What's an actor?"

"Someone who does what I just did."

"You get paid for that?"

"A hundred drachmas."

"One hundred drachmas for that little nothing? I'm impressed. Tell me, Thespis, my big shot, do you need an agent?"

24. "An associate producer is the only guy in Hollywood who will associate with the producer." (Fred Allen)

25. From correspondence between George Bernard Shaw and Winston Churchill:

Dear Winnie, here are two tickets to my new play. Bring a friend, if you have one. GBS

Dear GBS, sorry, but I can't make it to the opening night of your new play. However, I would appreciate tickets to the second night performance—if you have one. WSC

26. "I didn't like the play, but then I saw it under adverse conditions—the curtain was up." (Groucho Marks)

27. A man arrives at the theater to find another man lying across his seats.

"Sir, you're in my seats."

The man groans faintly, "Ohhhh!"

"I say, you're in my seats."

The man groans again a little louder, "Ohhhhhh."

"Sir, where are your seats?"

The man groans, "In the balcony."

28. Two stage managers, nearing the ends of their careers, were discussing the likelihood of there being some form of theatrical endeavor in the hereafter. The first stage manager consulted a friendly medium. Later the following exchange took place between the two stage managers:

SM1: "I have some good news and some bad news. The good news is that there is a wonderful theater in heaven—well equipped, spacious, plenty of wing space. In fact, there's a show opening tomorrow night."

SM2: "That's wonderful! So what's the bad news?"

SM1: "You're calling the show."

29. An old stage manager arrived at the Pearly Gates. As a reward for years of patience, discretion, and endeavor, St. Peter granted him a single wish. "I've never seen a perfect blackout—can that be arranged?"

St. Peter snapped his fingers, and the darkness descended. There was not a hint of spill from worklights or prompt corner. There was total silence, not a whisper, not a footstep, not a pin drop—just complete silence and total darkness. It lasted 18 seconds.

When the lights came up again, St. Peter was gone and the Pearly Gates had been struck.

SUGGESTED CLASSROOM EXERCISE

Have students apply a black marker to their personal copies to eliminate any of the entries above that they feel are sexist, racist, too vulgar, in bad taste, or not funny. Discuss the difference between knowing jokes/anecdotes and having a sense of humor.

APPENDIX D

Web Sites of Interest to Stage Managers

When everything is said and done, a lot more will be said than done.
—Anonymous

Here are a few Web sites referenced in the text with selected others. This is in no way a comprehensive list. The following are only a mouse click away at pearsonhighered.com/stern_ogrady.

Lists of Lists/Links

Ken McCoy, Ph.D. Stetson University
www2.stetson.edu/csata/thr_guid.html

Theater Services Listing
theaterservicesguid.com/directories/states.asp

Theatre Sound mailing list
groups.google.com/group/theatre-sound-list

Audio Terms

Rane Corporation
rane.com

Books, Publishers, and Book Stores

Cornell University Press
cornellpress.cornell.edu

Drama Publishers
quitespecificmedia.com

The Internet Theatre Bookshop
stageplays.com

Pearson Education, Inc.
mypearsonstore.com

The Playbill Store
playbillstore.com

Colleges/Universities

Brooklyn College
http://depthome.brooklyn.cuny.edu/theater

Case-Western Reserve University
case.edu/artsci/thtr

Fullerton College
http://theatre.fullcoll.edu/

Ohlone College
ohlone.edu/instr/theatredance

SUNY–Stony Brook
sunysb.edu/theatrearts/

Yale University
yale.edu/drama

Consultants

Theatre Projects Consultants
tpcworld.com

Costumes

Eastern Costume Company
easterncostume.com

Patternmaker
patternmakerusa.com

Directories of Theatrical Resources

Contacts (British)
contactshandbook.com

ESTA
esta.org

Theater Services
theaterservicesguide.com

Employment

Backstage Jobs
backstagejobs.com

High School Festivals

Fullerton College
http://theatrefestival.fullcoll.us/index.php

Ohlone College
ohlone.edu/instr/theatredance/hstheatre.html

Lighting

A. C. Lighting
aclighting.com

Altman Stage Lighting Company, Inc.
altmanltg.com

Bulbtronics
bulbtronics.com

Colortran-Leviton Controls Division
leviton.com

Diversitronics, Inc.
diversitronics.com

Electronic Theatre Controls, Inc.
etcconnect.com

High End Systems, Inc.
highend.com

Martin Professional, Inc.
martin.com

The Phoebus Co., Inc.
phoebus.com

Rosco Laboratories, Inc.
rosco.com

Strand Lighting
strandlighting.com

Strong Entertainment Lighting
strongint.com

Tomcat USA, Inc.
tomcatglobal.com

Vari-Lite, Inc.
vari-lite.com

Vincent Lighting Systems
virtualightstore.com

World's Greatest Lighting Manufacturers (Lighting Internet Service)
ewholesalelightingblog.com/2/lighting-manufacturers.html

Lighting Instrument Template

fieldtemplate.com

Magazines/Newspapers/Information

American Theatre Magazine
tcg.org

Back Stage
backstage.com

Contacts (UK)
spotlight.com/shop/product.asp?product=36

Dramatics
schooltheatre.org

Hollywood Reporter
hollywoodreporter.com

Lighting Dimensions
sciencecentral.com/site/426624

Live Design
livedesignonline.com

Plays
http://en.wikiquote.org/wiki/theatrical_plays_and_musicals

TDR (The Drama Review)
http://mitpressjournals.org/loi/drama

The Technical Brief
technicalbrief.org

Opera Scores

Cook Music Library
dlib.indiana.edu/variations/scores/scores.html

Organizations

A.S.K. Theater Projects
askplay.com

Educational Theatre Association
schooltheatre.org

International Association of Venue Managers, Inc. (IAVM)
iavm.org

International Code Council (ICC)
iccsafe.org

Stage Managers' Association (SMA)
stagemanagers.org

Stage Managers' Association (UK)
stagemanagementassociation.co.uk

USITT (United States Institute for Theatre Technology)
usitt.org

Publishers, Plays, and Musicals

Baker's Plays
bakersplays.com

Dramatic Publishing Company
dramaticpublishing.com

Dramatists Play Service, Inc.
dramatists.com

Eldridge Publishing Company
histage.com

The Heuer Publishing Company
hitplays.com

Institute for Readers Theatre
readers-theatre.com

Show Control

RCS Sound Software
rcsworks.com

Richmond Sound Design
richmondsounddesign.com

SM Equipment

Illumineering
nifty-gadgets.com

Tools for Stagecraft
toolsforstagecraft.com

Zee Medical, Inc.
zeemedical.com

Sound

Audio Manufacturers, list of
auldworks.com/theater/proaud1.htm

Clair Brothers Audio
clairsystems.com

Clear-Com Intercom Systems
clearcom.com

Crown International, Inc.
crownaudio.com

Eastern Acoustic Works
eaw.com

JBL Professional
jblpro.com

Mackie Designs, Inc. (mixer manual can be downloaded free)
mackie.com

Meyer Sound
meyersound.com

Nady
nadywireless.com

QSC Audio Products, Inc.
qscaudio.com

Rane Corporation
rane.com

Sennheiser Electronic Corporation
sennheiser.com/sennheiser/home_en.nsf

Shure Incorporated
shure.com

Sound Effects

Gefen Systems
gefen.com

Hollywood Edge
hollywoodedge.com

Sound Dogs
sounddogs.com

The Sound Effects Library
sound-effects-library.com

Sound Ideas
sound-ideas.com

Special Effects

MDG Fog Generators, Ltd.
mdgfog.com

Theaters

ACT San Francisco
act-sfbay.org

Theatrical Supplies

Dudley Theatrical
dudleytheatrical.com

ESTA (Entertainment Service and Technology Association) (lists/links of suppliers)
esta.org

Gala Systems
galainfo.com

International Theatrical Truss Corp.
ittcusa.com

Jeamar Winches
jeamar.com

Musson Theatrical TV Film
musson.com

Stage Decoration & Supplies, Inc.
stagedec.com

Tools for Stagecraft
toolsforstagecraft.com/index/htm

Unions

Actors' Equity Association (AEA)
actorsequity.org

AFM Local 47
promusic47.org

American Federation of Musicians
afm.org

American Federation of Television and Radio Artists (AFTRA)
aftra.org

American Guild of Musical Artists (AGMA)
agmanatl.com

American Guild of Variety Artists (AGVA)
agvausa.com

International Alliance of Theatrical Stage Employees (IATSE)
iatse-intl.org

Local One (formerly Local 922) IATSE
iatse-localone.org

Screen Actors Guild (SAG)
sag.org

Society of Stage Directors and Choreographers
ssdc.org

Teamsters Local 399
hollywoodteamsters.org

If you should find a Web site, not listed above, that is particularly useful to stage managers, please advise. See the Reader's Comments Form, page 319.

SUGGESTED CLASSROOM EXERCISE

Ask each student to visit a few sites on the preceding list, then report to the class on usefulness of each site to stage managers.

APPENDIX E

What Would You Do?

If you can't be a good example, then you'll just have to be a horrible warning.
—Catherine Aird

Here are some situations—unexpected—from the experience of stage managers. They are presented for use in classrooms with the hopes that students may work through possible strategies for dealing with them. The remarks in brackets are not intended as solutions, but refer to paragraphs in the text where related information may be found or similar situations described.

1. You are working on a non-Equity off-Broadway play with a relatively new production company. They have hired you and signed a contract to pay you $500/week while the show is performing. Unfortunately, the company loses half of its backing and delays opening, first for two weeks and then five weeks. You have already done three weeks of rehearsals and tons of prep work, but you won't get a penny unless it opens. Do you stick with the show, perhaps missing out on a more stable job or abandon it? What would you do?

Jazmin Hupp
Former BFA student
State University of New York at Purchase
Current Director of Awesome for Tekserve,
the independent Apple computer store in NYC

[Equity contracts specify rehearsal pay for stage managers. See page 238 for a listing of Equity offices, and pages 241–242 for phone numbers to call to reach the regional Stage Managers Committee and discuss the problem if it is an Equity situation. Be aware that outside of union situations, you are on your own to ensure that any contract you might sign protects you.]

2. You are stage managing the big musical show of the season and are working with a well-known SM-turned-director. Once rehearsals begin, he treats you like a coffee-go-fer and turns to his choreographer for all his stage management issues, who, in turn, hands them off to you. You have a discussion with the director about the situation and he apologizes, but then he continues to do the same. What would you do?

Katherine Chin
SM, Ryerson Theatre School, BFA2003
Toronto, Ontario

[See page 9 on conversational strategies.]

3. It is the second night of *The Three Musketeers*, with a beautiful opening night the evening before. It is an entirely female cast. The actors' call is 6 p.m. for an 8 p.m. curtain tonight. At 4:30 p.m., you receive a phone call from the county hospital. The woman playing Porthos has fallen off a horse and will not be able to do the show tonight. You have a sold-out house, only a three-day run, and the other 15 members of the cast are ready to perform. Oh, by the way, there are eight choreographed fights that Porthos performs in the show. What do you do?

Sarah Chandler
PSM/MFA Candidate, Virginia Tech
Blacksburg, Virginia

[Page 202 explains how a similar incident at the Atlanta Opera was handled.]

4. You are calling a professional show; the house is *sold out*. You have a substitute light-board operator who takes the first cue of the show. The lighting equipment malfunctions, causing the gobo turners in the rig to spin out of control. Nothing the board op does stops it. Do you (a) stop the show to fix the problem, (b) hope that this will stop in the next cue, or (c) have someone cut the power to these instruments even though you know they are used as the general front wash throughout the show? What would you do?

Zack Brush
Freelance SM
Santa Cruz, California

[See page 183 for procedures to follow when expected effects don't follow the cues you've called.]

5. You are stage managing a touring ensemble in *The Human Show*, an original play that is extremely physical. On your last stop, the director will be able to see the production in performance for the first time since the show opened nine months earlier. The cast is goofing off preshow and one of them falls on his face. He claims to be fine, but you notice that his eye is looking a bit puffy, and you get him a cold pack. At the five-minutes call, with a packed house and an eager director out front, you see that the actor (who still claims to be fine) has an eyelid that has swollen to the size of a golf ball and has turned black and blue. He has been hiding his bloody nose and has admitted to another cast member that he cannot feel the teeth on the right side of his face and that he feels a bit dizzy. What would you do?

Marielle S. Thorne
Non-AEA career SM
Terrace Theatre, Kennedy Center, Washington, DC

[See pages pages 43–44 for posting of callboard listing of nearest clinic and first-aid information.]

6. You are calling a black box show when the fire alarm goes off. You evacuate the theater in the middle of a scene only to find out that the system is malfunctioning. There is no fire. Someone from the alarm company is coming to turn off the alarm, but as of now you have bright flashing fire alarms on all sides of your black box. Do you risk ignoring the fire law by covering the flashers? Do you call the show with the flashers on? Do you hold for the alarm company to come? When the audience returns and you resume, do you start at the beginning of the scene or right where you left off? What would you do?

Jazmin Hupp
BFA student
State University of New York at Purchase

[See pages 229–230 for "Stage Manager's Fire/Evacution Checklist" and relationship to local fire departments.]

7. As stage manager for *Of Mice and Men*, you are at the end of a very long dress rehearsal at a college theater. The gun that is supposed to shoot Lenny does not go off (again). The Equity actor playing George gets upset, begins yelling, and slams the gun down on the set. This infuriates the technical director (faculty member), who rushes to the stage to fiddle with the gun. You hear a shot ring out, and the TD is holding his hand while blood drips from his grip. What would you do?

Name Withheld
Student SM
Name of School Withheld

[*Pages 152–153 give tips on safety in using firearms.*]

MY TEACHING STRATEGY

Students conduct e-mail interviews with three or four working stage managers. Prior to correspondence, students must submit a list of possible questions. Upon approval, I give the students the e-mail addresses of stage managers. Students prepare a report summarizing their findings, which they present to the class.

Mark E. Mallett, PhD
Assistant Professor of Theater Arts
The Richard Stockton College of New Jersey, Pomona, NJ

APPENDIX F

Directing a Community Theater Play

The checklist I use

Marty Nemko*

[Of course, I'd vary these, depending on the theater, play, cast and crew, etc.]

ONE YEAR BEFORE OPENING

Pick the play YOU want to direct. Find a theater company willing to let you direct it.

Cast a wide net to recruit the best possible cast and crew. Good people are hard to find—especially in community theater, where cast and crew usually are paid little or nothing.

FOUR MONTHS OUT

Read the script a number of times.

Meet with set designer. Have a ground plan ready for the production meeting.

Purchase scripts for cast and stage manager. Scan the script into an editable Microsoft Word file and add a draft of the blocking and business. (Use the ground plan and little toy soldiers or chess pieces to help you envision it.)

THREE MONTHS OUT

Hold auditions. Make casting decisions both on acting ability and how easy the actors are to work with, whether they contribute or detract from esprit de corps. Before casting someone, call directors they've acted for.

If possible, require actors to get off book by the first rehearsal. Their having received the scripts with the first-draft blocking will help them get off book. Requiring them to get off book fast enables the rehearsals to focus on creating great theater, not memorizing lines. Most actors will still need line calling but it will be minimized.

E-mail the tentative schedule, taking into account all actor, stage manager, and director conflicts.

TWO MONTHS OUT

Hold your first production meeting. Present your artistic vision to your set, costume, lighting, and sound designers, and prop master. Solicit the theater's artistic director's input.

Meet with your public relations person. Identify angles to use with the media.

Meet with your group sales person. These people are critical to filling houses. Include pitching organizations serving low-income people for free tickets to the preview performance.

SIX WEEKS OUT

Hold first rehearsal. Establish your rules (my rules are: rehearsals start on time, the schedule is subject to change, input is welcome, the draft blocking is cast not in stone but Jell-O, most notes are communicated by e-mail, and unless an actor objects, I may send actors notes during the run). Rather than having them do an in-the-chair read-through, I have them read while walking the draft blocking. After that first rehearsal, have a bonding party.

Get the cast solid on lines, blocking, and business as soon as possible.

Retain a videographer to make the trailer and to record a performance for the theater's archive.

FOUR TO FIVE WEEKS OUT

Work the scenes. Each rehearsal focuses on two or three five-to-ten-minute chunks (usually French scenes), each usually worked three times. Catch them doing something good: When I see something I like, without stopping them, I say "Good" or "keep it." If it's something I don't like and I can say it in a pleasant word or two, I may do so. But most notes are communicated via e-mail when I get home from rehearsal.

Coach actors one-on-one, as needed.

Meet again with production staff to get progress reports and provide feedback. Meet with set builder to gain final agreement on the plan.

Write copy for the Web site, show program, third-party ticket sellers, etc. Get it approved by the PR person.

Meet with prop master to decide on how to decorate the lobby. Get headshots from actors.

TWO TO THREE WEEKS OUT

Dress the set (furniture, walls, floors).

Costume parade, publicity photo shoot, trailer shoot.

Post trailer on the theater's site, third-party ticket seller sites, Facebook, YouTube, and Twitter.

Introduce and revise props, ensure their efficient placement.

Run acts and then the full play. Focus on pacing and acting issues.

ONE WEEK OUT

Cue-to-cue with sound and light operator.

Tech Saturday: Full run-through with tech, no stopping if possible. Notes. Pizza/salad, then another full run-through with tech, no stopping. (Costumes optional.)

Dress rehearsals.

Preview performance.

Opening night.

THE SECOND-TO-LAST PERFORMANCE

Record the performance to create archival DVD.

FINAL PERFORMANCE

Cast/crew strike party.

---

*Dr. Nemko is a director and president of the Board of Chanticleers Theatre, Castro Valley, California; chanticleers.org.

GLOSSARY

The terms compiled in this glossary are the special vocabulary of the stage manager.

Abstract Set Nonrepresentational set that suggests rather than simulates appropriate surroundings.

Accent Emphasis placed on an action or phase of a play by lighting or staging technique.

Achromatic Lens A lens that transmits light without separating it into its spectral colors. Lenses should be achromatic.

Acoustics The qualities of sound transmission within a theater.

Act Curtain *See* Curtain.

Acting Area That part of the stage used by actors during the performance; may be extended to aisles or elsewhere if the action of the play takes place there.

"Actor on" Rehearsal The rehearsal at which the cast gets on stage with the set for the first time. Primary purpose is to get the actors acclimated to moving on stage and backstage. May be a complete run-through or a cue-to-cue rehearsal.

Adaptor Short length of cable with a different type of plug on each end (i.e., twistlock to pin, or pin to stage plug); also, a plug inserted into a socket so that it will accept a different type of lamp base.

Ad-Lib (1) Anything said by actors on stage other than the lines of the script; (2) to extemporize in a performance or interpolate impromptu remarks possibly because of a lapse of memory, as a reaction to an unplanned incident, or to cover a late entrance.

AEA Actors Equity Association. Union for stage actors and stage managers.

AFTRA American Federation of Television and Radio Artists. Radio and TV entertainers' union.

AGVA American Guild of Variety Artists. Nightclub entertainers' union.

Amateur Anyone whose work in or for the theater is without financial reward.

Amber A popular yellowish-orange color.

Ampere Unit of electric current; one ampere is the amount of current sent by one volt through a resistance of one ohm.

Amphitheater An oval or circular building with rising tiers of seats about an open space.

Analog Signal sent from control to dimmer by way of intensity of electrical current (compare to digital).

Analog Input Channels Allows input from manual console to computer/memory console that has no manual slider control of channels.

Analog Input Switches User-programmable switches that can cause a variety of actions to occur at the touch of a switch (also called "macros").

Anchor To fasten to the floor.

Angel One who invests money in a production.

Antagonist Adversary of the hero or protagonist.

Ante-pros Lighting instruments hung in front of the proscenium; front-of-house positions.

Anticipate React to a cue that has not yet occurred (e.g., actor falls before shot is fired; actor turns to door before knock).

Antique To make props or set pieces appear old.

Appliqué Ornamentation cut from one material and applied to another.

Apprentice Individual who works in the theater for the learning experience, usually not paid.

Apron The part of the stage in front of the proscenium.

Arbor Metal frame supporting counterweights in system for flying scenery.

Arc Spotlight Spotlight in which the source of light is an arc of electric current jumping a small gap between two carbon sticks; the carbon sticks are either hand-adjusted or driven electrically to remain a constant distance apart; an iris shutter is used to control the size of the beam or to shut it off completely.

Arena Theater A theater having the acting area in the center of the auditorium with the audience seated on all sides *See also* Theater in the Round.

Arm A batten supporting a curtain; usually a short batten used for wings.

Asbestos Curtain Fireproof curtain located immediately in front of the front curtain. In some areas it is required by law that this curtain be raised and lowered in sight of the audience during a performance. Also called fire curtain and fireproof curtain.

Aside Dramatic device in which the character speaks directly to the audience while other characters on stage supposedly do not hear him or her.

At Liberty Euphemism for unemployed.

ATPAM Association of Theatrical Press Agents and Managers. Union for theater publicists and house managers.

Audition Tryout performance before producers, directors, casting directors, or others for the purpose of obtaining a part in a production; may be acting, singing, or dancing.

Auditorium Lights *See* House Lights.

Auto Sketch One of several CADD programs (Trademark by Autodesk).

Baby Spot Small spotlight, usually 100, 250, or 400 watts; lens is ordinarily 5 inches, 4½ inches, or smaller in diameter.

Backdrop A large area of painted canvas fastened to a batten and used for a background that hangs straight (e.g., *sky drop, woodland drop, lake drop,*); contrast to Cyclorama, which is not painted but lighted.

Backing Light Illumination behind a set used to give a lighting effect on a backdrop.

Backing Unit Any piece or pieces of scenery placed behind an opening (*door, window,*) to limit the view from the audience of the offstage areas.

Backlight To focus lighting instruments on the backs (shoulders) of actors to produce emphasis or separation from background.

Backstage (1) The entire area behind the curtain line: stage, dressing rooms, green room (2) any part of the stage outside of the acting area during a performance.

Baffle Metal or wood screen used to prevent light spill. *See also* Louvers.

Balcony Front Spotlights Spotlights that are mounted on the front of the balcony or related locations to light the acting area.

Barn door A metal shutter with doors to control light spill.

Batten (1) A length of rigid material, usually wood, fastened to the top and bottom of a drop or leg; (2) the 1 x 3-inch lumber used to construct scenery; (3) the wood or pipe on a set of lines to which scenery or lights are fastened.

Beam, Ceiling Beam in ceiling of an auditorium in which spotlights are concealed.

Beam Front Spots Spotlights mounted high in the beams (or prepared slots) of the auditorium ceiling for the purpose of lighting the acting area from above.

Belaying Pin A hardwood pin or pipe used in pin rails to tie ropes from gridiron.

BEP Break-even point.

Bit Part Small role in a production, rarely with more than two or three lines. *See also* Walk-On.

Black Light Light that causes certain colors and materials to glow in the dark.

Blackout Closing of a scene, act, or the play itself, usually on a particularly effective line, by a sudden extinguishing of the lights. Used frequently in musical revues.

Blacks Black draperies or curtains.

Bleed When a prior color is seen through a subsequent coat, it is said to bleed.

Block A pulley or pulleys in a frame, part of counterweight flying system.

Blocking Movement of actors in the acting area.

Blocking Notation Written description of actors' movement.

Boards The stage. "To walk the boards" means to appear on stage.

Bobbinet Transparent curtain of silken texture. *See also* Scrim.

Book Play manuscript. In musical productions, the libretto without the music.

Boomerang Color wheel. A box attached to a lighting instrument to hold color frames. Makes color changes convenient. *See also* Color Box.

Border Scenery: An abbreviated drop at the top of the set, which masks the flies from the audience. May represent sky or foliage. Lighting: Row of overhead lights on stage. First row behind the proscenium arch is called the concert border, X-Ray border, or first border. Others are numbered from down- to upstage: second border, third border.

Border Lights Strips of lights mounted in a metal trough divided into compartments with individual color frame holders. Instruments are normally wired into three or four different circuits and are used for general lighting in the stage area.

Bottle Slang for lamp that is used in a stage lighting instrument.

Box Set Traditional set of three walls.

Brace Cleat A small metal plate attached to the frame of a flat. A stage brace is hooked into it to brace a flat.

Brace, Stage An adjustable device made of two lengths of the 1 × 3-inch wood held between clamps, used to support scenery from behind. A forked iron hook fastened to one end of the brace is twist-hooked into a brace cleat attached to the unit requiring support, and an iron foot at the other end of the brace is secured to the floor by means of a stage screw.

Break Character To say or do anything, as an actor, during a rehearsal or performance, that is not consistent with what the character portrayed would say or do.

"Break a Leg" Traditional wish of good luck exchanged between theatrical people prior to opening night curtain instead of "good luck."

Breakaway Scenery or props that disappear, break, or change form in full view of the audience.

Bridge A long, narrow platform hung from the grid immediately adjacent to a light pipe or attached to it, for the purpose of allowing a technician access to lighting instruments.

Bridge Lights Those lights that are mounted on the bridge.

Bridge, Paint A long narrow platform hung from the grid at the back wall, upstage from which a scenic artist may paint scenery or drops attached to a frame on the wall.

Bring Up To increase the intensity of the lights. *See also* Dim In.

Build Accumulation and gradual acceleration of tempo, emotional intensity, and action by dramatist, actors, or director at any point in a play, but particularly in the approach to the climax.

Bump It To hit the floor forcefully with flown scenery in order to trim scenery.

Bump Up To bring lights up as fast as possible.

Burn To transfer sound data onto a hard drive.

Burn In The first red glow emitted by the filament of a lighting instrument before full intensity light is emitted.

Bury the Show To strike sets, costumes, and props after the final performance.

Cable Flexible wire for conducting current from dimmers to lighting units or effects equipment.

CADD Computer-aided design and drafting, used by theater designers.

Cage Wire enclosure used to separate lighting equipment or sound equipment from the stage.

Call (1) Notice to actors backstage announcing the amount of time before the curtain, normally half-hour call, 15-minute call, and five-minute call; (2) notice of rehearsal or performance placed on the callboard and reiterated by the stage manager.

Call Boy Individual who gives calls to the actors. It is advised that the stage manager do this herself or himself.

Callboard Bulletin board for actors.

Candlepower Illuminating capacity of an instrument.

Carpenter Stagehand responsible for handling scenery, building and repairing the set.

Cast (1) Players in a play; (2) to select actors to play roles.

Caster A small wheel used to make scenery movable.

CD Compact disk, used for sound effects.

Ceiling A large horizontal canvas-covered frame hung on two or more sets of lines, used to close in the top of an interior set. Book ceiling: built in two pieces that fold together at the middle (book-like) parallel to the footlights, to permit flying. Roll ceiling: canvas is attached to front and back battens and rolled around them for storing and transportation.

Ceiling Plate A plate for bolting together and hanging a ceiling piece.

Center Stage The area in the center of the acting area.

Central Staging Placing the audience area on all four sides of the acting area. *Compare to* Peephole Stage *and* Horseshoe Stage.

Chalk Line A long length of string rubbed with chalk that is snapped to transfer a straight chalk line to floor or flat.

Characterization Delineation by dramatist of a role in a play or portrayal by an actor of a role on stage.

Charge Artist Individual responsible for painting drops.

Cheesecloth An open-weave cotton cloth sometimes used as scrim.

Chew the Scenery To rant and rave on stage.

Cinemoid A colored plastic sheet used for producing color in light.

Clamp Most lighting instruments come with a C-type clamp to fasten them to a pipe. There is a similar cable clamp used to hold heavy quantities of cable to a light batten, but this is most frequently done with tape.

Claque Paid members of an audience hired to applaud.

Clavilux An instrument invented by Thomas Wilfred for throwing upon a screen varying patterns of light and color that permit combinations analogous to the successive phrases and themes of music.

Clear, Please (1) Order to strike props or get out of the way; (2) warning that the curtain is going up.

Cleat Metal hardware used for securing flat.

Clew A metal plate that holds several lines so that they can be handled by a single line.

Climax That part of the central action, usually near the close, in which tensions are greatest and in which the theme is finally and fully revealed.

Clinchplate A metal plate used to back clout nails.

Clip Cues To speak one's lines before the preceding actor has had time to finish the cue phrase. This usually destroys the meaning or effectiveness of the final words.

Clipboard A board with a metal clamp on the top for holding plots, cue sheets.

Clout Nails A type of nail used in scenery construction, which bends to hold materials together when it strikes the clinchplate.

Color Box A metal container of six color frames that can be attached to the front of a spotlight for color changes. Some of these are controlled remotely from a switchboard or from the spotlight. *See also* Boomerang.

Color Frame A metal, wood, or cardboard holder for the color medium in the front of a lighting instrument. More frequently called a gel frame.

Color Medium A transparent material, such as glass, gelatine, or cinemoid, that is placed in front of lighting instrument to produce color.

Color Wheel A device to make color changes. A large, cumbersome wheel mounted on the front of a spotlight that has four to six openings for different colored gelatines. It may be manually operated by the spotlight operator or it may be motor driven.

Come Down To move toward the downstage area, or toward the audience. *See also* Downstage.

Comedy (1) Style of drama characterized by the humorous and amiable; (2) a play in which the protagonist fights a winning battle.

Composite (1) Several pictures showing an actor in various costumes and poses; (2) part of an actor's résumé.

Concert Border Lights mounted on the first pipe upstage of the proscenium.

Connector A device for connecting two cables together or a cable to a switchboard or unit. Each connector consists of two parts, a female or receiving part and a male that has studs or prongs that fit into the female. Multiple connectors are female connectors to which more than one male connector can be fastened. A number of units can be attached to one cable easily by use of branchoffs or multiple connectors.

Contour Curtain A curtain that is gathered up in scallops.

Conversation Piece A comedy in which there is much talk and little action.

Corner Iron Right-angle iron strap or L-shaped plate used for support or reinforcement.

Corner Plate A triangle of 3/16- or 1/4-inch plywood used to reinforce corners of flats in scenery construction.

Counterweight System Mechanical use of weights to help balance heavy scenery or curtains.

Cover Understudy (British and opera).

Crash Box A box filled with broken glass or small metal parts used for sound effects.

Crisis Turning point in a play.

Crosspiece Horizontal batten in a flat.

CRT Cathode ray tube, the TV-like screen that is appearing in more and more control booths as the window into the computer control board.

Cue (1) A signal in dialogue, action, or music for an actor's action or speech or a technician's duty backstage; (2) a signal given by the stage manager to commence light, sound, special effect, or curtain; (verb) to send such a signal.

Cue Sheet A list of the exact cues for the execution of specific duties by the crew.

Cue-to-Cue Rehearsal A rehearsal in which large stretches of dialogue without light or sound cues are skipped. Actors deliver the "warn" line dialogue through the line after the "go" cue line. May also include lines before and after special effects, quick costume changes, prop handling problems, and set changes.

Curtain A hanging drapery that conceals the stage or scene from the audience. It may rise, part, fold, drape, or sink. Also called front curtain, main curtain, act curtain, house curtain, flag, and rag.

Curtain Line (1) An imaginary line across the stage that marks the position of the front curtain when it is closed; (2) the last line of a scene or act that is the cue for the curtain to close.

Cut (1) To remove a line or lines from a script; (2) order to stop rehearsal.

Cut Drop A drop that has pieces cut out or is edged to represent leaves, foliage, or other decoration.

Cut Line A trip line that is cut to release the asbestos curtain in case of fire.

Cutout *See* Ground Row.

Cutting List A list of the pieces of wood with their dimensions needed for scenery and set pieces.

Cyclorama (Cyc) A huge, seamless backing sheet of material, usually white, that can be lit to indicate sky. Sometimes it is hung in a semicircle with the sides coming well downstage to enclose the acting area.

Cyclorama Lights High-powered individual reflector-type border lights mounted on a castered frame (or hung from a light batten) to light the cyclorama.

Dark Night(s) Period when theater is not open to the public.

Dead Spot Area in acting area that is insufficiently lit.

Diffused Light Nearly shadowless light.

Digital Signal sent from control to dimmer via ones and zeros (compare to analog).

Dim To decrease the intensity of the light on the stage by means of rheostats or dimmers. Also called takedown. *See also* Takedown.

Dim In To increase the intensity of the light. Also called dim up or bring up.

Dimmer An electrical device used in a switchboard to regulate current. Types: resistance, slide, plate, transformer, vacuum, remote control, silicon rectifier.

Dip in Intensity Unplanned lowering in intensity of stage lighting.

Direct Beam Lensless projection equipment used to cast shadow or project translucency on a screen, cyclorama, or flat.

Discovered at Rise On stage when the curtain goes up.

Distemper Paint made by mixing dry pigment with size. Scene paint.

DMX512 Standard protocol for communication between consoles and dimmers.

Dolly A low truck with casters used for moving scenery, set pieces, or theatrical equipment.

Dome A permanent plaster cyclorama.

Dope Glue used for attaching canvas flats.

Douser Cutoff device in arc light or follow spot.

Downstage Toward the footlights (or if no footlights, toward the pit, apron, or audience).

Draw Curtain A type of curtain suspended from an overhead track that opens from center to each side. Also called a traveler curtain.

Dress Parade On stage, under the lights (preferably before appropriate flats) check of costumes to be worn by each character.

Dress Rehearsal Final rehearsal before opening.

Dressing a Set Adding minor decorations to the set, usually the ornamental touches as opposed to functional props that must be on the set for use of actors.

Drop *See* Backdrop.

Drop Curtain A curtain that rolls up from the bottom.

Duck Strong cotton material.

Dutchman A strip of material, usually muslin, about three inches wide, which is used to cover cracks where flats meet. Masking tape is sometimes called instant Dutchman.

Duvetyn Velvety cotton fabric.

Effect The impression given to an audience of a particular thing by a technical achievement, e.g., a rainbow produced by lights, wind produced by a windmachine.

Electrician The operator of the control board and lighting instruments. Not necessarily an electrician in the nontheater meaning of the word. Also called boardman, lighting technician, or tech.

Elevations (1) Working drawings of the flats of a setting; (2) risers, platforms that give variety to the stage level.

Elevator Stage A section or sections of the stage floor that can be lowered and raised by hydraulic process.

Entr'acte (1) Intermission; (2) short scenes performed before the curtain.

Entrance Actor's appearance on stage.

Epilogue A scene that follows the end of the play.

Equity *See* AEA.

Expressionism From a school of thought that developed in Germany in the late nineteenth century. Really an extension of Impressionism and opposed to Realism and Naturalism. Expressionists are concerned with producing an inner emotional, sensuous, or intellectual reaction. It is this inner emotion that they try to express, and they maintain that it does not necessarily bear a relation to the outer aspect of life.

Exteriors Settings painted to represent outdoor scenes.

Facing Decorative trim, painted or applied around doors, windows.

Fade In Gradual dim up of light or sound.

Fade Out Gradual dim out of light or sound.

Fall Rope used with block and tackle.

False Blackout A blackout that occurs within a scene but does not call for a scenery or prop change. Usually denotes passage of time. *See also* Blackout.

False Proscenium An inner frame especially built for a production to close down a large proscenium, to mask lighting equipment or to give special design to the production. *See also* Proscenium.

Fantasy Play unrestricted by literal and realistic conventions of the theater and usually distinguished by imaginative uses of the supernatural and the mythological.

Farce Play designed only for entertainment and laughter; there is no serious or sincere attempt to depict character nor is there genuine concern with probabilities or realities.

Farce-Comedy A form halfway between farce and comedy that contains elements of both.

Feedback Undesirable noise in sound system; sometimes caused by microphone being too close to speaker.

Filament Image Projection of filament from spot, to be corrected by adjustment of spot or diffusion.

Fill Light Addition of light to blend areas or reduce shadows.

Fire Curtain *See* Asbestos Curtain.

Fireplace Unit A fireplace frame made to fit a flat opening.

Fireproof Curtain *See* Asbestos Curtain.

First Border *See* Border.

Flag *See* Curtain.

Flaking Paint coming off a flat that needs to be refinished.

Flameproofing Solution sprayed or brushed on flats or fabrics to retard flames.

Flash Pot A box device in which a smoke or flash effect is created, also called flash box.

Flat A wooden frame covered with canvas used as a scenic unit. It may be from 10 to 20 feet in height and vary in widths. The widest flat is usually 5 feet 9 inches wide so it will go through the 6-foot openings in freight cars. This one is called a "six" or full flat. Other flats are named by their conventional widths.

Flat Paint Paint that absorbs light, opposed to glossy, which you would not want to use generally for scene paint.

Flies The space above the stage occupied by sets of lines and hanging scenery.

Flipper A small piece of scenery hinged to a larger flat.

Float To lower a covered flat by placing the foot against the bottom rail and allowing it to float down so it is lying flat on the floor. The flat will fall slowly because of air resistance.

Floodlights Light units that give a general diffused light. Also called olivette.

Floor Cloth Canvas or duck covering for the stage floor. Also called ground cloth.

Floor Plan A scale drawing of a stage setting showing the position on the floor of the walls, windows, and other openings.

Floor Plate Metal plate with ring used for tying lines to the floor.

Floor Pocket A metal-covered opening in the stage floor that contains a receptacle for large stage electrical plugs and is metal covered.

Flown Term applied to condition of scenery that has been raised into the flies.

Fly To lift scenery above the level of the stage floor using lines from the gridiron, out of view of the audience.

Fly Curtain A curtain that is raised and lowered.

Fly Gallery A narrow bridge or gallery running along the side of the stage, well above the floor, from which are operated ropes secured to the pin rail.

Fly Man Name applied to any stagehand who is to fly scenery.

Fly Rope *See* Lines, Fly Rope.

Flyboy(s) Rigger(s).

Follow Spot A spotlight on a movable joint, operated so as to follow a player on the stage with a beam of light.

Foot To apply one's foot to the bottom rail of a prone flat or ladder so that another stagehand can raise it.

Foot-candle A unit for measuring the illumination given by an instrument: It is equal to the amount of direct light thrown by one international candle on a square foot of surface, every part of which is one foot away.

Foot Iron A steel brace bolted to the bottom of a piece of scenery or set piece so that it can be fastened to the stage floor by means of a stage screw.

Footlights Strip lights, a source of illumination for the acting area, which may be portable, permanent, open-trough type, or disappearing. Being used less and less in modern theaters.

Fortuny System Indirect lighting, using spotlights focused on colored silk fabrics. The silk redirects the light to the stage. It is shadowless, diffuse, and allows for subtle color changes but is impractical because of expense and space required.

Foul To cause scenery or lights hung in the flies to become entangled with each other.

Fourfold Four flats hinged together.

Fourth Wall Name given to the hypothetical wall of separation between the stage and the audience in a proscenium theater.

Foyer Entrance hall into a theater. *See also* Lobby.

French Scene The division of an act in which the number of characters is constant. Entrance or exit of character (s) marks the beginning of the next French scene.

Fresnel Type of spotlight using a Fresnel lens or step lens. Lens is named for French physicist Fresnel who developed it for lighthouse beacons. The Fresnel produces an even field with soft edges. Compare to P.C. and Leko.

Front Curtain *See* Curtain.

Frost Translucent gel used to diffuse light.

Full Maximum intensity of lighting or sound.

Full Stage The entire area of the stage that can be used as the acting area.

Funnel A cylinder of cardboard or thin sheet metal fastened perpendicularly to a square of the same material. Also called snoot or highhat.

Fuse A strip of metal with a low melting point, usually in an insulated fireproof container, which breaks when the current becomes too strong.

Gaffer Stage crew head.

Gaffers Tape A tape used for spiking, and for holding cables in place. Usually has an adhesive that does not leave a residue when removed from the stage.

Gagging Slang for unauthorized improvisation or revision of lines by an actor.

Gain Volume control on an amplifier.

Gallery Highest balcony in a theater.

Gang (1) To hook together; (2) to move two dimmers together.

Gel Frame A metal, wood, or cardboard holder for the color medium, which is placed in front of a lighting instrument. Also called color frame.

Gelatin (Gel) Thin, transparent sheet of material for producing colored light.

Generic CADD One of several CADD programs (Trademark by Generic Software, Inc.).

Ghost A streak of light that falls from a light source and falls where it is not wanted. *See also* Spill.

Ghost Load An offstage lighting instrument used to load a resistance dimmer so that it will dim out an onstage instrument properly.

Gimp Tacks Small roundheaded tacks used for furniture upholstery.

Gimp Tape A decorative upholstery tape used as a finish strip on the edges of furniture.

Give Stage To move on stage so that the center of interest will be thrown to another actor.

Glare Light reflection too uncomfortable for the audience.

Glass Crash *See* Crash Box.

Glow Tape Luminous tape that glows in the dark. Used backstage to help actors and crew who must function without a worklight. Usually made of vinyl or plastic. Sometimes written Glo-tape.

Glue Burn Stain on flats caused by glue.

Glue Gun Small, hand-held electrical device for heating and applying glue.

Go Order to take a cue, execute an effect.

Go On To enter on the stage.

Go Up To forget one's lines and to be unable to resume without assistance.

Gobo (1) Metal plate with pattern used in lighting instrument to project pattern on cyc or lighting effect on flat; (2) a louver, usually of metal, used to prevent spill from lighting instrument.

God Mic Public address microphone.

Good Theater Any piece of business that clicks with the audience, or that communicates surely and easily with the audience.

Gopher (Gofer) A production assistant who gets his or her title from the fact that he or she is frequently sent to "go fer" something.

Grand Drape Curtain extending the width of the stage opening, which is hung just back of the proscenium and in front of the front curtain. It can be lowered to cut the height of the stage opening.

Grand Valance The first drapery border in front of the main act curtain, usually of the same material.

Green Room Waiting or reception room, behind, near, or under the stage, used by authors, directors, and actors to meet their public. So called because the first "retiring" room in Covent Garden Theater in London was all in green. Most professional theaters do not have green rooms today, but many little community and university theaters provide such meeting places.

Gridiron (Grid) The framework of steel or wooden beams above the stage, which supports the rigging used in flying scenery.

Grip A stagehand who assists the master carpenter in moving settings.

Grommet Metal eyehole, usually found at the top of drapes and through which ties are run.

Ground Cloth *See* Floor Cloth.

Ground Plans Layout of the stage showing location of set, properties, and lights for a production. *See also* Floor Plan.

Ground Row (1) A row of lights on the floor to light lower area of a cyc or drop; (2) a low profile of scenery designed to represent rocks, earth, or skyline. It stands self-supported on the ground, usually in front of the cyc, and is used to conceal the base of the cyc, the lighting equipment, and cables, as well as to help give the illusion of depth and/or horizon.

Grouping Placing the cast about the stage.

Guy Line Rope or wire from high scenery to floor used to steady or strengthen.

Gypsy A dancer, usually one who moves from show to show, or from one summer stock company to another.

Half Hour Warning by the stage manager a half hour before the curtain goes up.

Ham An actor who is bad or pretentious, or both.

Hand Prop Any property that is handled by the actor during the course of the play, but particularly those props that the actor carries onto the stage as opposed to those that are discovered. *See also* Properties.

Handle A word that an actor adds to the beginning of a line that was not originally written in the script (e.g., *Oh, gee, gosh, well, but)*.

Hang To install or refocus lighting instruments, as in "to hang the show."

Hanger Iron Hardware for hanging scenery. It has a ring attached to one end of a steel plate that is bolted to the scenery.

Hanging the Show Putting up the sets of a play: e.g., flats, doorways, lights. So called because originally the show was set with wings and backdrops that had to be hung from the grid. Also called mounting.

Hard Patch Lighting technician physically connects cable to dimmer or control.

HBV Hepatitis B virus.

Head Block Three or more pulley blocks framed together and placed on the grid-iron above the outer edge of the fly floor. The ropes from three or more loft blocks come together at the head block and pass down to the pin rail. Also called lead block.

Heads Up Order to watch for moving scenery.

Highhat *See* Funnel.

HIV Human immunodeficiency virus.

Hold (1) To sustain an effect for audience response; (2) to pause in delivering a line so that audience can react.

(To) Hold Book To prompt, take blocking notation, and make notes on line changes and cues during rehearsals.

Hood *See* Funnel.

Horseshoe Stage A stage that is surrounded on three sides by the audience. Compare to Peephole Stage or Central Staging.

House The auditorium and front of the theater, as contrasted with the stage and backstage areas. Also used to refer to the size of the audience, as in "How's the house?"

House Lights Electrical fixtures that provide light for the audience. Sometimes called auditorium lights.

Humheads Audio workers.

Hummers Audio workers.

Hung Up Condition of being unable to continue one's lines or business because another actor is ad-libbing or because another actor has already taken the position you were to take.

IATSE International Alliance of Theatrical and Stage Employees. Union for stagehands.

Impressionism Theory that productions should be concerned with artistic interpretation rather than with reality. Strives for psychological reaction by use of color and line.

In One, Two, Three "In one" is the area on stage just upstage of the curtain line 5 or 6 feet. "In two" is the first area plus the next five or six feet upstage. "In three" adds the next 5 or 6 feet upstage or full stage.

Ingenue Young girl in a play, usually providing the love interest.

Inner Proscenium *See* False Proscenium.

Inset A small scene set inside a large one.

Interiors Sets representing indoor scenes.

Iris Shutter A manually operated shutter for varying the size of a light beam emitted from a lighting instrument.

Jack A triangular device made of wood that is hinged to the back of a ground row or other set piece for the purpose of bracing it from behind.

Jackknife Stage Two portable stages with narrow ends parallel to foots, and on pivots. When one stage has been used, it is swung offstage into the wings. From the wings on the other side of the stage the second stage is swung into position on the acting area. The jackknife stage permits quick changes of scenery, as do elevators and revolving stages.

Jog A narrow flat.

Juicer Electrician.

Juvenile Player of youthful roles.

Keep Alive To store scenery or properties so that they will be readily available.

Key Light The main source of light.

Keyboard A switchboard, usually with slide controls.

Keystone A small piece of 3/16- or 1/4-inch plywood cut in the wedge shape of a keystone and used to reinforce joints in scenery.

Kill (1) To take an article off a set; (2) to extinguish lights or stop sound effects or other effects.

Klieglight Trade name for spotlights.

Lamp Source of light. *See also* Bottle.

Lamp Dip Lamp coloring lacquer that gives a durable translucent color tint.

Lash To bind two flats together with a lash line.

Lash Cleat A small metal hook on the frame of a flat, behind which a lash line is thrown to bind the flat to the edge of another flat.

Lash Line Length of #8 sash cord fastened to the back of a flat and used to lash flats together.

Lash Line Eye The metal eye to which the lash line is secured.

LDI Lighting Dimensions International—an annual trade show at which manufacturers of theatrical equipment, not only lighting, display their wares and hold workshops.

Lead Principal role in a play, or actor or actress playing the role.

Lead Block *See* Head Block.

Left Stage The area on stage at the actor's left as he or she stands center stage facing the audience. Stage left.

Leg Drop A drop from which the entire center portion has been omitted.

Legit Popular abbreviation for the legitimate stage, live theater as opposed to movies.

Leko Once a brand name, now a generic term for any ellipsoidal reflector spotlight. (Compare to Fresnel and P.C.)

Lekolite Trade name for spotlight.

Lens Glass cut for the purpose of condensing and concentrating the rays of light from lamp source and reflector.

Level (1) A platform, set of steps, or ramp that raises the playing space above the level of the stage (also called risers, elevators, and platforms); (2) an imaginary line drawn across the stage at any distance from the curtain line but parallel to it.

Lid Top of platform or ceiling.

Light Batten A pipe or batten to which lighting instruments are clamped and along which lighting cables are run.

Light Plot Sequence of light changes from beginning to end of the play, with lines or business that immediately precede each change. Each change is described.

Light Towers Poles mounted at the sides of the stage or audience area to mount lighting instruments. Also called light trees.

Light Tree Tower of pipe or wood used to hang lighting instruments in the wings.

Lightwright Database program by Rosco that manages lighting designer's reports (Trademark by Rosco).

Limelight Invented in the mid-1820s, limelight (burning a cylinder of lime) was used in lighthouses and theatres. Performers on stage in the limelight were in the spotlight or center of attention. That's how the expression "in the limelight" came to be.

Line, Lines Speech or speeches in a play.

Line (of Business) Type of role or roles in which an actor specializes.

Line Drawings Blueprints from which sets and set pieces can be constructed without reference to any other drawings or specifications.

Lines, Fly Rope The ropes from the grid that raise and lower scenery. One end is attached to the batten and the other is secured on the fly gallery. Three ropes are usually used on each batten. The nearest one to the gallery is called the short line. The one in the middle is the center line. The farthest is the long line.

Linnebach Projector A large metal box with concentrated light source for projecting pictures from a gelatin or glass slide.

Lintel Horizontal crosspiece over door, window, or arch.

Live Weight Weight of moving body as opposed to weight of inert body.

Load, Electrical (1) Amount of current used in a circuit; (2) electrical equipment to be connected to a line.

Load-In Process of moving all of a company's equipment (scenery, props, costumes) into a theater. *See also* Take-In.

Load-Out Process of moving all of a company's equipment out of a theater.

Lobby That part of the theater between the entrance and the last row of seats, usually separated by a wall and doors. *See also* Foyer.

Lobster-Scope A spotlight effect machine producing a flicker of light.

Loft Block A pulley block in the gridiron through which a line can be run.

LORT League of Resident Theatres.

Louvers (1) Concentric rings of thin metal strips fitted to the front of a projector to cut off all but the straight beam of light (also called spill rings and baffles); (2) parallel strips of wood or metal used to mask a light source from the audience.

Luminaire Lighting instrument.

Macro Key One key on console that can be programmed to sequence two or more keys.

Make Fast To tie off securely or fasten any line.

Manager There are various types other than stage manager. Producer: sometimes called manager. House Manager: responsible for all details in management of the theater building. Business Manager: handles money, payrolls, accounts, contracts. Company Manager: responsible for the company, usually on the road. Personal Manager: acts as a representative for an author or actor.

Manual Override Ability to modify cue during computerized execution of that cue.

Manuscript (ms) Written or typed play, or the book of a musical. Usually used in rehearsal.

Mark It Order to record level of intensity of light or sound cue.

Martingale A two-fer or branchoff connector. Two lines with female plugs spliced into one line with a male plug used to connect two instruments to one cable. (I have heard this term pronounced "Martin-dale" in supply houses on the West Coast. If any reader knows the origin or correct spelling of this term, please let me know. Thanks.)

> As a lighting technician who used to spend a lot of time horseback riding, it seems to me that a two-fer bears a good deal of resemblance to an accessory used frequently in horseback riding (English style) to keep the saddle from sliding back on the horse (leather straps with rings or buckle which attach to the top of the saddle and the girth). It is called a martingale. Perhaps this will shed some "light" on the matter.
>
> Barbara Middlebrook
> *Lighting Technician*
> *Astoria , NY*

Mask (1) To hide from sight, or to conceal from the audience; (2) any sort of cardboard or sheet metal slide to be placed in the guides of a spotlight to restrict the light to various shapes. Also called a mat.

Masking (Piece) A piece of scenery used to conceal backstage from the audience.

Mat *See* Mask.

M.C. Master of ceremonies, introducer of acts or participants in a variety program.

ME Master electrician.

Medium *See* Color Medium.

Melodrama An exaggerated, romantic, exciting, and improbable play. Incident and situation are important; characterization is not.

Memory Board Lighting board with built-in computer that remembers cues.

Mezzanine (1) Sometimes the first balcony of a theater having more than one; (2) the first few rows of the balcony when separated from the balcony proper.

Mic Abbreviation for microphone.

MIDI Musical instrument digital interface—a standard for keyboard-computer interface allows any MIDI keyboard to communicate with computers.

Mike Slang for microphone.

Milk It Dry To squeeze the maximum laughs out of a line, bit of business, or situation.

Mopboard Baseboard.

Motivation Reason behind all stage action and speech. The skill with which the director and actors find the motivation for characters and incidents will determine the quality of the play.

Mounting *See* Hanging the Show.

Movement Passing of actors from place to place on stage. *See also* Blocking.

MR-16 Low-voltage 75-watt tungsten-halogen lamp.

Mugging Excessive facial contortions during a performance.

Mule Block A block with pulley used to change the horizontal direction of a line.

Mullion Slender vertical bar between windows.

Multiple Pin Connector A female receptacle that accepts three male pin connectors.

Muslin Material frequently used for covering flats.

Naturalism Same in external form as Realism but emphasizes the natural function in life as opposed to Realism, which is more selective.

Newel Post that supports handrails of steps, also called newel post.

Notices Reviews, dramatic criticism.

Offstage Area backstage, outside of the acting area.

Ohm Unit of electrical resistance.

Olio A mixture, medley, miscellaneous collection. Usually variety acts following an old-fashioned melodrama.

Olio Curtain A curtain that rolls up from the bottom. Also called drop curtain.

Olivette *See* Floodlights.

On Stage Inside the acting area.

O.P. Opposite prompt, usually the left side backstage.

Open Cold To give the first public performance for critics without out-of-town tryouts or invitational previews.

Orchestra Lower floor of the auditorium.

Organic Blocking Process of blocking in which the director allows the actors to move at will and then uses their movement as the basis for his blocking.

OSHA Occupational Safety and Health Administration.

Out Front (1) The part of a theater that is beyond the front curtain—lobby, box office, seats; (2) any area occupied by members of the audience.

Outlet Box Heavy metal fireproof box containing two to four female receptacles, porcelain insulated.

Overture and Beginners, Please The British equivalent of "Places, please."

P.A. System Public address system. Microphone and loudspeakers, or any sound amplification equipment.

Pace To the theater what tempo is to music. The timing of lines and business. Not to be confused with speed.

Paper Tech A crew-only technical rehearsal to iron out the mechanical bugs.

PAR Type of lamp used in both amateur and professional theater lighting.

Parallel A collapsible frame support for a stage platform.

Part (1) Character assigned to an actor in a play; (2) typewritten portion of a play that pertains to an actor's scenes and contains all of his lines and cues. *See also* Side.

Patch *Verb:* To connect cables between luminaire(s) and dimmer, or between any electrical instrument and control. *See also* Hard Patch and Soft Patch. *Noun:* Connection of cables and dimmers or controlling devices.

Patch Panel A plugging panel used to interconnect dimmers and outlets, also called plugging panel.

Pay Out Order to allow rope to pass through hands.

P.C. Plano-Convex spotlight. Compare to Leko and Fresnel.

Peephole Stage Stage with definite division between acting area and audience, such as a proscenium arch. Also called a picture frame stage. Compare to Central Staging and Horseshoe Stage.

Periactus A three-sided revolving apparatus painted with scenery.

Period Plays Costume plays of other eras.

Perspective Drawing Rendering of floor plan and elevations to perspective of audience.

Phantom Load Added resistance to a dimmer so that it will dim out a spot too small to dim ordinarily.

Picture Frame Stage *See* Peephole Stage.

Pigtail *See* Martingale.

Pilot Light Dim light used by stage manager to follow prompt script.

Pin Rail A rail with holes in it, into which wooden pins are placed to secure lines. *See also* Fly Gallery.

Pipe Batten *See* Batten.

Pipe Clamp An adjustable metal jaw for mounting lighting instrument on pipe battens.

Pit Sunken space in front of stage, usually where orchestra performs.

Pivot Stage *See* Jackknife Stage.

Places, Please Signal given by stage manager to the cast for taking their respective positions preparatory to the rise of the curtain.

Plano-Convex Type of lens or type of spotlight using that type of lens.

Plant (1) Member of the acting company who is placed in the audience for the purpose of fostering the illusion that the audience is taking part in the performance; (2) a prop on stage at curtain rise, particularly one concealed from the audience.

Platform A collapsible and portable unit used to add levels to the stage, or to provide an additional acting area.

Playing Space Stage space, inside or outside the set, visible to the audience and used for acting during the play.

Plot (1) List of what is required of each technical department in order to make a play work (light plot, sound plot, property plot, costume plot, special-effects plot; (2) planned action or intrigue of a play.

Plug (1) A scenic unit placed in or in front of another piece of scenery to change it. For example, an arch for one act may be changed for the next act by placing in it a window plug or a fountain plug; (2) a male connector with insulated handle, with two strips of copper along the side to make contact with similar strips in the outlet box.

Plugging Box Portable outlet box.

Position An actor's place on the stage as set by the director.

Practical Something that is usable. For example, a pair of French doors might be constructed so that only one opens. The one that does open is the practical one.

Preset To place props, costumes, or any materials in position prior to curtain or prior to use.

Preset (or Preselect) Switchboard A switchboard where one or more complete changes can be set up in advance without interfering with the lighting of the scene in progress.

Preview Performance given prior to formal opening.

Principals Actors who carry major roles in a production.

Problem Play Play built around a difficulty of society. Its characters personify the various forces and their conflict is the subject matter of the play.

Producer The individual (amateur or professional) who accepts the responsibility for obtaining the personnel and the materials to make theater happen.

Profile Board Plywood, 3/16 inch or ¼ inch, used to edge a flat.

Projector Directional floodlight, using a metal parabolic reflector to project parallel light rays.

Prompt Script A script used by prompter. Distinct from promptbook in that it has only the script but does not include plots and other production information.

Prompt Side (P.S.) Side of the stage from which the stage manager runs the show, usually the right side.

Promptbook Book of the play including all business, action, plans, and plots needed for the production. *See also* prompt script.

Prompter One who stands in the wings or out of sight of the audience, and assists actors with their lines and cues. Usually utters only the first few words of a line that an actor forgets, or significant words of the line.

Prop Box Box kept offstage in which props are stored.

Prop Table Table offstage where props are set prior to the curtain. Actors are conditioned to obtain their hand props from the same place on the table at each performance, and return their props there if they carry them offstage.

Properties (Props) Articles used for a play—hand props, trim props, and set props.

Proscenium The wall dividing the auditorium from the stage.

Proscenium Arch The edge of the opening of the proscenium.

Proscenium Opening The opening in the proscenium through which the audience views the play.

Protagonist Hero of a play or the character who carries its principal idea.

Protocol Language in which signal is sent from control to dimmers.

Put-Together A rehearsal at which all elements of the production are brought together in their appropriate sequence.

Q2Q Cue-to-cue. *See* Cue-to-Cue.

Quartz-Iodine A long-life lamp used in lighting instruments.

Quick Study Hurried and technical memorization of a part and its business by an actor, usually in an emergency when a part must be learned at a moment's notice. Also refers to an actor to whom memorization comes easily.

Quiet, Please Order for silence.

Rag *See* Curtain.

Rail The top or bottom board in the frame of a flat. *See also* Pin Rail.

Raked Stage A stage slanted down toward the audience.

Raking (1) Placing the side walls of a set at an angle to improve the sight lines; (2) slanting stage area, platform, or audience seating area to improve sight lines.

Ramp Inclined platform.

Rant To deliver lines in a shouting, melodramatic, and extravagant manner.

Read-Through Rehearsal at which the script is read from beginning to end.

Realism Fidelity to nature or real life. Representation without idealization. Adherence to actual fact.

Reflectors Shiny metal surfaces used in spotlights and projectors in back of the light source to intensify the light and give it direction: spherical, ellipsoidal, or parabolic.

Rehearsal Repetition of scene or practice of a production in private, preliminary to public performance, and for the perfection of that performance.

Rep Company Company playing repertory.

Repertory Collection of plays, operas, or parts that may be readily performed because of familiarity with them on the part of a cast or actor. A repertory company is one in which, instead of performing one play continuously, there are several productions ready and they are varied each night or week. Usually the same actors have parts in several productions.

Reprise Repeat of a musical number.

Resistance Dimmer A type of stage dimmer used to decrease intensity of lighting instruments.

Return Piece A flat attached to the downstage corner of a set to mask the wings. It is parallel with the curtain and runs offstage.

Reveal *See* Thickness.

Revolving Stage One or more circular stages (mounted on top of the permanent stage) electrically or manually revolved to effect scene changes or special effects.

Right Stage The area on stage at the actor's right as he stands center stage facing the audience. Stage right.

Ring Down To drop the front curtain on the last scene or act. Based on an old theatrical custom of ringing a bell to denote the closing of the show.

Risers *See* Level.

Road Irons Angle irons placed at corners of flats to protect them when they must be moved frequently as on tour.

Road Show A theatrical production that tours several cities and towns.

Rococo Overelaborate style of decoration.

Roll Curtain A curtain that rolls up from the bottom. Also called olio curtain and drop curtain.

Rondel *See* Roundels.

Rosin Box A box, large enough to stand in, containing rosin used by actors or dancers to rosin shoes or slippers.

Round, In-the- Staging a play with audience on all sides of the stage, even if the shape of the stage is rectangular or square.

Roundels Circular heat-resisting glass color media.

Royalty Compensation to authors and composers paid for permission to perform their works.

Run Length of a stage engagement or the total number of performances.

Runway Extension of stage into audience area.

Saddle Iron A narrow strip of iron used to brace the bottom of a door flat. Also called door iron and sill iron.

Safety Factor Safe percentage by which load on ropes, cables, and dimmers may be exceeded.

SAG Screen Actors Guild. A union for actors working in filmed entertainment.

Sandbags Canvas bags filled with sand used to weight lines or the jacks behind scenery.

Satire A form of comedy in which sharp derision is aimed at an idea or individual.

Scene (1) Setting of an action; (2) division of an act or play.

Scene Dock A storage area for flats and other scenic units, usually located in either wing area of the stage.

Scioptican Device used to create moving effects such as clouds, flames or waves.

Scrim A finely woven material through which light may or may not be seen, depending on how it is lit. Also called theatrical gauze and bobbinet.

Selvage The edge on either side of a woven or flat-knitted fabric, so finished as to prevent raveling.

Set To prepare the stage for the scene that is to be performed.

Set Dressing Props arranged to decorate the set. Also called trim props.

Set of Lines A unit group of ropes hanging from the gridiron used to fly scenery. There are usually three or four lines in a set.

Set Piece A unit of scenery standing alone.

Set Props Props that stand on the stage floor, or other props not carried on by the actors. *Compare to* Hand Prop.

Set Up To erect a set and install related equipment.

Shift To change scenery and properties from one setting to another.

Shoe A block of wood enforcing the joint between toggle and stile.

Show Curtain A drop or curtain behind the front curtain that is painted to give atmosphere to the particular play being presented.

Showcase Theater A theater whose main purpose is to obtain paid work for members of the cast.

Shtick Slang: business, usually comedy business.

Shutter An apparatus mounted on the front of a spotlight, or designed into it, which cuts entirely, or in part, the rays of light. There are iris, combination, funnel, and slide shutters. Also called cut-off.

Side Page of an actor's part. Usually half the size of a standard typewritten sheet. When bound together, called sides.

Sight Lines Lines, painted or imagined, that divide area the audience can see from area the audience cannot see.

Sitting on Their Hands Phrase used to describe an unresponsive audience.

Situation Relationship of characters to one another or to a condition. A play may have a series of situations. The basic situation refers to that one problem that is central to the play.

Size Water A thin solution of glue and water used in mixing scene paint.

Sky Drop A drop painted blue to represent the sky.

Slider The individual channel control on a manual board or submaster on a memory board controlling groups of channels.

Smoke Pocket Steel channels on each side of the proscenium arch that guide the ends of the asbestos curtain.

Snatch To hook or unhook flown scenery during a scene change.

Snatch Lines Adjustable ropes or chains used to fasten scenery to a counterweighted batten.

Sneak To bring in a light or sound cue imperceptibly.

Snoot *See* Funnel.

Snow Cradle Device for making snow effect.

Soft Light Diffused light with little or no shadow.

Soft Patch Cables of alternative luminaires are all plugged into patch panel, but selection of active cables is done remotely from control board. *See* Hard Patch.

Soubrette A minor female part in comedies whose characterization calls for pertness, coyness, coquetry, or intrigue, and is frequently a show part.

Sound Effects Sounds performed offstage in relation to stage action.

Space Stage Method of staging plays with lights focused on actors so that no setting is necessary.

Spacing Rehearsal The first day in the theater, the company goes through the whole show not for acting or tech, but to look at it in the space. Anything is changed that doesn't look good due to sightlines, set pieces, and anything else not available in the rehearsal hall.

Spelvin, George Fictitious name used on a program by an actor whose real name already appears in the program. George Spelvin was first used by a minor actor who doubled in the cast of *Brewster's Millions* in 1907. The play was so successful that its author, Winchell Smith, continued to have George Spelvin listed in the rest of his productions for luck. Harry Selby is another name that is similarly used.

Spike To mark the position of a set piece on the stage floor, usually with tape.

Spike Marks Those marks, colored crayon, luminous paint, or tape used to help stage crew position set pieces. Infrequently used to help actors determine where they should be.

Spike Tape A cotton cloth tape used to create temporary markings on stages and sets.

Spill Unwanted light due to a poorly focused or shuttered spotlight. Sometimes spill is unavoidable because it is emitted from a lighting instrument that cannot be shuttered.

Split Stage Two or more scenes placed on stage simultaneously.

Spot Line A single rope specifically rigged from the gridiron to fly a piece of scenery that cannot be handled by the regular lines.

Spotlight Lighting instrument designed to produce a concentrated beam of light.

S.R.O. Standing Room Only.

Stage Entire floor space behind the proscenium arch.

Stage Brace *See* Brace, Stage.

Stage Call Meeting of the cast and director on stage to discuss problems before a performance or rehearsal.

Stage Directions Instructions in the script concerning movements and arrangements on the stage.

Stage Manager The individual who accepts responsibility for the smooth running of the production on stage and backstage in prerehearsal, rehearsal, performance, and postperformance phases.

Stage Pockets Outlet boxes distributed about the stage, usually sunken into the floor and equipped with self-closing slotted covers.

Stage Screw (Peg) A large, tapered screw with a handle used to secure stage braces to the floor.

Stage Wait Period of time when there is no dialogue or action on stage, usually an undesirable situation caused by a late entrance or a dropped line.

Stage Whisper A stage convention in which one actor whispers loud enough for the entire audience to hear, but is assumed to be heard only by those to whom he or she is whispering and not by other actors on stage.

Stagehand An individual who is always present backstage when an actress or actor has to make a quick change in the wings.

Stand By An order to be alert for a cue.

Standby Understudy.

Stands Metal devices for holding and mounting spotlights, floodlights, and projectors.

Star Leading actor or actress.

Stile The vertical piece of wood that forms the side in the frame of a flat.

Stock Resident company of players performing one play nightly for a week and rehearsing another play for the following week.

Stock Scenery Flats and other scene units kept on hand for repeated use.

Straight Refers to a role or performance that is natural, normal, and uncolored by eccentricities.

Strap Hinge A hinge with long tapered flaps used for hanging windows and doors.

Strike To clear the stage of scenery, props.

Strip Light A long, troughlike reflector with sockets for lamps of small wattage, or a row of individual reflectors housed in a rigid sheet-metal structure. Used to produce general illumination.

Stroboscope An instrument for producing the illusion of motion by a series of pictures viewed in rapid succession.

Subtext Meaning underlying the lines.

Supernumerary (Super) An extra or walk-on in a production. A person who merely appears in a mob scene or in the background, and who has no individual lines of his own to speak.

Swatch Sample of material or paint.

Sweep A method used for setting up and cutting circles or arches.

Switchboard A combination of switches, dimmer plates, and fuses for controlling light. Also called dimmerboard.

Tab A sheet of canvas or other material, framed or unframed, narrower than a drop but suspended like a drop, used chiefly for masking offstage spaces. Also called a leg.

Tableau Curtain A curtain gathered up in an ornamental arch. *See also* Curtain.

Tag Term for the final speech of a scene, act, or play, serving as a cue for the curtain.

Take-In Process of moving all of the sets and set pieces for the forthcoming production to the acting area for the first time and setting it all up as it is supposed to play. *See also* Load-in.

Take It Out Order to raise scenery.

Take Stage To move into an area of greater prominence on the stage with other actors yielding focus.

Takedown *See* Dim.

TCI *Theatre Crafts International* (magazine).

Teaser (1) Scenery border suspended from the grid just back of the front curtain used to mask from the audience anything in the flies or edge of a ceiling piece. It can be raised or lowered to change the height of the stage curtain. It is often used in place of a grand drape; (2) any short drop suspended above to mask.

Tech *See* Technical Rehearsal (Tech) *or* Technician (Tech).

Tech Rider Document containing technical requirements of a touring show.

Technical Director Individual responsible for construction of scenery and set pieces.

Technical Rehearsal (Tech) A rehearsal at which the technical aspects of the production are integrated.

Technician (Tech) An individual who runs lights, sounds, or special-effects equipment.

Template A pattern made of cardboard or plastic—most useful to the stage manager are those for furniture and lighting instruments.

Template Table A special type of workbench used in the construction of flats.

Theatrical Gauze *See* Scrim.

Theater in the Round Acting area is usually round and audience is all around stage with aisles to stage through the audience. *See also* Arena Theater.

Thickness A width of lumber or other material attached to the edge of an opening—doorway, arch, window—to give the edge the effect of depth or thickness. Also called reveal or return.

Three-Dimensional Scenery Scenery that will be seen from all sides and is therefore finished on all sides.

Three-fer *See* Two-fer *and* Add One

Three Fold Three flats hinged together.

Throw Distance between lighting instrument and surface to be lit.

Throw It Away To give no particular emphasis or expression to a speech or line in a play.

Thrust Stage Acting area of stage that extends into the audience, or the audience is seated on three sides of the apron.

Tie Off To secure lines to hardware or the pin rail.

Time Sheet Record kept by stage manager of exact times of each act, scene, and scene change.

Timed Fader Computer control of cue capable of running at a distinct rate.

Title Role Character whose name appears in the title of the play, usually the most important role.

Toggle (Bar) The crosspiece in the frame of a flat.

Top It To build or increase the volume or emotional intensity of a line to a greater level than the previous line.

Tormentor Long, narrow curtains or flats, upstage on either side of the proscenium arch, used to mask the wings.

Tormentor Lights A number of spotlights mounted on a vertical pipe batten on either side of the stage, just behind the tormentors.

Trades Newspapers and magazines devoted to the theater, or any other special interest.

Tragedy Drama in which the protagonist fights a losing battle.

Translucency A sheet of treated, thin material. When backlighted, may be used to produce silhouette effects.

Traps Trapdoors that open into the basement trap room and permit the use of sunken stairways, scenery, or actors rising from or sinking into the ground.

Traveler A curtain that opens to the sides.

Treadmill Stage Machine device consisting of belts running on the stage floor, on which scenery or actors may give the illusion of traveling over a distance.

Trim To hang and adjust drops or borders so that the lower edge is parallel to the floor.

Trim Props Trim properties that are placed within the set or hung on the walls of the set for ornamentation.

Trip To elevate the bottom of a drop or other flown scenery with an auxiliary set of lines, to make it occupy a space approximately half its height. Tripping is used on a stage where there is not enough fly space to get a unit out of sight by taking it straight up with one set of lines.

Trip Line A line or lines to a batten used to adjust its position.

Truck A dolly.

Tungsten-Halogen Long-life lamps used in lighting equipment.

Turkey A show that is a failure. The term originated when bad shows were opened on Thanksgiving Day to clear expenses and make a little money in the two or three holiday performances. Any badly cast or badly produced show.

Turntable Moving stage, revolving stage.

Twist Lock Electrical connectors that have to be twisted into place and therefore cannot easily be withdrawn. They are especially useful where cords must lie on the stage floor and are in danger of being kicked out of an outlet.

Two-fer Martingale or multiple connector. Two female plugs spliced into one male plug in order to plug two lighting instruments into a single cable. *See also* Martingale.

Two Fold Two flats hinged together. Also called a wing.

Typecasting Selecting actors for roles because they resemble in real life the characters they will portray.

Ultraviolet Light *See* Black Light.

Understudy An actor who must be present or on call, know all the lines and businesses, but who appears only when the person playing that role is taken ill or for some other reason cannot appear.

Uni-Par Can Plastic par can that accepts Par 46, 56, and 64 lamps.

Unit Set Set built of scenic units that can be used together in various combinations to form different settings.

Upstage (1) Away from the footlights or audience; (2) to move upstage of another cast member and thereby compel that cast member to turn his back to the audience if he wishes to speak to the "upstager."

USITT United States Institute of Theatre Technology—national organization that studies the technology of theater and disseminates information about it.

Valance Teaser or border.

Vampire Trap Double-faced section of a flat that revolves on a pivot for fast escapes or disappearance of props.

Velours Curtains used to dress a stage, made of velour, usually consisting of a backdrop with wing curtains for side masking.

Velveteen Imitation velvet material used for draperies.

Voltage The measurement of the force needed for the flow of electricity.

Wagon, Stage A low platform on wheels or casters on which a set can be placed and then moved quickly into place.

Walk the Curtain To walk behind the curtain as it closes to ensure that it closes properly.

Walk-On A very small part, with or without lines.

Walk-Through A rehearsal in which actors get out of their chairs and walk through their movements on stage.

Walk Up To raise a flat from the floor to a vertical position, by hand.

Wardrobe (1) Costumes and all articles of dress of a play or production; (2) room in which costumes are stored or fitted.

Wardrobe Person The person in charge of costumes and their upkeep.

Warn A signal that a cue is due within a short time, usually within a minute.

Watt A unit of electric power equal to a current of one ampere under one volt of pressure.

Wing *See* Two Fold.

Wings (1) Space outside the acting area, at the right and left of stage; (2) draperies that hang at the sides of the stage to mask the offstage areas.

Work Light Light for the stage area used during rehearsals, scene shifts, and construction. Work lights are usually controlled by a wall switch instead of from the dimmerboard.

Working Drawings Blueprints made from the designer's drawings. *See also* Line Drawings.

Yoke The metal, U-shaped support that holds a lighting instrument.

Zip Cord Lightweight household electrical wire that should not be used for stage lighting, except for practical lights on the set.

Zoom Ellipsoidal luminaire that can be focused manually or remotely.

SUGGESTED CLASSROOM EXERCISE

Write on the chalkboard those slang theatrical terms, with definitions, used at your theater that are not found in the glossary. Add definitions to your department handbook.

READER'S COMMENTS FORM

Does this book meet your needs?

Did you find it easy to read and understand?

Was it organized for convenient use and application?

Was it complete?

Was it well illustrated?

Was it suitable for your theater?

The name of your theater:

Type (circle one): professional—educational—community—children's—religious

Your name and job title:

Did you use this book (check appropriate lines):

- ☐ As an introduction to the subject?
- ☐ For advanced guidance on the subject?
- ☐ As an instructor?
- ☐ As a student?

Your comments:

☐ I wish to make reference to Chapter ________________

I feel additional information or examples should be included in the area of ________________

____

Please attach additional pages for your comments if necessary.

Perhaps in your work you have discovered a management procedure, a method, or a technique that would be of help to future stage managers. Insights into the peculiarities of dance, ballet, opera, ice shows, theme parks, dinner theater, puppetry, magic, variety shows, and festivals would be especially appreciated. Your comments or additions could help to improve the next edition of this manual.

Send to: THE STAGE MANAGER P.O. Box 109, Chautauqua, NY 14722-0109; contact at lawrencestern@netzero.com, arogrady@hotmail.com

INDEX